Praise for Previous Books by the Authors

By DOUGLAS GRAY and JOHN BUDD

The Canadian Guide to Will and Estate Planning

"The authors have done a masterful job . . . This is a shelf reference every Canadian taxpayer and every Canadian family should have."

Globe and Mail

"An informative, practical guide . . . The authors . . . cover all the bases."

The National Post

"This guide promises a general, practical, and objective overview of the issues, options, and terminology involved in estate planning. Fortunately, it delivers on all counts."

CA Magazine

By JOHN BUDD

Second Property Strategies

" . . . *Second Property Strategies* is a godsend for anyone who owns real estate in addition to a principal residence . . . The explanations are in detailed but conversational language . . . and, drawing on more than 20 years in tax and estate planning, he highlights key non-financial concerns in transferring valuable property to children."

The Financial Post

Canadian Guide to Personal Financial Management (with Deloitte & Touche)

" . . . a global examination of taxes, income and wealth in the life of a family. Rating: Excellent."

Globe and Mail

By DOUGLAS GRAY

The Canadian Snowbird Guide

" . . . an invaluable guide to worry-free part-time living in the U.S. . . . by one of Canada's bestselling authors of business and personal finance books . . . most comprehensive book to address issues for retired part-time residents of the United States . . . "

Globe and Mail

" . . . I hate to sound like a cheerleader for Gray and his *Canadian Snowbird Guide,* but RAH! RAH! RAH! Regardless . . . the book is a complete how-to written in his characteristically thorough style . . . Gray delivers the goods right where the Snowbirds live. If you or someone close to you winters in the U.S., you should have this book . . . "

Business in Vancouver

" . . . Gray has written a reference book, thoughtful and complete, and prepared with the authoritative research skills and knowledge of a fastidious solicitor . . . as practical as a sunhat on a Tampa afternoon, and that alone warrants it a place on every southbound RV's bookshelf."

Quill and Quire

Mortgages Made Easy

" . . . Gray's latest endeavour is a good educational tool . . . no legalese here, just some good ol' street level English that explains—mostly for the benefit of novices—all the real and perceived complexities of mortgages . . . "

Calgary Herald

Making Money in Real Estate

"Gray delivers the goods. It is all-Canadian, and not a retread book full of tips that are worthless north of the U.S. border. It's chock-full of practical street-smart strategies and advice, pitfalls to avoid, samples, what-to-look-out-for checklists and information."

Business in Vancouver

The Complete Canadian Small Business Guide (with Diana Gray)

" . . . This guide is truly a gold mine . . . taps into the authors' extensive expertise . . . an encyclopedic compendium . . . the bible of Canadian small business."

Profit Magazine

" . . . Detailed, very informative, scrupulously objective as well as being written in a style that is refreshingly clear of jargon . . . This one is a 'must-buy' . . . "

BC Business

Home Inc.: The Canadian Home-Based Business Guide (with Diana Gray)

"Should be required reading for all potential home-basers . . . authoritative, current and comprehensive."

The Edmonton Journal

The Complete Canadian Franchise Guide (with Norman Friend)

" . . . This book tells it like it is, a realistic look at franchising and what it takes to be successful. The information provided is clear, concise, practical and easy to apply . . . "

Canadian Franchise Association

Raising Money: The Canadian Guide to Successful Business Financing (with Brian Nattrass)

" . . . The authors have combined their formidable talents to produce what may be *the* definitive work on raising money in the Canadian marketplace . . . written in plain language, with a user-friendly question and answer format, and contains invaluable checklists, appendices and information sources . . . a definite keeper for potential and practicing entrepreneurs alike . . . "

Canadian Business Franchise

Risk-Free Retirement: The Complete Canadian Planning Guide (with Graham Cunningham, Tom Delaney, Les Solomon and Dr. Des Dwyer)

" . . . This book is a classic . . . will be invaluable for years to come . . . it is arguably the most comprehensive guide to retirement planning in Canada today . . ."

Vancouver Sun

Books by the Authors

By JOHN BUDD

Second Property Strategies

Canadian Guide to Personal Financial Management (co-authored with Deloitte Touche)

The Canadian Guide to Will and Estate Planning (with Douglas Gray)

By DOUGLAS GRAY

REAL ESTATE

Making Money in Real Estate: The Canadian Guide to Profitable Investment in Residential Property

Real Estate Investing for Canadians for Dummies (with Peter Mitham)

The Complete Guide to Buying and Owning Recreational Property in Canada

The Canadian Landlord's Guide: Expert Advice to Become a Profitable Real Estate Investor (with Peter Mitham)

101 Streetsmart Condo-Buying Tips for Canadians

Mortgages Made Easy: The Canadian Guide to Home Financing

Home Buying Made Easy: The Canadian Guide to Purchasing a Newly-Built or Pre-Owned Home

Condo Buying Made Easy: The Canadian Guide to Apartment and Townhouse Condos, Co-ops, and Timeshares

Mortgage Payment Tables Made Easy

The Complete Canadian Home Inspection Guide (with Ed Witzke)

SMALL BUSINESS

The Complete Canadian Small Business Guide (with Diana Gray)

Home Inc.: The Canadian Home-Based Business Guide (with Diana Gray)

The Canadian Small Business Legal Guide

Raising Money: The Canadian Guide to Successful Business Financing (with Brian Nattrass)

The Complete Canadian Franchise Guide (with Norm Friend)

So You Want to Buy a Franchise (with Norm Friend)

Be Your Own Boss: The Ultimate Guide to Buying a Small Business or Franchise in Canada (with Norm Friend)

Start and Run a Consulting Business

Start and Run a Profitable Business Using Your Computer

Marketing Your Product (with Donald Cyr)

Have You Got What It Takes? The Entrepreneur's Complete Self-Assessment Guide

PERSONAL FINANCE/RETIREMENT PLANNING

The Canadian Snowbird Guide: Everything You Need to Know About Living Part-Time in the USA or Mexico

The Canadian Guide to Will and Estate Planning (with John Budd)

Risk-Free Retirement: The Complete Canadian Planning Guide (with Dr. Des Dwyer, Tom Delaney, Graham Cunningham, and Les Solomon)

Software Programs

Making Money in Real Estate (jointly developed by Douglas Gray and Phoenix Accrual Corporation)

The Canadian
Guide to Will and Estate Planning

**Everything You Need to Know Today to Protect
Your Wealth and Your Family Tomorrow**

The Canadian Guide to Will and Estate Planning

FOURTH EDITION

DOUGLAS GRAY, BA, LLB AND **JOHN S. BUDD, TEP, FCPA, FCA**

New York   Chicago   San Francisco   Athens
London   Madrid   Mexico City   Milan
New Delhi   Singapore   Sydney   Toronto

1 2 3 4 5 6 7 8 9   QFR   22 21 20 19 18 17

ISBN   978-1-259-86341-7
MHID   1-259-86341-7

e-ISBN   978-1-259-86342-4
e-MHID   1-259-86342-5

This publication is designed to provide accurate and authoritative information in regard to the subject matter covered. It is sold with the understanding that neither the author nor the publisher is engaged in rendering legal, accounting, securities trading, or other professional services. If legal advice or other expert assistance is required, the services of a competent professional person should be sought.

—*From a Declaration of Principles Jointly Adopted by*
a Committee of the American Bar Association and
a Committee of Publishers and Associations

Library and Archives Canada Cataloguing in Publication
Names: Gray, Douglas A., author. | Budd, John S. (John Simpson), 1945– author.
Title: The Canadian guide to will and estate planning : everything you need
  to know today to protect your wealth and your family tomorrow / by Douglas
  Gray and John Budd.
Description: 4th edition. | New York : McGraw-Hill Education, [2018] |
  Includes index.
Identifiers: LCCN 2017022804 (print) | LCCN 2017023949 (ebook) | ISBN
  9781259863424| ISBN 1259863425 | ISBN 9781259863417 (alk. paper)
Subjects: LCSH: Wills—Canada. | Estate planning—Canada.
Classification: LCC KE808 (ebook) | LCC KE808 .G73 2018 (print) | DDC
  346.7105/4—dc23
LC record available at https://lccn.loc.gov/2

McGraw-Hill Education books are available at special quantity discounts to use as premiums and sales promotions or for use in corporate training programs. To contact a representative, please visit the Contact Us page at www.mhprofessional.com.

CONTENTS

CHAPTER 1: *What Is Estate Planning?* // 1

Regardless of your age, the issue of estate planning, in conjunction with your will, is an essential element of life planning. However, at different stages of your life, certain issues may arise that require different estate planning strategies.

Stages of Estate Planning Over Your Lifetime • Top 10 Pitfalls to Avoid in Will and Estate Planning

CHAPTER 2: *What Assets Will You Have?* // 9

You could be quite surprised once you assess the current and projected value of your estate. After you read this chapter and complete the net worth statement in Appendix D, speak to your professional advisor and decide on the best approach to meet your wishes.

How Much Are You Worth? • Government Pension Plans • Pension Plans Funded by Your Employer • Your Own Tax-Sheltered Pension Plans • Using Your Home as an Additional Source of Income • Insurance for Your Present and Future Needs • Are Your Deposit Monies, RRSPs, RRIFs, Annuities and Insurance Funds Protected Against Default? • Keeping Track of Risk • Key Issues with Digital Assets and Estate Planning

CHAPTER 3: *Building Your Estate* // 39

Three Elements of Wealth Accumulation: Saving, Investing and Preserving Capital

CHAPTER 4: *Understanding Wills* // 49

It is estimated that only one out of three adults has a will, which means that two-thirds of Canadians die with their wishes unmet. A will is an important legal document that can ensure that your assets will be distributed to the beneficiaries of your choice in the way you wish.

What Happens If There Is No Will? • What's in a Will? • Reflecting Your Wishes—Special Clauses in Your Will • Writing a Memorandum to Your Will • Keep Your Will Current • How to Change Your Will • Revoking Your Will • Is Your Will Valid in the U.S. for U.S. Assets? • Preparing a Will • Benefits of Using the Services of a Trust Company • The Complementary Document—Power of Attorney • Protecting Yourself in All Circumstances • Selecting an Executor • Selecting a Trustee • Selecting a Guardian for Your Children • Impact of Family Law Legislation • Fees and Expenses • How to Avoid Your Will Being Contested

CHAPTER 5: *Understanding Powers of Attorney and Living Wills* // 81

You will probably want to give authority to others to act on your behalf at some point in your life. Whether it is to help or take charge of financial situations or medical care, the power of attorney is the document that will allow you to choose your designate and set out the guidelines you wish to be followed.

Designating Power of Attorney • Living Wills

CHAPTER 6: *Understanding Trusts* // 97
Trusts are a very common way of dealing with a range of personal choice, family or business options and, as you will see, are not just for the rich with complex financial affairs.

Types of Trusts • The Creative Use of Living Trusts • Creating a Testamentary Trust • Selecting a Trustee • Benefits of Using the Services of a Trust Company • What Are the Fees and Expenses? • Outlining Everything in a Trust Agreement • The Tax Implications of a Trust

CHAPTER 7: *Understanding the Probate Process* // 115
While not all estates must go through the probate process, most estates do. Basically, the probate process ensures that your executor, or the administrator of your estate, is legally confirmed and that your will is approved by the courts.

What Is Probate? • Administration of the Estate • Responsibilities of the Executor/Administrator • Fees for Executors • Potential Liability of the Executor • Joint Ownership • Making the Most of It—Reducing Probate Fees

CHAPTER 8: *Death and Taxes* // 133
Don't be fooled—just because there is no inheritance tax, as such, in Canada, the beneficiaries of your estate will incur a significant amount of tax in the settling of your estate unless you do an effective job in planning your estate for tax minimization.

The History of Estate Taxes in Canada • Capital Gains Taxation in Canada • Capital Gains Taxation on Death • Capital Gains Taxation on Gifts During Your Lifetime • Other Taxes That Could Be Payable by an Estate

CHAPTER 9: *Dealing with the Tax Department and Estate Administration* // 155
The final "moments of reckoning," in terms of estate administration, are the filing of your final tax return. It is your executor's responsibility to see that all of your debts are paid—even the ones to the Canada Revenue Agency.

Income Tax Returns for the Deceased • Special Tax Rules Applicable to Deceased Taxpayers • Tax Returns to Be Filed by the Executors for the Estate • Winding up the Estate

CHAPTER 10: *Tax Planning Strategies* // 167
Tax "planning" as opposed to tax "evasion" is perfectly legal. While this chapter won't make you an expert, the odds are that at least one of the strategies outlined will help you minimize the future taxes payable in your estate.

Your Primary Tax Planning Goals • Your General Estate Planning Objectives • Transferring Property to Your Spouse • Utilizing the $800,000 Plus Capital Gains Exemption for Small Business Corporation Shares • Utilizing the Farm Property Rollover • Estate Freezing • Using Family Trusts for Income Splitting and Estate Planning

CHAPTER 11: *Tax and Estate Planning If You Own U.S. Assets* // 181
As if the tax laws of one country weren't enough, you may be subject to the tax laws in both Canada and the United States if you live in the U.S. part-time or own property or other investments there.

Do U.S. Tax Laws Apply to You? • Residency and the Tax Treaty • Summary of Guidelines Regarding Filing a U.S. Income Tax Return • The IRS Wants Your Number • The IRS Has Your Number • Deadlines for Filing with the IRS • Rental Income from U.S. Real Estate • Selling Your U.S. Real Estate •

U.S. Gift Tax • Possible Simultaneous U.S. and Canadian Taxes on Death • The Canada/U.S. Tax Treaty • Strategies for Reducing U.S. Estate Tax on Your U.S. Assets

CHAPTER 12: *Vacation Properties* // 203

Vacations are a time to relax and forget your worries. Financial concerns and capital gains taxes should be the last thing on your mind. This chapter will provide some ideas for dealing with vacation properties in your estate planning.

Keeping Things in Perspective • The Principal Residence Exemption • Will Planning and Your Vacation Property • Planning Strategies for Your Vacation Home • Should You Pay Tax Now or Later? • Buying Life Insurance to Cover Future Tax Liabilities • Using a Corporation to Own Your Vacation Property

CHAPTER 13: *Privately-Owned Businesses* // 221

With more than 100,000 family businesses in Canada, they have been the driving force building and sustaining our economy from Confederation to the present time. This chapter will help you create an effective succession arrangement and estate plan.

The Importance of Having a Plan • The Planning Process • Tax Planning in the Family Business • Shareholder Agreements • Creditor-Proofing Your Business

CHAPTER 14: *Charitable Giving and Philanthropy* // 241

Many of the greatest works of art are on display in public art galleries and museums for all to enjoy because of the philanthropy of past Canadians. Charitable donations can be made in many different ways—cash, works of art, marketable securities. Choosing the best method will maximize your income tax saving.

Tax Incentives for Charitable Gifts • Types of Donations • Private Foundations • Pitfalls to Avoid and Tips to Consider When Estate Planning

CHAPTER 15: *Life, Health and Disability Insurance* // 257

You must choose according to your needs from among the many types of life, health and disability insurance. The type of insurance you choose can play an important role in your estate planning strategy.

Identifying the Need for Life Insurance • Types of Life Insurance • Choosing an Insurance Agent • Choosing a Life Insurance Company • Comparison of Group Insurance Over Individual Insurance • Income Tax Treatment of Life Insurance • Health and Disability Insurance • Business-Related Insurance

CHAPTER 16: *Selecting Professional Advisors* // 279

Selecting the professional advisors that "fit" you is vital to protect your tax and estate planning interests. This chapter will outline the qualities and qualifications to look for in a lawyer, an accountant, a financial planner and other financial and investment advisors.

General Factors to Consider When Selecting an Advisor • Selecting a Lawyer • Selecting an Accountant • Selecting a Financial Planner • Other Financial and Investment Advisors

CHAPTER 17: *Selecting Retirement Residences and Care Facilities* // 305

Whether by choice or circumstance, you may need to enter a retirement residence or care facility in your later years. Use this chapter and the checklists to plan and choose wisely.

Where Do I Start? • What Is a Retirement Residence? • What Is a Care Facility? • Regulations, Licensing and Accreditation

CHAPTER 18: *Planning Your Funeral* // 313
In the midst of the grief and sorrow of losing a loved one, responsibilities have to be faced and decisions made consistent with the philosophical and spiritual beliefs of the deceased. Information in this chapter will help you make those decisions wisely and with confidence.

What Is a Funeral? • Arranging Your Funeral Services in Advance • Make Your Funeral or Memorial Service More Memorable • Expressions of Sympathy • When Death Requires an Autopsy • Documents and Permits • Support Services • Making the Arrangements Yourself • Selecting a Funeral Provider • Understanding Funeral Costs • The Funeral Service • Burial or Cremation? • The Availability of Financial Benefits and Assistance • Organ Donations and Medical Research

APPENDIX A: *Sources of Information* // 335
One of the challenges of research is to know where to start. This Appendix will save you a great deal of time, energy, money and hassle.

APPENDIX B: *Samples* // 341
Samples of documents discussed throughout the book will provide you with some more ideas, but these are for illustration only and must not be used as do-it-yourself documents.

APPENDIX C: *Charts* // 355
The handy charts in this Appendix will provide some points of comparison on topics discussed throughout the book.

APPENDIX D: *Checklists* // 363
These checklists will help you take stock of your current situation and focus on your future goals.

GLOSSARY // 405
The definitions here will ensure that you and your professional advisors are speaking the same language.

INDEX // 413

ABOUT THE AUTHORS // 425

READER INPUT AND EDUCATIONAL SEMINARS // 426

ACKNOWLEDGMENTS

We are indebted to many individuals who have given generously of their time and expertise in the preparation of this book. We are also grateful for the helpful assistance given to us by various federal and provincial governments, insurance, funeral and trust companies, and financial planning, tax and legal experts.

✳

FROM DOUGLAS GRAY: I would also like to thank Richard Brunton, CPA, Kelly Strachan, EA, and Ali Khan, CPA, of Brunton-McCarthy CPA Firm, Chartered in Boca Raton, Florida, for their generous feedback on cross-border tax issues.

I would also like to express my appreciation to Dr. Peter Singer, Director of the Joint Centre for Bioethics at the University of Toronto, for his consent to use selected parts of his consumer information material on living wills. Thanks also to the Canadian Life and Health Insurance Association (CLHIA) and Irene Klatt, Director of Education, for consent to use some material from the CLHIA consumer education booklets. I would also like to express my appreciation to the International Association for Financial Planning for permission to use some of the information from their consumer brochure, "Selecting a Financial Planner."

I would like to thank Alaura Ross, a lawyer and expert on probate and estate matters with the office of the Public Guardian and Trustee of British Columbia, for her review and constructive suggestions on several chapters of the book. My thanks also to Isabela Zabava, a lawyer and expert on planned giving for the B.C. Cancer Foundation, for her review and helpful feedback on the chapter on charitable giving. In addition, I would like to express my thanks to Ken Chong, CPA, of DMCL in Vancouver for his feedback on tax issues.

✳

FROM JOHN BUDD: As with the previous editions of this book, I want to express my deep appreciation, first and foremost, to my wife, Susan, whose continuing love, sage advice and support over the years enabled me to achieve my career goals and so much more. This accumulated experience during my many years in public accounting and since 1997, in the investment management business, has provided the insights to co-author this book. I am also grateful to my many long-time clients and friends for their loyalty and friendship over many years, and for providing so much intellectual "fuel for the fire" because of their complex financial, tax and estate planning situations. I am also especially grateful to my colleagues at Cumberland Private Wealth Management Inc. for their insights on investing and wealth management.

Due to space limitations, we could not incorporate all of the comments and suggestions received from the many experts who were kind enough to review the various drafts of this fourth edition. Accordingly, we take full responsibility for any errors or omissions that may have slipped through the cracks.

PREFACE

When you think of estate planning, what is the first step that comes to your mind? If you said preparing a will, that is the response that most people give. It is correct that a will is the foundation to building an estate plan. However, estate planning involves a lot more issues and decision-making than simply preparing a will. It also includes building your net worth so that you will actually have an estate when you die, as well as dealing with important issues such as: steps to minimize, delay or avoid taxes and fees on death; health care considerations; powers of attorney and living wills; provincial family law implications; gifting; setting up trusts; selection of the right executor; trustee, and guardian; giving to charities and much more.

Legislation and practices in all these areas are constantly in flux. In this fourth edition, we have fully updated, revised and expanded the content to keep it current, fresh and relevant. Information on changes to tax legislation in Canada and the U.S. has been fully amended to reflect the most current changes. We have further updated legislation in non-tax areas throughout the text to keep you up to date.

Depending on your financial, marital, family, business and health situation and your long-term wishes, the steps you take to do an estate plan could be simple or complex. Everyone's situation is unique. As your needs and circumstances change over time, you will need to review and modify your estate plan. The process is a dynamic and fluid one and requires a regular update on an annual or more frequent basis, depending on events and stages in your life. Many people have accumulated substantial wealth, although they may not think of themselves as wealthy. For example, over time assets could include a home, cottage, company pension plans, RRSPs or RRIFs, TFSAs, investments, art or jewellery. Added to this net worth could be the possibility of receiving an inheritance. The combined net worth could be significant. If strategic planning based on expert professional advice is not done, one of the principal beneficiaries could be the Canada Revenue Agency (CRA). Without proper planning, an excessive amount of income tax could end up being paid to the CRA at the expense of those individuals or charities that mean more to you.

This book was written for those who want a general, practical and objective overview of the issues, options and terminology involved in estate planning. That way, people are better prepared to determine their estate planning needs, select their advisors wisely, organize their financial affairs and make prudent and well-informed decisions. This book is the most comprehensive guide available for the layperson in Canada. It is based on the authors' professional legal, tax and investment experience advising clients over many years, questions that the authors have encountered through giving seminars and media interviews across Canada; review of relevant government legislation; extensive research; and discussions with other professionals involved directly or indirectly in tax and estate planning and other facets of wealth management.

However, this book is simply a guide. It does not provide legal, tax or investment advice, but merely gives some general information to enhance your awareness. The appendix samples are for illustration only. The documents are not intended to be modified and used personally under any circumstances. Their use could result in the document being deemed inappropriate or legally unenforceable, depending on your personal situation and province.

This book is not a "do-it-yourself" guide. That is why you need to seek out and obtain competent professional advice on a customized basis. There is no other logical or appropriate way to ensure your needs are properly met. The contents of this book will provide you with more knowledge to make your advisory meetings more productive and relevant. This will save you time, money and stress.

This book provides general information only for the common law provinces, that is, excluding Quebec. The laws relating to wills, trusts, powers of attorney, living wills, and probate fees vary from province to province. In addition, the legal terminology can also vary from province to province.

Although the chapters are mutually exclusive, the contents and issues are interrelated. In 18 chapters we cover the stages of estate planning; determining your assets and income now and in the future; and understanding wills, powers of attorney, trusts, living wills and probate. We also discuss death and taxes; dealing with CRA; tax planning strategies; special tax and estate planning issues if you own U.S. assets; vacation properties; and the family business. The final chapters include charitable giving; life, health and disability insurance; selecting professional advisors; selection of retirement residences and care facilities and planning your funeral. The format of the book includes sections at the end of each chapter on where to get more information and frequently asked questions.

In the appendices you will find a wealth of information to assist you. For example, in Appendix A there is an extensive resource list, contact numbers to save you time and hassle, and a list of helpful and informative websites. There are also samples, charts and various checklists, including checklists that will provide you with the questions to ask or consider. The extensive glossary will help you understand the jargon.

Finally, on page 426 there is a section inviting reader input and contact information about seminars that we offer. Since the first edition of *The Canadian Guide to Will and Estate Planning* was published, we have been delighted by the support and positive response. The feedback from readers, reviewers, industry and those attending our seminars has been encouraging and constructive. This has contributed towards the book being a national best-seller and we sincerely appreciate it. Clearly, there is a need in Canada for practical information on the wide range of issues to consider when estate planning.

We hope you enjoy this book and find it practical and helpful.

Douglas Gray, BA, LLB   Vancouver, B.C.

John Budd, TEP, FCPA, FCA   Toronto, Ontario

August, 2017

The Canadian Guide to Will and Estate Planning

What Is Estate Planning?

"Knowledge is power."

SIR FRANCIS BACON

INTRODUCTION

Estate planning refers to the process required to transfer and preserve your wealth in an orderly and effective manner.

A properly drafted will is the foundation of a strategic estate plan. From a tax perspective, your estate planning objectives include

- minimizing and deferring taxes on your death so that most of your estate can be preserved for your heirs
- moving any tax burden to your heirs to be paid only upon the future sale of the assets

There are various techniques to attain the above objectives, including:

- arranging for assets to be transferred to family members in a lower tax bracket
- establishing trusts for your children and/or spouse to maximize future tax savings
- setting up estate freezes, generally for your children, which reduce the tax they pay in the future on the increased value of selected assets
- making optimal use of the benefit of charitable donations, tax shelters, holding companies or dividend tax credits
- taking advantage of the benefits of gifting during your lifetime
- minimizing risk of business creditors encroaching on personal estate assets
- having sufficient insurance to cover anticipated tax on death
- utilizing effective tax strategies for business owners
- avoiding probate fees by having assets in joint names or with a designated beneficiary

The above techniques will be discussed in more detail in other chapters.

STAGES OF ESTATE PLANNING OVER YOUR LIFETIME

Regardless of your age, the issue of estate planning, in conjunction with your will, is an essential element of life planning. There are different stages in a person's life though, when certain issues may arise that require different estate planning strategies. Here are some of the key stages.

The Young Family

In this stage, you are just starting to accumulate assets and possibly raise a family. Preliminary planning is important. Do a financial status review, needs assessment and wish list to help in will preparation and estate planning. Various checklists in Appendix D will assist you. Consider these steps:

- Draw up a list of all your assets and liabilities, current income and expenses, and projected income and expenses over the next five years.
- Outline a five-year plan in terms of what goals and needs you have during that time.
- Assess your life and disability insurance protection to make sure it is adequate for all your present and projected needs.
- Review your savings programs such as Registered Retirement Savings Plans (RRSPs), Tax-Free Savings Accounts (TFSAs), and education funding programs for your children, such as Registered Education Savings Plans (RESPs).
- Decide on how you would like your assets to be distributed in the event of your death and do up a list. You and your spouse may want to do separate lists and then compare notes and come to agreement.
- Select an executor and trustee of your will by referring to Chapter 4, "Understanding Wills." The advantages of using a trust company are covered in Chapter 6, "Understanding Trusts."
- Decide on a guardian for your young children. This is obviously a very important decision and great care should be taken in the selection; refer to Chapter 4, "Understanding Wills."
- Consult with a lawyer, accountant or trust company on matters to do with wills, estate planning and trusts. Refer to Chapter 16, "Selecting Professional Advisors."

The Mature Family

In this stage, your priorities and needs are changing. Your children are adolescents or in their twenties, so the issue of the guardianship and education of your children is not so imperative as before. You are probably in your peak earning years and may have accumulated considerable assets. You may be separated, divorced, re-married, or living common-law, all associated with considerable legal and estate planning implications, as outlined next:

- Assess your financial status, and personal and life needs, goals, priorities and wishes. This is an ongoing process. In projecting your future financial income, for example, you could be receiving a large inheritance. You may want to buy a cottage or chalet as a second home.
- Review your will. This should be a periodic process anyway, at least annually, as cautioned before. Changing circumstances could necessitate reviewing your will more frequently than just once a year. Changing marital status situations or children from a previous marital or common-law situation presents new legal implications. Your will could be challenged by a dependent from a past relationship or current spouse's children from a previous marriage. There could also be a challenge for maintenance from a previous spouse. Your responsibility may not end on your death, depending on the laws of your province. Make sure you obtain legal advice.
- Re-assess your professional advisors on a regular basis. As your circumstances and financial situation become complex, you may need more skilled advisors or additional ones. This includes your lawyer, professional tax accountant, investment advisor, financial planner and trust company.
- Consider how your investments (including RRSPs and TFSAs) have been performing and, with the help of your investment advisor, work out a realistic plan to achieve a long-term investment goal. Most likely, you will not be able to rely on Old Age Security, the Canada Pension Plan, or a pension from your employer (if indeed you will even have one) to meet your living expense requirements when you retire. Now is the stage of your life when you need to start building up an investment portfolio that will support you in your retirement years.
- Re-assess your executor. In the first stage discussed previously, your financial situation needs may not have been so complex. That could have changed dramatically over the years. Consider the benefits of having a trust company as an executor and trustee.
- Consider a special trust. You may have had a trust earlier, for your young or special needs children. You may now wish to have a trust for many other reasons, discussed in other chapters. For example, a *spousal trust* is usually created to provide a spouse with income during his or her life only or until he or she remarries. The capital is then passed on to the children on the spouse's death or remarriage. A *spendthrift trust* provides income to a beneficiary without allowing access to the capital. This trust might be created because the person is financially irresponsible. The trust terms can give the trustees the discretion to release the capital when the person has matured and shown financial responsibility, or for some other worthwhile purpose. Another type of trust is called the *sprinkling trust*. In this situation, income is divided amongst various family members over time, rather than being given all to the spouse.

A more detailed discussion of trusts is covered in Chapter 6, "Understanding Trusts."

The Older Family

In this stage, you could be approaching retirement or planning early retirement. As you and your spouse get older, there could be health or medical concerns. Your assets are probably nearing their peak. Your children may be married and may or may not need your financial support. Alternatively, you may have a child who is out of work, or divorced or separated, perhaps asking for financial support for themselves or their children. Consider the following:

- Assess your financial status, and personal and life needs, goals, and priorities. You may wish to travel, or to become a "Snowbird" and live in the U.S., Mexico or elsewhere for up to six months a year. If so, refer to the latest edition of Douglas Gray's book, *The Canadian Snowbird Guide: Everything You Need to Know About Living Part-Time in the USA and Mexico*, published by John Wiley & Sons. You may wish to sell your existing home, and move to a condominium in a quiet retirement-oriented community. Many people "cash out" by doing this, in other words, have so much equity in their home that after their new purchase they still have lots of money left. If you are considering buying a condo, refer to Douglas Gray's book, *101 Streetsmart Condo Buying Tips for Canadians*, published by John Wiley & Sons.

- Review your will. You need to balance the needs of your spouse against those of your children. You may wish to enjoy your lifestyle and retirement fully and leave whatever is left to your children. Alternatively, you may wish instead to leave a trust for your grand-children or give additional money to a favourite charity or other worthwhile cause. If your children are already financially independent, these options may be attractive. You may want to completely disinherit a child for other reasons. Make sure your lawyer words the will carefully to minimize any chances it could be contested.

- Re-consider your executor and trustee—you want to make sure your executor still fulfills your needs fully. Immediate family or relatives may not be the best choice as executor or trustee. There could be personalities in your family that you know would result in conflict. You may therefore wish to retain a trust company to act as your executor and trustee. You could name a responsible family member as a co-executor and co-trustee if you so wished. The issues surrounding these choices are discussed in other chapters.

- Obtain professional advice on minimizing taxes as the size of your estate could have considerable tax consequences. Federal and provincial income taxes are due when you die, as well as deemed disposition of capital gains, potentially seriously depleting your estate. As mentioned before, you need to obtain advice from your lawyer, professional tax accountant, investment advisor, financial planner, and trust company.

- If you or your spouse are 65 or older, consider whether you should be holding the owner-ship of your non-RRSP investment portfolio, real estate, or other assets by means of a *joint partner trust* or an *alter ego trust*. These types of trusts would leave you in much the same position as if you continued to hold the personal legal ownership of your investments, real estate and other assets, however, a *joint partner* trust or an *alter ego trust* might reduce probate fees, and could simplify the administration of your estate. You should also plan for a time when you may not be capable of looking after your own legal and financial affairs, i.e. enduring power of attorney. Refer to Chapter 6, "Understanding Trusts."

Top 10 Pitfalls to Avoid in Will and Estate Planning

Two out of three adult Canadians do not have a will. Over 50 percent of them have children. One out of four Canadians will die suddenly. You can't take the risk that the CRA will be your primary beneficiary because of poor tax and estate planning and lack of the will to prepare a will.

There are some classic pitfalls to avoid when preparing your will and doing your estate planning. Throughout this book, we will point out many of the key risk scenarios and explain how to strategically plan and prevent them from occurring.

Here are just 10 of the many pitfalls for the unwary and unprepared.

Not Updating Your Will and Not Having a Power of Attorney and a "Living Will"

Many people have a will prepared and forget about updating it. So much can change in terms of your circumstances, assets, beneficiaries and wishes that you need to review your will on an annual basis at a set time, e.g. your birthday, the first of the new year or some other memorable time. Also review your will when any major change occurs in your life, e.g. divorce; death of a spouse, executor or beneficiaries; etc.

You need to have three key documents as a minimum for your estate planning protection. A will, of course; a power of attorney in case you are mentally incapacitated (accident, stroke, disease); and a "living will." This generic term means having a document that covers your financial, healthcare and end-of-life wishes if you are unable to do the decision-making yourself. Depending on the province, this document could be called an advance direction, healthcare proxy, representation agreement, etc.

Not Selecting the Right Executor, Trustee or Guardian

Being an executor of a will can be very time consuming, stressful and complex. Many people are inappropriate for handling that responsibility. Some people don't even ask the executor if he or she is prepared to assume that role; they just name the person in the will. The executor could predecease them or move to another province or country. Consider the benefits of using a trust company as an executor or co-executor and having an alternate executor. You need to be prudent when selecting a trustee for your financial protection and decision-making. Similarly, the choice you make for the guardian of your children on your demise lasts a lifetime. You want to avoid hassles that will leave negative memories.

Not Having Sufficient Financial Resources to Cover Taxes, Expenses, and Debts

Poor estate planning could result in the estate being drained at death, leaving little, if any, assets for distribution to beneficiaries. There are ways of minimizing this risk by advance planning— for example, by holding assets in joint names; by gifting before death; by designating beneficiaries of life insurance policies or RRSPs, RRIFs, or TFSAs; and by having sufficient life insurance while you are still medically eligible to obtain insurance.

Premiums for insurance to cover anticipated capital gains tax, for example, could be paid for by yourself, or by those who will be the major beneficiaries of an asset triggering capital gains tax, e.g. family cottage or shares in a business.

Not Taking a Strategic Approach to Estate Planning If You Are Self-Employed

If you are operating a small business and die, many negative situations could result unless proper planning is done. For example, if your business goes under, your estate could be depleted due to claims by business creditors, or because you signed personal guarantees to lenders, suppliers or a landlord. You should consider a buy/sell agreement secured by insurance, so that the company has sufficient resources to pay your estate out. There are many other strategic options to separate your personal assets from business exposure. In addition, you should consider estate freezes.

Not Taking the Necessary Steps to Protect Your Estate from U.S. Taxes

If you own any U.S. real estate (e.g. you are a seasonal "Snowbird" or have vacation or investment property), U.S. publicly traded stocks and bonds, or certain other kinds of U.S. assets, you need special tax planning strategies. Properly done, you can save most, if not all, of any U.S. estate taxes otherwise applicable. Otherwise, your executors could end up paying U.S. estate tax at the time of your death that could be as much as 50 percent of the market value of your U.S. assets, with little or no tax relief against the Canadian capital gains taxes that become payable upon your death.

Not Adopting an Investment Strategy for Your RRSPs and Other Investment Portfolios That Is Consistent with Your Estate Planning Goals

Without proper investment planning and implementation, there might not be enough assets in your estate to accomplish all the bequests that are set out in your will.

Not Understanding and Utilizing the Benefits of Trusts

Many types of trusts can go into effect during your life or on your death. These trusts serve a variety of different purposes, all relating to saving on taxes, minimizing exposure to creditors, or discouraging someone from challenging the bequests in your will or your provisions for others—e.g. trusts for minor children are set up to look after the needs of your children until they are adults.

Not Taking Full Advantage of Second-Property Tax Strategies

If you own a vacation home, you want to set up tax planning strategies to minimize or eliminate the tax consequences of leaving the property to other family members, and to set up the arrangement strategically to keep peace in the family.

Not Preparing and Updating a Personal Inventory and Information List

This step is very important. Many executors do not have any information available, which results in frustration, delay, expense and potential legal problems. You do not want to leave that stressful legacy on your demise. You need to prepare a current, complete and accurate inventory with details of your financial and personal information and update it as circumstances change. This inventory would include, for example, assets, liabilities, income sources, personal and family information, names of key contact people and advisors, insurance policies, funeral wishes, business information and special instructions or guidelines for the executor. You also want to have a record of your digital assets to avoid unnecessary hassle and expense for your family and executors. You don't want to leave unanswered questions.

Not Obtaining Professional Tax and Legal Advice

With customized strategic tax and estate planning techniques, you can definitely maximize the net assets available for those you want to remember, by eliminating, minimizing, or delaying tax. You can also avoid potential legal problems, e.g. someone challenging your estate to obtain a financial benefit or increased benefit. There are special situations where customized tax and legal strategies are required, e.g. common-law relationship, blended families, etc. Skilled advice is cheap money for peace of mind and prudent planning. Otherwise, the government coffers could be significant and happy financial beneficiaries.

You want to ensure that your professional advice is integrated and that you use appropriate specialists—for example, an estate lawyer, tax accountant (CPA), insurance broker, financial planner or portfolio manager, etc.

SUMMARY

This chapter is a brief overview of some of the points you need to consider in estate planning. Review other chapters to obtain an overall context and more detail on the issues and tips to consider, depending on your stage and circumstances in life. Complete the checklists in Appendix D and review the other material contained there. Refer to the website: *www.estateplanning.ca*. Make sure, as we reinforce throughout, that you obtain skilled, professional legal, tax and financial planning advice on an ongoing basis.

What Assets Will You Have?

"It is better to live a rich life than to die rich."

SAMUEL JOHNSON

INTRODUCTION

You could be quite surprised once you assess the current and projected value of your estate. After you read this chapter and complete the net worth statement in Appendix D, speak to your professional advisor and decide on the best approach to meet your wishes. This chapter covers generating and protecting existing and future income sources as well. Naturally, maximizing net income is the basis on which your net worth, and therefore estate, will be created.

Obtain objective professional advice before you embark on any particular course of action. How to select professional advisors is covered in Chapter 16. The quality of the advice you rely on will profoundly affect your financial well-being, peace of mind, quality of lifestyle and amount left in your estate.

This chapter will provide an overview of the most common income and asset topics, including:

- determining your personal assets
- government pension plans
- employer/union pension plans
- your own tax-sheltered pension plans
- using your home as an additional source of income
- insurance
- making sure that your funds are protected
- how to avoid potential financial risk areas
- where to get more information

9

HOW MUCH ARE YOU WORTH?

Complete the net worth statement in Appendix D. The statement addresses a wide variety of assets that you may currently have, such as a primary or secondary home, car, boat, paintings, investments, money, equity in a business, personal effects, etc.

GOVERNMENT PENSION PLANS

Here is a brief overview of the key federal and provincial government pension or financial assistance programs and guidelines that you should be familiar with. They can be modified periodically, of course, so obtain a current update of regulations and criteria relevant to your circumstances. In addition, there could be exceptions to the general guidelines outlined. For more information and assistance, including eligibility benefits, indexing and payment outside of Canada, contact Service Canada at *www.canada.ca* for online information and locations of local offices.

Keep in mind that the OAS, GIS, SPA and CPP benefits are not paid automatically. You have to apply for them. You can arrange to have these funds automatically deposited into your bank account.

Old Age Security Pension (OAS)

The OAS pension is a monthly benefit available to anyone 67 years of age or over (or from age 65 if you were born before January 1, 1962). OAS residence requirements must also be met. An applicant's employment history is not a factor in determining eligibility, nor does the applicant need to be retired. You have to pay tax, federal and provincial income tax, on your OAS pension. Higher-income pensioners also repay part or all of their benefit through the tax system, referred to as a clawback. This clawback is taken off the OAS pension at source, based upon the previous year's tax return income. Contact your local HRDC office or Health Canada for the current amount of the clawback (see Appendix A for contact information). This amount could be increased by the government over time.

All benefits payable under the *Old Age Security Act* are increased in January, April, July and October of each year based on increases in the cost of living as measured by the Consumer Price Index (CPI).

Guaranteed Income Supplement (GIS)

The GIS is a monthly benefit paid to residents of Canada who receive a basic, full or partial OAS pension and who have little or no other income. GIS payments may begin in the same month as OAS pension payments. Recipients must re-apply annually for the GIS benefit. Thus, the amount of monthly payments may increase or decrease according to reported changes in a recipient's yearly income. Unlike the basic OAS pension, the GIS is *not* subject to income tax.

Allowance for Surviving Spouse

The allowance is over and above the Guaranteed Income Supplement for qualifying individuals aged 60 to 64. It is designed to recognize the difficult circumstances faced by many widowed persons and by couples living on the pension of only one spouse. Benefits are not considered as income for income tax purposes.

Provincial Social Security Supplement Programs

Some provinces have guaranteed annual income systems. If you are 65 years of age or older and you receive the federal Guaranteed Income Supplement, you might qualify for additional provincial benefits which ensure that your income does not fall below the province's guaranteed income level.

To apply for provincial assistance, contact your provincial government. For a list of addresses and telephone numbers of provincial offices for seniors, refer to Appendix A.

Canada Pension Plan (CPP)/Quebec Pension Plan (QPP)

The CPP is a contributory, earnings-related social insurance program. It ensures a measure of protection to a contributor and his or her family against the loss of income due to retirement, disability and death. The plan operates throughout Canada. Quebec has its own similar program, the Quebec Pension Plan (QPP), which is closely associated with the CPP. The operation of the two plans is coordinated through a series of agreements between the federal and Quebec governments. Benefits from either plan are based on pension credits accumulated under both, as if only one plan existed.

Benefits paid by the CPP are considered as income for federal and provincial income tax purposes. You must apply for all CPP benefits and should apply at least six months before you want to receive it.

A CPP retirement pension may be paid at age 60. However, the contributor must have wholly or substantially ceased pensionable employment. Contributors are considered to have substantially ceased pensionable employment if their annual earnings from employment or self-employment do not exceed the maximum retirement pension payable at age 65 for the year the pension is claimed. Once 65, a pensioner is not required to stop work to receive a retirement pension.

All CPP benefits are adjusted in January each year to reflect increases in the cost of living as measured by the Consumer Price Index.

PLANNING TO PROTECT ● *Reducing Tax Through Income Splitting*

Doris and Chester wanted to reduce their aggregate present and future tax hit by splitting their income. This meant shifting income from the higher-income spouse to the lower-income spouse. Chester made a higher income. The purpose of the exercise was to have Chester's income taxed at a lower marginal tax rate or have the income taxed in Doris' existing lower marginal tax rate.

After obtaining expert professional advice, the couple arranged with Canada Pension Plan (CPP) to have the benefits split 50/50 in Doris' favour. Otherwise, Chester would have received substantially more retirement income than Doris. Doris did not previously have any CPP coverage. In addition, Chester started to place a substantial portion of his annual RRSP into a spousal RRSP. The reason for this was to transfer income to the lower-income spouse in order to minimize post-retirement taxes. Chester was still able to deduct the full amount of the RRSP annual contribution from his higher taxed income. As a consequence of the above steps, Doris and Chester estimated that they would save at least 10 percent on the combined retirement tax bill.

In addition to this tax saving, a further income-splitting tax benefit is available to Chester and Doris. Because they are age 65 or older, they are allowed to allocate some or all of eligible pension income to their spouse or common-law partner, for tax return filing purposes. One would do this if the spouse/common-law partner is in a lower income bracket. Eligible pension income includes pensions from registered pension plans, RRSPs, and RRIFs.

● ●

CPP Disability Pension

To receive a disability pension, a contributor must have had to stop working because of his or her medical condition, must have made sufficient contributions to the plan and must be under the age of 65.

A contributor is considered to be disabled under CPP if he or she has a physical or mental disability which is both severe and prolonged. *Severe* means that the person cannot regularly pursue any substantially gainful occupation. *Prolonged* means that the disability is likely to be long continued and of indefinite duration, or is likely to result in death.

A disability pension begins in the fourth month after the month a person is considered disabled. It is payable until the beneficiary turns age 65, or recovers from the disability (if this occurs before age 65), or until the beneficiary dies. When the recipient of a disability pension reaches age 65, the pension is automatically converted to a retirement pension.

CPP Surviving Spouse's Pension

A spouse of a deceased contributor or a person who lived in a common-law relationship with a contributor before his or her death, may be eligible for a survivor's pension. To qualify, the deceased must have contributed to the CPP during at least one-third of the number of calendar years in his or her contributory period. If the deceased's contributory period was less than nine years, then at least three years' worth of CPP contributions are needed. If the contributory period was more than 30 years, at least 10 years' worth of contributions are required.

To qualify for a benefit, the surviving spouse must be 45 or more years of age. There are some exceptions for those younger than 45 years. As regulations can change, find out the current status.

CPP Death Benefit

A death benefit may be paid to the estate of a deceased contributor, if contributions to the CPP were made for the minimum qualifying period. This minimum period is the same as for a surviving spouse's pension. The death benefit is paid, as well, where there is no will or estate. In this case, the benefit is usually paid to the person or agency responsible for funeral costs.

The death benefit is a lump-sum payment equal to six times the monthly retirement pension of the deceased contributor up to a maximum of $2,500.

Veterans' Pension

Veterans Affairs Canada provides a wide range of services and benefits to war veterans and former members of the Canadian Armed Forces. Assistance is in the form of disability pensions, survivors' pensions, and help with funeral and burial expenses. For more information, contact Veterans Affairs Canada at *www.canada.ca* for more information and the location of a local office. You must apply for all pensions or services provided by Veterans Affairs Canada.

Social Security Programs from Other Countries

In many countries, nationality is an important criterion in determining eligibility for social security benefits. Noncitizens may be required to meet special conditions before they can receive a pension, and the payment of benefits to noncitizens living abroad may be severely restricted or even prohibited. Through the social security agreement between Canada and selected countries, including the U.S., citizens and noncitizens are entitled to those benefits on the same conditions as the citizens of the other country. Most important, Canadian residents may start to receive benefits from the other country.

Most social security programs require contributions during a minimum number of years before a benefit can be paid. There may also be requirements for contributions in the period just before application for a benefit. People who have contributed to the programs of another country may not have sufficient periods of contributions to meet such requirements. Under the Canada-U.S. agreement, periods of residence in Canada and/or periods of contributions to the CPP may be used to satisfy the eligibility conditions of the other country's social security system.

PENSION PLANS FUNDED BY YOUR EMPLOYER

Ask your employer about the exact benefits you will receive, how they will be structured, and how soon you could receive them. Some employers have more than one plan. Some employers will also include extended health and dental plan coverage as well as life insurance coverage after you retire.

Registered Pension Plans (RPPs)

These are the most heavily regulated by the government. The two main types of plans are defined benefit and defined contribution. The plan could be "contributory," where you and the employer contribute payments, or "non-contributory," where the employer pays the full amount due each year.

DEFINED BENEFIT PLAN

This type of plan promises you a pension of a specific amount of money, based on your years of service and/or salary. For a long time, the conventional wisdom was that there is no risk that your pension funding could be affected by economic or market fluctuations, as the employer must set aside, by law, enough money, separate from other employer funds, to capitalize the specific pension they have promised you. In theory, the pension fund will therefore exist even if the employer ceases to operate. Future benefits could be limited of course in that event. If the pension fund investments do poorly, the employer must compensate by putting extra money into the fund, assuming of course that the corporation has the financial means to do this. One of the effects of the 2007 to 2009 economic meltdown was that a number of previously strong corporations went under, and so did their funding of their employees' defined benefit pension plans. With the market collapse, combined with historically low interest rates, many pension plans found themselves under-funded, and unable to meet their future pension payment obligations to their members. History repeats itself, so it's wise to keep in mind that an entitlement under a defined benefit pension plan is not necessarily 100 percent assured.

There are two forms of defined benefit plans:
1. **Accruing benefits plan.** This plan can vary considerably, depending on the employer. Some offer a pension based on a percentage (e.g. 2 percent) of your average salary over

your final three or five years of employment. This amount is then multiplied by your years of employment with the company. Other plans average all your earnings during your employment with the firm, not as attractive an arrangement as the previous one, based on your most current (higher) tax earning years. Basing payments on your later years will therefore result in increased pension payments.

Some employers offer a supplemental pension plan to extend the amount of pension from the RPP pension ceiling set by Canada Revenue Agency (CRA).

2. **Flat benefit plan.** This type of plan bases the calculation for pension purposes on a flat amount per month for each year of employment, for example, $30/month.

Some of these two types of plans include partial or full indexing for inflation; however, these kinds of plans are increasingly rare. If this is your situation, verify if this provision is guaranteed, or possibly required by provincial legislation, rather than optional on the part of the company.

DEFINED CONTRIBUTION PLAN

These plans are sometimes referred to as "money purchase plans." The employer promises to contribute a certain amount to your pension account annually, for example, 3 to 6 percent of your annual salary. A specific amount of pension, however, is not promised. You may be able to make your own contributions. Your employer invests the contribution on your behalf. The amount of your pension will vary depending on the value of your pension account on retirement. If your employer invests well, you will receive a greater retirement income benefit. If not, you get a lower amount. Your risk is related to the success of the pension fund manager, stock market performance, and interest rates between now and retirement, and afterwards as well.

VESTING

Vesting means that the pension credits that you have earned are locked in, so that you won't lose these benefits if you change your job. Ask your employer or the federal or provincial pension authorities responsible for your plan. Depending on the regulations, you might have to have been in the plan for two to five years or more before it can be vested.

If you quit your job, you can let your vested credits remain with your employer, rather than taking out the amount in a lump-sum, which would be taxable income. If the vested credits remain, you could receive a retirement pension that could net more than you otherwise could have earned. It all depends on your needs and circumstances of course, and what you want to do with the money. Alternatively, you could transfer the money into a locked-in RRSP. Although you can't withdraw it until your normal retirement age, you would control how it is invested. You must use the funds to provide retirement income, which would normally require you to buy a life annuity or a Life Income Fund (LIF). An LIF could allow you to wait until the age of 80, if you want, before buying a life annuity. Check what regulations and options apply in your case.

Deferred Profit Sharing Plans (DPSPs)

These plans are also regulated by government but are less restrictive than RPPs. They are similar to a defined contribution RPP in the sense that the amount you receive relates to the amount of the employer contribution and how effectively the money was invested.

DPSPs are different from RPPs in that the employer is only allowed to contribute half the amount permitted in a defined contribution plan. If there is an annual profit, the employer is obligated to make a minimum contribution. No contribution is required if the company shows a loss that year. Another difference is that you may not have to wait until retirement to withdraw money from the plan.

Group RRSPs

Some employers prefer not to have the regulatory controls of an RPP or DPSP, but still provide an employer-sponsored pension plan. Typically, the employer contracts with a professional money manager to establish an RRSP for each employee, with the administration fee normally borne by the employer. The employer could then increase your salary and deduct the increase to put into the individual RRSP. You benefit through this form of forced savings plan, plus you will receive more net pay each month, as the employer can withhold less for tax deductions due to the RRSP set-off. The disadvantage is that you do not normally have the freedom to select your RRSP investments. The phrase group RRSP is a misnomer, in the sense that although it is set up for a group of employees, each RRSP is individual.

YOUR OWN TAX-SHELTERED PENSION PLANS

Registered Retirement Savings Plans (RRSPs)

TYPES OF RRSPS

There are three main types of RRSPs:

- **Deposit plans.** These are offered by banks, trust companies, credit unions and life insurance companies. This would include term deposits or Guaranteed Investment Certificates (GICs). Terms range generally from one to five years. Vary the dates that your money comes due to average out changes in interest rates.
- **Managed plans**. In this type of plan, which would include ETFs and mutual funds, your money is pooled with others in a diversified portfolio of stocks, bonds, real estate and other

assets. Alternatively, you may have a singular plan managed just for your investments. The value of the assets can vary, depending on the market.

- **Self-directed plans**. In this example, you would be responsible for managing your own portfolio, subject to various restrictions. The funds are held by a bank or a trust company. You can purchase for your plan a wide variety of assets, such as stocks, bonds or mortgages.

Many retired people prefer to opt for the deposit plan or managed plan in conservative investments, so that preservation of capital is foremost.

TYPES OF RRSP WITHDRAWAL OPTIONS

At some point you will have to turn your RRSP savings into retirement income. If you have RRSP funds transferred from a pension plan, you may be subject to pension legislation. For example, you may be required to purchase only life annuities with your funds. Some provinces have approved various alternatives to life annuities. They are called Life Income Funds (LIFs) and/or Locked in Retirement Funds (LRIFs). You basically have three RRSP withdrawal options:

- **Lump-sum withdrawal**. As all the money you withdraw is taxable in the year you receive it, most people don't choose this option unless there is an urgent need. You may prefer to take out smaller amounts with low taxable consequences for specific purposes. The more you take out, the less money is available for future retirement income and potential growth in your retirement plan.
- **Registered Retirement Income Fund (RRIF)**. Covered in more detail in the next section, a RRIF allows you to defer tax on your money, similar to your RRSP.
- **Annuities.** Annuities provide regular income for life or for a specific period and are covered in more detail later.

Registered Retirement Income Fund (RRIF)

A Registered Retirement Income Fund or RRIF has become a very popular retirement income option because it provides the flexibility to control your retirement income and investments. Like a RRSP, you can select the investments you want, adjust your income payments or take lump-sum withdrawals at your pleasure. You can have a self-directed RRIF if you want. Like a RRSP, a RRIF can grow tax-free, if you have income or growth types of investments. A RRIF is like a RRSP in reverse. Instead of putting in money each year, you withdraw money that is taxable income. You have to draw a minimum mandatory amount. There is no maximum payment level. Obviously, the higher the payments you take, the sooner your funds will be depleted. RRIFs can continue for the lifetime of the holder or their spouse. You have to make a conversion from a RRSP to a RRIF by the end of your 71st year, although you can do it at age 65 if you prefer if, for example, you need to qualify for the Pension Income Credit.

Your choice of RRIF will have an important impact on meeting your retirement needs. Consider the amount of income you anticipate you will require in the short and long term, and how long your savings will last.

TYPES OF RRIF WITHDRAWAL OPTIONS

There are various options for withdrawing your RRIF. As you are permitted to have more than one RRIF, you might want to balance your withdrawal options customized to your needs. Not all institutions provide the options listed below:

- **Level payout**. Payments are the same each month, for example, over a 25-year period. Although it is similar in some aspects to an annuity, you have control at all times.
- **Fixed-term payout**. Used by people who want to use up the funds in a shorter time frame, e.g. 10 to 15 years, frequently due to ill health.
- **Minimum payout**. This option maximizes your investment by allowing the funds to grow in a compounding tax-free environment. You can set up your RRIF at the end of your 71st year, for example, with payments to commence the following year. You don't have to take any payments in the calendar year it is funded. If your spouse is younger, you can set the formula based on his or her age, as there are advantages to this.
- **Interest-only payout**. In this case, you would receive interest only until the deadline arrives for minimum withdrawals. At this point your capital will start eroding, therefore growth will not occur. In the meantime though, you would have preserved your capital.
- **Indexed payout**. Payments are increased annually based on a projected inflation rate, for example, 3 to 5 percent.
- **Smoothed payout**. Payments are adjusted so that you receive higher payments in the early years and lower payments in the latter years. The schedule of payments is calculated based on actuarial projections.

FACTORS TO CONSIDER WHEN MAKING YOUR RRSP OR RRIF SELECTION

You can continue making RRSP payments up to your 71st year if you want, when you have to convert to a RRIF or an annuity or a take a lump-sum withdrawal. Key considerations as to the type of RRSP or RRIF relate to placing your funds in no-risk to high-risk types of investments. Consider the following factors:

- **Safety**. As you are retired or nearing retirement, preservation of capital is a primary consideration, followed by income or growth strategies that will at least neutralize inflation. You don't want to speculate. Spread any risk by diversifying your portfolio, unless you simply want money market funds such as Guaranteed Investment Certificates (GICs), Canada Savings Bonds or term deposits. Products that could result in your losing money would negatively affect your retirement lifestyle or impair your peace of mind.

- **Diversification**. As you mature you want to move into more stable and secure investments. Equity-based mutual funds or actual stocks tend to be too risky for many people who either don't understand the market or feel anxious about the risk of eroding their capital, with little time for recovery. On the other hand, if you have some "extra" money, you may wish to place some of it in more growth-oriented investments.
- **Rate of return**. The lower the risk, the lower the return; the higher the risk, the higher the potential return. To preserve your capital, you will probably opt for safety and certainty. However, by actively considering your options and checking out the competition thoroughly, you could still get possibly 1 to 4 percent more return without much risk of impairing your capital. Over time, this extra percentage could make a considerable difference, by compounding tax-free in your RRSP or RRIF.
- **Liquidity**. Having access to a certain amount of your money when you need it, or if interest rates increase considerably, allows you to take advantage of that opportunity.
- **Fees**. Normally not an issue for people with deposit funds, such as GICs and term deposits etc. If you have a self-directed RRSP or RRIF, a managed plan such as a mutual fund, or a personally managed portfolio, the issue of fees for management is a consideration.

Annuities

An *annuity* involves putting a lump sum of money into a plan that provides a regular income for life or for a specified period. There are some limitations to be aware of relative to RRIFs. With an annuity, you have no income payment flexibility or opportunity to manage investment options to possibly increase your retirement income. There could also be little or no inflation protection unless you have the annuity indexed for inflation. The amount an annuity pays is determined by your age and the interest rates at the time of purchase. Annuities are a viable option if you can't or prefer not to manage your own money, as you can with a RRIF.

Term certain annuities are sold by various institutions, including banks, trust companies, credit unions and insurance companies. Life annuities are sold only by life insurance companies. Ask about deposit insurance protection, estate preservation and fees on any RRIF or annuity before you invest.

TYPES OF ANNUITIES

There are the two main types of annuities:

1. **Term Certain Annuity to Age 90 (TCA90)**

   This annuity provides regular periodic payments that can continue until your ninetieth year. Payments are normally level, but can usually be indexed for inflation. If your spouse is younger than you are, you can purchase the TCA90 to continue after your death until your spouse's ninetieth year. If you die before 90 and do not have a spouse, you can make arrangements for the payments to go to your estate. Some issuers offer a TCA90 with an alternative to a fixed rate of return. In this option, the yield and payments are adjusted periodically with interest rate charges. You can also get up to age 100 (TCA100) if you want.

2. **Life Annuity**

A life annuity provides regular payments that will continue for the rest of your life, no matter how long you live. When you die however, any money left in the annuity goes to the issuer, not your estate. The exception would be if you arrange an annuity that has a guaranteed payment period.

There are various types of life annuities. Here is a sampling of the most common ones:

- **Straight life annuity.** This type of annuity is for an individual only, and provides you with the highest amount of income for each dollar of premium, in terms of monthly or annual payments. However, it only lasts for your lifetime, when the annuity payments stop, unless you have a guaranteed period. This type of plan might be suitable for people who have no dependents.

- **Life annuity with a guaranteed period**. This provides a guarantee that you or your beneficiary will receive back all of your investments plus full interest if you wish, even if you only live for a short time. Alternatively, you may have the guarantee period set up to provide income payments for a fixed time frame, such as 5, 10 or 15 years from the start of payments to you, or until you or your spouse reach a certain age, e.g. 90. The longer the guaranteed period, the lower the payments.

- **Joint and last survivor annuity**. This annuity provides a regular income as long as either spouse is living. Payments can continue at the full amount to the surviving spouse, or they can be reduced by any stipulated percentage on the death of either spouse or specifically at your death. Selecting the reduction option will result in higher payments while both spouses are alive. Although this type of plan results in less income for each dollar invested in the annuity, to many people the additional benefits are worth it.

- **Installment refund annuity**. If you die before you have received as much money as you paid for the annuity, this annuity will continue income payments to your beneficiary until they equal the amount you originally paid.

- **Cash refund annuity**. In this annuity, rather than your beneficiary receiving continued income payments, as in the above example, they receive a lump-sum payout instead.

- **Indexed life annuity**. This provides for annuity payments that either increase each year automatically from 1 to 5 percent, for example, based on the return of a specified group of assets. Although this provides you with some protection against rising living costs due to inflation, it will also reduce your payments in the early years.

- **Integrated life annuity**. If you wish, you can integrate your Old Age Security (OAS) payments with your annuity. With this annuity, you would receive substantially increased annuity payments until age 65, at which time the payments will reduce by the maximum OAS entitlement at the time you purchased the annuity.

USING YOUR HOME AS AN ADDITIONAL SOURCE OF INCOME

Many Canadian seniors prefer to remain in their own homes as long as possible for a variety of reasons, including their support network of neighbours, friends, church, or other regular social activities.

This desire is not always matched by their capacity to pay for it, however. It is not uncommon for seniors to be house-rich and cash-poor.

Although contributions could have been made to private pension plans, government pensions or RRSPs, there could still be insufficient financial resources for the seniors' needs or wants, such as being a Snowbird and living in the U.S. Sunbelt states. Other seniors may not have the savings income mentioned, and rely only on federal Old Age Security (OAS) income along with possibly a federal Guaranteed Income Supplement (GIS). Some of these federal or provincial programs involve a means test. Many seniors with fixed savings have had their purchasing power eroded by inflation. The home is the single largest form of "savings" for seniors, especially if they can tap into the equity that has accumulated, for lump-sum and/or on-going income, without having to make monthly payments.

Many seniors think that a home cannot readily be converted into an income source unless the home is sold, a very stressful scenario to some. Other seniors, by circumstance or choice, elect to sell the home, buy a condominium, in many cases in a retirement area, and have considerable cash left over for their financial and lifestyle needs.

There are options for seniors who want to stay in their own homes but need or wish to supplement their income. One option is to rent out a self-contained basement suite to provide income. Another is to rent out spare rooms in the house, in other words have boarders who share common kitchen facilities and washrooms. In many cases the rental income may not give rise to any additional personal income tax, because it can be offset against a percentage of the house expenses. The above options may provide additional benefits in the form of companionship and the feeling of security. This latter benefit could be particularly attractive if the owner is a Snowbird, or is frequently away on trips. On the other hand, some seniors resent the loss of privacy. Municipal by-law regulations could also technically restrict having tenants. In many cases these regulations are flexible, depending on current municipal policy regarding enforcement, and extenuating circumstances of the owner.

Reverse Mortgages

Reverse mortgages, reverse annuity mortgages or home equity plans are similar concepts that have been available for a number of years to seniors or early retirees across Canada. Over the years, many people have built up considerable equity in their houses, townhouses or condominiums. Many Canadians have decided to turn their largest asset into immediate cash and/or ongoing revenue and still remain in the home.

The basic concept behind these various plans is simple. You take out a mortgage on part of the equity of your home (debt-free portion of your home), and in exchange receive a lump-sum amount of money and/or a monthly income for a fixed period or for your life, and if you are married, for the life of the surviving spouse. This latter example is sometimes referred to as a reverse annuity mortgage (RAM), as part of the money obtained from the mortgage is used to purchase an annuity. When you sell the home, or when you die, or if you are married, when your surviving spouse dies, the mortgage plus accrued interest must be repaid. You do not have to make any payments in the meantime. Any balance left in residual equity in the home after the sale would belong to the senior or his or her estate.

Here are some of the features of the various reverse mortgage options:

- Reverse mortgages, RAMs and other home equity programs are readily available through a variety of agents and brokers. This permits you to compare and contrast in a competitive marketplace and end up with a plan customized for your specific needs. Look on the Internet under "reverse mortgage" or "CHIP program."

- The CRA has decided that the home equity lump-sum payment and monthly annuity payments are tax-free, as long as you live in your home. If you select a monthly income annuity that continues after you have moved out of your home, the income from the sale may be subject to favourable prescribed annuity taxation rules. The current ruling on the various means-tested programs, such as the federal Guaranteed Income Supplement (GIS), is that receiving the annuity will not interfere with your eligibility for, or reduction in, the GIS. As tax laws and regulations change, make sure you obtain current independent advice from a tax accountant and the CRA on this issue.

- As you retain ownership, you benefit from any appreciation in value of the home over time, that is, you get an increase in equity. For example, if your property goes up 10 percent a year in value, and you locked in the mortgage on your property for the reverse mortgage or RAM at say 8 percent, then you are technically ahead in terms of the interest differential. In reality, because you are not making regular payments on your mortgage, the interest on it is being compounded, therefore in practical terms, ultimately eroding the increasing equity. This could substantially reduce your estate. The reduction could be partially offset by an attractive average annual appreciation in property value.

Although many of the reverse mortgages, RAMs and related plans operate in similar ways between various companies, they vary as to interest rates and other specific conditions. Here are some points to consider:

- What are the age requirements to be eligible for the lump-sum or annuity plan?
- Do you need to have clear title on your home?
- Can you transfer the mortgage to another property if you move?
- What percentage of your home equity is used to determine the reverse mortgage or RAM, and what percentage of that is available for a lump-sum payment and annuity?
- Is the interest rate on the mortgage fixed for your lifetime or duration of the annuity, or is it adjusted and how regularly and using what criteria?
- If the reverse mortgage and lump-sum is for a term period, what are the various terms available?
- What if the equity of the home on sale is insufficient to pay the mortgage and accrued interest? Are you or your estate liable for the shortfall?
- Can the agreement of the term be extended if the home has appreciated in value?
- Can you move out of the house, rent it and still maintain the home equity plan?
- What if you already have a mortgage on the house?
- If the annuity is for life, is there a minimum guaranteed period of payment or will payments stop immediately upon the death of the recipient and/or the surviving spouse?
- How will the income received under the proposed plan be taxed, if at all?
- Will the income received affect your eligibility under any federal or provincial housing or social programs?

The process of obtaining a reverse mortgage or RAM takes about four to six weeks on average. This would include home appraisal, annuity calculations and other matters. As mentioned, because these plans are fairly complex, it is essential you obtain independent legal and tax advice in advance and thoroughly compare the features and benefits.

Renting Out Part of Your Home

You may choose to rent out a basement suite and are entitled to offset the rental income you receive against a portion of your house-related expenses.

PLANNING TO PROTECT ● *Omar Offsets Rental Income Against Expenses*

Omar received rent of $300/month ($3,600 a year) from the rented area of his home. His total house-related expenses were $14,400 a year, and the rented area represented 25 percent of the total home square footage, therefore $3,600 of the total expenses ($14,400 x 25 percent). The rental income, therefore, would be offset by expenses, leaving a zero taxable income. Like Omar, in all instances you should obtain advance tax advice from a professional accountant.

• •

If you are renting out part of your home, check with your provincial government to obtain information and booklets about your obligations and rights as a landlord. You would be governed and regulated by that legislation. For example, some provinces have rent control, others do not. You ideally want to have a tenancy agreement that supplements the provincial legislation, and deals with your policy on smoking, pets, noise and the number of people living in the suite.

Your municipality has the authority to regulate zoning and determines whether a residence is single family zoned. Technically, therefore, you could contravene a municipal zoning by-law by renting out a part of your home to a non-relative. If you hear the word "illegal suite" then, it simply means it technically contravenes the existing municipal by-law on the issue. The contravention has nothing to do with provincial legislation (dealing with landlord-tenant matters) or federal legislation (dealing with income tax). Each level of government is independent of the other.

Check with your local municipality. It could be that certain areas in the municipality are encouraged to have rental suites. Alternatively, the municipality may have the technical restriction but it is not actively enforced, unless there is a complaint by a neighbour. If a municipal inspector does investigate, you normally have a right to appeal. One of the grounds of appeal is economic hardship for you the owner, and serious inconvenience for the tenant. Some municipalities may have a moratorium (temporary freeze) on enforcing the by-law because of a shortage of rental accommodations, and/or general recessionary hardship of property owners that need a "mortgage helper" to meet payments.

Some provincial governments have programs to encourage home renovation in order to create rental suites. In addition, the Canada Mortgage and Housing Corporation (*www.cmhc.ca*) has some programs for renovation to accommodate handicapped or elderly people.

Operating a Business Out of Your Home

Many people intend to start part-time or full-time businesses out of their homes. This is a growing trend for reasons including eliminating daily commuting to work, lifestyle choice, retirement opportunity, supplementing salaried income, testing a business idea, or saving on business overhead (by writing off house-related expenses). Keep in mind that you need competent tax and legal advice before you start up. The last thing you want is potential risk, which could impair your retirement funds and lifestyle. You need to obtain a GST/HST number if you have over $30,000 in income in your business or are paying GST on items you purchase and want to set off against GST you are charging. Check with your accountant and closest GST office (CRA), the contacts for which are available in Appendix A.

Expenses may be claimed for the business use of a work space in your home if either:

- The work space is your principal place of business for the part-time or full-time self-employed aspect of your career (you could have a salaried job elsewhere; it is not required that you meet people at your home), or
- You only use the work space to earn income from your business, and it is used on a regular and continuous basis for meeting clients, customers or patients. In this case you could also deduct expenses from an office outside the home.

PLANNING TO PROTECT ● *The Tax Advantages of Carmen's Home Business*

Carmen has always wanted to be her own boss. At the age of 50, she accepted an attractive early retirement package from her employee. Carmen considered various types of small businesses, but finally decided to start a craft business out of her home. She worked very hard and made good money, but she was frustrated at having to pay the taxes she did. Carmen had not obtained any tax advice and was not taking off all her home office deductions.

Had Carmen obtained professional tax advice at the outset, she could have netted a lot more "take home" after-tax income. She may still be able to claim some or all of the expenses that she missed, as the CRA allows you to send in an amended return and to carry business losses back to any of the three preceding years, and forward for up to 20 years in the future. There are many legitimate home office expenses that one can write off. The most obvious ones are a percentage of the house insurance, property taxes, utilities, mortgage interest and maintenance. In broad terms, if the home expenses were $30,000 in total and 20 percent of the home square footage was used as an office, the deduction would be $6,000 from business income.

• •

You may be able to claim 100 percent of the cost of the expense or a depreciated amount over time, depending on the item. To clarify what you can deduct and how to do it, as well as other home business tax issues, speak to your tax accountant. Speak with your lawyer about the various legal issues when starting a business. How to select professional advisors is covered in Chapter 16.

INSURANCE FOR YOUR PRESENT AND FUTURE NEEDS

Confirm what type(s) of insurance you have and make sure that you have the right type and amount of insurance for your present and future projected needs. Refer to Chapter 15 on the types of insurance products available. Also, complete the projected insurance income section in Appendix D.

ARE YOUR DEPOSIT MONIES, RRSPS, RRIFS, ANNUITIES AND INSURANCE FUNDS PROTECTED AGAINST DEFAULT?

Depending on how and where you invest your money, it may or may not be protected. Making sure your retirement investments and insurance benefits are protected is naturally a matter of concern as some banks, trust companies, credit unions and insurance companies in Canada have ceased to operate. Here is a brief overview of your protection. Make sure you verify all the information in this section to ensure it is current, accurate and relevant to your situation.

Protection of Canadian Deposit Monies, RRSPs, RRIFs and Annuities

- **Bank or trust company deposit plans.** Deposits would be protected by the Canada Deposit Insurance Corp. (CDIC), up to a certain amount. In Quebec, it is referred to as the Quebec Deposit Insurance Board. Your RRSP deposit or RRIF, regular savings or chequing funds on deposit, or term deposits would be automatically insured for up to $100,000 for each separate account. Each deposit (in the form of an RRSP or otherwise) must mature in five years or less. If you have more than $100,000, you can divide your funds among several separate CDIC member financial institutions. Some banks and trust companies have subsidiaries that are separate CDIC members, resulting in a ceiling of $100,000 each. For information and confirmation, contact CDIC at 1-800-461-2342 or *www.cdic.ca*.

- **Credit union deposits.** Deposits in a credit union are protected by a deposit insurance plan in that particular province. Each province can vary in its protection for deposits— savings, chequing or term deposit, or RRSP or RRIF with term deposits or GICs less than five years. Depending on the province, the protection could be from $100,000 to unlimited protection, that is, 100 percent. Contact a credit union in your province to enquire, or phone the CDIC number noted in the previous point to obtain contact numbers for the credit union deposit insurance head office in your province.

- **Life insurance deposits.** Deposits in a life insurance company would be covered by an industry-operated protection plan called Assuris (*www.assuris.ca*), up to certain limits and in certain situations, depending on the nature of the investment. The limit for policies registered under the *Income Tax Act*, such as RRSPs, RRIFs, Tax-free Savings Accounts (TFSAs) and pension policies, is $200,000, and $200,000 for non-registered policies, such as cash value of a life insurance policy. For information and confirmation, contact Assuris at 1-866-878-1225 or *www.assuris.ca*.

- **Managed funds.** Generally, these funds are protected if in an RRSP in the form of deposit funds, e.g. term deposits or GICs under five years. Mutual funds have no protection as such, due to the nature of the pooled investment. However, the fund's investments are segregated from the assets of the fund manager, in case the fund manager ceases to operate.
- **Self-directed plans.** Such plans are not protected against the default of the institution holding them. However, certain investments in the plan, such as term deposits or GICs under five years, could be protected. The amount of the protection depends on the institution, e.g. bank, trust company, credit union, brokerage firm. Refer to the deposit ceilings discussed earlier for these types of institutions and verify for current accuracy.

  If it is an investment dealer (e.g. brokerage firm) that ceases to operate, there could be protection for certain investments in your self-directed plan up to $1 million under an industry plan called the Canadian Investor Protection Fund (CIPF). The CIPF is sponsored by the Investment Industry Regulatory Organization of Canada (IIROC) and is the only compensation fund approved by the Canadian Securities Administrators for IIROC dealer members. Mutual fund companies or investment advisors not associated with a member broker are not covered by this particular fund. For further information and a list of current IIROC/CIPF members, contact your broker or the CIPF office in Toronto at (416) 866-8366 or *www.cipf.ca*.

- **Life insurance.** If a company that is a member of the Assuris protection plan makes promises in a life insurance, health insurance, money-accumulation or annuity policy to pay either a fixed, or at least a minimum amount, of money to a person or on a person's death, and that company goes under, you could be protected up to a certain amount. For example, if you have term life insurance protection, the limit is $200,000 or 85 percent of the promised death benefit, whichever is higher. For life annuity and disability income policies with no options of a lump-sum withdrawal, Assuris guarantees that you will retain up to $2,000 per month, or 85 percent of the promised monthly income benefit, whichever is higher. For health benefits other than disability income annuities, Assuris guarantees that you will retain up to $60,000 or 85 percent of the promised benefits, whichever is higher. For further information and confirmation, contact Assuris at 1-866-878-1225 or *www.assuris.ca*.

- **Creditor-proofing.** If you have personally guaranteed loans for an incorporated company, or you operate an unincorporated business, you could be exposed to claims from potential creditors. Funds placed with certain types of products from life insurance companies or with trust companies in Quebec could be protected from creditors. Obtain advice from the institution involved and verify it with your lawyer.

PLANNING TO PROTECT ● *Are Fiona's Investments Safe?*

Fiona owned $300,000 in RRSP Guaranteed Investment Certificates (GICs). She recently consolidated all of her GICs into one four-year fixed term, which was held in one account under her name. She had them deposited with a small regional bank. Recently she heard rumours that the bank could be having some regulatory difficulties in terms of its financial stability, but she automatically assumed that she would be protected for the full amount of her RRSPs. Fiona had heard that the Canadian Deposit Insurance Corporation (CDIC) protected investors, so she felt secure. She wanted to stay with the bank because they offered her .5 percent more to move her RRSPs from her larger, previous chartered bank.

If Fiona does not make a prompt change in her investment structure, she could be out $200,000 in the event that her current bank has financial difficulties. She is only protected for up to $100,000. What she should do is move her RRSP immediately to a large and stable national bank. That is her first line of defence. The other thing she should do is place her RRSPs in separate accounts not exceeding $100,000 each. That way each account would be covered by the CDIC protection of $100,000. An additional benefit of this strategy is that it provides flexibility. The other issue is that she is locked in at present for an additional four years in her current RRSP. This type of planning does not allow for any flexibility. In retrospect, after determining her needs, she could have staggered her RRSPs from one to five years and had some in smaller denominations for shorter terms in the event of an emergency. It should be a last resort to collapse an RRSP, however, as there is a tax holdback by the institution to remit onto the CRA. An alternative plan would be to borrow from the new lender that will be holding the RRSP.

● ●

KEEPING TRACK OF RISK

There are many forms of risk that could affect your financial net worth, cash flow, lifestyle and estate. There are ways to eliminate, minimize or control each of these risk areas by knowledge of them, research, and prudent decision-making. Having a diversified investment portfolio is one way. If you are retired or planning retirement, these 12 key risk areas are particularly important to know. Statistically, if you retire at 55 years of age, you could live to 85 and have 30 years of retirement—almost as long as your working life. Some of the potential risk areas are inter-related, but are segmented out because they should be specifically identified as risk with financial implications, directly or indirectly. By obtaining customized financial planning advice, you should be able to anticipate and neutralize many of the risks outlined.

Currency Risk

This is a particularly important issue for Canadian Snowbirds. If the Canadian dollar drops in value relative to the U.S. dollar, you will obviously notice an increased cost of living due to the reduced purchasing power of your Canadian money when you convert it to U.S. currency. The value of the Canadian dollar is dependent on many variables, both national and international. If it goes down 5 percent, you have lost 5 percent of purchasing power in the U.S.

Inflation Risk

This is one of the most serious financial risks to those in retirement. Although both Canada and the U.S. currently enjoy very low inflation rates, that can change and change rapidly. Inflation eats away at your purchasing power. Inflation at 5 percent will reduce your purchasing power by 50 percent in less than 15 years. If you have investments that have interest rates or value that is keeping up with the rate of inflation, or you have annuities or RRIFs indexed for inflation, then your purchasing power would at least remain constant. If you have a fixed income, the inflation issue is particularly onerous.

With Canada or provincial savings bonds, inflation would erode the purchasing power of the bond as well as the interest. You also have to look at your real rate of return on your money, after tax and inflation is factored in. If you were earning 2 percent interest and were taxed at 35 percent, your net return only is 1.3 percent. If inflation was 3 percent, you would actually be losing purchasing power with your money, that is, you would be in a negative position by 1.7 percent.

Deflation Risk

In this example, if there is a severe or prolonged economic downturn or recession, you could have the risk that the value of your assets will drop accordingly.

Interest Rate Risk

Interest rates in Canada and the U.S. have been very volatile over the past 15 to 20 years on any type of interest-sensitive financial investment. In the early 1980s the prime rate was in the double digits, up to 22 percent. This was of course attractive for people with interest income from term deposits, mortgages or bonds. However, since the mid-1990s, rates have been in the low single digits. Interest rate risk can cut both ways, however. For example, if you set your lifestyle needs based on high interest rate returns, your lifestyle will be negatively affected when rates fall. Or if you lock yourself into a fixed-rate bond when rates are low, and then interest rates increase, the value of the bond investment will go down when you try to sell it. If you have a locked-in annuity bought at a low interest rate, and if rates go up and inflation along with it, your purchasing power and lifestyle will be affected.

Government Policy Risk

Governments in Canada and the U.S. are constantly changing the tax or pension laws, depending on the political philosophy of the party in power and other economic pressures. One example is the clawback of the Old Age Security pension resulting in lower payments if the recipients' income exceeds a certain amount. This amount could be lowered over time. The Guaranteed Income Supplement could be reduced or eligibility criteria tightened up. The federal government could again change the age that you are required to convert your RRSP to a RRIF, or they could change the minimum annual withdrawal amount on your RRIF. Federal and/or provincial income taxes could be increased or decreased, depending on how much income you have and what tax bracket you are in. If you are a Snowbird, the U.S. government could bring in legislation that could increase taxes paid by non-U.S. residents, or a state could increase an estate tax on death on real estate or U.S. assets that you own.

Repayment Risk

This type of risk comes in several forms. One form of risk is not being repaid what you are owed when it is due, or when you want your money. For example, if you buy bonds, the issuers' ability to repay you depends on whether they have the money. Although bonds issued by municipalities, corporations or governments rarely default, there are several levels of credit risk normally involved. Agencies such as Standard & Poor, Moody's, and Fitch rate the credit risk of various bonds, which generally range from AAA to D. These ratings indicate the repayment risk you are taking with a particular bond issue.

Considering that a few insurance companies have gone under in the past, you don't want to risk losing money you might be expecting from insurance proceeds, cash surrender value funds, disability insurance payments or annuities. Contact the Canadian Life and Health Insurance Association (CLHIA) in Toronto (Appendix A). Ask about the independent ratings for the various member companies that you might be considering. Also make sure the insurance company is a member of the CLHIA so you are protected by Assuris. This coverage was discussed in the previous section.

Another form of repayment risk is receiving your invested money back sooner than you expect or want. For example, if you lock in a bond with a 3 percent yield, and the going rate (yield) falls to 1 percent, you would not be able to replace that bond with a new one at the same yield if the bond issuer redeemed or called the bond earlier than anticipated. Many corporate bond issuers have this right a certain number of years after the bond was issued. Most government bonds cannot be called.

Market Cycle Risk

Many markets are cyclical, such as the real estate market, stock market and bond market. Depending on where your investment is at any point in the cycle, you could run the risk that your investment could slowly or rapidly diminish in value. If you wanted or needed to sell it, you could lose money. Being aware of the market and the direction of the cycle is obviously important. Generally, the longer you are able to hold an investment (i.e. your time horizon), the less the risk. The shorter the term you intend or are able to keep the investment, the higher the risk a market correction could impair your investment return.

Economic Risk

The economy obviously has an effect on investments such as real estate or stocks. Generally speaking, the more buoyant the economy, the more buoyant the price of real estate and stocks and vice versa. However, keep in mind that economic cycles are not generally in sync with stock market cycles. For example, when the economy and the stock market have both been down due to recession, the stock market usually hits bottom a full six to nine months before the economy bottoms and starts to recover.

Lack of Diversification Risk

The risk here is having all your assets in one specific kind of investment, such as real estate or only a few bonds or stocks. You are not protected if that asset drops in value, in terms of having alternative assets to buffer the loss. If you spread the risk you lower the risk, for example, having different asset types as well as different investments within each type.

Lack of Liquidity Risk

Liquidity refers to the speed at which you can sell your asset, either at all, or at a fair price. For example, if you need to sell your home or stocks and the market has dropped, you could still sell but it could take much longer and you are going to obtain a lower price. Negative media about stocks and real estate can have a dramatic short-term effect on the market, as potential buyers become nervous. Less demand means lower prices.

Taxation Risk

This risk affects your lifestyle if increased taxation erodes away your anticipated retirement income. This form of risk could arise from new taxation policies including taxing income at higher levels, to including part or all of income currently exempt from taxation, to taxing RRSPs or RRIFs in some fashion other than when you take the money out. Naturally, all the above possible initiatives would result in a strong public demand to rescind them. Economic pressure on federal or provincial governments to reduce their respective debts, however, could result in all areas of personal income being subject to review for additional tax.

Pension Risk

This type of risk takes various forms. One possibility would be for federal or provincial governments to reduce the net amount of pension you receive through Old Age Security, Canada Pension Plan or Guaranteed Income Supplement, through taxation, increased taxation, clawbacks based on your other income, reduction in amount of money or more restrictive eligibility criteria. Another form of risk is that a pension fund manager does not invest money prudently, and the return to the pension fund is less than expected. Or an employer does not make any profit in a particular year (or goes bankrupt) and therefore does not contribute anything to the pension fund, or possibly an employer reduces or eliminates some pension plan collateral benefits such as life insurance or health and dental plan coverage for cost-saving reasons.

KEY ISSUES WITH DIGITAL ASSETS AND ESTATE PLANNING

In this age of technology, almost everyone, regardless of age, has a large digital footprint. However, many people do not give any consideration to their digital assets when thinking about a will or power of attorney or overall estate planning. It is just taken for granted.

Think about a personal doomsday scenario for a moment. If you were to die suddenly or had a stroke and were mentally incapacitated for a long time, how would anyone know the complete blueprint of your whole digital history and life? How would your executor, or your attorney under a power of attorney, or your heirs know where to try to start the search process? It would create significant adverse consequences, stress, and frustration, and cost time and money to attempt to re-create your digital asset profile, let alone being legally authorized to access it. Also, people frequently change their contact IDs or usernames and passwords.

All of this real and potential risk can be avoided with prudent advance planning as set out below. The discussion focusses on the personal. If you have a business, the urgent need for digital assets planning is magnified by many multiples.

What Are Digital Assets?

The types of digital assets can vary widely, and include online files stored on many different types of online websites or programs and devices that can only be accessed by user account IDs and passwords:

- Online account information for websites and programs
- Social network accounts, such as LinkedIn, Twitter, Facebook, Instagram, etc.
- Loyalty account programs such as Aeroplan, Air Miles, retail stores, pharmacies, etc.
- Financial transaction or business accounts, such as PayPal, Amazon, eBay, etc.

- Email and webmail
- Financial documents or information online such as personal and business banking, credit cards, investments and utilities
- Automatic monthly or annual bank account withdrawals for membership or subscriptions
- Computer equipment access or unlocking codes for various products, such as Apple and Samsung or other brand electronic devices, such as cell phones, tablets, laptops and desktops, as well as ID numbers, etc.

Who Has a Legal Right to Access Your Digital Assets?

During your lifetime, you are the sole authority for access and use. However, if you die or are mentally incapacitated due to disease, stroke or accident, does your executor under your will or attorney under your power of attorney have the automatic right to stand in your shoes digitally speaking? The short answer is "no" and possibly a partial "maybe" in certain situations. For example, Google permits you to set an alternate authorized access user, and some other companies have similar options. You want to eliminate all this uncertainty.

The other factor is that whenever you set up an online account, you need to agree to the terms of the service agreement with the online service provider. The executor and attorney under a power of attorney must legally act in compliance with the service agreements of each particular digital asset.

In addition, your estate documents, including a will and power of attorney as well as separate signed memorandum, must specifically authorize the executor or attorney to access your digital assets and set out any instructions or limitations for that role.

Importance of a Digital Estate Plan

You need to set up a plan to ensure that your digital assets are properly dealt with and managed according to your wishes, on your demise or incapacitation. Otherwise, your digital assets could be subject to identity theft or content theft, or be compromised in other ways, or simply not be legally accessible by a designated person.

A plan will provide a legal structure and procedure for ensuring that specifically designated people have the legal right and authority to assume your position as the owner and user of the digital assets.

The plan should include your authority and wishes to be set out in your will and power of attorney documents.

Developing a Digital Estate Plan

If you are using a trust company or a lawyer specializing in estate law, they would provide proactive guidance to you for completing a digital asset plan. They would have first-hand experience with the legal and estate challenges and issues of people dying or being mentally incapacitated and not having prepared a digital estate plan, or of the plan being out of date or incomplete.

Here are some suggestions on dealing with digital assets to protect your estate and your interests and wishes, in the event of your demise or during your life if you are mentally affected by illness or injury.

PREPARE A CURRENT DIGITAL ASSET INVENTORY
AND KEEP IT UPDATED AND LOCATED IN A SAFE PLACE

Create a detailed inventory of all your electronic digital data with log-in usernames, account numbers, IDs and passwords. Make sure you keep it current with any log-in or password changes.

Divide your inventory list into different categories so it is easy to follow.

Keep the inventory in a safe place and secure. This could also be your safety deposit box. Even if your executor does not have your key access, once your executor satisfies the bank that the executor is the legal executor, the bank would drill open the safety deposit to get access. You may wish to have two lists, with one list of passwords only and another separate list for account numbers in case a list was stolen, for example, if your home was broken into, and one list was found. Of course, you would want your lawyer's office to keep a copy in their legal file, as they would presumably also have copies of your other legal documents, such as your will and power of attorney. That way, your lawyer can protect your interests by controlling access to your digital inventory when it is given to your legal executor and attorney of your power of attorney.

Appendix D in this book has a sample detailed personal inventory checklist to complete as well.

CONSIDER AN ONLINE VAULT

This option is like a digital safety deposit box. There are a number of programs available that allow you to store your private data and manage your digital assets. In addition, you can use these sites to store copies of your important legal and estate planning documents, such as your will, power of attorney, living will, insurance policies, etc.

As noted previously, Appendix D is a detailed personal inventory to complete. Including that document in your online vault, as well as keeping a copy in your regular safety deposit box and giving a copy to your lawyer, would provide the blueprint of all your assets and liabilities and key contact information.

The obvious benefit to your lawyer, executor or attorney under a power of attorney is that they could access all your key documents and access information in a complete and timely fashion.

Some of the companies offering digital vaults include Dropbox, My Vault, Everplans, PasswordBox and ShareFile. You can do a Google search for other companies as well.

DRAFT INSTRUCTIONS FOR DIGITAL ASSETS ACCESS AND USE BY YOUR EXECUTOR OR ATTORNEY FOR YOUR POWER OF ATTORNEY

Your lawyer should draft a specific clause in your will and power of attorney documents specifically permitting access to your current, past, and future digital assets and by whom. You want to make it clear what your intent is, and that the executor, or attorney under a power of attorney, should have the same access as the account holder had during his or her lifetime for all of the person's digital accounts.

This should include a broad statement of intent for digital assets access and usage. In addition, it is recommended that you create a separate memorandum as well with specific instructions for each account, or any limitations, and attach a current list of all your digital assets. This memorandum could be addressed to your executor, your attorney under a power of attorney, your lawyer, and your heirs setting out your wishes. For your protection, these memoranda could be kept in your legal file at the office of the lawyer who prepared your estate legal documents.

As your will could be filed in court as part of the probate process and be available to the public access, you obviously don't want to put specific digital asset details in that document. A memorandum of wishes is not filed as part of the normal probate process. Your estate lawyer will provide customized advice.

CONSIDER HAVING A DIGITAL EXECUTOR

Your general executor for your will may or may not have the computer technology skills to understand, access or deal with your digital asset instructions, including managing your online presence as may be required or desired. One option is to consider a specific person with electronic skills whom you trust and have confidence in, who could be named just for dealing with those issues, under the overall directions of your general executor. Whoever has access will be dealing with very personal information. If you are using a trust company as an executor or attorney under a power of attorney, or trustee under a trust, the designated party will have the broad resource expertise available. Your estate lawyer will advise you as to the most appropriate option in your circumstances.

WHERE TO GET MORE INFORMATION

- Refer to Appendix A, "Sources of Information," for helpful contact numbers for provincial and federal government departments and seniors' organizations.
- Refer to Appendix D for checklists to complete including personal information record, current financial net worth, and current and projected retirement monthly income and expenses. Also refer to the projected financial needs checklist in Appendix D and where your retirement income will come from.

- Refer to the list of websites that might be of interest to you. These are found in Appendix A.
- Contact the banks and credit unions for consumer information books.
- Refer to the website: *www.estateplanning.ca*

SUMMARY

In this chapter, we have given an overview of the primary revenue sources available to you. In addition, we have outlined the various existing assets that you might have. By completing the various checklists in Appendix D, along with the personal information record, you will have a very complete sense of your financial and related affairs.

We also covered the types of protection available for selected investments, as well as ways of assessing investment risks. By being aware of these issues, you will maximize the asset value of your estate.

❓ Frequently Asked Questions

1. *How do I know if my bank deposits are protected from the bank going under?*

   The Canadian Deposit Insurance Company (CDIC) is a federal Crown corporation. You are protected up to a maximum of $100,000 for each separate deposit in the event that the bank or trust company goes into bankruptcy or otherwise compromises your funds. However, the deposit money criteria have to be followed to be eligible for a claim. For example, equity mutual funds are not covered. Credit union deposit fund protection is also available and varies depending on the province.

2. *What is a reverse mortgage?*

   A reverse mortgage is a source of raising funds by placing your primary residence as security. Generally the funding takes the form of a cash advance or annuity or a combination, up to a pre-determined value of your home. You don't make any payments, as long as you live in the house. When the house is sold, the reverse mortgage company receives the principal amount owing plus interest from the sale proceeds. You should make sure that your estate would not be financially liable for any shortfall on sale. Due to the compounding effect of the mortgage, the aggregate debt load can accumulate quickly over time. You need to be a certain age, generally 55 years or older, and have a clear title to the home in specified cities.

3. *Am I eligible to obtain Old Age Security (OAS) and Canada Pension Plan (CPP) if I decide to live outside Canada part-time or full-time?*

   If you have paid into the CPP program, you are eligible for the pension regardless of whether you live outside of Canada for any length of time. You are also eligible for OAS pension as long as you have lived in Canada for 20 years before you depart. If you are living outside Canada for up to six months a year, there is no deduction at source. If you are living full-time outside of Canada and are no longer a resident of Canada, there could be a withholding deduction from source. This could range from a complete waiver of deduction up to 25 percent depending on the country of your full-time residence.

4. *How does inflation impact on my investment return?*

   Fortunately, we are in a position of low inflation in Canada. Nevertheless, inflation erodes your purchasing power. If your nominal or stated investment return is 4 percent and inflation is 3 percent, then your real return, adjusted for inflation, is only 1 percent, and that's not even taking into account the income taxes payable on your investment income.

5. *At what age do I need to convert my RRSP into an RRIF and what are the implications?*

You need to convert by the end of the year in which you turn 71 years of age. The implication is that in an RRSP, you have the advantage of tax-free compounding of your money, without the need to take any out. Once you convert to an RRIF, you are required to withdraw a minimum amount each year on which you will be taxed, depending on your marginal tax rate.

Building Your Estate

"My greatest fear is that I will outlive my money."

INTRODUCTION

If any of us actually knew when the grim reaper was going to come calling, there would be, perhaps, something to be said for living the high life, eating up one's capital and sipping the last drop from the last bottle of champagne just before taking your final breath. There is undeniably a school of thought that believes it is quite acceptable to start using up your principal as you get older, because, as they say, "You can't take it with you" or "The hearse doesn't have a trunk." The unfortunate thing about these common expressions, however, is that they imply it is not only acceptable, but preferable, to use up one's capital with age. Eating up your capital as you grow older, however, is hardly practical.

Even if you did have an accurate "personal death clock"* (a rather grim thought), would you really want to deplete all of your capital and sip the last drop of champagne in the nick of time? Is there no one to whom you would want to leave something? Are there no charities to which you would like to make a bequest? The fact is that the majority of Canadians do wish to pass something along to their family, friends, and favourite charities, and therefore, the idea of using up one's capital is not very sensible.

The truly frightening consequence of eating into your capital is that you could live longer than you had expected and your living expenses (possibly in a supported living centre for seniors) may turn out much higher than you estimated, especially in the last few years of your life. What will happen then? Will your children, grandchildren or other relatives come to your financial rescue?

Check out www.deathclock.com for a statistical estimate of your life expectancy, based on U.S. mortality tables.

They might like to; however, it is possible that they will be struggling themselves to cover their own living expenses. One of the interesting consequences of people living so much longer than ever before is that many in their late eighties or nineties have children who are senior citizens struggling to get by on a pension and income from their investments.

Looking ahead 10, 20 or 30 years, what if you no longer have enough money to cover your living expenses in a retirement residence and you have no family or other safety net to fall back on? Will the provincial or federal government come to your rescue? Don't count on it.

With the Baby Boomer generation moving into their seventies, the percentage of the total population that is over 60 and retired is getting higher every year. Statistics Canada has reported that by 2036, Canada's population could exceed 40 million. By then, the entire Baby Boomer generation will have reached age 65 and the number of senior citizens could more than double, outnumbering the amount of children in the country for the first time.

This population ageing trend is already putting a tremendous strain on the country's social services, from health care to assisted living, in addition to the ever increasing CPP and OAS obligations. Another consequence of the ageing population is that the percentage of the population representing people who are actually working and paying the bulk of the country's income tax revenue and other taxes is getting smaller each year. It is also conceivable that with the falling birth rate, the actual number of taxpaying working Canadians could start to shrink.

The writing is on the wall. Regardless of how old you are, the time is now to start accumulating wealth so that you will be as financially independent as possible when you retire. Furthermore, you will be building an estate to leave to your family, friends and selected charities.

THREE ELEMENTS OF WEALTH ACCUMULATION: SAVING, INVESTING AND PRESERVING CAPITAL

There are three elements of successful wealth accumulation: *saving*, *investing* and *preserving capital*. If you only do one without the others, you will likely fall short of your financial goals. The first two elements, *saving* and *investing*, are especially important in your working years. The third, *preserving capital*, is important throughout your life, but becomes even more imperative as you grow older.

It may seem obvious that *saving* is a key element of wealth accumulation. However, a large number of Canadians do not save at all, or if they do, their savings are focused on meeting relatively short-term goals, such as buying a car. Even with such tax incentives as Registered Retirement Savings Plans (RRSPs) and Tax-Free Savings Accounts (TFSAs), most Canadians simply do not save enough for retirement. Saving money means forgoing current consumption in order to have a better life in the future, but the vast majority of people may not have the ability or willpower to save in a meaningful way.

Investing is not the same as *saving*, but the two go hand in hand. If you simply set aside a portion of your income in a savings account or GIC, you will probably not even keep pace with inflation, because interest rates are so low. With interest rates still at historically low levels, you could actually lose ground over the years (after income taxes) in terms of the purchasing power of your accumulated savings. *Investing* means being prepared to take on a certain amount of risk with your money in order to achieve a reasonable return in excess of the inflation rate, whether it involves investing in stocks and bonds, real estate or a business. Understanding the risk associated with various kinds of investments is critical to your success. Also, the level of investment risk you take must make sense in relation to your personal circumstances, including your overall financial position, your age, your income and your financial goals.

In the previous chapter, we discussed different kinds of assets that you may have in your estate, such as an investment portfolio, your home, life insurance and, during your retirement years, various pension entitlements. Will all of this be enough to see you through the rest of your life? Unfortunately, for all too many, the answer is no. Often, this is due to a lack of willpower over the years in setting aside money for investment purposes or disregarding the guiding principle of *preserving capital. Preserving capital* is not only one of the three elements of wealth accumulation, but also one of the cornerstones of sound financial planning. As explained above, the population ageing trend is straining the economy, and to deplete any significant portion of your capital as you grow older may lead to major financial issues late in life at a time when family or government assistance might not be available. Therefore, the principle of *preserving capital* is one that should constantly be followed in managing your own financial affairs.

Analyze Your Financial Position

Where should you start the process of building your estate? First, you need to understand where things stand right now from a financial perspective. Take stock of your current financial position by completing the checklist and worksheets in Appendix D.

Next, think of various "what if" situations in 5, 10 or 15 years in the future and how you will prepare for them.

Will You Continue Working?

Is it likely that you will still be working after age 60, 65 or 70? If so, in your financial projections, you should factor in the income that you could be earning. You may not need to start dipping into your RRSP or other investment portfolios quite so soon.

Even if your current job involves a mandatory retirement age, that does not necessarily mean you have to stop working entirely. Perhaps your employer is willing to make an exception to have you continue on a part-time basis, or there may be some entirely different type of work for which you are suited. Many people find that full-time retirement is not all it is cracked up to be. After all, it only takes so much time to do those jobs that you have been putting off for years, such as clearing up the furnace room and the garage. And, like the authors of this book, you might be fairly useless at golf, so the last thing you need is more time on your hands for frustrating days on the links.

As mentioned earlier, with our ageing population, it will become increasingly difficult for people over 65 to make ends meet from their pension income or investment accounts. Even having a source of income from a part-time job can make an enormous difference to one's standard of living after retirement.

Think about the "capital equivalent" of earning $30,000 a year from some type of full- or part-time work during your sixties or seventies. If you follow a "rule of thumb" recommended by investment advisors to limit annual cash withdrawals from an investment portfolio to no more than 4 percent of the portfolio value, discussed later in the chapter, an income of $30,000 is almost like having an extra $750,000 in your investment portfolio from which you are withdrawing 4 percent a year (i.e. $30,000). This by no means implies that you should simply rely on a part-time job to get you through your retirement years, as it is still imperative to maintain a solid investment portfolio. However, if your health (and/or your spouse's health) allows you to keep working through your sixties into your seventies, and you believe that the work will generally make you happy, this additional income can make a significant difference to your financial position in years ahead: you will be able to continue saving, investing and preserving capital, and avoid spending and depleting your savings early on in retirement.

What Is the Estimated Future Value of Your RRSP and Other Investment Portfolios?

Estimate how much money you may have in your RRSP and in any non-RRSP investment accounts in 5, 10 or 15 years, using conservative annual rates of return. Do several different projections using "best case" and "worst case" rate of return scenarios.

Sit down with an investment advisor and discuss the kinds of investment strategies that you could follow. Generally speaking, the more equity-oriented (i.e. stocks) your investment portfolio, the higher the returns will be over the long run, as compared to bonds. However, bear in mind that stocks generally fluctuate in value far more than bonds and other income-type investments. What sort of roller-coaster are you prepared to ride in terms of the fluctuation in the value of your investment portfolio from month-to-month and year-to-year?

Statistically, the stock market has produced a return equivalent of 8 to 10 percent per annum over most (but not all) 10-year time periods going back 100 years, based on a 10-year average. However, be careful that you do not get a false sense of security or comfort from the stock market averages. Even for the majority of 10-year time periods where the stock market has in fact produced an average per annum return of 8 to 10 percent, there were many gyrations in the year-by-year returns.

Some 10-year time periods have also been pretty grim, such as the 10 years ending December 31, 2008, as a result of a world-wide financial crisis. For countless millions, the drop in the value of their investment portfolios in 2008 wiped out all of the gains made in the previous nine years. History repeats itself, so it's only a matter of time before this happens again, but hopefully not for many years.

The good news is that markets don't stay down forever. In fact, at the time we wrote the third edition of this book in 2011, many people's investment portfolios were already back to where they were before the credit meltdown and stock market crashes of 2008 and early 2009. Nevertheless, these events threw a monkey-wrench in the financial plans and forecasts of millions of people. They had counted on their savings growing to a certain level in order to retire at a particular age and to supplement any pension income with money from investment portfolios. After the financial turmoil of 2008 and early 2009, those plans needed to be revised.

You also need to be cognizant of the investment risk associated with bonds. In the writers' experience, we have found that a common misconception is that if interest rates go up, then bond prices will also go up. In fact, as interest rates rise, a bond's current market value will generally go down.

PLANNING TO PROTECT ● *Bonds Also Involve Investment Risk*

Alastair bought a $10,000 government bond that will mature in 10 years, which is paying interest at 3 percent per annum. A year later, the economic outlook has improved, money is tighter, and the going rate (yield) for government bonds maturing nine years later has become 5 percent, not 3 percent.

The good news is that Alastair's bond will still be worth $10,000 if he holds it to maturity, nine years later (i.e. 10 years from when he purchased the bond), provided of course that the government does not default on its obligation. (Canadians can take some comfort in the fact that there has never been a bond default by the Canadian federal government or by any of the provinces. The same cannot be said for certain other countries, such as Greece, Spain, Italy and Portugal.)

For Alastair, the bad news, so to speak, is that because bond yields rose to 5 percent a year after purchasing the bond, the actual market value of his bond will have dropped to something less than $10,000. The lower market value will reflect the fact that any purchaser of his bond would want to achieve a 5 percent yield on the bond until maturity, but the actual interest payments are fixed at only $30 per annum for every $1,000 of face value (i.e. $300 of annual interest payments on the bond's $10,000 face value). Therefore, the market value of Alastair's bond will have declined in value to an amount where the $300 annual interest payment equates to a 5 percent yield.

Unless you consider yourself an expert in the markets, and in forecasting the economy and interest rates, you should have a professional manage your investment portfolio, whether it be stocks, bonds or a combination of both. There are many hazards for the unwary. If anything, the proliferation of investment information on the Internet and television has made it ever more difficult for people to determine what is, and what is not, relevant. A number of investment management choices open to you are outlined in Chapter 2, as well as the various kinds of risks that you need to be aware of.

Withdrawing Money from Your Investment Portfolio

Up until now, you may have been in a saving and investing mode, and you have not had to withdraw any money from your investment portfolio(s). However, for most people, the day will come when regular withdrawals from their RRSPs, RRIFs, TFSAs and other investment accounts will be necessary in order to make ends meet. In fact, there is a mandatory minimum annual withdrawal when you reach age 71 and you have to convert your RRSP to a RRIF (as discussed in Chapter 2).

We are often asked: "How much can I safely withdraw (in percentage terms) each month or year from my investment portfolio without impairing the portfolio and eroding my capital?" The answer is "It depends."

A rule of thumb used by many financial planners and investment advisors is that cash withdrawals from an investment portfolio should not exceed 3 or 4 percent of the total portfolio value. The rationale is that a balanced portfolio of stocks and income-type investments (e.g. bonds and preferred shares) can reasonably be expected to generate a total return averaging somewhere in the 4 to 8 percent range over the long run. (By *total return*, we mean dividend income on those stocks that are dividend-paying, interest income on bonds, plus capital gains, net of capital losses.) However, although the average return may fall into this range over a 5- or 10-year time period, in some years the actual return will be higher and in others lower.

The danger in withdrawing too much from your investment portfolio is that the stock market and/or bond prices may be in a slump, forcing the sale of securities at an inopportune time in order to raise the necessary amount for your regular cash withdrawal. Depending on how much cash you take out, and by how much the investment portfolio has fallen in value, it may not be possible for your investment portfolio to ever get back to its previous pre-recession level.

Another rule of thumb is that the overall mandate for your investment portfolio should be set in such a way that there will be sufficient *yield* to cover the regular cash withdrawals that you will be making. By *yield*, we mean periodical-type income such as dividends and interest income on bonds. When we refer to a portfolio's yield, we do not take into account the capital gains that we hope to achieve. Capital gains (and capital losses) are "lumpy" and cannot be predicted.

PLANNING TO PROTECT ● *Consider How Much to Withdraw Each Year*

Miriam is a widow in her late sixties. She is financially well off; however, she does not live extravagantly. She has lived in the same house in southwestern Ontario for the past 30 years, and the house is mortgage-free. The house is currently worth about $750,000.

Miriam also has an investment portfolio worth $1 million. She receives a survivor pension from her late husband's company pension plan of $3,000 per month, as well as a CPP survivor pension and the Old Age Security. Miriam is financially astute, but she does not consider herself an expert in the world of investments. Her investment portfolio consists of various stocks, bonds, income trusts and preferred shares, and it is managed for her by a Canadian investment firm on a discretionary basis. (*Discretionary* means that the portfolio is managed in accordance with a particular investment mandate that Miriam and her investment advisor have agreed upon and confirmed in writing. Miriam's permission is not required in advance for each purchase or sale that is carried out in her investment account.)

Miriam's investment portfolio is "balanced," which involves a 50-percent ceiling on the portion of her portfolio that can be invested in stocks or other equities. The other 50 percent is placed in conservative income-type investments such as bonds, and possibly some preferred shares.

Miriam's investment advisor has told her that it is reasonable to expect the total return (net of fees and other costs) to average somewhere in the 4 to 7 percent range over the long run, after taking into account the investment firm's fees and any other costs. In terms of incoming cash flow, some of the stocks are dividend-paying, which, along with the bonds and some preferred shares, currently produce a yield of about $20,000 per annum. (This figure does not take into account any projected capital gains, net of capital losses.)

The investment advisor believes that it is important for Miriam to preserve capital, and he has recommended that her cash withdrawals not exceed the portfolio's yield of $20,000 per annum (i.e. 2 percent of the current portfolio value). If the future unfolds as he hopes, the per annum average total return (including capital gains) should be in the 4 to 7 percent range, leaving something on the table for the portfolio to grow in value and to outpace inflation. In that way, in future years, the portfolio value will be higher, and therefore Miriam's 2 percent annual cash withdrawals will be somewhat higher each year as well.

The investment advisor's recommendations appear to make sense and follow the conventional wisdom. However, Miriam wants to withdraw $50,000 a year so as to be able to take more trips and enjoy life a little more. The investment advisor is concerned that cash withdrawals at a 5 percent annual rate may harm the portfolio and, sooner or later, cause an erosion of capital, particularly if the stock market falls off and takes a long time to recover.

Miriam appreciates her investment advisor's concerns, but she thinks that he isn't seeing the big picture. Miriam feels that her house is far larger and more luxurious than what she wants or needs, and she plans to sell it and move to something smaller in a few years. Her children are grown up and living on their own. The house is in a desirable neighbourhood and is expected to continue to appreciate in value. Miriam is not overly concerned if her cash withdrawals from her investment portfolio do cause a decline in value at some point, because she still has her house. Most likely, the house will keep going up in value—and the appreciation is tax-free as well, because of the *principal residence exemption* in the *Income Tax Act*. It is only a matter of time before she sells it.

● ●

This case study is intended to show that there are no pat answers to questions such as "How much money can I safely withdraw each year from my investment portfolio, while still preserving capital?" Each situation is different. However, whatever you do, you should review your situation with a financial planner or an investment professional. Be sure that you outline your full financial position, as well as your intentions regarding what assets you may be willing to sell in the future (such as your house) and how and where you want to live in the future.

Where to Get More Information
INTERNET
Refer to the following websites:
- *estateplanning.ca*
- *homebuyer.ca*
- *retirementplanning.ca*
- *snowbird.ca*
- *smallbiz.ca*

BOOKS
Thousands of books have been written on the topics of investing, retirement planning and wealth preservation:
- Visit your local bookstore or library, paying particular attention to recently published books. Newer books have the advantage of reflecting the authors' and experts' perspectives on what has transpired in the past few years and what it means for ordinary people in planning their financial affairs and managing their investment risk.

One of the authors, Douglas Gray, has written several relevant books relating to real estate and owning a business that could be helpful references, including the following titles:

- *The Canadian Guide to Buying and Owning Recreational Property in Canada*
- *101 Streetsmart Condo-Buying Tips for Canadians*
- *The Canadian Landlord's Guide: Expert Advice to Become a Profitable Real Estate Investor* (with Peter Mitham)
- *Making Money in Real Estate: The Canadian Guide to Profitable Investment in Residential Property*
- *Real Estate Investing for Canadians for Dummies* (with Peter Mitham)
- *The Complete Canadian Small Business Guide* (with Diana Gray)
- *The Canadian Snowbird Guide: Everything You Need to Know About Living Part-Time in the USA or Mexico*

SUMMARY

In this chapter, we have shared a few of the key principles regarding growing one's net worth, namely the importance of *saving, investing* and *preserving capital*. By paying attention to and following through on each of these three concepts, you stand a better chance of having a decent standard of living throughout your life, as well as being able to leave an estate to your intended beneficiaries.

It is imperative to analyze your current and future financial position, keeping in mind that you may continue working after retirement. While planning investment strategies that utilize equity-oriented investment portfolios, exploring non–equity-oriented options (i.e. bonds) is also important. Regardless of what you plan to withdraw from your investments each year or how you estimate your RRSP and other investment portfolios, it is highly recommended that you consult a professional when making important financial decisions.

❓ Frequently Asked Questions

1. *How much can I safely withdraw from my investment portfolio each year after retirement while still avoiding serious erosion of my capital?*

    As discussed in the chapter, a typical rule of thumb suggested by investment advisors allows for an annual 3 or 4 percent withdrawal from your investment portfolio. Depending on your assets, however, you may be able to utilize more of your capital per year if your financial situation allows for it. Make sure to consult a professional financial advisor whenever making major financial decisions involving your investment portfolio.

2. *The chapter discusses preserving capital as a cornerstone of financial planning throughout one's life. Is this concept, however, less important for someone with a high net worth?*

    Generally speaking, *preserving capital* is a guiding principle that one should follow, especially during retirement, but there are certainly exceptions to the rule. For example, someone who has a net worth that appears to be far higher than what is necessary to preserve that person's standard of living for the rest of his or her life, taking inflation into account, may consider beginning an orderly process of transferring wealth to the next generation or to selected charities. For wealthy individuals, this may indeed make sound financial sense. There may be significant savings in potential capital gains taxes or estate taxes arising on death by reducing your net worth during your lifetime.

Understanding Wills

> "Say not you know another entirely 'til you have divided
> an inheritance with him."
>
> JOHANN KASPAR LAVATER

INTRODUCTION

Over the course of your life you will sign many documents. Your will is the most important document you will ever sign. Everyone should have a will, unless you have no assets, liabilities, spouse, children, family or friends. A will is the basic legal document that can ensure that your assets will be distributed to the beneficiaries of your choice in the way that you wish, instead of by a government formula in the absence of a will; in a timely and efficient manner, rather than a delayed fashion causing a burden to your family; and with effective estate planning so that the least amount of tax is payable. Estate planning and will planning should be interrelated to achieve the optimal attainment of your needs and wishes. There are no estate taxes or succession duties in Canada at this time, however income tax on your RRSPs and RRIFs and unrealized capital gains may arise on your death.

In addition, your children can be cared for by a guardian of your choice if you have that in your will. If you didn't have a will or clause on that issue in the will, the government and courts would determine who would care for your children.

It is estimated that only one out of three adults has a will, which means that two-thirds of the time when people die their wishes are not met. Depending on the circumstances, the provincial government, through the public trustees' offices, may become involved in administering the estate and appointing a guardian for the children, if both parents have died. There are various reasons why people fail to prepare a will. Some procrastinate by nature or have busy lives and simply never prioritize getting a will done. Others do not appreciate the full implications of dying without a will or even put their mind to the issue. Some resist the reality that they are mortal. The finality of death is discomforting to some and therefore there is a resistance to dealing with issues that face the prospect. Preparing a will and dealing with estate planning issues certainly faces the issue of mortality in a direct way.

Of those that do have a will, many do not review it regularly or modify it based on changing circumstances. People first think of their will at predictable stages of the life cycle, such as at marriage, divorce, the birth of a first child, the first time they fly without their children, or upon news of the sudden death of a friend or relative. Once the will is completed, they then forget about it. Not updating it can be as bad as or even worse than not having a will at all. It could cause the beneficiaries a lot of grief, stress, time and expense when those problems could so easily be avoided by regular will review and updating. Other people draft their own will, which has potentially serious implications if it is not done properly.

Your will comes into effect only after your death and is strictly confidential until that time. You can rewrite or amend the will at any time. In fact, keeping your will up to date cannot be overemphasized, as circumstances can change at any time. A will should be reviewed every year ideally at the same time, for example, on the first day of the New Year or some other special date on a routine basis. In addition, you should review your will if your family needs or marital status have changed, your assets increased or decreased, you have moved to a new province or a new government tax or other legislation has been introduced.

The laws and terminology relating to will preparation or estate planning can vary from province to province. Federal income tax legislation changes on an ongoing basis. Seek professional advice as outlined in Chapter 16, "Selecting Professional Advisors."

In this chapter, we will provide an overview of some of the key issues to consider including:

- what's in a will
- preparing a will
- revoking a will
- selecting a guardian
- impact of family law legislation
- fees and expenses
- avoiding family feuds
- avoiding spousal disputes

- what happens if there is no will
- changing a will
- selecting an executor, trustee and lawyer
- benefits of using the services of a trust company
- the validity of your will in the U.S.
- where to get more information
- understanding the rights of dependents
- how to avoid your will being contested

WHAT HAPPENS IF THERE IS NO WILL?

If you don't have a will, or don't have a valid will, the outcome could be a legal and financial nightmare and an emotionally devastating ordeal for your loved ones. Not having a will at the time of death is called being *intestate*. It means you have not left instructions how you want your assets to be dealt with on your death and you have not appointed anyone to be legally in charge of your estate. Accordingly, provincial legislation covers that situation. The court eventually appoints an Administrator. If no family member applies to act as Administrator, the Public Trustee or Official Administrator may be appointed. Your estate will be distributed in accordance with the formulas of the laws of your province, which are inflexible and will most likely not reflect either your personal wishes or the needs of your loved ones.

While the law attempts to be fair and equitable, it does not provide for special needs. A home or other assets could be sold under unfavourable market conditions in order to effect the necessary distribution of assets that the law requires. In addition, the settling of your estate could be a lengthy and expensive matter. Your heirs could end up paying taxes that might have easily been deferred or reduced. There may not be sufficient money in the estate to pay the taxes. Your family could be left without adequate cash for an extended period of time. During this period, your assets may suffer loss or destruction due to a lack of proper safeguards. There may be a delay in the administration of your estate and added costs such as an Administrator bond, a bond that is similar to an insurance policy in case the Administrator makes a mistake. Refer to Appendix C for an overview of how the courts will distribute your estate if you don't have a will.

If you have children and die without a will appointing a guardian for your young children, and there is no surviving parent who has legal custody of the children, provincial laws come into effect. The Public Trustee becomes the guardian and manager of the assets of your estate that your children are entitled to. The provincial child welfare services may become the guardian of their care, upbringing, education and health. A relative or other person can apply to the court for an order appointing them as guardian. It is up to the court's discretion as to what decision would be in the best interests of the child.

Dying without a will, if you have minor children and are separated, divorced or living common-law, can result in a bitter legal custody battle. A person could be appointed guardian who you personally would not have approved. The whole experience could be unpleasant, costly, protracted and traumatizing to the children. This scenario could be avoided by seeking legal and other professional advice, preparing a will, and setting out your wishes in it.

WHAT'S IN A WILL?

Depending on the complexity of your estate, your will could either be a simple will in its content and length, or a complex lengthy one. Following is an outline of the main contents of a basic will.

Identification of Person Making the Will

The *testator* (person making the will) states their address and a declaration that the document is their last will and testament.

Revocation of All Former Wills and Codicils

A *codicil* is a supplementary document to a will that may change, add to or delete wording from the original will.

Appointment of an Executor and Trustee

An *executor* is a person or a corporation whom you can trust to administer your estate, in other words, settle the affairs of your estate and ensure your instructions in the will are followed. More detail on selecting an executor is discussed later. Also refer to Appendix D for the duties and responsibilities of an executor. You may need to appoint a trustee of your will if you have included trust provisions. The provincial Public Trustee may also agree to be appointed executor and must be in your will. Trusts are set up in a situation where the testator does not wish to give an immediate lump-sum gift to a particular beneficiary, or the beneficiary is an infant and not legally capable of managing his or her own affairs. A trustee is responsible for seeing that the instructions in the will with respect to the trust are carried out. If the estate is small and relatively simple, the executor is usually appointed the trustee as well. If the estate is large or complicated with many trust provisions, a trust company is normally selected as a trustee. Refer to Chapter 6 on understanding trusts.

Authorization to Pay Outstanding Debts

This would include funeral expenses, taxes, fees and other administrative expenses and debts before any gift of property can be made.

Disposition of Property

A major function of your will is to dispose of your property to those individuals or organizations who you would like to receive part of your estate. This objective is accomplished in two ways:

GIFTS OF SPECIFIC PROPERTY

It is common for people to leave a particular item of property or cash legacy to a particular person. If you want to give personal *bequests*, that is, specific articles of personal property or sums of money to specific people, you must state so expressly in your will. The same follows if you want to *devise*, or give, a specific piece of real estate to a specific person. You should only include in your will major assets and articles of sentimental value, such as family heirlooms. You can attach a separate piece of paper, referred to in your will as a *Memorandum* or *Letter of Direction*, which lists how you would like your minor personal possessions to be distributed. Request that this list be used as a guideline by your executor. Describe the item in sufficient detail to clearly distinguish it from the rest of your property and identify the beneficiary by his or her full name and address.

GIFTS OF CASH LEGACIES

When giving cash legacies, you should periodically review the amount to be given to ensure that it is still sufficient and that it reflects your intentions. A gift of $15,000 included when your will was made in 2010, is not the same as a gift of $15,000 today. You may wish to increase the value of specific cash legacies every few years to account for the eroding power of inflation. You should also make sure that there will be sufficient funds in your estate to cover any cash legacies. This is especially important if most of your assets are jointly owned with your spouse, with a right of survivorship. This means that if you die before your spouse, those jointly-owned assets (e.g. joint bank accounts, investment portfolios and your home) would pass directly to your spouse by "operation of law," without going through your estate. That is one reason why you would need to make sure that you have some assets in your own name, if there are specific cash bequests that you want to make under your will.

Specific personal bequests are made first and property disposed of in this manner does not form part of the *residue* of your estate. A beneficiary must be alive in order to receive a gift. However, your will could specify that the gift should go to the beneficiary's heirs-at-law in the event of the beneficiary's death.

If you dispose of the bequest item during your lifetime, the gift under your will is void. The beneficiary receives nothing, and is not entitled to receive the cash equivalent.

GIFT OF THE RESIDUE OF YOUR ESTATE

The *residue* of your estate is what is left after all debts, funeral and administration expenses, taxes and fees have been paid and gifts of specific property and cash legacies have been made. You need to grant your executor the power to sell or convert any part of your estate into money at such times and in such a manner that he or she thinks best in order to wind up the estate.

There should be a *residuary clause* stating what should happen to the balance of the estate. If there is no residuary clause, then any property not already disposed of will fall under the rules for an intestacy. The residuary clause covers all the assets you may have acquired since the making of your will.

In making the gift of the residue, it is important that you provide for alternate beneficiaries in case the first named beneficiaries do not outlive you.

Appointment of a Guardian for Minor Children

It cannot be overstated how critical it is if you are a parent with minor children, to protect their best interests, in terms of their care and upbringing in the event of your death. A lot of thoughtful planning should go into this process, including the prudent selection of a guardian. Discussion on selecting a guardian will be covered later.

Funeral Instructions

Some people detail in their will their instructions regarding funeral arrangements and the disposition of the body. These instructions are not legally binding on the executor, for various legal reasons. You should therefore express your wishes in your will for the consideration of those who make the actual arrangements, but more importantly, inform your executor and immediate family of your funeral arrangement wishes while you are still alive. You can also make pre-arrangements. In practical terms, your will is generally not located and read until after the funeral has already occurred. Your comments in the will simply reinforce what you have stated verbally on the issue.

Attestation Clause

This clause states that the will was properly signed according to the required legal formalities in your province, basically, that it was signed in front of at least two witnesses who were both present at the same time, and who both signed in your presence and the presence of each other.

REFLECTING YOUR WISHES—SPECIAL CLAUSES IN YOUR WILL

You may wish to include special provisions in your will relating to the disposition of your property and the administration of your estate. Consult a lawyer who specializes in wills and estates to assist you in identifying and preparing special provisions with respect to your personal situation. There are many types of special provisions including:

Alternate Beneficiaries and 30-Day Survivorship Clause

Where spouses die together or within a very short time of each other, if they have wills leaving everything to each other without naming alternate beneficiaries, the situation is similar to not having a will at all. Although uncommon, a disaster could occur, such as a car or plane accident. In other words, neither spouse has provided for the possibility that the other spouse may not be able to benefit from the estate. The benefit of naming alternate beneficiaries is to avoid the risk that your estate could be faced with a partial or complete intestacy, that is, as if no will existed. Earlier, we discussed what happens if you don't have a valid will. Table 1 in Appendix C shows how your assets would be disposed of. A 30-day clause provides that in order for your beneficiary to benefit from your estate, he or she has to survive you by 30 days. If a married couple dies together, and it is impossible to determine who died first, it is presumed that the younger spouse survived the older spouse.

Trusts

If you want to give someone a gift but do not want them to have direct control of the property, you may want to set up a trust provision in your will to manage the gift. One example among many where you would use a trust,would be with a minor child. Trusts are discussed in more detail in Chapter 6, "Understanding Trusts."

Disinheriting a Child or Spouse

There could be situations where you want to leave a family member or spouse out of your will or provide for a reduced bequest. Many people think that can be easily done. However, in many cases, that is a myth. Some provinces have legislation permitting the courts to vary the will, in certain situations, if an eligible party (e.g. child or spouse) objects to being disinherited. An eligible party could also contest the amount given in the will as insufficient.

The courts in each province have the discretion to review the facts and either vary the will or not. Each individual case is decided on its own merits. Some general guidelines that the courts have followed in such situations are:

- that moral obligations of the testator are taken into account
- that the testator's stated reasons for not providing for a particular beneficiary can be ignored
- that the claimant's financial needs are not necessarily a criterion in order for the claimant to be successful
- that the division of family assets on divorce (assuming that the claimant is not currently divorced and does not have a legal separation agreement) is a criterion for determining a benchmark for fairness.

If you are thinking of disinheriting someone or giving one child proportionally less than another, you definitely need skilled legal advice to legally accomplish your objectives. Establishing an *inter vivos* trust or selectively gifting assets during your lifetime are two such methods.

Leaving Someone a Life Interest

For various reasons, you may wish to leave someone the income and enjoyment of the asset (e.g. house), rather than giving the asset itself. This person is called a *life tenant*. In this situation, on the death of the life tenant, another beneficiary (e.g. children) could receive the asset. For example, you may want to set up the above provision in case your surviving spouse remarries (e.g. if it was your second marriage), to ensure that your children from the first marriage eventually receive the asset. In this example, you may not have any children from your second marriage.

Powers of Executor or Trustee

Your will sets out the various powers that you are giving to your executor or trustee to enable them to manage your estate without the need to obtain approval from the court. This could include the right to make investments in areas that otherwise would not be permitted by provincial legislation.

Encroachment on Capital

If you have appointed a trustee to administer your estate, you may want him or her to be able to take money from the capital if necessary in the trustee's opinion. This right has to be clearly stated. For example, you may wish to give the capital beneficiary (e.g. dependent child) or life tenant (e.g. spouse) additional funds based on need and circumstances.

RRSPs and RRIFs

If you have an RRSP or RRIF and have not designated a beneficiary, there could be a considerable tax hit on your death, which in some situations, may not be shared fairly or proportionally by your heirs. At that time, all funds would be paid to the estate and would be taxed as income received as of the date of your death. However, if you designate your spouse as a beneficiary, then your spouse would be able to rollover or transfer, the monies to his or her own RRSP or RRIF within 60 days after the end of the year in which the money is received.

For various tax reasons, your spouse may or may not want to take advantage of the above option. He or she may prefer to take none or just some of the RRSP or RRIF funds on a rollover basis. For example, the surviving spouse might project that the deceased spouse would have a lower marginal tax rate than the surviving spouse would have on his or her subsequent death. By naming a spouse as a beneficiary in your will, you have given your spouse the benefit of various options based on specific tax advice they would obtain at the time.

There are considerable tax implications however, if you are specifying a beneficiary of your RRSP or RRIF, if the beneficiary is not your spouse, or a financially dependent or disabled child or grandchild. That is because there would be no rollover option and taxes would have to be paid. The issue of how the taxes are paid should be set out in the will. Otherwise, the estate could be liable for the taxes if the beneficiary refuses to pay for the taxes. If the estate is not large, this could deplete the estate considerably. Consider making it clear that the beneficiary is only to receive the RRSP or RRIF proceeds if he or she agrees to be responsible for any taxes. In that event, the projected taxes, e.g. 30 percent, would be taken from the proceeds and remitted to the CRA.

Organ Donation

If you are interested in donating your body or organs, you may wish to specify that in your will. However, you also want to complete the organ donation documentation separately from your will, as the donation would be immediate and your will may not be read for several weeks after your death. Notify your family, executor and doctor of your wishes, as decisions have to be made promptly at death.

Refer to Chapter 18 on planning your funeral for more information. Also refer to Appendix A for a list of provincial organ donation agencies.

Funeral Instructions

It is recommended that you specify your funeral wishes in the will including the nature of funeral or memorial service; where internment or cremation is to take place; and the approximate cost of your funeral. Make sure that your executor and family know your wishes in advance. You can also pre-arrange your funeral.

Protecting Your Children's Inheritance

When you are planning your estate, you also want to consider the issue of provincial family law legislation. You should obtain legal advice on anticipating downside scenarios in the event that any of your currently married children separate or divorce. Your inheritance could become part of any matrimonial property settlement, which is not what you would have wanted. There are various ways of dealing with this type of risk assessment, including establishing a testamentary trust.

Understanding Rights of Dependents

Every province has legislation to protect the rights of a spouse and dependents. Whatever your financial and legal obligations during your lifetime, these also continue on your death, in many cases. Naturally, this would have an impact on how your estate is distributed if you did not deal with these issues in your will. Your will could be challenged. This is covered later in this chapter. Generally, a *dependent* is someone who relied on you for financial support immediately prior to your death. This usually includes a spouse and dependent children. Children could include children of blended families, common-law or legal marriages and children with special needs. In some provinces, it also includes a common-law spouse, parents and grandparents.

WRITING A MEMORANDUM TO YOUR WILL

When you are outlining various bequests, it could take a lot of space to explain the exact way in which you want those bequests to be distributed or how decisions are to be made in the event of conflict, for example, if two children want a particular personal item that has not been specifically named, or a child does not want a particular personal item that has been specified. You may wish to draft a memorandum of your wishes in more detail as a supplement to your will. This document would outline your wishes and intentions. Copies of this memorandum would be given to your executor and family members.

You should review and if need be, revise your memorandum from time to time. As the document is not a will as such, merely a statement of your wishes, it provides guidance to the executor only. It does not have the legal effect of a will.

KEEP YOUR WILL CURRENT

You can cancel or change existing wills or make new wills as often as you would like before your death, as long as you are mentally competent.

It is not only important that you make a will, it is equally essential that your will is kept current and that it reflects your current wishes and intentions. An outdated will may be worse than having no will at all. You should look over your will at regular intervals if any of the following events has happened:

- you have married, separated or divorced since the making of your will
- you have entered a "common-law" marriage (with opposite- or same-sex partner)
- death of a beneficiary
- death of an executor, trustee or guardian
- birth of a child or grandchild who you would like to benefit under your will
- marriage, divorce or death in your immediate family
- there is a change in the competency of a beneficiary, executor or trustee
- a substantial change in the value of your personal assets, or you have acquired, inherited or sold an important piece of property
- you have additional dependents, such as a child or elderly parent
- a change in the tax laws
- you have moved to or acquired real estate in another province or country
- your executor, trustee or guardian has moved away or is no longer willing or able to act
- you have changed your life insurance coverage
- you have changed your mind concerning the provisions of your will or distribution of your estate

HOW TO CHANGE YOUR WILL

Every time you want to make changes in your existing will, you don't need to make a new will. If you are making minor alterations to a will, you can execute a separate amending document called a codicil if, for example, you are only changing one or two clauses in your will, such as a specific bequest or name of executor. A codicil is a supplementary document that refers to and alters the original will, adding, deleting, qualifying or limiting certain provisions in the will.

To be valid, the codicil must be executed in a similar fashion as a will. Don't make changes on the original will. It is not worth the risk as you could void it.

If you want to make major alterations to your will or if you have several codicils, it is advisable to revoke your existing will and draw up a new one. Otherwise, it could be confusing interpreting your wishes.

REVOKING YOUR WILL

You can revoke or cancel your will in a number of ways. You can voluntarily revoke all or a portion of your will. Alternatively, that process could occur automatically in certain situations. You need to know when a will is revoked so that you can replace it with a new will. Here are only five ways that a will could be revoked.

Making a New Will

You can voluntarily revoke your will by making another valid will. Your new will should contain a clause revoking all previous wills and codicils. By law, the most recent valid will governs. If you have made a new will, you should either physically destroy your old will or write "revoked and replaced by a new will" across it.

Destruction

You can voluntarily revoke a will by physically destroying the original version, for example, tearing it up. You must be capable of forming the necessary intent to destroy the will. If you are no longer mentally competent, the revocation will not be legally effective.

Written Intention to Revoke

You can voluntarily revoke your will by a written declaration of an intention to do so. The declaration must be completed the same way as a will. In other words, it must be in writing and be signed by you in the presence of at least two witnesses who, in turn, sign in your presence and each other's.

If you revoke a will this way, you will no longer have a valid will. You would therefore die intestate unless you make a new will.

Marriage

A will is automatically revoked by law if the testator enters into a legal marriage after the will has been made. Depending on your provincial legislation, a common-law marriage may or may not have the effect of revoking an existing will. Any time a testator marries, therefore, the existing will would no longer be of any effect in the event of the death of the testator.

There is one exception to the rule relating to a legal marriage, that is, where there is a declaration in the will that it was made in contemplation of a future marriage to a specific person named in that will. If you are getting married, you should make a new will in contemplation of the marriage or as soon after the marriage as possible. You should consult a lawyer as a very specific language is required. If you do marry without making a will expressly in contemplation of marriage, and never make a new will, you will die intestate. Your estate will then be disposed of in a manner that very likely will not reflect your wishes.

Separation or Divorce

In most provinces, the entire will is not invalid in the event of divorce or separation, only the parts of the will that give any powers or property to the testator's estranged or ex-spouse. The will is interpreted as if the spouse died before the testator. Therefore, the spouse would not be able to take part of the estate or act on the testator's behalf. The definition of a spouse for the purposes of this provision usually means any person considered by the testator to be his or her spouse, generally applied to both legally wedded and common-law spouses.

Like the rule that marriage automatically revokes any existing will, the law presumes that where there has been a marriage breakdown, your will no longer reflects your current intentions regarding your spouse, the disposition of your property or the administration of your estate.

An exception to this rule exists where a contrary intention is expressed in the will that states any gifts, appointments or powers given to the spouse are to remain even in the event of a judicial separation, divorce or nullity of marriage. If you are anticipating a separation or divorce you should consult a lawyer to ensure your will reflects your wishes. As mentioned earlier, provincial legislation can vary, so check.

PLANNING TO PROTECT ● Updating Will and Beneficiary Designations

David recently re-married. He had been divorced about three years earlier, but had never signed a separation agreement dealing with financial matters. He did his own uncontested divorce to save money on legal fees, as he had been separated for more than a year. He did not have any children from his first marriage.

David had previously named his ex-spouse as his designated beneficiary in his RRSP and his insurance policy. He forgot that he had done that.

It is important for David to promptly notify the insurance company and financial institution in writing, that he wishes to change the beneficiary from his ex-wife to his new wife or his estate. There are probate and other tax considerations to explore in terms of the pros and cons of those options. Divorce automatically revokes designations in a will, but not necessarily in RRSP and insurance contracts. In addition, David should make a new will with a clear statement revoking all previous RRSP and insurance beneficiary designations.

Is Your Will Valid in the U.S. for U.S. Assets?

The following explanation is general in nature and you should seek professional advice, customized to your specific situation, from a U.S. and a Canadian lawyer skilled in wills to ensure that there is no conflict of wills. When you are dealing with more than one will, the situation is fraught with potential perils, unless your U.S. and Canadian lawyers coordinate the contents of each will and any amendments to them.

In general terms, if you have a valid will that is legally enforceable in your province, it would probably also be valid in the U.S. state in which you have assets. Possibly you are a Snowbird with a condo in a Snowbird state or own recreational property in the U.S.

There could be a serious problem if you have two wills. Because there are different legal jurisdictions between Canada and the U.S., there could be, in theory, a challenge about the contents of the will by a beneficiary (or someone who would like to be one), in one will jurisdiction but not in the other one. Standard boilerplate clauses in wills state that the most recent will automatically revokes any and all previous wills. You can imagine the problem if you inadvertently included that clause in a U.S. will. It would automatically nullify your Canadian will!

Other options to consider for your U.S. assets might be for your Canadian lawyer to include specific terms in your Canadian will relating to your U.S. property or assets and have affidavit attestation of the witnesses of your will at the same time. All this must be done in conjunction with feedback from a U.S. lawyer, expert in will matters in the state where you own assets. Another option is to have a U.S. lawyer transfer your U.S. property and other assets into joint names, with right of survivorship, so that your U.S. assets would automatically go to your surviving spouse and bypass probate. You could consider having your U.S. property in a living trust or revocable trust. This bypasses your estate, and therefore probate procedures, as the trust is not in the deceased's name, but a trustee's name. There are also immediate as well as future U.S. and Canadian capital gains tax and U.S. gift tax implications to consider, if you change the form of ownership of your U.S. assets. Check into the pros and cons of these options in your personal situation.

As mentioned earlier, if your will has been correctly executed in your provincial jurisdiction and has the appropriate clauses, then it should be valid for your assets under the laws of most U.S. states. Check this out in your specific case. It could then be admitted to probate, once the court has been satisfied that the will has been properly witnessed. If you do not have any assets in the U.S. because you are renting, the issue of a valid U.S. will is not applicable, as there would be no U.S. probate procedures on death.

Preparing a Will

There are basically three ways to have your will prepared: writing it yourself, having a lawyer do it for you, or having a trust company arrange for a lawyer to do it for you. A brief overview follows. When you read the reasons for seeing a lawyer, you will see the compelling need to protect your estate and personal wishes by doing so.

The Holograph Will

This type of will is signed only by the person making it. There are no witnesses. In addition, the will has to be written entirely in the handwriting of the person making the will. The disadvantages of this type of will, of course, are that the person making it could have been under duress (e.g. pressure to write it by someone else), it could be confusing in terms of the wishes and intent, the writing could be illegible, or it could be altered by some unscrupulous person. In addition, you obviously would not have had the advantage of legal and tax advice on optimizing your estate planning strategies. The risk of this type of will being challenged or deemed invalid is very high.

Some provinces do not recognize this type of will. However, there could be exceptions in those provinces based on extenuating circumstances, such as someone in the armed forces on active duty.

The Self-Written Will

This is the poorest choice, because it could have many defects and inadequacies that could result in a legal, financial and administrative nightmare for your family, relatives and beneficiaries. How you expressed your wishes may very well be legally interpreted differently than what you intended due to ambiguity. Worse still, the clause in the will could be deemed void or the whole will could be considered void for various technical reasons. Some people do their own will by drafting it from scratch or using a "standard form" of will format purchased in book or stationery stores. It is false economy, and depending on your situation, you or your family could have a lot to lose. Many people assume that a "simple" will completed by themselves will suffice. As discussed elsewhere what may appear to be a simple estate to a lay person could require more in-depth decisions and wording based on professional advice. There are better and inexpensive alternatives to provide you with peace of mind, as outlined in the next two professional alternatives.

PLANNING TO PROTECT ● Don't Make the Same Mistake as Sam!

Sam thought he would save money so he bought a "will kit" on the Internet. He and his wife had three children between 5 years and 14 years of age. He also had his own small business and various other assets. The family home was in his name.

Sam rode his bicycle to work and one day he was killed by a distracted driver. His family thought that he had taken care of everything. Unfortunately, he had not. His will was invalid as he only had one person witness it, who was a relative. He had been too busy to arrange for a second witness and thought it was just a lot of unnecessary "red tape" anyway.

As a consequence, the provincial government public trustee's office stepped in. Under the will legislation of the province, the assets of Sam's estate had to be distributed according to a formula. This formula would not have made Sam happy. As there was no valid will, his spouse had to get approval by the public trustee's office to administer the estate. This cost Sam's wife a lot of time, money and aggravation. As the children were minors, the public trustee's office became involved and determined in a bureaucratic manner what was in the children's best interests. Again, none of these decisions would have made Sam happy. The memories of this lack of proper planning on Sam's part lasted for a very long time.

The Lawyer-Drawn Will

Wills, in almost all cases, should be prepared by a lawyer familiar with wills who is qualified to provide legal advice and is knowledgeable on how to complete the legal work required in drafting a will.

Depending on the complexity of the estate however, a lawyer may not have the expertise to advise you on other non-legal issues, for example, tax, investments and retirement. Enlist the expertise of the other specialists, for example, a professionally qualified accountant who specializes in tax, specifically a Chartered Professional Accountant (CPA). Look on the Internet for accountants with these designations. Better still, ask several people you know and respect for their financial and business acumen to give you the names of the professionals whom they use. How to select a professional accountant and lawyer is covered in Chapter 16, "Selecting Professional Advisors."

If you are selecting a financial planner as well, make sure you check credentials, expertise and reputation. Ask for referrals from your lawyer or accountant and have any advice verified for the tax, legal and administrative implications by your lawyer, accountant and trust company. How to select a financial planner is covered in Chapter 16, "Selecting Professional Advisors."

When selecting a lawyer, check with the lawyer referral service in your province, listed on the Internet. The initial consultation is either free or a nominal fee, for example, $10. Ask to speak to a lawyer who specializes in wills. You can phone the lawyer referral service again and get a different lawyer's name. Ideally, have appointments with two or three lawyers, so you can make a comparative judgement. Use the same cautious approach, a minimum of two interviews, when selecting an accountant, financial planner or trust company, unless a particular individual or firm has come highly recommended from someone you know and trust. Write down your questions beforehand so you don't forget them and prioritize them. Refer to the will preparation checklist in Appendix D. Review and complete this before you go for the appointment.

The legal fee for preparing a "basic" will is relatively modest, generally between $500 and $1,000 per person. If your estate is complex, of course, this fee could be much higher because of the additional time and expertise required. A "back-to-back" will is a duplicate reverse one for husband and wife and is generally a reduced price.

The Trust Company Will

For a very long time, various estate planning services, including will preparation, executor and trustee functions, and estate administration, have been offered by trust companies, such as Royal Trust, Canada Trust, and National Trust. However, in the past several decades, many trust companies were acquired one by one by various Canadian banks. Royal Trust was absorbed into the Royal Bank, National Trust by the Bank of Nova Scotia, and Canada Trust by TD Bank. In such cases, however, the businesses of such trust companies are being operated as separate divisions of the banks that bought them. For convenience, we will refer many times to "trust companies." Such references are meant to include the trust company operations of the various banks that offer these services.

A trust company can offer extensive services in terms of will and estate planning, generally in conjunction with a lawyer of your choice, or they could recommend one. Always make sure you obtain independent legal advice. A trust company is invaluable when there is a trust set up as part of your estate planning, as well as a need for them to act as your executor. Everyone's needs vary and after obtaining advice you may not require a trust company. Compare a minimum of three trust companies before deciding who to deal with. Look on the Internet and do a Google search under "trust companies." The benefits of using the services of a trust company are discussed in Chapter 6, "Understanding Trusts."

BENEFITS OF USING THE SERVICES OF A TRUST COMPANY

Many people prefer to name a trust company in the will as their executor for a variety of reasons. Refer to Appendix D for details of the extensive duties and responsibilities of an executor. Compare a trust company to the capabilities of a personal friend, relative, or family member acting as an executor in your given situation. You may choose to select a private executor as a co-executor with the trust company, or have a designated trust company named as an alternate, if the named executor is unwilling or unable to act. There are various options you can explore and discuss with your lawyer.

Experience and Expertise in Will and Estate Planning

A large portion of any trust company's operation involves acting as an executor. A trust company's staff can advise you on a regular basis in terms of coordinating your will with the other financial affairs as they are closely interrelated, and in conjunction with your legal and tax advisors. Part of estate planning involves establishing objectives for estate distribution, taking into consideration any legislation concerning provision for dependents. In addition, planning involves determining what taxes would be payable by the estate or beneficiaries and considering procedures for minimizing or providing for these taxes. More discussion on estate planning is covered later.

Continuity of Service

The appointment of a trust company ensures continuity of service during the full period of administration of the estate. This is particularly important if the estate involves a trust responsibility that might have to be administered for many years (e.g. if you have young children or a mentally disabled child). A trust company will designate only their most experienced staff to deal with the administration of estates. Staff must combine both business ability and capacity for human understanding and empathy, enabling them to deal tactfully and fairly with each beneficiary.

Accessibility

A trust officer is assigned a specific estate and is personally responsible for providing customized and responsive service.

Full Attention to the Needs of Your Estate

The operation of your estate administration is smooth as a defined infrastructure and continuity exists. If a layperson is an executor, his or her attention to the executor duties could be influenced by other personal interests, age, ill health, procrastination or excessive stress due to the demands of fulfilling expectations in an area where they have no experience or expertise.

Providing Portfolio Management

A trust company can provide expertise for your estate's investment needs, such as cash management or operating a business. Since most trust companies are now owned by large banks that also offer investment management services, it may make sense, depending on your situation, for a separate investment firm or firms not associated with the trust company, to be engaged to manage your estate's investment problem(s). In that way, the trust company officials handling your estate could be more objective in assessing the performance of your investment manager(s) and in making changes where appropriate than if the investments were being managed "in house" or by an affiliated investment firm. A lot depends on your situation, the level of your net worth, and which trust company/bank you intend to use.

Ensuring Control When That Is Important

There could be instances when a professional, neutral and experienced executor or trustee deals with issues in the will that require an element of control, for example, releasing funds over time to an adult child who lacks financial responsibility. Another example would be the management of a business until the appropriate time to sell it. Trust companies have access to this type of expertise and, generally, can competently deal with most situations that might come up.

Confidential Nature of the Estate Administration Business

Trust company staff is trained to treat the estate administration and related client business in the strictest confidence.

Sharing Responsibility

If you decide to nominate a friend as a joint executor, the trust company assumes the burden of the administration but works together with your other executor to make joint decisions. In this type of situation, the executor fees could be split proportional to the respective contribution of time and expertise.

Financial Responsibility and Security

Most trust companies in Canada are well established and are backed by substantial capital and reserves. Reputable trust companies also strictly segregate estate assets from their general funds. Also, a trust company is covered by insurance if there is a mistake or oversight due to negligence or inadvertence.

Funding Capacity

A trust company can work with your family to provide for their immediate financial requirements and needs immediately after your death.

Specialized Knowledge

Due to the increasingly complex nature of tax and other legislative issues relating to an estate, as well as a wide variety of options available, a trust company employs a staff of experts to review and advise on matters that arise.

Acting as a Trustee

Briefly, acting as a trustee means that the trust company protects your ongoing interests after you die. One example would be managing your investments or capital and making payments to designated beneficiaries as required over time. If there are minor children; a child who is mentally incapacitated and expected to remain so; children from a previous marriage; or situations where the estate assets have to be controlled for an extended period of time, for example, a trustee could be giving out necessary funds from your estate over a period of 20 years or more.

Group Decisions

If vital matters come up that involve a major decision, a trust company will utilize the collective expertise of a variety of senior staff and specialists to arrive at a decision.

Fees and Savings

Most trust companies will enter into a fee agreement at the time your will is prepared. Trust company fees are determined by legislative guidelines and the courts in most provinces, however a separate agreement can deal with additional charges or fees. The same guidelines also apply to a private executor. The topic of executor fees is covered later in this chapter. There can also be savings due to efficiency by having an experienced trust company perform the executor duties. This would not, of course, include fees involved in ongoing estate management, or the maintenance of trusts set up during the will planning process and included in the will. You can obtain quotes from the trust company in advance, or let the co-executor negotiate the fee on the testator's death. You should also give the personal co-trustee the power to change the corporate trustee.

Avoiding the Possibility of Family Conflict

In any family situation there could be personality or ego conflicts, or friction due to issues dealing with control, power, money, distribution of family possessions or assets, resentment due to past financial favours to certain children, or forgiveness of loans to others, unequal distribution of the estate to family members or a multitude of other potential areas of conflict. A trust company acts as a neutral, objective and professional catalyst in pre-empting, ameliorating or resolving potential disagreements affecting the administration or distribution of the estate. Based on practical experience, a trust company would understand and anticipate the many potential personal, family, financial, emotional and psychological dynamics that may be operating following a death and the administration of the wishes set out in the will.

Peace of Mind

There is a great reduction in stress to know that the estate will be administered competently, professionally, promptly and in accordance with your stated wishes. An experienced trust company can provide this peace of mind and security.

There are clear advantages to using the services of a trust company in many situations, not only to act as an executor but also as a trustee. You may wish to appoint a spouse or family member as a co-executor or co-trustee in certain situations. Remember to interview a minimum of three trust companies before you decide which one you would prefer to deal with. Always have your own lawyer who you can obtain independent legal advice from on will or trust matters. Make sure your lawyer has expertise in this area.

THE COMPLEMENTARY DOCUMENT—POWER OF ATTORNEY

Many lawyers draft a power of attorney at the same time that they prepare a will. The purpose of a power of attorney is to designate a person or a trust company to take over your affairs if you can no longer handle them due to illness or incapacitation, for example. Another reason is that you may be away for extended periods on personal or business matters. Considering the benefits of a power of attorney is important if you have substantial assets that require active management. You can grant a general power of attorney over all your affairs or a limited one specific to a certain task or time period. You can revoke the power of attorney at any time in writing.

If you do not have an enduring power of attorney and are unable to manage your financial affairs due to illness, accident or mental infirmity, an application has to be made to the court by the party who wishes permission to manage your affairs. If another family member does not wish to perform this responsibility, a trust company can be appointed, with court approval. The person or trust company who assumes this responsibility is called a committee, guardian or similar terminology, depending on the province. Committee duties include filing with the court a summary of assets, liabilities and income sources, with a description of the person's needs and an outline of how the committee proposes to manage the accounts and/or structure the estate to serve those needs. In addition, ongoing asset management is required to meet any changes in circumstances, as well as recordkeeping and accounting functions, all subject to the direction of the court.

A more detailed discussion of powers of attorney is covered in Chapter 5, "Understanding Power of Attorney and Living Wills."

PROTECTING YOURSELF IN ALL CIRCUMSTANCES

To reinforce the necessity to obtain a legal consultation before completing or re-doing a will, just look at some of the many reasons legal advice is specifically required because of the complex legal issues and options involved:

- you are separated from your spouse but not divorced
- you are divorced and want to re-marry
- you are divorced and paying for the support of your former spouse and children
- you are living common-law, will be entering a common-law relationship or leaving an existing one
- you have a same-sex partner
- you are in a blended family relationship, with children of each spouse from previous relationships
- you have children from a previous relationship and an existing one
- you own your own business or are part-owner with other partners

- your estate is large and you need assistance with estate planning long before your death to reduce or eliminate taxes on your death (discussed later)
- you have a history of emotional or mental problems such that someone could attack the validity of your will on the basis that you did not know what you were doing when you signed the will, or were not capable of understanding the financial matters covered in the will
- you want to have objective, unbiased and professional advice rather than making choices in a vacuum or possibly being influenced by others who have a vested interest in the contents of the will
- you want to live in the U.S. or elsewhere for extended periods of time (the issue of your technical domicile, or permanent residence at the time of your death has legal and tax implications in terms of your will)
- you own or plan to own real estate in the U.S. or elsewhere
- you have a will that was signed outside Canada or plan to do so
- you want to forgive certain people for debts they owe you, or make special arrangements for the repaying of debts or mortgages to your estate should you die before the debt or mortgage is paid back to you
- you want certain events to occur that are complicated and have to be carefully worded, such as having a spouse or friend have a certain income or use of a home until they re-marry or die and at that time the balance of money or house goes to someone else
- you want to set up a trust arrangement to cover various possibilities (discussed later)
- you want to make special arrangements to care for someone who is incapable of looking after themselves, or has shown themselves unable to apply sound financial or other relevant judgement (a child, an immature adolescent, a gambler, an alcoholic, a prodigal child, a spendthrift, or someone who has emotional, physical or mental disabilities or limitations or who is ill)
- you wish to disinherit a spouse, relative, or child for a variety of reasons. (For example, you may have lent a lot of money to one child out of several and the money was not repaid and promises were broken and a serious estrangement occurred. The debt substantially reduced your estate. Another more positive reason is that all your children are now independently wealthy and don't need your money. You may therefore want to give the majority of your estate to charitable causes.)
- you wish to appoint a guardian to look after your children in case you and your spouse die together
- you have several children and you want to provide the opportunity for one specific child to buy, have an option to buy, or receive in the will the house, business, farm or a specific possession or asset of your estate, and want to set up the appropriate procedures and wording to enable your wishes to occur

As you can see, when projecting your circumstances in the near future, there could be many different reasons to consult with a legal expert on the topic of wills.

SELECTING AN EXECUTOR

One of the most important decisions you will make is your choice of *executor* to fulfill your instructions in your will. Your executor acts as your "personal representative" and deals with all the financial, tax, administrative and other aspects of your estate. This would include assembling and protecting assets, paying outstanding debts, projecting future cash needs, handling all tax requirements, distributing the assets of the estate, and acting as a trustee for the ongoing management of the assets of your estate. For a more detailed outline of the duties and responsibilities of an executor, refer to Appendix D. As you can see, it would be difficult to find a layperson or family member who could adequately fulfill all the qualifications that might be required, in terms of having the range of skills and expertise needed. An executor should either be an expert or retain specialists in diverse areas such as law, income tax, real estate, asset evaluation and management, accounting, financial administration and insurance. Not only can the process be time-consuming and complicated, it can also expose the executor to personal legal liability if errors are made. The executor is accountable to all beneficiaries.

A will takes estate planning only so far. It is up to the executor to settle the estate to the satisfaction of the beneficiaries. Generally, there are two kinds of executors. One type is the professional executor, such as a lawyer, accountant or trust company. The other type is the inexperienced layperson, generally a relative or family friend familiar with your personal life.

Many people consider being asked to be an executor an honour, a reflection of the trust and respect in the relationship. Unfortunately, in the emotional context of a death, however, conflicts can and do occur between executors, or co-executors, and beneficiaries. The conflicts can arise as a consequence of the executor being perceived as being overzealous or indifferent; being authoritarian or showing favouritism; lacking necessary knowledge and either making decisions too hastily or delaying for too long; or lacking tact, sensitivity or insight in terms of the necessary interpersonal dynamics required.

An executor can (and should) retain the services of a lawyer, accountant and tax expert and can also retain the services of a trust company as an agent. Another consideration is for you to appoint a co-executor. If the will names more than one person to administer the estate, they are referred to as co-executors. They have equal rights and responsibilities for the administration of the estate. For example, you could consider having a spouse and a trust company as co-executors. In addition, if you are naming an individual as an executor or co-executor, make sure you have an alternate executor in the event the first one is unwilling or unable to act.

As a practical matter, most Canadians' estates are not large or complicated, and most often, it makes good sense to name one's spouse as executor, or if there is no surviving spouse, one's adult children as co-executors. Although lacking in professional expertise (unless you happen to have a lawyer in the family), the executor(s) will engage a lawyer experienced in wills and estates to advise on everything that needs to be done, and to guide them through the entire estate administration process until the estate is wound up.

SELECTING A TRUSTEE

You may want to have a trust set up and operable during your life. This is generally called an *inter vivos trust*. You would need to have a trustee manage the trust. A separate type of trust, one that is operable upon your death as outlined in your will, is generally referred to as a *testamentary trust*. Both are discussed in more detail in Chapter 6.

Through your will, you can appoint an individual or trust company to administer assets of your estate that you identify for later distribution. The benefits of using the services of a trust company as an executor or trustee were discussed earlier in this chapter. For example, you may wish to appoint a trustee to manage a portion of your assets for an extended period of time. If you are selecting a layperson to be the executor, you may not want the same person to be the trustee. There could be a potential conflict of interest and different skills could be required. You can also set up trust funds in a variety of ways, depending on your objectives. You may wish the beneficiaries to have regular monthly payments of the income generated from the original capital of trust money. This could be the situation if you are leaving money to an educational or charitable organization. Conversely, you could have a monthly payment provision in favour of a surviving spouse.

If you are setting up a trust for young children, payments are usually made to parents or guardians for the maintenance and education of the child. You may want to include a provision allowing the trustee to take from (or encroach on) the capital of the trust fund, in specific circumstances, to meet the needs set out in the trust provisions. Another option is to invest the trust funds until a specified event and then release the total funds. If a child had shown themselves to be financially irresponsible, you may wish to have the funds held until he or she was more mature, for example, 35 or 40 years old. If you wish to keep a trust for someone secret, there are various ways of doing that. If a will is probated, it is a public document, so for secrecy purposes a trust would be required. Speak to a lawyer who is experienced in dealing with trusts. Also, refer to Chapter 6, "Understanding Trusts."

Trustees are normally given the power in the will to undertake many duties, including taking in money, investing money, selling assets and distributing the estate proceeds in accordance with the trust terms. The trustee must maintain a balance between the interests of income beneficiaries and beneficiaries subsequently entitled to the capital, unless the trust says otherwise. In addition, a trustee should maintain accounts and regularly issue accounting statements and income tax receipts to beneficiaries, make income payments to beneficiaries, and exercise discretion on early withdrawal of capital where permitted, to meet special needs of beneficiaries. Finally, the trustee makes the final distribution of the trust fund to beneficiaries on the death of the income beneficiary and/or upon beneficiaries reaching certain ages designated in the terms of the will, or based on other conditions in the will.

You can see why trust companies perform a vital role. An individual may not have the long continuity required, due to death or lack of interest or ability, for the 10, 15, 20 or more than 25 years required. It would certainly be an onerous role to place on a sole individual. Speak to your lawyer, and if you know any other lawyers or Chartered Accountants who work in the tax and estate planning area, ask them if they can recommend any trust companies. Otherwise, do your own research by looking on the Internet and checking the Yellow Pages of the phone book under trust companies. Remember to compare three before making your final selection.

Selection of the right executor for your needs will enhance the smooth disposition of your assets and administration of your estate. It will also reduce the stress your family will be under. Selection of the wrong executor for your needs will result in the opposite outcome. A trustee performs separate tasks but in certain situations, for example, a trust company could perform both roles. To be on the safe side, use professionals to act as an executor or trustee, or appoint a family member to be a co-executor or co-trustee if the circumstances warrant it. When establishing a trust, particularly an *inter vivos* trust, you have to weigh the total cost of setting up and administering the trust against the tax and other benefits.

SELECTING A GUARDIAN FOR YOUR CHILDREN

If you are a parent of young children, it is in your children's best interests to thoroughly plan for their upbringing and care in the event of your death. When you appoint a guardian of your young children in your will, you are really just making a request, as your wishes are not legally binding as children are not property and therefore cannot be willed. The law attempts to determine what is in the best interests of the children. In practical terms, if the guardian is willing and able to perform the responsibilities, the courts will generally uphold your wishes. Make sure you name an alternate guardian in case the first one is unwilling or unable to assume the responsibility, or predeceases you.

Obtain the consent of the main and alternate guardians after discussing the matter with them. It is recommended that you leave with your will, in your safety deposit box or in safe-keeping with your lawyer, a letter detailing your wishes with regards to raising your children. This would include fundamental issues such as religion, education, values and general upbringing. Your wishes, of course, should also be discussed with the guardian.

You may wish to consider appointing different people to be the trustee and guardian of the children, thereby eliminating any potential conflict of interest. The trustee is responsible for protecting the child's inheritance by minimizing the erosion of the capital set aside in the trust, unless circumstances justify otherwise, of course. A guardian on the other hand, is frequently attempting to obtain more funds for the upbringing, care, health and education of the child. It is crucial that the guardianship issue be dealt with in the will, but is particularly important if only one parent has legal custody of the children.

Planning for the issue of guardianship includes selecting and appointing the guardian, creating assets in the estate to be available for the trustee to meet the children's financial needs, and appointing a trustee to administer and invest the trust funds on behalf of the children. One way of making sure there is sufficient money for the trust is to purchase life insurance. Make sure you update your will as your guardianship needs or decisions change.

IMPACT OF FAMILY LAW LEGISLATION

Legislation involving your obligations to others on death can vary depending on the province. Existing marriage partners have rights in all provinces. Common-law couples may have rights in some provinces. Same-sex, common-law partners may have rights in some provinces. In all provinces, children have rights and in some provinces this is extended to parents, grandchildren and grandparents. Children born in a common-law relationship or out-of-wedlock have rights.

Under the *Income Tax Act*, common-law couples have the same rights as married couples in terms of being a beneficiary under an RRSP or RRIF. In other words, income tax on those assets is deferred until the death of the surviving spouse.

There are various ways that you can protect your rights or wishes. This would include a marriage or pre-nuptial contract, joint ownership of property or bank accounts, and stating the beneficiaries in your will. In addition, you could specify your legal or common-law spouse on your power of attorney documents and name them as designated beneficiaries in your RRSPs, RRIFs and insurance policies. Another option is to establish a living or testamentary trust. Based on customized legal advice that takes into account your provincial legislation, you can eliminate or minimize uncertainty or undesirable outcomes in the event of your death.

Avoiding Spousal Disputes

The best way to avoid problems is to anticipate them and plan accordingly. Depending on your situation, you may be faced with any of the following relationship scenarios—"traditional" marriage (male/female), same-sex marriage, common-law marriage, same-sex relationship, separated spouse and spouse from divorce.

TRADITIONAL MALE/FEMALE MARRIAGE AND SAME-SEX MARRIAGE

You want to have a will that covers your spouse and children, if applicable. This could include "back-to-back" wills, where the surviving spouse receives all the assets. If you don't have a will, provincial law will give your legal spouse rights to your estate based on a formula. This varies from province to province. For example, two-thirds to your spouse and the rest divided equally among your children. Refer to Appendix C for a comparison of the provincial laws on dying intestate. In most provinces, couples can prepare a marriage contract or pre-nuptial agreement if desired, protecting assets brought into the marriage, or of course make a will.

COMMON-LAW RELATIONSHIP

Common-law spouses generally do not have any rights to property under provincial family legislation or intestacy law, but they could have a claim for ongoing support. Common-law spouses have similar rights to married couples in terms of RRSPs and RRIFs being transferred with income tax being deferred until the death of the surviving spouse. CPPs (Canada Pension Plan) are similar, if they designate their partner as beneficiary and spouse. In order to protect your common-law partner, as well as yourself, you should consider:

- owning property jointly. That way the property automatically goes to the survivor on death, bypassing the will
- designating each other as beneficiaries in your wills, RRSPs, RRIFs, TFSAs, other non-registered investments and insurance
- designating each other in your enduring power of attorney documents, advance directives or health care proxy. These are similar concepts to a "living will"
- developing a co-habitation agreement covering support and property issues in the event of separation or death

SAME-SEX RELATIONSHIP

Over the past decade, the law has evolved significantly in this area, including same-sex marriage. Same-sex couples have been granted rights by the courts, and legislation has changed in most jurisdictions. This all has an impact on estate planning issues. However, as mentioned with reference to common-law couples, you want to structure and document your financial affairs to protect your mutual financial interests. If this relationship scenario applies to you, and you are not legally married, check with your legal, financial and tax advisors as to the current pending or existing relevant legislation.

SEPARATED SPOUSE

The act of separation does not nullify the contents of your will with respect to your spouse. You cannot write your spouse out of your will if you are still legally married, unless you have signed a separation agreement or a marriage contract. If you are separated, you want to obtain legal advice, and then promptly:

- update or prepare a new will
- cancel any power of attorney or advance directives documents and do up new ones
- re-register any assets owned jointly, e.g. if property, sell it or change to tenants-in-common. If you have a joint bank account, open up your own personal account
- change the names of designated beneficiaries for your RRSPs, RRIFs, TFSAs, non-registered investments, pension, insurance and annuities

DIVORCED SPOUSE

A will prepared prior to your divorce is not automatically revoked. However, there is an impact on a couple of provisions in the will. Any bequest or asset left to your ex-spouse is revoked. Also, your ex-spouse cannot act as an executor. If you did not have a co-executor, your lawyer would have to apply to the courts to have an executor appointed.

You should always draft up a new will concurrently with signing the separation or divorce agreement. At the same time, review all your other financial affairs and beneficiaries, as outlined earlier under "Separated Spouse."

FEES AND EXPENSES

There are various fees associated with probating a will or settling an estate or dealing with a trust. The main ones are:

Executor's/Administrator's Compensation

In most cases an executor or administrator is entitled to a fee for his or her time and services provided. The maximum fee is normally 3 to 5 percent of the value of the estate, depending on the time and skill involved, even if it drags on for years. The beneficiaries or the court have to approve the accounts prepared for compensation and the amount comes out of the estate. An executor who is also a beneficiary could be denied a fee unless the will makes it clear that the gift to the executor is given in addition to, not instead of, executor's fees.

Legal Fees

A lawyer can assist in locating and collecting assets; make any necessary application to court and prepare related documents; get the assets transferred into the name of the executor or administrator; prepare accounts; distribute funds; obtain releases; and file tax returns.

Legal fees are considered a proper expense and may be paid out of estate funds, subject to approval of the court or the beneficiaries. A lawyer may charge a fee for itemized services rendered, or a lump-sum fee of generally up to 2 percent of the value of the estate for certain basic services. This is a maximum percentage, not a standard rate. If any legal issue arises, such as the validity or meaning of a will, or where an application to the court is made, legal fees will be extra and are normally billed out at the lawyer's hourly rate. This could be between $200 and $500 plus an hour, depending on the degree of expertise required and prevailing rates in your community.

Probate Fees

These are also known as *court fees* and are established by provincial legislation. They do not form part of the executor's compensation nor do they include legal fees associated with administering the estate. The probate fees can range from low to high depending on the province. For example, Alberta has the lowest fees and Ontario, the highest. It is the value of the estate that is used as a base when determining the probate fee that is paid to the provincial government. Refer to Appendix C for a chart comparing provincial probate fees. As these can change at any time, ask for the current fees.

Trustee Fees

These would generally be negotiated separately, especially if a trust company is involved, and confirmed in writing.

Additional Fees and Costs

Naturally, income–tax related costs are extra.

Contesting the Fees Charged

If a beneficiary of the estate feels that the administration fee charged by an executor is excessive, he or she can ask the executor to *pass accounts* in a court of law. The executor must present an accounting of the work done to the court and ask a judge to set the fees. The final fee may be higher or lower than the fee that the executor initially requested. When there are infant beneficiaries, the executor may be required to pass accounts because minors cannot give their approval for the actions of the executor.

If the executor or beneficiary believes the legal fees are excessive, they too can be challenged. This is called *taxing* or assessing a lawyer's account. It is generally taxed in front of the Registrar or master at the court house. Check the procedures in your community.

HOW TO AVOID YOUR WILL BEING CONTESTED

Anticipate Who Might Contest Your Will

Think of who might challenge the content of your will. It would be primarily people who feel that you should have included them but didn't, or did include them but did not give them much, or you had restrictions on the access to or timing of receipt or nature of the bequest. This could include children from an earlier relationship whether common-law or marriage, children with special needs, relatives or current spouse. In some provinces, parents and grand-parents also have rights.

Get Expert Legal Advice in Advance

You want to speak to a lawyer who specializes in will and estate law. They have the expertise and experience to protect your interests. For example, they could insert special clauses explaining the rationale why certain beneficiaries were excluded, or included but with restrictions or reduced bequests. This field of law is a highly specialized area. How to select such a lawyer is covered in Chapter 16, "Selecting Professional Advisors."

Minimize Amount in Your Estate

If you feel your will could be contested by someone, there are various options to consider as outlined below to bypass the estate, and therefore deplete the value of your estate covered by your will. Any lawyer, acting on behalf of someone planning to contest your will, could advise the client to forget about it, if research showed there was nothing left in the estate of consequence. Many of these options have been covered in more detail in other parts of the book. Keep in mind that under provincial legislation, only what is in the estate is at risk. If you have very little in your estate, then of course you don't have much at risk.

One way of minimizing your estate assets is by applying different strategies based on professional advice. For example:

- dedicated beneficiaries of RRSPs, RRIFs, TFSAs, other registered and non-registered investments, and life insurance
- joint ownership of bank accounts and property. In most cases, on your death, the asset is automatically owned by the other joint owner
- gifting to others while you are still alive
- setting up living or *inter vivos* trusts

WHERE TO GET MORE INFORMATION

There are many sources of information available to you as follows:

- Obtain advice from a lawyer skilled in will matters. Contact your local lawyer referral service for names or look for lawyers on the Internet who advertise their speciality in the area of wills. Refer to Chapter 16, "Selecting Professional Advisors."
- Obtain advice from a professional accountant (such as a Chartered Professional Accountant (CPA)) with tax expertise. Refer to Chapter 16, "Selecting Professional Advisors," for sourcing information.
- Obtain advice from a qualified credentialled financial planner. Again, refer to Chapter 16, "Selecting Professional Advisors."
- Contact the various banks and trust companies for consumer publications relating to will matters.
- Refer to Appendix B for a sample will and codicil. These are for illustration purposes only. Do not adopt them for your own needs, as you require customized legal and tax advice to protect your wishes.
- Refer to Appendix D for a will preparation checklist and chart of how your assets would be distributed if you did not have a will or a valid will.

SUMMARY

It is human nature for some people to procrastinate when dealing with complex personal or financial issues. Other people think of illness, death and grief when they think of the subject of will and estate planning. When reflecting on the subject in a more objective fashion though, the benefits are overwhelming. The consequences of not dealing with these issues are equally overwhelming.

A will should be customized for your specific needs and updated on a regular basis. As a will is a legal document, the wording and necessary clauses to reflect your wishes should be approved by your lawyer.

The consequences of not having a will are not the type of memory or legacy most people would choose to inflict on their children, spouse or relatives. During the natural grieving process, one does not want one's family and friends to deal with the stress and uncertainty of not having had a will. Memories should be cherished for all the right reasons, including the foresight, consideration and love reflected by having a valid will that reflects current realities. Simply put, there is no logical reason not to have a will.

❓Frequently
❗Asked Questions

1. Can the executor witness the will?

Yes, provided the executor is not also a beneficiary.

2. Can a beneficiary witness the will?

No. If a beneficiary or the spouse of a beneficiary signs as a witness to the making of the will, the will is valid, but the granting of the gift left in the will to the witness, or to the witness's spouse, is void and is not given to the stated beneficiary.

3. Can I change my will after I have signed it?

Yes. You can make minor changes by making a codicil, which must be signed and witnessed in the same way as a will. Do not erase or alter the will itself. If you want to make major changes, make a new will.

4. What happens to my will if I get married or divorced?

A will is automatically revoked when you get married, unless it states that it is made in contemplation of marriage. If you leave something in your will to your spouse and then are divorced, your will takes effect on your death as though your former spouse died before you, in other words, didn't exist. The exception is if it is clear from the wording of the will that you did not intend this to happen.

5. What if someone has been left out of the will?

If a will does not adequately provide for a spouse or a dependent or adult child (natural through a married or common-law relationship, or adopted), he or she may apply to the court for a variation of the will to make a fairer distribution. Consult a lawyer promptly if you are considering such an action. In order to be considered, court proceedings generally have to be started within a certain time period from the commencement of the probate process.

Understanding Powers of Attorney and Living Wills

"It is an equal failing to trust everybody and to trust nobody."

18TH CENTURY ENGLISH PROVERB

INTRODUCTION

At some point in your life, you will probably want to give authority to others to act on your behalf in certain situations. However, as provincial legislation can vary, the following content represents general guidelines only. Obtain specific advice for your province and circumstances from a lawyer.

This chapter covers the most common type of legal authority given to others, the power of attorney (PA). In addition, there will be a discussion of a "living will," an increasingly popular and important option. Topics covered include:

- the various types of powers of attorney
- choosing your attorney
- responsibility and powers of the attorney in different situations
- paying your attorney
- revoking the attorney powers
- types of "living wills," legalities, changing your mind
- the differences between a "living will," regular will and PA
- the implications of living part-time outside of your home province
- where to get more information

DESIGNATING POWER OF ATTORNEY

What Is a Power of Attorney (PA)?

Many lawyers draft a PA at the same time that they prepare a will. A PA designates a person or a trust company to take over your affairs if, for example, you can no longer handle them because of illness or incapacitation. This is referred to as an *enduring power of attorney*. You may be away for extended periods on personal or business matters, and want to give someone the authority to sign documents on your behalf regarding the sale of your home while you are away. This is normally referred to as a *specific power of attorney*, and is limited in scope and time. Considering the benefits of a PA, it is especially important if you have substantial assets that require active management. You can revoke the PA at any time in writing.

What If You Don't Have a Power of Attorney?

If you do not have a PA and are unable to manage your financial affairs because of illness, accident, or mental infirmity, an application has to be made to the court by the party who wishes permission to manage your affairs. This party is referred to as a *committee*. A committee's rights and actions are governed by provincial legislation and monitored by the provincial Public Trustee office under direction from the court. The purpose of this approach is to protect the financial and health interests of the person who is incapacitated. However, as bureaucracy, delays, expense and loss of autonomy result when the government intervenes, this can all be avoided if you have the proper PA.

Committee duties include filing with the court a summary of assets, liabilities and income sources, along with a description of the person's needs and an outline of how the committee proposes to manage the accounts or structure the estate to serve those needs. Continuing asset management is required to meet any changes in circumstances or needs, as well as record-keeping and accounting functions, all subject to the direction of the court.

For further information about a Public Trustee's duties, contact your provincial government Public Trustee Office.

Types of Powers of Attorney

There are several types of PAs as discussed following.

GENERAL POWER OF ATTORNEY

This document gives authority to someone else to look after all your affairs, generally of a financial nature. You would have the option of giving all the powers right now, but protecting yourself by not giving a copy of the original document to the attorney unless you needed to. The other alternative would be to have a PA that would only be triggered on a certain specified event.

Unless the PA had an enduring feature to it, e.g. would continue to be valid if you were mentally incapacitated, then it would be void if you were mentally incapacitated. Depending on your province, the document has to be very specific in its terminology in order to be enforceable.

PLANNING TO PROTECT ● *Ruth Wants to Help Her Father, But...*

Ben was age 77 and had a few minor strokes or TIAs (transient ischemic attacks). He was on medication. Then suddenly he had a major stroke that left him incapacitated. Ben was a widower and had one daughter, Ruth, who lived nearby. When Ruth tried to handle her father's affairs, she found that she was unable to deal with anything. She could not even stop Ben's mail, let alone access his chequing account to pay his bills, cancel his apartment lease or admit him to a nursing home. Out of frustration, Ruth contacted the provincial public trustee's office to ask for guidance. As Ben was not mentally competent, the public trustee's office took over all his affairs. Ruth applied for and was accepted as an administrator under the direction and control of the public trustee's office.

If Ben had paid out a few hundred dollars to have a lawyer draw up an enduring power of attorney document for personal care and property, all the above would have been avoided. Ruth would have been listed as her father's agent or attorney and would have been able to conduct all of the matters that needed to be handled promptly. The public trustee's office would not have entered the picture, as they would have had no authority to do so. It would have saved a lot of time, money and hassle and given Ruth the opportunity and autonomy to make responsible decisions about her father's needs without being monitored and regulated by government.

● ●

LIMITED POWER OF ATTORNEY

There could be situations where you want to give the authority to someone to look after a specific matter for you, e.g. selling a home or doing some transactions relating to securities during a specific time period. Generally, the criteria for the authority are very clearly spelled out. This type of limited attorney powers is generally not valid in the case of your mental incapacity.

PLANNING TO PROTECT ● *Maria Uses a Limited Power of Attorney to Sell Her House While Vacationing*

Maria decided to leave the country for a visit to see her grandchildren. As she wanted to sell her home while she was away, she gave her niece, Anita, a power of attorney limited to the right to sell the house during her absence. This document was limited in time, specified what power was being given and the minimum purchase price and terms acceptable. The house was sold and transferred without any difficulty. Those involved in the transaction—the purchaser, realtor, lawyer, mortgage company and provincial land registry office all accepted Maria's power of attorney as a legitimate proxy authority for Anita to conduct Maria's housing transaction.

• •

BANK POWER OF ATTORNEY

If you want to grant a PA to a trusted friend or relative to act on your behalf on financial matters, the financial institution generally requires you to sign its own legal forms, regardless of any other document that you have prepared.

The financial institutions are particular about whether a document really reflects a customer's current intentions, whether the document is a general or specific PA, and whether it includes an enduring clause or not. The enduring clause would normally state that the document would still be valid and your proxy power to the attorney would "endure" in the event of mental incapacity. Basically, the institution wants to see you personally and watch you sign their own documents rather than accept a document purporting to grant attorney proxy to others that they did not see you sign.

CONTINUING POWER OF ATTORNEY FOR PROPERTY

In this type of document, you give authority to an agent or proxy to represent your interests in financial matters. This document would remain valid even if you are mentally incapacitated, and it must be reviewed every three years unless it contains a clause to the contrary. It is sometimes referred to as an enduring PA.

CONTINUING POWER OF ATTORNEY FOR PERSONAL CARE

In this type of document, you are giving your authority to an agent or proxy to make decisions regarding your health and medical treatment in the event that you are mentally incapacitated, or unable to look after your health affairs. Other terminology for similar documentation includes living will, advance medical directive, representation agreement, health care proxy, etc., and are discussed later in more detail. The words "living will" are just a generic term.

If you are considering this type of PA, put your instructions in words your attorney can understand. The word "attorney" does not mean "lawyer." It means anyone whom you appoint as your agent or proxy. For example, if you tell your attorney you don't want any "heroic measures" to keep you alive, your attorney might not know what that means. Try to give examples of what you want or don't want to happen and under what circumstances. With advances in medicine, measures that might be considered by some to be "heroic" today could become commonplace in a few years' time, with high recovery rates. Here are some guidelines to consider when preparing your documentation:

- **Explain your instructions.** You might think of saying, for example, that you don't want to be "hooked up to a machine." Remember, machines that assist in breathing can be used temporarily in emergencies during surgery. That's not the same as being dependent on a machine to live.
- **Be clear and specific.** You may want to give certain instructions depending on the physical or mental condition you might be in and whether the condition is permanent. Think about whether you want different degrees of treatment in different circumstances, for example, if you are conscious or unconscious, physically mobile or bedridden, able or unable to recognize loved ones.
- **Be aware of the different degrees of illness or *condition*.** For example, you might give instructions in case you have a stroke, but you may have a mild stroke or a very severe one. Your instructions might be quite different, depending on the quality of life you could have after the stroke. Be careful about the instructions you give regarding medication. For example, you might have a very serious infection that could kill you, but it may be easily treated with an antibiotic.

    If you've already made a living will or advance medical directive, you can make the content of this documentation a part of your instructions in your continuing power of attorney for personal care. Living wills and advance medical directives are documents people write that say, in advance, the types of medical treatment they would choose or refuse if certain things happen when they cannot make decisions themselves. Your PA may include these documents.

- **Discuss your instructions with your attorney.** Make sure your attorney understands your instructions. Talk about your values and wishes. If you decide to give instructions about medical care, talk to your doctor and other health care providers about your health and what kinds of medical treatments you might face.
- Seek legal advice for peace of mind that the documentation and your wishes are clear and enforceable.

Choosing Your Attorney

You may want an attorney for different purposes:

PROPERTY

The first thing to do is to choose an attorney to make decisions in your absence with regard to your property. An attorney is someone who will make decisions for you when you are no longer mentally capable. As mentioned, the word "attorney" does not mean "lawyer." The attorney can be a relative, a friend or someone else. You can choose anyone you want as your attorney as long as he or she has reached the age of majority. This age varies between provinces and territories and is either 18 or 19.

Many trust companies are prepared to act as attorney for a fee. Some individuals choose this option because they want an attorney who is professional and impartial. To help you decide who your attorney should be, here are some general guidelines:

- **Think about the person.** Does he or she know anything about money matters? Will your attorney accept the responsibility? Do you know the person well? Do you trust him or her completely with your financial decisions and management of your property?
- **Talk to the person.** Ask that person whether he or she is willing to be your attorney. Talk about what the responsibilities will be. Explain why you are doing this. Discuss how you want your affairs handled.
- **Consult with other people.** Before you decide, you may want to talk to your family or close friends. Although you are not required to consult with a lawyer, it is a prudent and recommended idea. You may also want to talk to a financial planner or other trusted advisors, provided they are impartial and concerned only with your best interests.

You can name more than one person to be your attorney for property. If you do this, you may decide they will share the job or divide their responsibilities. Or, you could name one person as your attorney and another person as a substitute or backup, who could step in if your first choice resigns, gets sick or dies.

But if you name two people to be your attorneys and do not say how they should make your decisions or who should make which types of decisions, the law says they must make all your decisions together, that is, unanimously.

If you decide that your attorneys are going to make decisions together, it's a good idea to specify how disagreements get resolved. You might say that in a case of conflict, one attorney's decision would override the other's (although this would seem to defeat the purpose of having two attorneys). Otherwise, your attorneys might have to go to court and the judge will decide. You can see why getting advance legal advice is highly recommended.

PERSONAL CARE

The person you select for your attorney for your property may not be the same person for your personal care. There are different skills and attributes involved. Consider the following:

- **Think about the person.** Does he or she know you well enough to make personal care decisions for you? Do you trust your attorney to accept the responsibility and follow your instructions or wishes even if he or she may disagree with what you want?
- **Talk to the person.** Ask that person whether he or she is willing to be your attorney. Talk about what the responsibilities will be. Talk about why you are doing this. Discuss your instructions.
- **Consult with other people.** You are not required to consult a lawyer, but it is a good idea to do so. You may also want to talk to your doctor especially if you have complex health concerns. A discussion with your close family is also a good idea.

You can make the same person your attorney for both personal care and property, if they meet the requirements for both. But you should think about whether that person is suitable to make decisions in both areas. A person who can make decisions about your health care, for example, may not know a lot about finances. It can put a lot of pressure, responsibility and potential liability for financial decisions on one person.

Your Attorney's Responsibilities

There are different responsibilities and duties of an attorney for property or personal care.

PROPERTY

Your attorney must:

- act with honesty and integrity and in good faith, for your benefit
- fully understand the powers and duties of an attorney
- encourage you to participate to the best of your abilities, in decisions about property
- consult from time to time with your supportive family and friends and with whomever is providing personal care to you. (This is important to ensure that needs and decisions are clearly understood.)
- act in your best interest by putting your financial needs and legal obligations first, without any obligations to others
- keep accounts of all transactions and meet specified guidelines for how money may be spent on gifts, loans and charitable donations

PERSONAL CARE

Your attorney must:

- choose the least restrictive, least intrusive course of action that is available and appropriate
- encourage you to participate in your personal care decisions
- act honestly and in good faith
- follow the instructions you gave when you were capable unless it is impossible to do so
- try to establish regular personal contact between you and your family members and supportive friends
- as far as possible, help you become independent
- explain to you what powers and duties the attorney has
- consult from time to time with supportive family and friends, and with whomever is providing you with personal care

Powers of Your Attorney

Your attorney only has the amount of power that you have delegated, whether it be limited or general and whether specific to property or health. Also, the PA document has to comply with stringent requirements of your province in order to be enforceable.

Paying Your Attorney

In many cases, a PA does not have a fee associated with the services provided, especially if family members are involved. It really depends on the nature of the proxy and the individual. However, if a trust company or financial institution has a PA for your matters and is spending time acting on your behalf as your proxy, naturally there would be professional fees associated with that service. The issue of fees should be discussed at the outset and set out clearly in the proxy document to make sure there is no misunderstanding.

Revoking Your Power of Attorney

You can revoke a PA for property at any time as long as you are mentally capable. You do this in writing, in front of two witnesses. The rules on who cannot be a witness are the same as those for making a PA.

There are two ways to revoke a PA for personal care. If the PA is not *validated*, then the process of revoking it is the same as for property. If it is validated, the validation has to be cancelled before the PA can be revoked. *Validation* is a process by which your attorney can confirm that you are incapable and receive written proof of his or her authority from the Public Trustee office. A PA that is validated can be used even if you disagree with the decisions made by your attorney. Validation can be cancelled if you are no longer incapable.

If you revoke a PA for property or personal care, make sure to notify everyone to whom you've given copies of the documents or told about your PA, including your financial institutions and caregivers. It's a good idea to keep a separate list of these people.

If there have been big changes in your life, review your PA. For example, you may wish to review your choice of attorney if you marry, separate or divorce. You should review your PA for personal care if your health changes—perhaps you have developed an illness or a condition that affects your instructions. Review your continuing PA for property if your financial situation changes.

Finally, if you are moving from one province to another, you will need a new PA for that new province in most cases. Consult with a lawyer, your insurance company or those organizations that specialize in providing this kind of information and these services. If you are living part-time in the U.S. as a Snowbird, you will need to obtain a PA valid in the state you reside.

What to Do with Your Power of Attorney

You may wish to have it reviewed by an expert advisor. If it is not completed properly, it may not be valid.

It's a good idea to let people know that you've made a PA because you may not be able to tell them about it when you are incapable. You should therefore let anyone who will have to deal with your attorney(s) know who he or she is, how to make contact, and who has copies of the documents.

Depending on the type of PA you made, it is advisable to tell your family, lawyer, and any financial institutions you deal with, health care providers, and anyone else who provides you with care, who your attorney is and his or her address and telephone number. Remember to update them regarding any change in your attorney's address or telephone number.

You may give the original documents to your attorney(s) or keep them in a safe place where the attorney(s) can locate them quickly if necessary, e.g. a safety deposit box. Alternatively, you may leave the documents with a trusted third person, e.g. a lawyer or trust company, with written directions as to when they may be released to the attorney.

It is a good idea to keep at least one photocopy of the document. If possible, keep it with you together with the current address and telephone number of your attorney(s).

Make Sure Your Power of Attorney Is Valid for U.S. Assets

How valid your Canadian PA is in your Snowbird state, if you suffer a stroke or are otherwise incapacitated, depends on the terminology of the PA. There are two main types of PAs. One type would not be recognized in Florida, for example, and the other one might be. If you have a PA that gives someone a specific right to act on your behalf within a certain time period, e.g. selling a house in Canada for you, that is one type of PA. If you have a PA that gives someone authority to look after all your affairs if you are incapacitated, that is another type of PA. It is the second type that you have to be careful with regarding terminology. Here is an example under Florida law. The same issues could be applicable for any Snowbird states.

If it is a contingent or *non-enduring* PA, that is, it only takes effect when and if you become incapacitated, that type of PA is *not* recognized in Florida. If you have a *durable* PA, sometimes referred to in Canada as an *enduring* PA, then that type of PA *could* be valid in Florida. In that type of PA, you are appointing someone to be an attorney now, but it survives incapacity or disability. Non-enduring PAs are no longer valid in Florida, the premise being that if you give someone the right to act on your behalf, you have to have the right to revoke that if you are mentally capable, unless specific terminology in the PA deals with the issue of incapacity (e.g. enduring or durable). Naturally all PAs terminate at death, when your will takes over.

Even if your Canadian PA is technically acceptable in Florida, it may not be functionally useable. That is because the people who are being asked to accept the PA (e.g. transfer or sell property), will be naturally cautious about its validity and could refuse to recognize it because they are not familiar with the terminology or the content of the document. The more remote the area, the greater the chance of rejection. If you have a Florida PA dealing specifically with your Florida property and assets, and it is on a statutory form accepted and approved by the Florida government, then naturally that will make a huge difference in acceptance.

Although this example referred to Florida, the guidelines and cautions would be pertinent to consider for other U.S. states, particularly popular Snowbird states such as Arizona, Texas or California. You can see why you need to get legal advice from a lawyer in the U.S. state in which you have assets. Check also with your Canadian lawyer to make sure there is no conflict between your PAs in each country.

LIVING WILLS

In the previous section we briefly covered a continuing power of attorney for personal care. The following overview of living wills is based on the excellent consumer information material prepared by the Joint Centre for Bioethics at the University of Toronto, the leading source of helpful information on the topic. Contact numbers are located at the end of this chapter.

What Is a Living Will?

A *living will*, is a generic term, sometimes called an "advance medical directive," or other name, is a document containing your wishes about your future health or personal care. You make a living will when you are able to understand treatment choices and appreciate their consequences, that is, when you are *capable*. A living will only takes effect when you can no longer understand and appreciate treatment choices, that is, when you are *incapable*.

Living wills that meet certain technical legal requirements are also called "health care directives," "advance health care directives," "representation agreements," "mandates," "authorizations," "personal directives" and "powers of attorney for personal care," depending upon the province in which you live.

Difference Between a Living Will and a Regular Will or Power of Attorney

A regular will takes effect only after you have died, and directs how your *property* will be distributed among your heirs. Both a PA for property and a living will take effect while you are still alive, but unable to make decisions for yourself. A PA for property names someone else to make decisions for you regarding your finances and property. A living will contains instructions about your health and personal care, and may also name someone to make these decisions on your behalf, if you are no longer capable of doing so. A personal care PA gives authority for someone to make personal and health care decisions plus financial decisions relating to those issues, for example, incurring the cost of a private rather than semi-private hospital bed. However, in practical terms, a personal care PA and living will are synonymous documents depending on their wording and provincial legislation.

Why You Should Consider Making a Living Will

People complete a living will for two main reasons: to gain control over their future health care, and to relieve their loved ones from the burden of making difficult decisions for them. If you don't complete a living will, there might be conflict among family members about who should make decisions for you or what treatment should be given. Even if there is no conflict, it may be very difficult for your loved ones to make life-and-death decisions for you. If your loved ones feel they are making the decision you would have made yourself, they will be less likely to blame themselves. If you haven't told anyone what you want, no one will know.

However, to make a living will, you must consider the prospect of your own sickness and death and make plans for these events. Some people find this distressing as they have to face their own mortality. Each person should decide whether completing a living will is right for him or her. In almost all cases, preparing a living will provides peace of mind and clarity for all concerned and reduces stress and uncertainty.

Usually, a living will is part of a broader process called "advance care planning."

Types of Living Wills

Because instruction and proxy directives are complementary, your living will should, if possible, contain both of these directives. However, if you find that making decisions for a possible future illness is too difficult, then you may want to complete only the proxy directive. In this case, your proxy(ies) will make treatment and care decisions for you, based on their judgment as to what you would want, or would be best for you.

Or, if you do not have someone you trust to make decisions on your behalf, then you may want to complete only the instruction directive. If you do that, persons making decisions for you will be guided by your instructions in making treatment and personal care decisions for you. However, in practical and pragmatic terms, a decision would be made by the medical team in co-operation with the family based on the circumstances at the time.

PROXY DIRECTIVE

A *proxy directive* specifies who you want to make decisions on your behalf if you can no longer do so. The proxy should be someone you know and trust, and who understands your way of thinking about your health care treatment and personal care. This could be your spouse, partner, family member or close friend. This person should be capable of making health care and other personal care decisions and be willing to act as your proxy. As mentioned, a living will and personal care PA are very similar, if not identical, concepts. The distinguishing feature could be the power of the attorney to make decisions on care that could have financial implications to the person under care, for example, a private nurse or private room. The wording of the document and provincial legislation determine how a document can be enforced.

Because the proxy is responsible for carrying out your wishes, it is important that you discuss your wishes with your proxy. Otherwise, it may be difficult for your proxy to guess what your wishes might be.

You may name more than one person to act as your proxy, but you should state whether they should make decisions together as a group, or whether they should be given authority individually. In addition, you may want to indicate how disagreements between your proxies should be resolved. You might also want to name different proxies to make different types of decisions. Taking these steps can help to avoid conflict in case your proxies disagree about your treatment.

You may also wish, in your living will, to say whether you would want your doctors to follow the treatment decisions of your proxy, or your wishes as expressed in the instruction directive, if these two appear to be in conflict.

INSTRUCTION DIRECTIVE

An *instruction directive* specifies what health care or other personal care choices you would want your proxy to make in particular situations. You should express in the directive, in your own words, the values and beliefs that are the basis for your health and personal care decisions, in other words, your underlying personal philosophy.

Health care decisions are those made either by you, or by someone on your behalf, to consent or to refuse to consent to a treatment. Treatment refers to anything done for a diagnostic, therapeutic, preventive or palliative reason, e.g. comfort care.

Personal care decisions refer to decisions about those aspects of your daily life that are necessary for maintaining your health and well being. These include shelter, nutrition, hygiene, clothing, and safety.

Discussing the Living Will with Professionals

DOCTOR

It is a good idea to review your living will with your doctor. The doctor can ensure that you have understood the choices in the living will and that the instruction directive is suitable for your own health situation.

For example, a person with chronic lung disease will want to focus primarily on whether to go on a ventilator, e.g. breathing machine, if he or she develops respiratory failure. A person with kidney failure receiving dialysis will want to focus primarily on the situations in which he or she would want dialysis to be stopped. A doctor can help ensure that the living will you prepare is suitable for your medical circumstances.

LAWYER

It is a good idea to consult a lawyer with experience in this area. A living will is a legal document with serious legal implications. A lawyer can ensure that your living will is legally valid in your province. A lawyer's assistance may be particularly helpful if your capacity to make a living will is likely to be challenged, or if there may be disagreement among your family, or between your family and proxy.

Changing Your Mind About Your Wishes or Proxy

You can change your mind about your health care or other personal care decisions or your proxy at any time while you are still capable. If you change your mind, you should change your living will. Also, you should review your living will at regular intervals, such as once a year, and when there are important changes in your life—for example, if your medical condition changes, if you are admitted to hospital, if you marry or divorce or if your proxy dies. If you change your living will, replace all copies of the old one with copies of the new one. You should destroy the old copies so they do not get mixed up with the new copies of your living will.

Does Your Living Will Need to Be Followed?

Yes, it should be followed. The Canadian Medical Association has endorsed a policy supporting living wills and most doctors favour them. In provinces with specific legislation, people may be legally required to follow your living will. However, there could be circumstances in which you would not want people to follow your living will—for example, if there is evidence that you have changed your mind but have not changed your living will, or if there has been a medical advance that you did not know about when you completed the living will. In your living will, you can say how much leeway you want to give your proxy in following your wishes.

The Legality of Living Wills in Canada

Almost all provinces and territories have legalized the making of living wills. Living wills have different names and powers depending on the province in which you live.

For more detailed information, or to be sure that your living will is valid and enforceable, consult with a lawyer.

Since a living will speaks for you when you are no longer able to speak for yourself, other people must know that it exists. Give copies of your living will to your proxy, doctor, lawyer, and family members. If you review your wishes with these people and give them the opportunity to discuss your living will with you, they will be more likely to understand and follow your wishes. Do not put the only copy of your living will in your safety deposit box, since it will not be easy to gain access to it when needed. You may photocopy the living will once you have completed it.

The Joint Centre for Bioethics (JCB) has an excellent public information program. They also have samples of living wills that may be valid for your province. However, you still should consult with a lawyer to ensure it is compliant with your provincial requirements. Laws and regulations can change. Contact information for the JCB is given at the end of this chapter.

What If You Live Part-Time Outside Your Home Province?

If you reside in another province for part of the year, you need to ensure that the living will is valid in the other province. If not, you could have two living wills in Canada, each of which comply with the law of the province concerned. As you see, the JCB living will is valid in most provinces.

If you are residing part-time in the U.S., for example, as a Snowbird, you would need to have a living will that would be valid for your part-time home state.

Most states recognize a properly drawn living will or advanced directive. For further information, contact an organization called Caring Connections. The contact particulars are outlined at the end of this chapter. You can obtain sample advanced directives from them.

PLANNING TO PROTECT ● *Family in Conflict—*
Claire Had No Living Will

Claire was an 88-year-old Snowbird who spent part of the winter in Florida. She was healthy. One day as Claire was crossing the street, she tripped and fell and hit her head severely. Claire suddenly took a turn for the worse and fell into a coma. She was under life support for months without any chance of recovery. Her out-of-country emergency medical supplemental insurance coverage ran out and now her personal assets would be at risk for the shortfall. Her family was in conflict over whether to request that the heroic measures be stopped and let nature take its course. They wanted to do the right thing for their mother, but were in disagreement.

If Claire had signed a living will and health care proxy designed for her state, before she went into a coma, the family decisions would have been much easier. Living wills give guidance to the medical team and family members on the wishes of the patient in the event that he or she is in a terminal medical situation without any hope of recovery. In many U.S. states and Canadian provinces, living wills are recognized by government as a document that expresses the wishes of the patient. The medical team and family have discretion as to the appropriate decision on withdrawing life support.

What to Do with Your Living Will?

Make sure that the key people in your life know about your wishes and have a copy of your living will. This would include your spouse, of course, family members, doctors and lawyer. You may also wish to keep a copy in your wallet or purse. It is impractical for people to see the document or know about its contents, if you just keep a copy in your safety deposit box.

WHERE TO GET MORE INFORMATION

There are several sources of excellent information:

- **Joint Centre for Bioethics (JCB), University of Toronto** publishes a living wills information kit. The kit includes a sample living will, plus explanations and other interesting information. You can print off a free copy of their living will from their website if you prefer. They can be reached at:

  Joint Centre for Bioethics (JCB)
  University of Toronto
  155 College Street, Suite 754
  Toronto, ON M5T 1P8
  Website: *www.jbc.utoronto.ca*

- Refer to Appendix A, "Sources of Information," for contact numbers for provincial organizations dealing with advance directives.
- Refer to Appendix B for samples of a continuing power of attorney for personal care and property, and a living will. These documents are for **illustration purposes** only as you need to obtain current, customized professional advice.

SUMMARY

We have covered various issues in this chapter, including powers of attorney and living wills. There are many options available to you, but you need to obtain legal advice to be assured that your wishes are protected in writing.

❓ Frequently
∴ Asked Questions

1. *What is a power of attorney?*

This is a legal document within which you have granted a person or company to act on your behalf. There are different types of power of attorney, for example, for a specific purpose such as selling your home or a general purpose of looking after all your financial or health affairs if you are incapacitated. For your peace of mind, and to ensure that the document you sign is valid in your province, make sure that a lawyer prepares it.

2. *What if I don't have a power of attorney?*

This situation can result in serious problems if you are incapacitated. Your will only deals with your wishes on your death. However, in the absence of an enduring power of attorney, no one would have the legal authority to deal with your financial affairs. The provincial public trustee's office would enter the picture and look after your affairs or the court may appoint a family member to manage your affairs. The person appointed would annually account to the public trustee's office. You can avoid the cost of the court's involvement by keeping your power of attorney current.

3. *Is my power of attorney valid for my U.S. assets in the event that I am incapacitated?*

It would likely not be valid. Each state sets the law governing powers of attorney and the appropriate format and content required. For example, if your spouse attempted to use your provincial power of attorney to deal with your assets in the U.S., the bank or real estate company would likely not recognize it. They would feel uncomfortable with the unfamiliar and would not want to be exposed to liability. (Consult with a U.S. lawyer in the state where you hold U.S. assets.)

4. *What is a living will?*

A living will is designed for those who are concerned about the quality of life when near death. It is a written statement of your intentions to the people who are most likely to have control over your care, such as your spouse, family or doctor. The purpose of a living will is that it conveys your wishes, in the event that there is no reasonable expectation of recovery from physical or mental disability. In that event, you are usually requesting to be allowed to die naturally, and not be kept alive by artificial means or "heroic medical measures." The validity of a living will can vary depending on the provincial legislation.

Understanding Trusts

"Trust everybody, but cut the cards."

FINLEY PETER DUNNE

INTRODUCTION

You have probably heard of family trusts, private trusts, or corporate trusts. You may also have heard of offshore trusts or international trusts. There is a mystique about trusts as well as a lot of confusion about what they are and when they should be considered. Many people think trusts are just for the rich or for people with complex financial and investment affairs. That is not the case at all.

Trusts are a very common way of dealing with a range of personal choice, family or business options. As will be outlined in the following chapter, one or a number of trust options could meet your financial, estate and tax planning needs.

A trust arises when a person (known as the *settlor*) transfers legal title to property or assets to another person (known as the *trustee*), with instructions as to how the property is to be used for the benefit of named persons (known as the *beneficiaries*). The trustee could also be one of the beneficiaries. Although the trustee has legal title to the trust property, *beneficial ownership* rests with the beneficiaries. In other words, the beneficiaries actually own the trust property, even though the title is in the trustee's name.

In this chapter, we will outline:

- an overview of trusts
- an explanation of living or *inter vivos* trusts and examples of different types
- an explanation of testamentary trusts and examples of different options
- the benefits of using the services of a trust company
- fees and expenses

- the trust agreement
- tax implications
- where to get more information

TYPES OF TRUSTS

There are two main types of trusts: living trusts and testamentary trusts. A *living trust*, also referred to as an *inter vivos* trust, is established while an individual is alive, and comes into effect once the trust agreement is signed and the trust is funded. A *testamentary trust* is created under the terms of a person's will and therefore takes life on the person's death. It is funded with assets from the proceeds of the deceased's estate. These trusts serve different purposes and objectives and can have different tax implications.

You can set up trust funds in a number of ways. You may want the beneficiary to receive regular ongoing income generated by the capital of the fund, that is, the original trust money. This is a very common provision when leaving money to charitable or educational organizations. If you are setting up a trust for infant children, you may want your trustee to have the power to *encroach* upon the capital of the fund, in other words, use part or all of the trust money for your children's education and maintenance. You may wish to accumulate income within the trust fund and postpone payment of the entire fund until the occurrence of some specified event. This is called a *conditional trust*. For example, this trust could be used for minor children until they reach the age of 21, 26, or 30 for example. If you have an irresponsible adult child, you could have a condition that he or she can't access the entire fund until he or she reaches 40 years of age.

A trustee only derives certain limited powers by provincial statute. Therefore, your will should specify exactly what powers you want to give to your trustee in carrying out the provisions of the trust. For example, if you do not wish your trustee to be restricted in the type of investments available for the management of trust funds, you must provide your trustee with expanded investment powers in your will.

THE CREATIVE USE OF LIVING TRUSTS

There are a number of creative ways that you can use a living trust. Common uses would be for a family trust, estate freeze, managing retirement needs, avoiding probate, minimizing taxes, ensuring confidentiality, and structuring a divorce settlement. Here are some examples. Refer to Appendix B for a will with a testamentary trust provision, just as an example.

The Family Trust

A *family trust* is a very useful device for holding investments or other assets for the benefit of your children, or for other members of your family to whom you provide financial support.

If you have young children, you could build up an investment portfolio within a family trust, which will be used in the future to pay for their higher education costs. If the trust agreement and the transfer of assets or money into the trust are properly designed, significant income tax savings can be achieved over the years because capital gains realized on the trust's investments will be taxed in the hands of your children at lower tax rates than if such gains were taxable in your own hands.

The Joint Partner Trust

If you are age 65 or older, and you wish to leave your assets to your spouse or partner, you can do this by transferring your assets into a *joint partner trust* while you are alive. During your lifetime, you would continue to have the use of the trust's assets, and to receive any income or capital gains realized on such assets within the trust. The *Income Tax Act* allows assets to be transferred into a joint partner trust at cost, without triggering capital gains taxation.

On your death, the assets that are held by the joint partner trust will pass to your spouse under the terms of the trust, rather than under the terms of your will. A joint partner trust achieves a postponement in capital gains taxation on death, since the trust's assets are deemed disposed of at fair market value when the second partner dies. This is no different than if you left assets to your spouse under your will. However, assets being transferred after your death via a joint partner trust may not be subject to provincial probate fees, depending on the province in which you reside.

A joint partner trust can be used for a same-sex or opposite-sex spouse, or for a common-law spouse.

The Alter Ego Trust

An *alter ego trust* is similar to a joint partner trust, but is for people 65 or older who do not have a spouse or partner. At the time of your death, the trust's assets would be deemed disposed of at fair market value for capital gains taxation purposes. This is no different than for assets that you held personally at the time of death, where there is no surviving spouse.

Besides avoiding probate fees, another significant advantage of alter ego and joint partner trusts is that there is no requirement for obtaining court approval after your death, and no requirement to file a list of the assets that are passing to your intended beneficiaries under the terms of the trust. Even if there were no savings in probate fees, many affluent people 65 and older are using joint partner and alter ego trusts as a means of preserving secrecy regarding the level of their net worth and information on how their estates are to be distributed after their death.

PLANNING TO PROTECT ● *All in the Family—But the Parents*
Maintain Control!

Donny and Johnny operated a successful travel agency. After many years of hard work, it became clear that their two children would want to succeed them in the business. The children had natural business aptitude plus a strong work ethic inherited from their parents. They also liked the free and low-cost perks and familiarization trips. They wanted travel to be their vocation and avocation.

Based on feedback from their professional advisors, Donny and Johnny decided to do an estate freeze. As part of the plan, they arranged for a family trust to be created for the benefit of their children. They also converted their common shares into preferred shares at the fair market value and then issued new common shares to the family trust. The result of this procedure was that the common shares would initially have only a nominal value, e.g. $1 per share. Therefore, any future growth in the value of the business would accrue to the benefit of the children via the family trust, which in due course, some years from now, would distribute the common shares to the two children. As the parents were still actively involved in the business, they prepared a management agreement, giving them exclusive control over the day-by-day operation of the business. There are other protective steps the parents could take, for example, making their preferred shares voting shares, and ensuring that there are a larger number of issued preferred shares than the common shares, therefore giving them direct voting control of the corporation.

● ●

Providing for Family Members with Special Needs

If you have family members who are not able to handle their own affairs, due to mental or physical incapacity, or other reasons, a *living trust* could be established to provide for their lifetime financial needs. On the recipient's death, the residue of the funds in the trust could be left for some other purpose, such as a charity or a gift over to your other children. You also may set up a trust for a person receiving disabilities benefits so they don't lose their benefits. See a lawyer familiar with the special requirements of these types of trusts.

Giving to Charity

You may wish to set up a *charitable remainder trust.* In this situation, you could assist your charity of choice by donating a residual interest in a trust to the charity. The common format is for the capital in the trust to go to the charity on your death (the *residual interest),* and in the meantime, you receive the income earned from the assets in the trust. The trust could be structured so that you receive a donation tax credit when the trust is established, representing the projected fair market value of the residual interest (the *remainder*). If the capital is not going to be eroded during your lifetime, it is easy to project the remainder. Refer to Chapter 14, Charitable Giving and Philanthropy.

Managing Retirement Needs

With advances in medical science and people being more aware of healthy living and eating, the average life span has increased immensely over the years. It is not uncommon for people to live into their eighties and nineties.

However, with aging, many people do not feel comfortable managing their own affairs. Their children may not have good money management skills, may be very busy or live out of town. For these reasons, many people consider the benefits of a living trust, managed by a trust company and a responsible family member, as co-trustees. Assets are set aside and put into the trust. Normally it is structured so that the parents receive income for life, with the capital distributed to the children and/or grandchildren on the death of the second parent.

The trust could also have a provision stating that the capital of the trust could be used under certain conditions, such as greater financial needs dictated by health, for example, paying for a long-term care facility in a retirement home.

Avoiding Probate

As a trust bypasses the estate, it is not included in the probate process. Because of this, there are no probate fee or estate administration charges that would be paid.

Keeping a Gift Confidential

For a variety of reasons, you may wish to keep your gift confidential. By transferring assets to a living trust, alter ego trust, or joint partner trust, the assets are no longer part of the owner's estate on death. Because the probate process does not cover these assets, they would not be included in the public record when the will is probated.

There are several options available to maintain confidentiality:

SECRET TRUST

This is a direct gift in the will to someone who is required to use the money on behalf of the person you wish to benefit from the gift. A *secret trust* can also be set up during a person's lifetime. Remember "Pip" of Charles Dickens' *Great Expectations*? He was able to live the life of a "gentleman" by being a beneficiary of a secret trust. He suspected all along that his benefactor was Miss Havisham, only to find out much later that it was the escaped convict to whom he had shown kindness many years earlier. This is certainly one of the most famous "secret trusts" in English literature.

HALF-SECRET TRUST

This is named as a trust gift in the will, but the will does not mention who the beneficiary of the trust will be; only the trustee will know the purpose of the trust and who is to benefit. The trustee must be careful not to reveal the purpose of the trust, so discretion is very important.

If you wish to use either type of trusts in your will, you should seek the advice of a lawyer experienced in trusts.

Payments for Divorce Settlements

Divorce settlements where children are involved can be contentious. On the one hand, the spouse who is the primary caregiver needs to be able to rely on regular support payments for the children. On the other hand, the spouse who is paying the support wants to make sure that money is going for the purpose intended. As lump-sum support payments can be a source of disagreement, one way around the issue is to put available capital into a living trust agreement for the benefit of the children. The children would continue to get the support payments under the trust until they reached the age of majority. The age of majority varies depending on the provincial jurisdiction, e.g. 18 or 19.

For a sample of a living trust document, refer to Appendix B.

CREATING A TESTAMENTARY TRUST

Testamentary trusts are included in your will to take effect after your death. Common options include the spousal trust, trusts set up for minor children or grandchildren, providing for family members with special needs, discretionary trusts for children who are spendthrifts and gifts for charities. Here are some examples:

The Spousal Trust

In this situation, you set up a trust to provide income for the life of your spouse, with the capital remaining at the spouse's death to go to the children or grandchildren. This type of trust is common when a spouse is ill or incapacitated or lacks financial expertise. A variation of this format, if there are no children or grandchildren, is to leave the capital to charity, on the death of the surviving spouse.

PLANNING TO PROTECT ● *Jerry Protects Her Family Through a Spousal Trust*

Jerry was sophisticated in managing her financial affairs, but her husband, Ben, was not interested in financial matters. They had two children, Kurtis and Krysta. Jerry looked after all the household finances and investment decisions. As Jerry had a high-risk occupation as a deep sea diver, she was concerned over how Ben would manage financial matters if she were to die. She decided to set up a spousal trust for her husband in her will. All her assets would go into the trust. A trust company would be the trustee and would manage the trust in accordance with Jerry's wishes for Ben's benefit and the benefit of the children.

When Ben died, the remaining trust funds would go to the two children, assuming they had each reached the minimum age of 25. This arrangement gave Jerry the peace of mind of knowing that her husband and children would have their financial affairs well managed. It also was a prudent decision to protect her children's inheritance. If Jerry had not set up a trust, Ben could have re-married and on his death, his second wife could have inherited all of his estate.

Trusts for Minors

You may already have in your will that in the event that both parents die at the same time, or when the surviving parent dies, that a portion of your estate shall be held in trust for minor children or grandchildren until they reach a certain age. In the meantime, the trustee can pay out the income and encroach on the capital for specific needs of the children. Many people then arrange to have the money disbursed over various time periods as the children mature, for example, one-third at age 19, one-third at age 25, and one-third at age 30.

Trust for Charities

You may wish to set up a trust that provides family members with income for life, but on their death the remaining capital in the trust is distributed to a charity of your choice. For more detail, refer to Chapter 14, Charitable Giving and Philanthropy.

The Spendthrift Trust

You could have a child who has a history of financial irresponsibility. One solution is to set up a trust to control the funds or assets that the child would otherwise receive. The trustees would have the power to distribute as much of the income as appears reasonable for the child, with any excess income being re-invested in the trust. There could also be a power to use some of the capital as necessary in extenuating circumstances.

On the death of the child, the capital in the trust could go to the grandchildren, for example.

The Special Needs Trust

If you have a family member who is physically or mentally challenged and not able to manage his or her own affairs, you may want to consider a trust. That way, you would have the assurance that the needs of the child would be looked after from the interest on the capital of the trust, with encroachment powers on the capital in extenuating circumstances. Any excess interest would be re-invested in the trust and added to the capital.

If it appears that the trust would be operating for an extended time, it is prudent to consider the benefits of having a trust company as trustee or co-trustee.

SELECTING A TRUSTEE
Refer to the discussion on this topic in Chapter 4.

BENEFITS OF USING THE SERVICES OF A TRUST COMPANY
Refer to the discussion on this topic in Chapter 4. Trust companies can be used as executors or trustees or both.

WHAT ARE THE FEES AND EXPENSES?
There are various fees involved when dealing with a trust. You need to balance out the benefits of the trust to the cost of setting up, managing and distributing the trust assets. Although a living or testamentary trust can sometimes provide many estate and financial planning benefits and investment potential, the costs could be considerable.

You will need tax and legal advice from experienced professionals who are familiar with how to properly structure a trust document, be it in the form of a living or testamentary trust. Naturally, the more complexity involved, the higher the fees. Whatever form of trust you are considering, the set-up fees would probably range from a minimum of $1,500 to $3,000 and up.

The cost for managing the trust is covered by provincial trustee legislation. Some provinces establish a set maximum for managing an estate, while other provinces permit reasonable fees based on the skill, care and complexity involved, with limits set by the court. The fees are normally based on a percentage of the gross value of the trust being administered. However, in many cases, there can be a separate agreement between the parties that provides additional remuneration to the trustees.

When the trust is finally distributed, there is another fee charged for the disposition. Again, this is covered by provincial legislation or guidelines, with the possibility of having a supplemental agreement setting out different or additional fees.

OUTLINING EVERYTHING IN A TRUST AGREEMENT

This is a document which sets out the details of the trust arrangement. It names the trustees, defines the beneficiaries, outlines what property is being transferred, and establishes the criteria for distributing the income and capital from the trust. A living trust is contained in a separate legal document. In the case of a testamentary trust, the terms of the trust are outlined in the will.

One of the key elements of a trust is the powers that the trustees have to manage the trust. For domestic (within Canada) trusts, provinces have trustee acts which govern the operation of trusts, and give powers or guidance to the trustees and the courts. In the case of Quebec, the rules for managing a trust are set out in the *Civil Code.* If you are considering an international trust, it is governed by the laws of the country in which the trust is located.

The terms of the trust agreement, be it a living or testamentary trust, are critical to your needs being fully met. Some provincial trust legislation can be more restrictive and conservative than others, in terms of setting out the powers of the trustees and the nature of the investments permitted. The provincial government's conservative rationale could be for public policy reasons, in other words, to protect the beneficiaries of the trust from abuse of the trust powers. However, in most cases, you are permitted to override some of the restrictive aspects of provincial trust legislation and expand the powers given. You would do this by the additional powers you give the trustee in your will or trust document. The net effect could be that you could give a lot of discretion and autonomy to the trustee on how the trust is operated and the nature of the investments, for example, discretion on putting money into hedge funds or private equity investments, keeping a business operating rather than selling it, selling the property in the trust and investing the funds or collapsing the trust.

You can see why you need to retain highly competent professionals to prepare your living or testamentary trust clauses to meet your objectives. You want them to have the experience to anticipate and pre-empt any potential issues that could result in legal action. You want to think of contingency plans if the capital beneficiary dies before the income beneficiary, or the beneficiary dies before you or a condition that you set for receiving a gift is not met.

THE TAX IMPLICATIONS OF A TRUST

The following is a summary of the way in which trusts are subject to Canadian income tax, as well as the tax treatment of property transferred to and from a trust. Space limitations do not allow us to cover all of the tax rules that apply to trusts. In the context of the Canadian tax system, the expression "for every rule there is an exception" is all too true.

Taxation of a Trust as a Separate Entity

A trust is considered to be an "individual" for income tax purposes. Just like each of us, a trust must compute its income and capital gains from all sources both inside and outside Canada, in arriving at *net income* and *taxable income*. However, unlike "real" individuals, trusts are not allowed to claim any personal tax credits in arriving at tax payable.

The income tax rate(s) that applies to a trust depends on whether the trust is an *inter vivos trust* or a *testamentary trust* that qualifies as a "graduated rate testamentary trust." As explained earlier, an *inter vivos* trust is one that has been created by a person during his or her lifetime. A *testamentary trust* is a trust that came into existence after a person's death as a result of certain terms of the person's will.

In calculating the income tax liability of a testamentary trust, the same graduated tax rate schedules are used that apply to real individuals but only for the first 36 months after the person's death. After that, an ongoing testamentary trust is taxed at the top marginal income tax rates. The provincial tax rate depends on the province in which the trust is "resident." The province in which a trust is considered to "reside" is generally where the trustee resides, or in the case of there being more than one trustee, where the majority reside and carry out their duties. In the case of a trust that is resident in Quebec, Quebec income tax is calculated and reported in a separate Quebec tax return (TP-646-V).

For an *inter vivos* trust, the federal income tax is calculated using the top marginal income tax from the first dollar of taxable income. The lower graduated rates of tax that are applicable on a sliding scale for real individuals, cannot be used for *inter vivos* trusts. Therefore, the combined federal and provincial income tax rate for an *inter vivos* trust and for testamentary trusts after the first 36 months is about 50 percent, give or take a few percentage points, depending on the province of residence.

Treatment of a Trust as a Flow Through Entity

A trust can pay income tax itself, or it can be a *flow through* entity for income tax purposes. This depends on a number of factors relating to the nature of the trust, who the beneficiaries are, and on how the trustee(s) chooses to prepare the trust's T3 income tax return.

A detailed explanation of these tax rules is beyond the scope of this chapter. However, the basic principles are as follows.

DEDUCTION FOR INCOME PAID OR PAYABLE

If any of a trust's income (including capital gains) for a particular taxation year was *paid or payable* in the year to one or more beneficiaries, the trustee(s) has the right to deduct such amounts in arriving at the trust's net income for income tax purposes.

This is an optional deduction. The trustee(s) can choose to let the trust pay the income tax (which in the case of an *inter vivos* trust or a testamentary trust after the first 36 months will be at a flat rate of about 50 percent), or the trustee(s) can allocate the taxable income to one or more beneficiaries, and let them pay the tax. This can often result in a lower overall tax liability (e.g. if the beneficiaries have very little income from any other sources, and are in a low tax bracket). However, if the beneficiary is under the age of 18, the *income splitting tax* (so-called *kiddie tax*) may eliminate the potential tax saving.

BENEFICIARY CAN BE TAXED RATHER THAN THE TRUST

It stands to reason, that when *paid or payable* amounts are deducted by the trust they are considered to be *income* of the beneficiary (beneficiaries) to whom the amounts were paid, or became payable in the year.

MEANING OF "PAID OR PAYABLE"

The income of a trust is considered to have been *paid or payable* if the trust:
- makes income distributions directly to one or more beneficiaries
- makes a payment to a third party on behalf of, or for the personal benefit of, a particular beneficiary (e.g. tuition fees are paid directly by the trust to the school, college or university in respect of a particular beneficiary) *or*
- causes any remaining undistributed income or taxable capital gains of the trust to have become legally "payable" to a beneficiary by the end of the trust's taxation year (e.g. by issuing a promissory note as evidence of the amount owing to a particular beneficiary by the trust)

CHARACTER OF FLOW THROUGH
INCOME AND GAINS IS RETAINED

There are a number of special rules which ensure that the character of certain kinds of income and gains realized by a trust can be retained when they are allocated to a beneficiary. For example, dividends from taxable Canadian corporations retain their character, so that the beneficiary can claim the dividend tax credit. Similarly, capital gains can be flowed through to a beneficiary. This permits any capital losses of the beneficiary from other sources to be offset against the capital gains allocated from the trust.

PREFERRED BENEFICIARY ELECTION

The *preferred beneficiary election* allows income that has not become paid or payable in the year to one or more beneficiaries to be allocated none the less. This special election can only be made in limited circumstances where the beneficiary is disabled.

Transfer of Assets into a Trust

CASH TRANSFERS

Since there is no gift tax in Canada, cash can be contributed to a domestic or foreign trust without incurring any tax. However, there are other tax implications to consider. For example, if cash is transferred to a trust whose beneficiaries include the spouse of the donor, or any minors (e.g. individuals who are under the age of 18 or 19, depending on the province), the attribution rules may be applicable. This could have the effect of causing the income (or capital gains) of the trust to be taxable in the hands of the donor of the cash, rather than in the hands of the trust itself or a beneficiary.

TRANSFER OF ASSETS THAT HAVE APPRECIATED IN VALUE

If property is transferred to a formal trust (as opposed to a "bare trust"), it is generally considered to have been transferred for notional proceeds equal to the current fair market value of the property. This means that if the donor's adjusted cost base for the property was a lower amount, a capital gain would arise on the transfer. Alternatively, transfers to a joint partner trust or alter ego trust by a person aged 65 or older are considered to be made "at cost." Therefore, capital gains are not triggered on the transfer.

PROPERTY TRANSFERRED TO A SPOUSAL TRUST

Generally, a transfer of property to a trust that is for the exclusive benefit of one's spouse (and which meets certain conditions) will be treated as a rollover for capital gains purposes. Thus, no capital gain has to be reported by the transferor of the property. This is the good news. The bad news is that the spousal attribution rules will generally come into play, to cause any future income on the property, or capital gain realized by the trust on the sale of the property to be attributed back to the person who originally transferred the property into the trust.

PLANNING TO PROTECT ● *Tony Uses a Trust—*
But Incurs a Capital Gain

Tony has decided to set up a trust for the benefit of his two children. He decides to transfer some shares of a particular stock that he bought a year or two ago. He paid $10,000 for the stock, which is currently worth $50,000.

If he goes ahead with the transfer of the stock to the trust, he will have to report a capital gain of $40,000 in his income tax return for the taxation year in which the transfer occurs. Depending on his marginal tax rate and the value of the shares down the road, this trust may be worth the tax. He should consult a tax advisor for his optimum option.

● ●

TRANSFER OF PROPERTY TO A *BARE TRUST*

A *bare trust* is a particular type of trust where the beneficial ownership of the property held by the trust has been retained by the person who made the transfer. The trustee of a bare trust is little more than an agent, who is holding title to certain assets on behalf of a particular individual who retains the true beneficial ownership.

In such cases, a transfer of the legal title of property to a bare trust where there is no change of beneficial ownership, is not treated as a "disposition" for capital gains purposes. Therefore, no capital gain arises on the transfer.

Transfer of Property Out of a Trust to a Beneficiary

DISTRIBUTION OF PROPERTY TO A CAPITAL BENEFICIARY

If property is distributed out of a trust to a beneficiary who is entitled to share in the "capital" of the trust, the transfer is generally treated as a rollover for capital gains purposes. The trust does not realize any capital gain on the transfer, and the beneficiary takes over the trust's "cost" (for tax purposes) of the property. In effect, the trust's accrued capital gain on the property is assumed by the beneficiary, rather than being taxed in the trust as a capital gain at the time of the distribution. This does not mean that tax is being avoided—only that capital gains taxation is being postponed until the time that the beneficiary eventually disposes of the asset.

DISTRIBUTION OF PROPERTY TO AN INCOME BENEFICIARY

Normally, if a trust's income (or part of it) is being distributed to one or more beneficiaries, the distribution(s) will be made in cash. However, if property is transferred to a beneficiary as part of that person's entitlement to the "income" of the trust, it is treated as a disposition by the trust for proceeds equal to the fair market value of the property. Thus, any accrued capital gain at the time of the transfer would have to be reported by the trust.

You Can't Avoid It—Capital Gains Taxation Every 21 Years!

Most trusts (with the exception of certain kinds of spousal trusts) are subject to a "21-year deemed disposition" rule for capital gains tax purposes. This means that on the twenty-first anniversary of the trust's creation, and every 21 years thereafter, the trust is considered for Canadian capital gains tax purposes to have disposed of each and every asset in the trust for notional proceeds equal to the fair market value of the assets at that time.

This rule was introduced many years ago as an anti-tax avoidance measure, because the government of the day believed that trusts were being used improperly to hold assets in such a way that capital gains tax could be postponed indefinitely.

The 21-year rule poses a major obstacle to the use of a trust as a long-term ownership vehicle for one or more assets within a family. There is no counterpart in the case of property owned outright by "real" individuals, other than the deemed disposition on death, as outlined in Chapter 8, Death and Taxes. However, there is nothing that requires accrued but unrealized capital gains of real individuals to be subject to income tax every 21 years, as in the case of most trusts.

In spite of the 21-year deemed disposition rule, a trust can still be an extremely useful tax and estate planning tool in certain situations, as outlined in this and other chapters.

Foreign Trusts

For many years, the "offshore trust" was a favourite planning device for wealthy people who wished to protect assets from creditors, or simply to avoid Canadian income tax on the investment income and capital gains earned on assets held by the trust.

TAXATION OF FOREIGN ACCRUAL PROPERTY INCOME (FAPI) OF FOREIGN TRUSTS

There are now numerous anti-avoidance rules that are designed to curtail the use of offshore trusts by residents of Canada for tax avoidance reasons.

PLANNING TO PROTECT ● *Maurice Heads Offshore to*
Avoid Tax But Is Disappointed

Maurice is a wealthy resident of Canada who is fed up with our high income taxes. He has a very large investment portfolio, and he pays Canadian income tax at the top marginal rate on the interest income, dividends, and capital gains generated by such investments. Maurice likes living in Canada, and he does not want to move to some tax haven island, just to save tax. During a recent holiday in the Bahamas, he got the seemingly bright idea of setting up a trust in the Bahamas for his, his wife's and his children's benefit. He would then transfer several million dollars into the trust, and have the trust invest the funds outside of Canada in various marketable securities and international mutual funds.

Under this scenario, the trust will be subject to certain rules in Section 94(1) of the *Income Tax Act* that will cause it to be subject to Canadian income tax. Generally, this happens when cash or other assets are contributed to an offshore trust by a resident of Canada, and where one or more of the beneficiaries of the trust are also residents of Canada who are related to the contributor. As a result, any *foreign accrual property income* (FAPI for short) of the trust will be subjected to Canadian income tax, even though such income is being earned and accumulated offshore. FAPI is a defined term that includes various kinds of *passive* investment income such as interest income, dividends and capital gains on portfolio investments.

If Maurice goes ahead with his plan, he will be in for a disappointment. The savings in Canadian income tax that he hoped to achieve will not be realized.

• •

PLANNING TIPS FOR USING TRUSTS

Over the years, there have been many changes in the tax rules, designed to curtail the tax advantages of trusts. Nevertheless, there are still a number of opportunities. A trust can serve many useful purposes, even if there is no particular income tax advantage in using a trust. If you are motivated by the potential tax savings of using a trust, you should not let the "tax tail wag the dog." Trusts are complex, and costly to set and maintain year-to-year.

Here are a few planning tips:

- If you are creating a straightforward *inter vivos* trust to hold investments for the purpose of funding future tuition fees of your children, consider naming one or more individuals as the trustee(s) of the trust, rather than a trust company. This type of trust will likely only have a limited life (e.g. under 21 years) and does not involve the level of complexity or long-term responsibility that warrants the use of a trust company as the trustee.

- If you are going to use a trust as part of an estate freeze strategy for a family business, be extremely careful about whom you appoint as the trustees of the trust. You may want to use three trustees, along with certain "majority rule" provisions in the trust agreement, in order to ensure that the trust is not subject to the "revocable trust" rules in Section 75(2) of the *Income Tax Act*. You must also be careful how you get assets or money into the trust, otherwise Section 75(2) may come into play. Obtain advice from a tax professional who is familiar with this area of tax and estate planning.

- You may be thinking about putting some of your assets into a living (*inter vivos*) trust in order to avoid probate fees in your estate. Bear in mind that the transfer of assets to such a trust could be treated as a disposition at fair market value for income tax purposes. Therefore, capital gains tax could be triggered at the time that you create such a trust. This could be a steep price to pay, in order to save on future provincial probate fees.

WHERE TO GET MORE INFORMATION

There are several sources of information:

- Speak with professionals, such as a tax lawyer or Chartered Professional Accountant (CPA) who has experience in dealing with trust agreements and their tax implications. Refer to Chapter 16, "Selecting Professional Advisors," for the selection process. Remember to speak to several professionals before deciding. The importance of quality expert advice to meet your needs cannot be overemphasized.

- Speak with a lawyer with specific expertise in drafting living or testamentary trusts. Again, seek advice from several experts before making your decision. Refer to Chapter 16, "Selecting Professional Advisors."
- Contact various banks and trust companies found on the Internet and ask for any consumer publications they have available on trusts. Also ask for information about the services they provide and ask for a complimentary consultation. Obtain feedback from several firms before making your decision. Also, ask your professional advisors (lawyer, accountant, financial planner) for their recommendations.
- Refer to Appendix B for a sample of a living trust document and a sample will with a testamentary trust provision in it. These are for illustration purposes only and should not be used for your own purposes under any circumstances. You need customized professional legal and tax advice if you are considering a trust.

SUMMARY

In this chapter, we have covered the various types of trusts, benefits of using a trust company, fees and expenses, the trust agreement, tax implications and where to get more information.

As you can see, the range of benefits of using a trust in certain situations is very compelling. However, because of the legal and tax implications of setting up a living or testamentary trust agreement correctly, you want to obtain expert advice from a tax accountant and lawyer who deals in wills and estate matters. The law concerning trust provisions can be very complicated and the tax laws can change from time to time.

❓Frequently Asked Questions

1. What is a living trust?

This is a document, sometimes referred to as an *inter vivos* trust, which takes effect during your lifetime. There are numerous different types of trust arrangements, for example, a family trust or spousal trust. A trust is set up by placing assets in the trust, with the beneficiaries of the trust being the people you designate, e.g. your spouse and children. The trust is operated by a trustee, which might include some of the beneficiaries, but generally not. The purpose for setting up a trust can be for tax reasons as well as to provide a structure for controlling how assets are dealt with. Insulation against creditors in certain situations can also be a motivation.

2. *What is a testamentary trust?*

In this case, the trust is usually part of your will and takes effect only on your death. The same comments apply as in the previous question. There are many types of trust options. One of the most common types is a trust for minor children. In this example, the trustee would invest money for the children until such time as they are entitled to the funds under the will. In some cases, that could be the provincial age of majority, e.g. 19 years of age. In other cases, it could be spread out over various ages, e.g. one-third at age 19, one-third at age 25 and one-third at age 30.

3. *What is a spendthrift trust?*

This type of trust can be in the form of a living trust or testamentary trust. The person setting up the trust believes that the recipient, based on past experience, is not mature enough to handle his or her own financial affairs responsibly. The trustee will therefore control the release of money from the trust based on its purpose.

4. *How do I select a trustee?*

Very carefully. The trustee should be someone whose judgement has proven historically to be sound and objective. He or she should also be someone who has the acumen to handle the responsibilities and is willing to do so. The trustee could also be the executor of your will, e.g. your spouse or close family member. You can also appoint a trust company to be your trustee or co-trustee with your other selected trustee.

5. *What fees do I pay a trustee?*

Each province has legislation governing the maximum amount that a trustee can be paid for providing services, e.g. 5 percent of the total amount administered. However, there can be a separate agreement for payments over and above this amount, or for additional services. If there is more than one trustee, the trustees have to agree on how to apportion the amount claimed, up to the maximum amount permitted by law. If there is a dispute, the courts will determine what the fair amount is in the circumstances.

Understanding
the Probate Process

INTRODUCTION

When you die, everything you own or have any interest in, and all outstanding debts that you have, automatically make up what is referred to as your estate.

As you are no longer around to manage your own affairs, the law requires that someone act on your behalf to wind up your financial matters and administer the disposition of your estate. This process is discussed in this chapter.

The following topics will be covered:
- the concept of probate
- who administers the estate
- how is the estate administered
- responsibilities of the executor
- probate fees
- liability of the executor
- techniques of reducing probate fees
- where to get more information

WHAT IS PROBATE?

Probate is the process by which your will is legally approved by the courts under provincial legislation. It also refers to the required documentation as set out by provincial legislation and confirmed by the courts and includes the legal confirmation of the appointment of the executor.

Not all wills have to be probated. It depends on various factors, such as the complexity of the estate, the amount and nature of assets, the number and nature of beneficiaries, etc. For example, a will usually has to be probated in order to deal with real estate if not held jointly. In practical terms, most estates by circumstance or choice end up going through the probate process.

There is another reality that encourages people to have the will probated. If the executor did not go through this legal confirmation process, many people, regulatory or government agencies or banks could become concerned that the will is invalid, or possibly signed under duress, or that there could be a later will. Due to these potential concerns, various individuals or private or public sector organizations could refuse to recognize the executor's authority, unless the will was validated by the court. So, even if it was not technically required in a given situation to have the will probated, in practical terms it could be desirable.

ADMINISTRATION OF THE ESTATE

Executor

An *executor* (called an *executrix* if a woman) is the person who you name in your will as your personal representative. In fact, you may name two individuals as joint executors (co-executors) or a trust company or a combination of both. How to select an executor was covered in Chapter 4, "Understanding Wills."

Administrator (Administratix)

If you don't have a will or don't have a valid will, then under provincial legislation, the court will appoint a personal representative. This could be a family member or a relative of the deceased who is appointed by the courts and monitored by the courts.

RESPONSIBILITIES OF THE EXECUTOR/ADMINISTRATOR

There are numerous duties that an executor or an administrator has to perform. It can be an onerous task, requiring time, skill, commitment and human relations ability. It is important to have an understanding of how the probate process works. It is relevant whether you are considering selecting an executor or have been asked to be an executor.

Here is a brief summary of the various steps. For a more detailed outline of the executor's responsibilities, refer to the checklist in Appendix D. The following guidelines are general in nature, as there can be provincial variation, as well as different terminology and procedures.

Locate and Read Will

If you know you have been named the executor of a will, your first obligation is to obtain the original of the most recent will of the deceased. Hopefully, the testator has informed you where the will and other important papers are kept to assist you in your job as executor. If not, you must make a search of all the likely places where the deceased may have kept important papers and records to determine if the deceased left a valid will.

If the will is kept in the deceased's safety deposit box and no other person has co-access to the box, you will need to take the key, death certificate and your own identification with you before the bank or institution will allow you access to the box. A bank representative must open the box. If you do not have a key, the box can be drilled open on the premises. The will can only be removed from the bank or institution after proving that you are the executor named in the will, and an inventory of the box's contents has been made. The other contents of the box are not generally released until the probate and administration grant has been obtained from the courts.

Where a safety deposit box is held in joint tenancy with another person, such as a spouse, it may be transferred immediately to the sole surviving joint tenant upon presentation of a death certificate.

If only a copy of the will is located, check the will for the name of the lawyer or law firm who drew it up. Many people choose to keep the original of their will with the lawyer who prepared it. If a trust company is named as an executor, check with the deceased's contact at the trust company to see if they have the original in safekeeping.

A Wills Search usually takes several weeks and is a process by which an executor of a will or a lawyer can locate a will or codicil (amendment) to a will by checking with the provincial "will registry." There is a will registry in each province. When someone prepares a will, he or she sends a notice to the relevant department at the will registry confirming the latest will and its location (e.g. a law firm or bank safety deposit box). You will receive a Wills Search Certificate, which will state the location of any will or codicil made when notice of it was filed with the Provincial Registry of Vital Statistics. This certificate is required to be filed with your application for Grant of Letters Probate to prove that the will being submitted for probate is indeed the last will of the deceased.

If you can't locate a will, or the most recent will that you are aware of, the law presumes that the testator destroyed it if it was in his possession or never had a will. In these circumstances, the deceased is generally presumed to die intestate, unless a valid will is located. *Dying intestate* means that provincial legislation determines how the assets are distributed, by means of a set formula. While the legislation generally tries to approximate how most people would want their estates distributed and protect the interest of the minor children, it does not mirror how most couples deal with their estates or deal with special circumstances such as step-children.

Obtain the Death Certificate

You should apply immediately upon the testator's death for a death certificate, usually obtained from the funeral home director. This certificate is required to legally prove the death of the deceased and takes approximately one to two weeks to receive.

Make the Funeral Arrangements

Contrary to popular perception, the executor, and not the deceased or any surviving family member, has the right to determine how to dispose of the deceased's body. Any instructions regarding burial arrangements contained in the deceased's will are not legally binding on the executor.

A person takes the position of executor by virtue of his appointment in the will. However, since the will is not usually found until after the funeral arrangements need to be attended to, it may not be clear exactly who the executor is. Or if the executor is a trust company, it may not be familiar with the personal wishes and way of life of the deceased. In practical terms, the deceased's family usually makes the funeral arrangements.

Where the funeral services require immediate payment, the bank may agree to pay for funeral expenses directly out of the deceased's account. If the family pays for the funeral expenses, they are entitled to be reimbursed from the estate. Regardless of who makes the arrangements, the estate is only responsible for payment of reasonable funeral expenses that are in keeping with the deceased's way of life. Therefore the person who made the arrangements may be responsible for any additional extravagant expenses. Refer to Chapter 18, "Planning Your Funeral."

Arrange Immediate Funds for Survivors

The deceased's assets are immediately frozen until the Grant of Letters Probate is received, which legally entitles the executor to deal with the assets. However, depending on the circumstances, the bank may be able to make arrangements if this causes any problems.

The most obvious source of funds is from assets that pass outside of the estate and are therefore not frozen, such as bank accounts, property held in joint tenancy or property owned by a legally designated beneficiary.

For example, if the deceased and the surviving spouse kept joint bank accounts, the spouse would be able to transfer the account into his or her name upon presentation of a death certificate. All money in the account would pass to the spouse automatically by right of survivorship. Where the deceased had a life insurance policy or a pension plan, the named beneficiaries can apply to have the proceeds of the policy or benefits of the plan paid out directly to them.

Joint Ownership to Avoid Probate Fees—Maybe

Many people believe that by putting a particular asset into joint name (with right of survivorship) with one's spouse or with one or more adult children, this will avoid probate fees being payable on the asset, if the person dies before the spouse or before the child or children. On the face of it, this is usually the case, because the asset will pass to the surviving spouse or to the child or children outside the terms of the person's will by virtue of the right of survivorship feature of the joint ownership. However, this is not always the case.

There have been numerous court challenges to joint ownership with right of survivorship arrangements by individuals who believed that they were deprived of their rightful inheritance, and the courts have sided with them in a number of instances. In a number of decided cases, the courts have held that the principle of *resulting trust* was applicable, and notwithstanding that the legal title of the particular asset was in joint name with one or more children, the courts held that 100 percent of the particular asset formed part of the deceased's estate. Although every case is decided on the basis of the particular facts, generally such decisions were in situations where there was no clear evidence that the deceased had intended to transfer part of the *beneficial* ownership to his or her child or children when the particular asset was put into joint name. By holding that a particular asset was governed by the deceased's will, that meant a different distribution of that asset amongst beneficiaries than what would have happened under the joint ownership with right of survivorship documentation.

In situations where joint ownership with a right of survivorship is created between a parent and child, and there is written evidence at the time of the parent's intention to give the child a portion of the beneficial ownership, this will give rise to income tax consequences and possible capital gains tax being payable by the parent if the particular asset has appreciated in value.

If you are contemplating creating joint ownership of a particular asset with your spouse or with one or more of your children with the objective of avoiding future provincial probate fees, it is essential that you obtain both legal and tax advice before doing anything. There are a number of legal and tax issues to consider.

PLANNING TO PROTECT ● *Saving on Probate—*
Alice Unknowingly Cuts Out Her Children!

Bob and Alice recently married. It is a second marriage for both of them and both have children from their first marriages. Alice is thinking of putting all her assets into joint ownership with her husband in order to avoid probate fees. She has a will and in her will she has left over half of her assets to her children from the previous marriage. Alice feels secure that she has protected her wishes and the financial needs of her children.

Alice is in a precarious position. She does not understand the full legal implications of what she has done. It is a case of being "penny wise and pound foolish." Here's why. By combining all the assets under joint ownership, such as the house, bank accounts, etc., Alice has given her husband joint ownership during her lifetime and total ownership automatically at the time of her death. Therefore, she will have very little assets left in her estate that can be distributed in her will to her children. This defeats her objective. The amount saved on probate fees would have been about $2,000 in her province. The amount that the children will not receive in the above scenario would have been about $150,000.

In hindsight, what Alice should have done is obtain professional legal and tax advice before finalizing her plans. She could have held the house in tenancy in common with her 50 percent interest. That way, those assets would be deemed to be part of her estate and would be dealt with based on her wishes outlined in the will. She could have had a separate bank account which would not be considered a joint account. These would be available for her estate and would be covered by her will. In this situation, Alice's estate would have had to pay some probate fees, but with proper professional strategic advice, they would have been minimal. In fact, if Alice were 65 or older, she could have set up a joint partner trust during her lifetime (as outlined in Chapter 6) and avoided probate fees entirely on her death.

• •

If there are no funds available from assets that pass outside of the estate or pension income, the executor may have to arrange a loan for the surviving spouse until the estate can be distributed.

Notify Beneficiaries and Others

You are normally required by law to notify certain persons who have or who may have an interest in the estate that you will be applying for a Grant of Letters Probate and what, if any, their entitlement is under the will. Even where a will exists, anyone who could make a claim to the estate or the validity of the will must be notified. A notice of intent to apply for probate with a copy of the will attached may be required to be sent to any of the following persons and additional persons. Check for the current legal requirements from a lawyer in your province, as the following are general guidelines only.

BENEFICIARIES AND ALTERNATE BENEFICIARIES

These people should be notified even if the property referred to in a specific bequest no longer exists and there is really no actual gift to that beneficiary.

ALL HEIRS-AT-LAW

There would be individuals who would be entitled to inherit under an intestacy or partial intestacy. The reason for sending notice to this class of persons is that even if a will exists, it may be found invalid.

ALL PERSONS ENTITLED UNDER PROVINCIAL
WILLS VARIATION LEGISLATION

That means any surviving legally wedded spouse and all children of the deceased. This category includes a spouse who is separated or where divorce proceedings are in process, but not complete.

COMMON-LAW SPOUSE OF THE DECEASED

You need to exert your best efforts to locate this person if he or she was no longer living with the deceased, as the common-law spouse could still have legal rights to a claim.

If any person who needs to be notified is a minor, the notice must be delivered to the parents or guardians and to the Public Trustee. Similarly, where any of the above persons are mentally incompetent, the notice must be mailed to their Committee representative or anyone who is in charge of the mentally incompetent person's affairs and to the provincial Public Trustee. The Committee is someone appointed by the court to handle the affairs of a mentally incompetent person.

Letters Probate will not be granted unless you have completed this notice requirement.

You will also need to notify the deceased's employer, bank, pension office and insurance company as soon as possible after the deceased's death. You may need to request the post office to redirect mail to your attention. Credit cards, customer accounts, subscriptions and memberships should be cancelled or closed.

Prepare a List of Assets and Liabilities

One of the major tasks of an executor is to prepare a complete inventory of all the deceased's assets and liabilities, including their value, as of the date of death. This information is used in preparing the Disclosure Statement, which must be submitted in your application for a Grant of Letters Probate. Only those assets and liabilities that make up the deceased's estate must be listed on the form. Any assets that pass outside of the estate by right of survivorship under joint tenancy or by the designation of a named beneficiary do not have to be included in this document.

DETERMINE VALUE OF ASSETS

Depending upon the state in which the deceased's affairs were left, the job of determining what assets the deceased owned and the current value of those assets at the date of death may require considerable time and effort. A good starting point is a copy of the last income tax return filed by the deceased. This will tell you what income-producing assets the deceased owned. The following list will give you some specific steps you may have in completing this task:

- Write to insurance companies to determine the amount and the names of beneficiaries of all life insurance policies; complete and submit claim forms for the payment of proceeds.
- Locate any lists of the deceased's online bank accounts, investment accounts, etc., and the usernames and passwords. Refer to a discussion in Chapter 2 on making key usernames and passwords accessible by your executor on your demise.
- Write to banks, trust companies, credit unions, brokers, and any other places where the deceased may have had accounts.
- List and obtain the value of any securities, such as stocks and bonds.
- List the contents of the safety deposit box.
- Obtain a title search from the land registry office and determine the value of all real estate owned by the deceased, including any outstanding mortgages, leases or agreements for sale registered against the property.
- Obtain the amounts of any salary, holiday pay and group life insurance benefits owing from the deceased's employer.
- List and value all personal effects and household goods such as cars, boats, jewellery, furnishings, paintings and antiques.
- Determine whether there are any debts owing to the deceased.
- Determine if there are any private or government pension or death benefits available; complete and submit application forms. In particular, check with the local Canada Pension Plan office regarding eligibility for payment of a lump-sum death benefit and monthly survivor's and orphan's benefits.
- Determine the amount payable and whether a beneficiary has been designated for any RRSP, RRIF, or TFSA.
- Determine and value any business interests of the deceased. You will probably need the services of an accountant for this particular task.

It is important that all assets are valued as of the date of the deceased's death. Subsequent increases in value, such as interest earned on investments or a rise in the market value of real estate, should not be included.

Benefits may be available from Canada Pension Plan if the deceased had contributed to the plan for a minimum of three years. Eligibility depends on the age of the deceased and the length of time contributions were made in relation to the total available contributory period. A monthly Survivor's Benefit may be payable to a surviving spouse. See Chapter 2 for more details on the various pension benefits.

DETERMINE THE DEBTS AND LIABILITIES

You will also need to determine all outstanding debts and liabilities the deceased was responsible for at the date of his or her death. These debts must be paid before the assets of the estate can be distributed. A thorough search of the deceased's records and important papers should provide you with some idea of the deceased's liabilities. Common examples of liabilities include unpaid income taxes, medical expenses, funeral and burial expenses, charge accounts and credit cards, promissory notes, rent arrears, utility bills, car payments, bank loans, and sometimes loans from other family members.

Protect the Assets

As executor, one of your most important duties is to ensure the deceased's assets are protected from loss, theft or destruction until they are sold or distributed. If you fail to properly protect the assets and the estate suffers a loss, you may have to make good that loss.

TAKE THEM INTO POSSESSION

One way of protecting assets is by taking valuable papers, cash, securities, jewellery and similar items into your own custody. Or you may decide to move certain assets, such as household furnishings and antiques, to secured storage. In situations where surviving family members do not get along and may fight over what they believe they are entitled to, you might need to call a locksmith to change the locks on the deceased's residence(s).

INSURANCE PROTECTION

Another way of protecting assets is by insurance. All existing insurance policies on real estate, household contents, automobiles, boats, etc. must be examined to determine if that insurance is adequate. You should notify the insurance agent of the deceased's death and request that, as executor, your name be added to the policy. Where any real estate is vacant you must provide for its supervision and protection; for residential insurance contracts it is advisable to check whether the existing coverage remains valid if the premises are left vacant for an extended period of time. In most insurance policies, this would be in excess of 30 consecutive days.

The risk that the policy could be voided by the insurance company begins after the above time, unless certain requirements were met. The insurance company could deny any subsequent claim on the policy if there was damage to the premises, for example, due to vandalism, arson, theft, or pipes breaking during the winter and water damage occurring.

ONGOING PROFESSIONAL MANAGEMENT

If the deceased owned a business you must arrange for its continued and proper management. This could prove to be the most challenging aspect of the executor's role. You must also review and provide management for any investments of the deceased. For example, it is your responsibility to collect income from any stocks, bonds, mortgages, rents and other investments the deceased may have owned.

Advertise for Creditors

It is recommended that you publicly advertise for any creditors who may have a claim against the estate. By advertising, you can legally protect yourself from any future claims creditors may make after you have distributed the estate.

Creditors with a valid claim against the estate can recover their debt at any time, even after the estate has been distributed to the beneficiaries. If you advertise, the creditors would only be able to recover from the beneficiaries. If you do not advertise, you may be held personally liable to the beneficiaries for any successful claim.

To advertise for creditors, a general notice must be published to the effect that all creditors with claims against the estate of the deceased send their claims to you for settlement. Normally you would just advertise in local papers. The executor/administrator may give notice to a creditor claiming against the estate that he rejects the claim. The creditor then generally has six months to bring an action or the claim is forever banned.

Apply to Probate the Will

Apart from a few exceptions, in most cases you will need to arrange for probate of the will. The sooner you apply for probate, the sooner you will be able to legally deal with the deceased's assets and be able to transfer property and distribute the estate.

Basically, to apply for probate you will need to complete and execute a number of documents to be filed with the court. If you are considering probating an estate yourself, an application for probate requires a lot of detail work and may be initially rejected without legal assistance to ensure that all forms are completed properly.

Prepare and File Income Tax Returns

You have heard the old saying that "There are only two things certain in life—death and taxes." The primary type of taxes payable by the estate of the deceased are income and capital gains taxes. The executor is responsible for filing income tax returns on behalf of the deceased taxpayer and the estate. The topic of tax filing requirements and related tax issues are covered in other chapters.

Pay Debts and Expenses

You can't distribute the estate to the beneficiaries before you pay all outstanding debts of the deceased, funeral expenses, and the expenses of administering the estate and income taxes.

Administration expenses include, for example, the cost of probating an estate, safeguarding the assets, correspondence conducted on behalf of the estate, any legal and accounting fees, and your fees as executor. With large estates, and to avoid personal liability, it is customary for the executor(s) to obtain a Tax Clearance Certificate from the CRA, certifying that all income taxes owing by the deceased and the estate have been paid.

If there is not sufficient cash available, you must convert other assets into cash by either selling them, such as with a car or stocks, or by redeeming them, such as Canada or provincial savings bonds. Personal property from the residue of the estate should be used first to satisfy the cash requirements for the payment of debts and expenses, before using cash legacies and personal property that has been specifically bequested. Real property should only be used where you cannot raise sufficient cash from the personal property in the estate.

If the estate is insolvent, meaning that the amount of total liabilities is greater than the amount of total assets, you must pay the debts and expenses in the following order of priority:

- reasonable funeral expenses
- the cost of probate and administration, including legal, executor and accounting fees
- municipal and income taxes
- all other claims as of the date of death

You are also entitled to be reimbursed for any expenses you may have made on behalf of the estate in priority to taxes. Where the estate has insufficient funds to satisfy all the debts and expenses, neither the beneficiaries nor the executor are responsible to pay for any claims that cannot be paid by the estate.

Distribute the Estate

Once you have performed all the above duties, including obtaining a Tax Clearance Certificate from the CRA if considered necessary, you can arrange for the settlement and distribution of the estate. Before distributing the residue of the estate, you should pay out any cash legacies and transfer or deliver specific property gifted under the will. If there is insufficient cash available to pay the cash legacies you will need to sell or redeem other assets.

If the will provides for the setting up of any trusts, you must make the necessary arrangements. Otherwise, you can distribute the estate directly to the named beneficiaries. After all these other matters have been attended to, the residue of the estate then must be distributed.

Keep Accurate Records

You are accountable to the beneficiaries for the assets of the deceased, any monies that you received and all assets and monies that you distributed or paid out on behalf of the estate. It is therefore essential that you set up and keep accurate and complete accounting records, which are supported by invoices and receipts. A statement of accounts must be reviewed and approved by all beneficiaries before they provide the executor with final releases discharging the executor upon the final distribution of the estate. Beneficiaries who are minors cannot approve the accounts, and the executor will have to pass his or her accounts if there are concerns or he or she wants a release or discharge. The parents or guardians cannot sign for them. It is also possible to wait until the minor is an adult. He or she can approve accounts then and release the executor/administrator.

FEES FOR EXECUTORS

The amounts set out by provincial legislation are the maximum limits for these fees and are not necessarily the actual fees that will be allowed. In other words, you may not be entitled to the full percentage by law. In determining the appropriate executor's fee the following factors must be considered:

- the size and complexity of the estate
- the care and responsibility involved
- the executor's skill and ability
- how well the executor has administered the estate and whether the value of the estate has been increased
- the amount of work and time required in performing the executor's duties

Unless your fee has been provided for in the will, you must propose one to the beneficiaries who in turn must approve it. If the beneficiaries do not agree with your fee, and you are unable to negotiate a compromise, you will have to pass your accounts before the court.

When determining the executor's fee, the overall amount that can be charged is the same whether there is an individual executor or co-executor. Where there is more than one executor, the executors must decide among themselves how they will share the fee. If they cannot agree, they will have to apply to the court to settle the matter. The fee for a trust company is usually larger than the fee for an individual person because a trust company usually offers more expertise and has more resources available.

PLANNING TO PROTECT ● *The Best of Both Worlds*

Helen was a widow and only had one relative, Doris, who lived in the same city. Although Helen thought that Doris was very competent, she felt that the burden of dealing with complex estate matters would not be fair to anyone. Helen therefore decided to retain a trust company as a co-executor and asked Doris to be a co-executor. The benefit of this arrangement is that the trust company would look after all the technical and administrative details and Doris would be able to provide the personal insights and advice. Helen therefore arranged with the trust company to act as a co-trustee of her estate, along with Doris.

This arrangement gave Helen considerable peace of mind. The trust company fees for acting as a co-executor and trustee represented about four percent of the total estate. The provincial ceiling for trustee fees was 5 percent, excluding any private written agreement with the trust company for fees for additional services.

• •

Where the executor is also a named beneficiary under the will, the law presumes that the gift to the executor is normally given in consideration of that person performing the duties of the executor and therefore in substitution of any executor's fee.

An executor's job should always be viewed as a paid and not a volunteer job, even though an executor has the right to decline to take a fee. As you can see, this job usually requires a great deal of time and effort. Not only is taking on the job of executor a big responsibility, but the person doing this job may be held personally liable for any loss to, or claims against, the estate. Therefore, family members or close friends shouldn't be expected to undertake this heavy responsibility and work for free.

POTENTIAL LIABILITY OF THE EXECUTOR

There are many areas of potential legal liability exposure that an executor could face. Here is an overview of some of them:

Slow Distribution of the Estate

There is generally no absolute time period by which the estate must be distributed. The executor usually has a year of grace, known as "the executor's year," in which to deal with the affairs of the estate before the beneficiaries can bring an action against the executor for failure to satisfactorily perform the executor's duties. Even then this action will only be possible if the executor has not been performing his or her required duties. It may take several years to properly distribute the estate.

Wills Variation Legislation

An executor must wait for a certain period from the date the will is granted Letters Probate. Otherwise, the executor may be personally liable if the will is challenged, since under provincial wills variation legislation the surviving spouse and children of the deceased have the time set by provincial legislation to apply to the court to have the will varied.

Common-Law Spouse

Most provincial legislation provides that a common-law spouse of the deceased has a certain period from the date of the Grant of Letters of Probate to apply to the court for a share of the estate. Therefore, even where there is no will, it is advisable to wait this required period before distributing the estate if there is any possibility at all of such an application being made.

Creditors

By publicly advertising for creditors, you should be legally protected from any future claims by creditors against the estate after it has been distributed.

Canada Revenue Agency (CRA)

Under the *Income Tax Act*, you will be personally liable for any unpaid taxes, interest and penalties that may be payable by the estate if you distribute the estate before obtaining clearance certificates from the CRA certifying that all taxes, interest and penalties have been assessed and paid. In most cases, there are two different clearance certificates that can be obtained. One covers the period up to the deceased's death and the other covers the period for trusts established after the deceased's death.

Release from Beneficiaries

It is recommended that you obtain a properly executed release from every beneficiary before distributing the estate. Basically, you should get the beneficiary to release you from the job of executor by having the beneficiary acknowledge receipt of the gift, and review and approve of the accounts. You should then have the beneficiary agree in writing to give up any claims he or she may have against the estate and to indemnify you if necessary, in other words, to protect and free you from any personal liability for future claims against the estate for the value of the amount of the gift.

Duty to Act in Good Faith

This would include the responsibility to act without any conflict of interest or bias or unjustly enriching yourself to the detriment of the value of the estate.

MAKING THE MOST OF IT—REDUCING PROBATE FEES

Assets of your estate that are passed on through your will and go through the probate process are subject to probate fees. Some provinces have a ceiling, whereas other provinces do not. As a reminder, when an executor asks the court to confirm the executor's right to deal with an estate, the Grant of Probate fees are also due. Even if no will exists, the courts must formally confirm the authority of an administrator and a probate fee must still be paid. See Chapters 3 and 4 to determine what strategies you can use to reduce those assets which are subject to probate fees, thereby allowing more of your estate to go directly to your beneficiaries.

You can minimize the amount of probate tax payable on your death by removing assets that would otherwise fall into your estate. Clearly, if after professional consultation you choose to do this, you must be sure to leave enough assets or funds in your estate to pay the tax. These strategies have to be viewed, though, in the context of your overall tax and estate plan strategies.

One of the objectives of an estate plan is to keep taxes and expenses as low as possible and pay as much as possible to your beneficiaries. You don't want to automatically make decisions just to reduce probate fees. Other strategies could better suit your overall estate planning objectives. These strategies could save a lot more tax money in the long run thereby increasing the value of the estate for the beneficiaries.

For example, if you have a business, part of your estate plan could be to place most of your assets beyond the reach of potential creditors. Otherwise, in theory, your estate could be at risk of attack by your business creditors. In addition, you may not want certain assets to remain in the estate, since these could be frozen pending the probate of the estate. Obtain professional advice from your lawyer and accountant on the various issues that concern you, such as relinquishing control, your marital situation (particularly if you are separated or living common-law), whether you have children, tax consequences, legal or creditor considerations, and many other issues. There are some key techniques to move assets out of an estate before death or to automatically transfer them directly to a beneficiary at the time of death, thereby avoiding going through the will and probate.

Note that it may be possible to significantly reduce probate fees by having two wills. One will would deal with your shares of your business or your investment holding company, and the other will would be your "umbrella" main will covering everything else. Depending on which province you are in and certain other factors, it may be possible to avoid probating the first-mentioned will (i.e. the one covering your business or investment holding company), thus achieving a significant probate fee saving. The probate application for your main will would cover everything else, and probate fees would be payable only on those assets. You need to obtain skilled legal advice in this scenario in advance.

WHERE TO GET MORE INFORMATION

- Contact the various banks and trust companies and ask for consumer booklets dealing with the probate process.
- Check websites or contact your local bookstore or library.

- Speak to a lawyer skilled in wills and estate law by contacting your local or provincial lawyer referral service.
- In addition, search the Internet for lawyers who specialize in wills, trusts, and estates.
- Refer to Appendix A, "Sources of Information," for key contact numbers. Also, look at the checklist of executor duties and chart of provincial probate fees in Appendix C.

SUMMARY

We have covered the key issues that you need to know about the probate process including the responsibilities and liabilities of the executor, executor fees and where to get more information.

As you can see, there are many types of skills and responsibilities involved when being an executor. Protecting your assets might mean appointing a trust company as executor or co-executor. Good professional advice is also essential during the probate process in order to reduce probate fees and eliminate your risks as executor.

?Frequently Asked Questions

1. What is a letter of probate?

This is a formal document issued by a court, which confirms the validity of the will and the appointment of the named executor(s). In certain instances, the duties of an executor can be carried out without any court involvement, generally in very small and simple estates without any registered assets or real property (land, condo, etc.) not held jointly. The reality though, in a situation where the assets are registered, is that an official confirmation is required that the will is valid and the executor is the proper person to deal with the assets of the deceased. This would include land that has a bank mortgage on it, or even land without a mortgage, and items registered in provincial government registries of ownership, such as property or motor vehicles.

2. What are Letters of Administration?

Where the deceased died without a will, an existing will that is not valid, no executor was named in the will, or the executor has died, Letters of Administration are issued by the court to appoint an administrator for the estate. This person could be a spouse or relative approved by the court or a representative from the provincial government's public trustee's office. The appointment would be to take responsibility for the assets and distribution of those assets under the provincial legislation dealing with administration of estates.

3. *What are probatable assets?*

Probatable assets are all assets, such as real property, stocks, bonds, etc., which the deceased owned or held an interest in prior to death. The distribution of such assets is controlled by the will and the aggregate value of the estate covered by probate is generally subject to a probate tax. This tax is determined by each province, and therefore varies considerably.

4. *What are non-probatable assets?*

These are assets that the deceased owned or held an interest in prior to death, but which do not form part of the estate. These assets include real and personal property that was registered jointly with the right of ownership; that is, the survivor automatically takes the deceased's interest. An example would be a joint bank account with one's spouse. A life insurance policy with a named beneficiary would also be included. As they are excluded from probate, no provincial probate taxes apply.

5. *Can I receive funds from an estate immediately after death?*

If there is a will, the executor of an estate can normally arrange for some money to be released from a financial institution to be used for the maintenance of the deceased's spouse or dependents, until such time as the court grant is issued. If you have a joint bank account, you can take money out immediately. If there is an insurance policy and you are the beneficiary, you can receive money directly within about two to three weeks after application for payment. In the case of someone dying without a will, called intestate, a financial institution is understandably reluctant to advance funds from the deceased's account until the court appoints an administrator, or the public trustee's office is involved.

6. *Why advertise for creditors when settling an estate?*

One of the duties of an executor or administrator is to determine the debts of the deceased person. Part of this process involves advertising for creditors in a local newspaper where the deceased lived and/or carried on business. The executor/administrator could be held personally liable for distributing estate assets if advertising for creditors was not done beforehand, and a creditor lays a claim against the estate at a future date.

Death and Taxes

**"Tis impossible to be sure of anything
except death and taxes."**

CHRISTOPHER BULLOCK, 1716

INTRODUCTION

In order for you to do an effective job with your estate planning, you should have a general understanding of how your estate will be affected by "taxes." This book is not going to turn you into an expert in tax planning. However, it will help you identify a number of tax issues and planning ideas that you can discuss with your professional advisors. This may jump-start the estate planning process and save you some fees. Whatever tax savings you can achieve by planning your affairs in a tax-effective manner, the more of your estate will be left to pass down to your intended beneficiaries.

This chapter provides a brief historical perspective on estate taxes in Canada, and outlines the various kinds of taxes that can currently arise on a person's death, including:

- capital gains taxation of "accrued" gains at the time of death
- how capital gains and capital losses are calculated
- income taxes payable on RRSPs, RRIFs and other amounts at the time of death
- the tax treatment of gifts
- the capital gains consequences of "paper transactions" between family members when no money changes hands.

Taxes of various kinds have been a fact of life for every civilization down through the ages, and Canada is no exception. Charles Adams, author of *For Good and Evil: The Impact of Taxes on the Course of Civilization*,* makes the observation that "Taxes are the fuel that makes civilization run. There is no known civilization that did not pay tax." And down through the ages, taxes have been imposed on just about anything you can think of. For example, if you had lived in eighteenth or nineteenth century England, you would have had to pay a tax on the number of windows in your house. Charles Adams tells us:

> *[E]ach house was taxed at one shilling per window, provided the house had more than seven windows. This exempted the poor, consistent with English tradition. Taxpayers resorted to all kinds of avoidance devices, like boarding up windows until the assessors finished, and then opening them up again. In Edinburgh, a whole row of houses was built without a single window in the bedrooms. This tax lasted well into the nineteenth century.*

Just as taxes are a way of life, so is human ingenuity in trying to avoid paying them. Although we do not have a window tax in Canada, we do have an incredible array of taxes: income taxes, property taxes, sales taxes, harmonized goods and services tax (GST/HST), etc. Perhaps in a hundred years time, some of our taxes will seem as strange to our descendants as the English window tax is to us. The form of taxation has changed over the centuries, but human nature has not.

In the chapters that follow, we will outline some of the strategies that you could consider for minimizing, postponing, or avoiding taxes in your estate. Don't worry! Every technique outlined in this book falls into the realm of "legitimate" tax planning as opposed to improper tax avoidance or tax evasion. In fact, some techniques are actually outlined by the CRA in some of their published bulletins, circulars, and booklets, all of which are available at the CRA's website.

THE HISTORY OF ESTATE TAXES IN CANADA

There is no actual "estate tax" as such in Canada, however there are other taxes or fees that could be imposed on your estate, including income tax, probate fees, and perhaps even foreign estate taxes if any of your beneficiaries or assets are located outside of Canada. For most Canadians, the greatest tax exposure will be the income tax that must be paid on their Registered Retirement Savings Plans (RRSPs) and Registered Retirement Income Funds (RRIFs) at the time of death, and the income tax arising on any unrealized capital gains on assets owned at the time of death. First, a brief review of estate taxation.

---

*Adams, Charles. *For Good and Evil: The Impact of Taxes on the Course of Civilization* (New York: Madison Books, 1993), p.3.

Federal Estate and Gift Taxes Before 1972

An *estate tax* is a tax imposed based on the total value of a person's assets at the time of death, with various deductions and tax credits being allowed depending on the overall size of the estate, the type of assets, and the relationship of the beneficiaries to the deceased. Similarly, a *gift tax* is one that is imposed based on the value of gifts made by an individual during his or her lifetime, whether in cash or in property. Estate tax and gift tax go hand-in-hand. For example, if there were an estate tax but no gift tax, a person would be able to reduce or avoid estate tax at the time of death simply by transferring assets by way of gift during his or her lifetime to the intended beneficiaries such as a spouse, children or grandchildren.

Estate and gift taxes were imposed in Canada by the federal government up to the end of 1971. Such taxes were eliminated for deaths occurring after December 31, 1971. This was done in conjunction with the introduction of capital gains taxation in Canada. On January 1, 1972, Canadians became subject to income tax on capital gains that were earned after 1971. Up until December 31, 1971, capital gains were tax-free in Canada. With the introduction of capital gains taxation, came a rather unusual form of capital gains taxation on death—the "deemed realization."

1971 Tax Reform Introduction of Capital Gains Taxation

The 1971 Tax Reform came about after years of studies and Royal Commissions on how to "improve" the Canadian tax system. One of the recommendations of the Carter Commission was that capital gains be subjected to full income tax. Perhaps one of the reasons that the "rich got richer" before 1972 was that capital gains realized on stock transactions or on the sale of other investments were completely tax-free (provided that the person was not a dealer or trader in securities or a speculator in real estate). The Carter Commission recommended that capital gains tax be imposed not just on actual sales or transfers of assets during one's lifetime, but also at the time of a person's death, based on the appreciation in the value of the person's assets up to the time of death. In other words, the Carter Commission thought the tax system should be designed so that capital gains tax would be imposed whether you're "dead or alive."

Elimination of Federal Estate and Gift Taxes at End of 1971

Because the post-1971 tax system called for unrealized capital gains to be taxed at the time of death, it was thought that it would be "double taxation" if estate taxes were also imposed at the time of death. Therefore, estate taxes were eliminated as of January 1, 1972. Similarly, the federal gift tax was also eliminated for gifts made after 1971.

As a matter of interest, the rates of federal estate tax prior to 1972 were very high, which was one of the reasons that people often went to almost any lengths to plan their affairs so that estate taxes would be kept to a minimum. For example, the top estate tax bracket was reached when the aggregate taxable value of the estate was $300,000. The tax was $89,200 plus

50 percent of the value of the estate in excess of $300,000. Small wonder that people often entered into elaborate estate planning arrangements in order to avoid seeing up to one-half of their estate "confiscated" by the federal government in the form of estate tax!

Provincial Succession Duties and Gift Taxes

At the present time, there is no province in Canada that levies estate tax, succession duty or gift tax. However, this was not always the case. Before 1972, Ontario, Quebec and British Columbia imposed *succession duties*—a form of estate tax that technically speaking, was imposed on the beneficiaries of an estate. The provincial succession duty rates were generally not as high as the federal estate tax. Also, the rates varied depending on whether the beneficiary was related to the deceased, and if so, whether the relationship was that of spouse, child, grandchild or other relation. Similarly, gifts of cash or property during a person's lifetime were subject to provincial gift tax (as well as federal gift tax) depending on the province of the person's residence and certain other factors.

With the introduction of capital gains taxation on January 1, 1972, all of the provinces forecasted a drop in tax revenue from the repeal of estate taxes, and it was expected that it would be some years before the new "capital gains taxes" would fill the void. One reason for this concern was that under the new capital gains rules, people were allowed to use a valuation day of December 31, 1971 for the purposes of calculating taxable capital gains realized on the disposition of assets after 1971. In other words, the capital gains rules were designed so that any accrued capital gains that existed as of December 31, 1971 would never be subject to capital gains taxation because of the "valuation day" rule. In fact, someone who owns property, securities or other assets that were acquired prior to 1972 can still use the 1971 valuation date value in calculating capital gains.

From the viewpoint of the provincial governments, there would have been an unwarranted loss of "estate tax" revenue since in the case of individuals who died soon after 1971, the post-1971 appreciation in the value of the person's assets might be minimal. Therefore, little if any capital gains tax would be collected. Because of this, Ontario, Quebec and British Columbia continued to impose succession duties for a number of years into the 1970s. Moreover, the other provinces that had not previously imposed their own succession duties and gift taxes (because they had an estate tax revenue sharing arrangement with the federal government) introduced their own succession duties.

The good news is that the federal estate and gift taxes, and the provincial succession duties are now ancient history. By the late 1970s, all of the provinces had repealed their succession duty and gift tax legislation, primarily because the costs of administering the succession duty systems were not justified in relation to the fairly minuscule amount of revenue that was actually being collected. Furthermore, because of post-1971 inflation, the income tax revenue on taxable capital gains being reported in personal income tax returns was steadily rising. Therefore, the provincial governments decided that there was no further need for a separate system of taxes on wealth transfers.

Taxes Arising on Death

For most people, the greatest tax exposure on death exists with respect to the cash and investments that are sitting within an RRSP or RRIF. Generally speaking, the full value of these "registered" accounts at the time of death must be reported as "income" in the person's final income tax return. The amount of income tax actually payable will depend on the deceased's marginal income tax rate in his or her final income tax return. (However, there are a few important exceptions, such as when the RRSP or RRIF is transferred to a surviving spouse.)

Other assets can also attract tax in your estate. For example, if you own a vacation home that has appreciated in value, a taxable capital gain may eventually have to be reported by your executors in your final income tax return, because of the "deemed disposition" on death. Similarly, if you have a portfolio of marketable securities, some of the long-held stocks may have increased significantly in value. Such accrued but unrealized gains as of the time of death will give rise to income tax in your final income tax return, unless there are large enough offsetting deductions or tax credits, such as charitable donations.

CAPITAL GAINS TAXATION IN CANADA

For convenience, we often talk of the *capital gains tax*, when in fact, there isn't a separate tax on capital gains. Instead, it is actually *income tax* that is imposed on capital gains. There is a whole separate section of the *Income Tax Act* (Canada) that contains the capital gains rules. In order to understand the various planning strategies described in the following chapters, you need a general overview of how the capital gains rules work, and how the deemed disposition rules operate in the year of a person's death.

Capital Gains Terminology

At the risk of getting technical, there are a few terms and definitions that need to be explained.

DISPOSITION

You cannot have a *capital gain* for tax purposes unless you have had a *disposition* of property. Generally speaking, a disposition means any transaction that results in a change in the true beneficial ownership of property. A change in the *legal title* of property without any change in the beneficial ownership does not generally cause a disposition for capital gains purposes. The following case illustrates a situation where there would *not* be a disposition for capital gains tax purposes:

PLANNING TO PROTECT ● *Steven Avoids a "Disposition" for Capital Gain Tax Purposes*

Steven owns and holds the legal title to several houses, which he rents out. Desiring a degree of anonymity on the municipal tax rolls, Steven arranges for his lawyer to transfer the legal title to the properties into the name of "ABC Investments Inc.," a corporation that Steven has just incorporated for this purpose. Steven and ABC Investments Inc. enter into an agreement that stipulates that the corporation is simply holding the title to the properties as a "bare trustee" for Steven. Steven is still the beneficial owner of the properties, not the corporation. Therefore, Steven will continue to report the rental income and expenses in his personal income tax return.

● ●

DEEMED DISPOSITION ON DEATH

Although there was no disposition for capital gains tax purposes in Steven's situation, a disposition can occur for tax purposes in other cases simply because of a particular rule or rules in the *Income Tax Act* that "deem" a disposition to occur under particular circumstances. The particular "deeming" rule that we are most concerned with in the context of estate planning is the one in Section 70 of the *Income Tax Act*. This rule deems a person to have disposed of his or her property "immediately before" death for capital gains tax purposes. So in the above example, the houses held in the name of ABC Investments Inc. would be deemed to have been disposed of immediately before Steven's death, and would incur capital gains tax at that time.

Why *immediately before* death, rather than *at the time of death*? Isn't the government splitting hairs? Supposedly, this rule is worded in this way only for technical reasons, in order to ensure that any capital gains that are triggered as a result of a person's death will fall into the person's final taxation year that ends at the instant of death. (The people in Ottawa who drafted the legislation must have worried that a deemed disposition "at the time of death" might somehow fall through the cracks and not be included in the calculation of taxable income in the deceased's final income tax return.) For convenience, we will often refer to the deemed disposition as if it occurs "at the time of death" rather than "immediately before."

DEEMED DISPOSITION ON A CHANGE OF USE

A disposition also occurs for capital gains tax purposes in certain situations where the use of a property changes from *personal use* to *income-producing*, or vice versa.

PLANNING TO PROTECT ● *Taxation Without a Change
in Ownership or Exchange of Money*

Michael bought a condominium six years ago with the idea of using it as a rental property until such time that he might want to occupy it himself. The tenants have now moved out, Michael is selling his current house, and he is moving into the condo. For capital gains tax purposes, a *change of use* is occurring. The condo is ceasing to be an income-producing property and is being converted by Michael to a personal use property.

This constitutes a disposition for income tax purposes, which must be reported in Michael's income tax return for the year in which the change of use occurs. Depending on whether the condo has gone up or down in value, and whether or not Michael has claimed tax depreciation ("capital cost allowance") on the condo, he may have to pay income tax on recaptured depreciation and/or a taxable capital gain.

● ●

The above example illustrates that a taxable event can occur for income tax purposes under a fairly innocuous set of circumstances where there has not been any change in the real ownership of a property, and no money has changed hands.

Calculating the "Capital Gain" or "Capital Loss"

Once you have determined that there has been a disposition, the next step is to calculate the *capital gain* or *capital loss*, which is done in the following manner:

Proceeds of disposition	$_____	(A)
Less:		
Selling expenses	$_____	(B)
Less:		
Adjusted cost base	$_____	(C)
Equals:		
Capital Gain (A) minus (B + C)	$_____	

The term *adjusted cost base* is explained later. For example, in the case of real estate, it means your original cost, plus the costs of improvements made during the years you owned the property. A *capital loss* arises if the *adjusted cost base* and the selling expenses are greater than the *proceeds of disposition*.

Calculating the Taxable Capital Gain or Allowable Capital Loss

The amount that you must include in calculating your taxable income is 50 percent of the capital gain. When capital gains taxation was first introduced in 1972, 50 percent of capital gains had to be included in taxable income. In the 1980s, the inclusion rate was raised to 66 2/3 percent, and then to 75 percent. In 2000, the government reduced the inclusion rate to 66 2/3 percent and later in the same year to the 50 percent rate. Things have, therefore, gone full circle. Therefore, the *taxable capital gain* amount is back to being 50 percent of the capital gain. Similarly, an *allowable capital loss* is 50 percent of the capital loss amount.

Offsetting Capital Losses Against Capital Gains

Allowable capital losses can be offset against taxable capital gains. However, if the losses exceed the gains, the excess generally cannot be deducted against your other income. One of the few exceptions to this rule is where the loss relates to an investment in a Canadian "small business corporation." Another exception is where the cumulative capital losses exceed capital gains in the year of a person's death allowing the estate to use the excess against any type of income reported in the deceased's final tax return.

Determining the Proceeds of Disposition

Proceeds of disposition is the term used to describe the gross proceeds that you receive from the sale of an asset. In most cases, the determination of the proceeds of disposition is easy, since the sale is for cash. However, by definition, proceeds of disposition also includes the fair market value of something other than cash that you might receive in exchange for an asset that you dispose of, as in the following example.

PLANNING TO PROTECT ● *Even Trades Are Considered Dispositions, as Christopher and Bali Find Out!*

Christopher owns a small ski chalet in a highly desirable location, but he wants something bigger for his ever-expanding family. His neighbour, Bali, owns a large chalet in a somewhat less desirable location that would be perfect for Christopher. Both chalets are worth about the same. As it happens, Bali has recently separated from his wife, and wants something smaller. Christopher and Bali therefore decide to switch properties in a "barter transaction."

Unfortunately, from a capital gains viewpoint, this transaction is a disposition that must be reported in their respective income tax returns. Broadly speaking, Christopher's proceeds of disposition for the property that he disposes of is the fair market value of the chalet that he receives in exchange. Similarly, Bali's proceeds of disposition is the fair market value of Christopher's chalet. Assuming that Christopher and Bali are not related to each other, and they are dealing with each other at arm's length, the two fair market values and their proceeds of disposition amounts are the same.

Claiming a Capital Gains Reserve

Your proceeds of disposition is the gross selling price for an asset, even if part of the purchase price is paid in cash and the balance will be paid to you over time. However, if a portion of the sales proceeds is owing to you in a future year, you may be entitled to claim a *capital gains reserve* so as to spread your taxable capital gain over a number of years, as in the following example.

PLANNING TO PROTECT ● *Susan Uses a Capital Gains Reserve to Delay Her Tax*

Susan owns the shares of a corporation which makes widgets. She formed the company in 1985, with an initial investment of $100,000. She has agreed to sell the company to Anna, for $1 million. The terms of the deal call for $200,000 to be paid in cash at the time of closing. The balance of the purchase price ($800,000) is to be paid to Susan in four annual installments of $200,000 each.

Susan will have a capital gain of $900,000 on the sale of the shares (ignoring any possible "lifetime capital gains exemption," which will be outlined in Chapter 13). Since part of the sales proceeds is payable over the next four years, Susan can claim a capital gain reserve so as to avoid having to pay income tax on all of the capital gain in the year of sale. In the year of sale, she can claim a reserve equal to 80 percent of the capital gain, since 80 percent of the total sales price is payable after the end of the year. In effect, 20 percent of the $900,000 gain will be recognized in the year of sale, and 20 percent in each of the following four years.

• •

The capital gain reserve rules require that you report at least 20 percent of your total gain in the year of sale. By the end of the second year, you must have reported 40 percent of the gain, 60 percent by the end of the third year, and so on. In effect, the capital gain reserve mechanism does not allow you to spread out the gain over more than five years, regardless of how long the payment terms are for the sale.

Determining the Adjusted Cost Base

The second most important element of the capital gain calculation is the *adjusted cost base* of the property. The higher your adjusted cost base, the lower the capital gain, and the less tax you will have to pay.

The starting point in calculating your adjusted cost base for a particular asset that you own, whether it be shares of a corporation, real estate, or something else, is your actual cost of the property—in other words, what you paid for it. You also add to this amount any additional "capital" expenditures that you made on the property during the period of time that you owned it. The *Income Tax Act* also sets out various items that may have to be added or deducted in arriving at your adjusted cost base, depending on the type of asset and whether or not particular circumstances exist.

PLANNING TO PROTECT ● *Murray and Anne Determine Their Adjusted Cost Base*

Anne and Murray purchased a cottage 10 years ago to use for summer vacations and perhaps to rent out occasionally. They paid $100,000 for the cottage. The cottage was purchased jointly, and each of them contributed $50,000 to the purchase. Over the years, they spent $10,000 to add an additional bedroom, $5,000 for some new kitchen cabinets, and $4,000 for an electric heating system. They also figure that they have spent about $30,000 over the years on general repairs and maintenance.

They are now going to sell the cottage. In order to calculate their capital gain, their adjusted cost base would be determined as follows:

Original cost	$100,000
plus capital improvements:	
New bedroom	10,000
New kitchen cabinets	5,000
Electric heating system	4,000
Adjusted cost base	$119,000

The costs of repairs to the property cannot be included in calculating the adjusted cost base. Similarly, annual maintenance costs, and other recurring expenses such as annual property taxes, cannot be included. However, costs of improvements, such as new kitchen cabinets to replace open shelves, can be included.

Calculating the Income Tax on a Capital Gain

The amount of income tax that you would have to pay on a capital gain that you report in your income tax return depends on what income tax bracket you are in. Canada has a graduated rate system, which means that the rates of income tax rise as the level of your taxable income goes up.

We also have to pay provincial income tax, as determined by the province in which you reside as of December 31st of each year. All provinces except Quebec have tax collection agreements with the federal government which allow the federal government to collect the applicable provincial personal income tax. Separate calculations are made in your personal income tax return of the provincial income tax, and any applicable provincial tax deductions or credits. Quebec on the other hand, requires its residents to file a separate Quebec personal income tax return and to remit the applicable Quebec personal income tax directly to the Quebec Ministry of Revenue.

Canadians have the dubious distinction of being one of the most heavily taxed people in the world. If your taxable income is high and you are in the top income tax bracket and depending on your province of residence, your marginal income tax rate (on a combined federal and provincial basis) would be about 50 percent. The top rate is different in each province because of varying provincial personal income tax rates, and/or various provincial surtaxes and credits.

For illustration purposes, if we assume that you are already in the top tax bracket, or that the capital gain that you report in your tax return pushes you into the top bracket, the amount of income tax on a capital gain of $100 would be as follows:

Capital gain	$100.00
Taxable capital gain (50%)	$50.00
Personal income tax @ 50% rate:	$25.00

In other words, your effective rate of capital gains tax could be about 25 percent, assuming that you are in a 50 percent income tax bracket.

Estimating the Future Capital Gains Taxes in Your Estate

For estate planning purposes, you need to think about the *capital gains taxes* that will be imposed on your estate in the future. Tax rates change from year to year, and it is anybody's guess what the income tax rates will be a year from now, let alone in 5, 10 or 20 years. Estate planning is a long-term proposition, and there is no way of knowing how long we will live. Therefore, for purposes of estimating the amount of capital gains tax that could be payable by your estate in the future, it is probably best to err on the high side.

For someone with an annual taxable income over approximately $200,000, the effective rate of income tax (federal and provincial combined) on a $100 capital gain is currently in the range of 24 to 27 percent, depending on the province of residence.

Therefore, for estate planning purposes, we recommend that you use a capital gains tax rate of 25 percent in estimating the taxes that could be payable by your estate in the future.

CAPITAL GAINS TAXATION ON DEATH

The mechanism by which accrued capital gains as of the time of death are subjected to income tax is as follows:

1. A person is considered to have disposed of all of his or her capital property immediately before death and

2. The person is considered to have received proceeds of disposition equal to the fair market value of the property at that time.

While there are a number of exceptions to these rules, these are the two essential ingredients for a capital gain (or a capital loss) that must be reported in a deceased person's final income tax return. Thus, a *taxable event* can occur on death, even though no disposition of the person's assets actually takes place, and no actual proceeds of sale are received.

One of the most important exceptions from the deemed disposition rule is where a person's assets are left to a surviving spouse, either outright or in trust (if certain conditions are met). In such cases, there is a *rollover* for capital gains tax purposes, resulting in a deferral of tax until the surviving spouse disposes of the assets during his or her lifetime, or at the time of death. The spousal rollover rules are discussed in Chapter 9, which also describes what is involved in preparing a final income tax return for the year of a person's death, including the various special rules that apply.

Determining Fair Market Value

What do we mean by *fair market value*? Although this term is not defined anywhere in the *Income Tax Act*, the following definition has come to be accepted by the CRA and by the Canadian courts when rendering judgments on income tax cases:

[T]he highest price obtainable in an open and unrestricted market where the seller is under no compulsion to sell, and the purchaser is under no compulsion to buy.

In the case of publicly-traded securities, the fair market value can be readily determined in most cases simply by referring to the most recent stock trading prices. However, if an individual's shares in a particular corporation represent a controlling interest, it may well be that the fair market value of that person's shareholding is more than the fair market value of identical shares that are being publicly traded. There may be a *control premium* to reflect the fact that the majority shareholder has voting control of the corporation and is in a position to elect the board of directors and to "call the shots."

It is often difficult to arrive at the fair market value of real estate, especially property that is in any way unique, or where there are no recent sales of comparable properties that could serve as a guide. Where it is necessary to determine the fair market value of real estate that was owned by a person at the time of death, it is usually desirable to obtain a formal valuation opinion from a qualified real estate appraiser. A real estate agent may also be able to provide an estimate of the fair market value, but this will not carry as much weight with the CRA compared to a formal real estate appraisal.

Determining the Capital Gains Arising on Death

The deemed disposition on death at fair market value means that any accrued but unrealized capital gains (or capital losses) at the time of death must be recognized for income tax purposes, unless one of the various rollovers or exemptions outlined later is applicable.

PLANNING TO PROTECT ● *Determining the Taxes Due*
After David's Death

David passed away on January 15th. He was a widower, and under his will, he left his assets to be divided equally between his two daughters. At the time of his death, he owned the following assets:

	Fair Market Value	Adjusted Cost Base
Cash in bank	$15,000	$15,000
Canada Savings Bonds	75,000	75,000
T-Bills & GICs	30,000	30,000
RRSPs	80,000	N/A
Publicly-traded securities:		
Acme Inc.	15,000	11,000
Widget Company Ltd.	8,000	9,000
XYZ Inc.	19,000	13,000
Life insurance	50,000	N/A
Personal residence	300,000	60,000
Summer cottage	250,000	180,000
Total	**$842,000**	

N/A: Not applicable

The tax treatment of David's various assets at the time of death is as follows:

Cash, bonds and deposit accounts:

There is no capital gains tax on the cash, Canada Savings Bonds, T-Bills or GICs, since David's adjusted cost base is equal to the fair market value. However, there might be some accrued interest as of the date of his death that needs to be reported in his final tax return. We have ignored it in this example.

RRSPs:

David had cash and securities worth $80,000 in his registered retirement savings plan at the time of his death. Since he was not survived by a spouse, the full amount will have to be reported as income in his final income tax return. Thus, the income tax could be about $40,000, if the taxable income in David's final income tax return is in the top bracket.

Marketable securities:

David's shares of Acme and XYZ both went up in value, and there were accrued capital gains as of the date of death of $4,000 and $6,000, respectively. However, he was losing money on his Widget shares because they were worth only $8,000 compared to his cost of $9,000. Therefore, a capital loss of $1,000 would be reported on the Widget shares.

Life insurance:

The $50,000 life insurance policy will be paid tax-free to David's estate or to the named beneficiaries. As outlined in more detail in Chapter 15, life insurance is afforded generous treatment under the Canadian tax system. In particular, the proceeds of a life insurance policy that are paid as a result of the death of the insured person are not subject to income tax in the hands of the recipient.

Personal residence:

David's personal residence is worth $300,000, but his adjusted cost base (original cost of the house) is only $60,000. Although there is a gain of $240,000 as of the date of David's death, this gain will likely be tax-free under the *principal residence* exemption. The exemption is calculated under a formula that compares the number of years that the property can be designated as David's principal residence for capital gains tax purposes with the number of years that the property was owned by him.

Surprisingly, the principal residence exemption can be claimed on any property that is "ordinarily inhabited" by a person "during the year." The rules do not require that you occupy the property "throughout the year," which means that you can easily meet the occupancy test for a seasonal residence. However, the income tax legislation also stipulates that you can only designate one property as your principal residence in any given calendar year. Obviously, this presents a problem if you own more than one residential property, because the principal residence exemption cannot be used to fully shelter both properties from capital gains taxation.

The principal residence exemption is explained in more detail in Chapter 12 on vacation properties and the various estate planning strategies to minimize future capital gains tax exposure.

Summer cottage:

David's summer cottage is worth $150,000 and we have assumed that his adjusted cost base (original cost of the cottage) is only $80,000. Therefore, he had an accrued capital gain at the time of his death of $70,000. Since the appreciation in the value of his house was much greater than the cottage, it makes sense to use the principal residence exemption on the house. Therefore, the accrued capital gain of $70,000 on the cottage will be taxed in David's final income tax return.

Income taxes arising on David's death:

The income tax on David's RRSPs and accrued capital gains at the time of death can be calculated as follows:

Accrued capital gains and (losses):	
Acme Inc. shares	$4,000
XYZ Inc.	6,000
Widget Company Ltd.	(1,000)
Cottage	70,000
Total	$79,000
Taxable capital gains (net) — 50%	$39,500
RRSPs	80,000
Total taxable amount	$119,500
Income tax at say 45%	$53,775

(As noted earlier, the actual amount of additional income taxes owing in David's final tax return on the above "year of death" amounts will depend on what income tax bracket David is in, based on the amount of his other income from January 1st up to the date of death.)

• •

CAPITAL GAINS TAXATION ON GIFTS DURING YOUR LIFETIME

No Gift Tax in Canada

We said earlier that Canada no longer has any *gift tax*. This means that you can give away as much money as you like during your lifetime without any gift tax being payable. For example, you might like to send cheques for say $1 million to Doug Gray and John Budd in appreciation for the wealth of information contained in this book, and no gift tax would be payable! (We won't hold our breaths waiting for the cheques.)

Part of the rationale for not having a gift tax is that virtually all kinds of income and gains are subjected to income tax during a person's lifetime or at the time of death. Therefore, any "cash" that a person has must, in theory, represent "tax-paid" funds that are left over from income or capital gains on which income tax was previously paid.

Deemed Disposition for Capital Gains Purposes

Since we don't have a gift tax, you may be wondering if it is possible to avoid capital gains tax on death by giving away your assets during your lifetime. Unfortunately, a gift of assets during your lifetime is treated for capital gains purposes in much the same way as assets that are deemed to have been disposed of at the time of death. If you transfer an asset to another person (other than your spouse) by way of gift, you are considered for income tax purposes to have received proceeds of disposition equal to the fair market value of the property, even though you receive nothing in return. Because of this rule, any gift of property that has appreciated in value to someone other than your spouse will force you to recognize a capital gain in your income tax return. Here is an example of how a "paper transaction" can have undesirable tax consequences:

PLANNING TO PROTECT ● *Giving Gifts of Equal Value—Or Not?*

Chloe and Melissa are the best of friends and each of them has a daughter who is getting married. Chloe is going to give her daughter Marjorie and her husband-to-be $25,000 cash to help them save for a house. Not to be outdone, Melissa is going to give her daughter Joan $25,000 worth of shares of Microsoft Inc., which she bought in the early 1990s for only $1,000.

Chloe's gift will be tax-free (since we do not have any gift tax), but Melissa will have to report a capital gain in her tax return. Because she is transferring "property" rather than cash, she will be considered to have disposed of the Microsoft shares for proceeds of disposition equal to the current fair market value of the stock. Since her adjusted cost base (her cost) is only $1,000, she must report a $24,000 capital gain. Since 50 percent is taxable, the income tax could be about $6,000 assuming that Melissa is in the top income tax bracket.

• •

The above example illustrates just how different the tax effects can be where two individuals carry out similar transactions. In this case, a gift of cash attracts no tax, whereas a gift of an asset that has gone up in value carries a significant tax cost.

Non-arm's Length Transactions

The *Income Tax Act* has various rules that apply to transactions that are carried out by persons who do not deal with each other *at arm's length*. One such rule states that if a person disposes of an asset to another non-arm's length person for no proceeds, or for proceeds that are less than the fair market value of the property, the person making the disposition is considered for tax purposes to have received proceeds of disposition equal to the fair market value of the property. This rule is therefore similar to the one that applies to gifts.

Related Persons

What is meant by *non-arm's length*? Generally, if two individuals are *related to* one another, they are considered to be not at arm's length with each other. The *Income Tax Act* contains a detailed definition of "related persons," which includes the following relationships:

- brothers and sisters
- parent and child
- husband and wife

More distant relationships such as uncle and nephew, and cousins, are not caught by the related person definition. However, even in situations where two *unrelated* persons enter into a transaction that is not carried out on normal commercial terms, the tax legislation permits the CRA to determine that the parties to the transaction were not dealing with each other at arm's length, "as a question of fact."

Transactions Between Family Members

The non-arm's length rule in the *Income Tax Act* has tremendous significance for transactions that occur between family members. In effect, the requirement to recognize fair market value proceeds of disposition, regardless of whether any proceeds are actually received, forces capital gains to be recognized whenever an asset that has appreciated in value is transferred from one family member to another. There are some exceptions to this rule, such as transfers between spouses and others, which will be outlined in the chapters that follow. Let's look at how the non-arm's length rule operates in the following situation.

PLANNING TO PROTECT ● *From Father to Son—Is It Worth It?*

John is the owner of a company, John Manufacturing Inc. (JMI), which manufactures bathroom fixtures. He incorporated JMI 15 years ago, and paid $100 for 100 common shares that were issued to him upon incorporation. John took advantage of the lifetime capital gains exemption some years ago and carried out several transactions involving the shares of JMI, which resulted in him increasing the adjusted cost base of his shares of JMI by $800,000. Therefore, John's adjusted cost base for his shares of JMI is now $800,100.

John wants to transfer the ownership of the company to his son, Mike, who has been working in the business for many years. John believes in the credo that "something worth having is worth paying for," so he is not prepared to transfer the company to Mike for nothing. Since John's adjusted cost base for his shares is $800,100, he thinks that this would be a reasonable price for Mike to pay. He thinks that if he transfers the company to Mike at this price, no capital gains tax will have to be paid.

John is in for a surprise when he pays a visit to his tax advisor. Why? As mentioned above, John and Mike are considered to be dealing with each other on a non-arm's length basis, since they are closely related to each other. Therefore, regardless of how low a sale price John charges Mike for the shares of JMI, he will be considered to have received proceeds of disposition for capital gains tax purposes equal to the fair market value of the shares. The tax advisor therefore tells John that he should have a valuation done for the company before he decides whether or not to transfer any of the JMI shares to Mike.

Let's suppose that the accountant carries out a valuation and determines that the fair market value of John's JMI shares is $1,000,000. If John were to go ahead and transfer the shares to Mike at the originally proposed price of $800,100 (which is equal to John's adjusted cost base), John would still have to report a capital gain of $199,100. This is because his deemed proceeds of disposition would be $1,000,000 (the fair market value of the shares) notwithstanding the fact that the actual sale price would be lower.

The income tax on this gain could be about $50,000—perhaps too steep a price to pay in order to get the ownership of the company into Mike's hands.

• •

Chapter 13 deals with family business estate planning in more detail, and describes various succession planning strategies (such as estate freezing) that can be used to minimize the tax cost of transferring the ownership of a family business from one generation to the next.

OTHER TAXES THAT COULD BE PAYABLE BY AN ESTATE

Until now, this chapter has focused almost entirely on capital gains taxation at the time of death, and certainly for a large percentage of Canadians, this should be their prime focus in planning so as to keep future estate taxes to a minimum. But, this is not the end of the story.

Income Tax on RRSPs and RRIFs

If a Registered Retirement Savings Plan (RRSP) is in existence at the time of death, the full value of the RRSP must be reported in the deceased's final income tax return. An exception to this is where investments held in a RRSP or RRIF account have dropped in value after the date of the person's death until when such investments are transferred to the beneficiaries. In such cases, the amount of the drop in value can be claimed as a deduction in the deceased's final income tax return against the year of death RRSP/RRIF income inclusion.

Another very important exception to the rule regarding the full value of RRSP/RRIF accounts being included in the deceased's year of death taxable income is where the deceased was survived by a spouse, and the RRSP is transferred to the spouse. In that case, the income tax will merely be postponed, since taxes will be payable by the spouse as funds are withdrawn from the RRSP in the form of an annuity or as payments under a Registered Retirement

Income Fund (RRIF). Any amount remaining in a RRSP or RRIF at the time of the spouse's death would be subject to income tax at the time of the spouse's death.

Income Tax on Unrealized Income at the Time of Death

Various kinds of accrued income as of the date of death are also subject to income tax in a deceased's final income tax return. For example, if the deceased was a shareholder of a private corporation and a dividend had been declared but was unpaid at the time of the shareholder's death, the unpaid dividend would be taxable.

Chapter 9 mentions some of the special rules that apply to the preparation of tax returns for a deceased taxpayer, including several special *elections* that may reduce the income tax otherwise payable.

Probate Fees

As outlined in Chapter 7, most of the provinces impose a fee in connection with the filing of an application for Letters Probate for an estate. Probating a will involves filing an application with the applicable provincial court or judicial authority requesting that it certify that the will of the deceased is the person's valid "last will and testament." An executor's authority comes from the will itself. The Letters of Administration give the administrator the authority to administer the estate.

The rates of probate fees in various provinces, as well as some possible strategies for minimizing probate fees are discussed in Chapter 7.

Foreign Estate Taxes

Your estate could also be subject to foreign estate or inheritance taxes, if you own assets at the time of your death that are located in a foreign country. For example, Canadian residents who own real estate in the United States have an exposure to U.S. estate tax. The tax treaty between Canada and the U.S. provides some relief from the U.S. estate tax in many situations, but not all. This subject is summarized in Chapter 11.

PLANNING TIPS

One of the keys to developing an effective estate planning strategy is to know where you stand from a tax viewpoint. Here are some things to keep in mind:

- Make sure that you understand the basics of how capital gains are taxed in Canada.
- Don't forget that some of your assets, such as your RRSP or RRIF, will be subject to income tax at the time of your death, or on the death of your spouse. Make sure that you take such future taxes into account when deciding on the terms of your will and how you want your estate to be divided among your heirs.

- If you choose to designate a particular individual (other than your spouse) as the beneficiary of your RRSP or RRIF, bear in mind that the gross RRSP/RRIF proceeds will be paid after your death to that person. However, the income tax relating to the income inclusion of the RRSP/RRIF value at the time of death will be a liability of your estate, and must be paid out of the other assets of your estate.

- Prepare a personal statement of net worth, and do an estimate of the income taxes that would have been payable if you (and your spouse) had died yesterday. Remember to include the accrued capital gains on your investments or real estate (other than your principal residence).

- Next, do a projection of the taxes that could be payable in 5, 10 or 20 years, taking into account the estimated growth in value of real estate, company shares or other capital property that you own.

- Determine whether your estate may have an exposure to other taxes, such as U.S. estate taxes.

In Chapter 10, "Tax Planning Strategies," we will outline a number of ideas that may help you reduce or postpone the taxes that could otherwise be payable by your estate.

WHERE TO GET MORE INFORMATION

Information is contained at the end of Chapter 9, "Dealing with the Tax Department and Estate Administration," on some CRA publications that explain the various tax returns and special rules that are applicable to deceased taxpayers and their estates. A number of banks and trust companies as well as CPA firms provide free brochures on various tax and estate planning topics.

SUMMARY

In this chapter, we have given you a general understanding of Canada's most unusual form of estate tax, namely the taxation of unrealized capital gains at the time of death. We have covered some of the basic concepts of fair market value, disposition, deemed disposition, proceeds of disposition, adjusted cost base, and how to calculate capital gains and taxable capital gains.

In matters pertaining to taxation, the expression "for every rule there is an exception" is all too true. As with any book of this nature, we have had to leave out some of the special tax rules that apply in certain situations. If you think that your circumstances are the least bit unusual, it could be worth your while to have a specialist in tax and estate planning review your situation.

? Frequently
• Asked Questions

1. *Is there any estate or gift tax in Canada?*

Strictly speaking, we have not had any estate or gift taxes in Canada since the mid 1970s. However, there is a form of "estate tax" and "gift tax" when assets that have appreciated in value are gifted or bequeathed to another person. In that situation, income tax may become payable on a taxable capital gain (even though no money changes hands).

2. *If I decide to make a cash gift of, say, $100,000 to someone during my lifetime, or under my will, would any tax be payable by me or my estate, or by the recipient of the gift?*

Since there is no estate tax or gift tax per se, no tax would be payable by you or by your estate on such a gift. Similarly, the recipient of the gift will not be subject to any tax in Canada on the gift. However, there are few other things you should know:

(i) If you are making a cash gift to your spouse or to someone who is under the age of 18, and if the money is going to be used by the recipient for investment purposes, the *attribution rules* will likely come into play. These income tax rules could attribute their income (as well as capital gains in the case of a gift to a spouse) to you, so that such amounts would be taxable in your hands, not theirs.

(ii) If you are a U.S. citizen (residing in Canada), you are still subject to the estate and gift tax rules in the U.S. Internal Revenue Code. If the cash gift exceeds your annual U.S. gift tax exemption, and depending on what other gifts you made during the year, some U.S. gift tax could be payable. A cash bequest under your will would not attract gift tax. However, your net worth at the time of death could be subject to U.S. estate tax, depending on the size of your estate, whom you have named as your beneficiaries, and other factors.

3. *For capital gains tax purposes, how is "fair market value" determined, and what is acceptable to the CRA?*

This information is readily available from business newspapers and from the Internet for publicly-traded securities (stocks and bonds). Although stock prices fluctuate all the time, you should use the closing price at which the stock traded on the particular date that is relevant in your situation. In the case of real estate, a formal appraisal from a qualified real estate appraiser would carry the most credibility. However, rather than incurring the appraisal fee, many people simply obtain an "estimate of value" from one or two real estate agents in case the CRA questions the value.

4. Does it matter if I name my "estate" as the beneficiary of my RRSP, or one of my intended beneficiaries?

If you are married and you want your estate (including your RRSPs or RRIFs) to go to your spouse if he or she survives you, it is generally a good idea to specifically name the spouse as the beneficiary, rather than your estate. However, if there are other intended beneficiaries (e.g. one or more children), you should consider naming your estate as the beneficiary of your RRSPs or RRIFs. This is so that the income tax applicable to the RRSPs or RRIFs at the time of death will be shared equally by all of the beneficiaries (assuming this is what you intend). For example, suppose you have two investment port-folios that are both worth $100,000. One is a RRSP, and the other is not. You decide to treat your two grown children equally under your will. You decide that the easiest thing is to name your daughter as the beneficiary of the RRSP, and to name your son as the sole beneficiary of the residue of your estate. In that way, they will both inherit the same amount of money—or will they? Under this scenario, your daughter would receive the *gross* RRSP investment portfolio after your death. However, the income tax on the RRSP would arise in your final income tax return, and the tax would be payable by your estate. Therefore, this would reduce the amount that your son will inherit. Is this what you would have intended? Most likely you would have wanted your son and daughter to bear equally the taxes payable on your RRSP, so that on an after-tax basis, they each inherit the same amount.

Dealing with the Tax Department and Estate Administration

"In general, the art of government consists of taking as much money as possible from one party of citizens to give to the other."

VOLTAIRE

INTRODUCTION

Most people have never had to file tax returns for a deceased individual or an estate. In terms of your own estate planning, the filing of your final tax return(s) and any additional returns that are required for your estate or for any trusts created under your will are the final "moments of reckoning."

Our objective in writing this chapter is to help you understand the various tax return filing requirements, as well as:

- various elections and special tax rules that are applicable to deceased taxpayers and their estates
- the procedures that your executor(s) needs to follow in winding up your estate

One of the main responsibilities of the executor(s) of your estate is to pay all of your debts. This includes any income taxes that may be owing from previous taxation years that have been reassessed by the CRA, as well as the income taxes owing on your "final" income tax return.

The responsibility for filing tax returns with the CRA or any other tax authorities falls on the executor(s). However, this does not mean that the executor must prepare the returns himself or herself. Unless one of the executors has expertise in income tax matters, it is generally a good idea to hire an accountant or trust company to prepare the required return(s). The cost is relatively low, in relation to the advantage of ensuring that the returns are accurate and complete.

INCOME TAX RETURNS FOR THE DECEASED

Income Tax Return for Previous Calendar Year (If Not Already Filed)

April 30th is the normal filing deadline for Canadian personal income tax returns. This deadline is extended to June 15th in the case of individuals who have business income from a proprietorship or because they are active members of a partnership.

Depending on the time of the year when a person dies, the income tax return for the previous calendar year may not already have been filed. This is almost always the case for individuals who pass away in the first three or four months of the year.

In order to give the executor(s) of an estate more time to find the relative tax and financial information, the deadline for filing any income tax returns of a deceased person has been extended to the *later* of:

1. the normal filing deadline (e.g. April 30th or June 15th, as the case may be), or
2. six months from the date of death.

This is illustrated by the following example.

PLANNING TO PROTECT ● *Determining the Deadline for Filing Jimmy's Tax Return*

Jimmy was a chartered professional accountant who carried on his practice in partnership with two other CPAs. He died on March 31, 2017.

He had not yet started work on his 2016 income tax return, the normal filing deadline of which is June 15, 2017 (extended from April 30th, as explained earlier).

Because of the time of the year when Jimmy died, the deadline for filing his *2016* income tax return is September 30, 2017 (i.e. six months after the date of death), rather than his "normal" filing deadline of June 15th.

● ●

Final Stub Period Income Tax Return for the Year of Death

The executor(s) of an estate must also file a final income tax return for the deceased, covering the period January 1st up to the date of death. Some people refer to this as a *stub period* return, because it does not cover an entire calendar year. This is the all-important return in which any accrued capital gains as of the time of death must be reported (as explained in Chapter 8, "Death and Taxes"). Later in this chapter, we will outline various special rules that apply to the preparation of this return.

The normal filing deadline for the final stub period return is April 30th of the *following* calendar year (or June 15th in the case of someone with business or active partnership income).

PLANNING TO PROTECT ● *And What About Jimmy's Final Tax Return?*

Continuing with the previous example, Jimmy's final 2017 income tax return will cover the period January 1–March 31, 2017.

The filing deadline will be the *later* of six months after Jimmy's death (i.e. September 30, 2017) or the "normal" filing deadline, which is June 15, 2018. Therefore, June 15, 2018 is the deadline.

● ●

Usually, the beneficiaries and the executor(s) of an estate will want to wind up the affairs of the deceased as quickly as possible. This includes filing any necessary tax returns as soon as the relevant information on the deceased's income, capital gains, etc. is available. One of the practical problems in filing the final tax return early is that the CRA forms for the current year's tax return are not yet available. They do not usually come out until November or December.

In Jimmy's case, the executors might have all the information they need in order to file his final income tax return for the period January 1 to March 31, 2017 at the same time they are filing his 2016 return (e.g. in September, 2017).

The CRA has been willing to accept final stub period returns for deceased taxpayers on the previous year's tax return form, if the current one is not yet available. However, the individual preparing the tax return must make whatever modifications are necessary to reflect current year changes in income tax rates, exemptions, credits, etc. This isn't really very feasible, since professional tax return preparers use computer software to prepare tax returns, and one cannot change the tax rates and exemptions, etc. that are embedded in the software program. The executor(s) might have no choice but to prepare the final return manually on the previous year's tax forms, if they are in a real hurry to file the return before the CRA forms and the current year T1 programs are available.

In our experience, it is more trouble than it is worth to try to file the final stub period return using the previous year's tax form, unless the return is extremely simple. For the sake of a few months delay in winding up the estate, the executor's job would be made a lot easier by simply waiting until the new tax forms are available.

Special Rights or Things Return, If Applicable

Certain kinds of unrealized income of the deceased at the time of death (e.g. unpaid dividends on shares) that are subject to income tax in the deceased's final year can be reported by the executor(s) in a separate income tax return, rather than in the person's final income tax return. This separate return is referred to as a *rights or things* return.

The reason for reporting unpaid dividends and other rights or things items in a separate return is to shift income that would otherwise be taxed at the top marginal income tax rate in the "normal" final return, to a separate rights or things return, taking advantage of the graduated income tax rates once again. A second advantage is that the same personal tax credits can be claimed in the deceased's regular final return. The filing deadline for a rights or things return is the same as for the final stub period return, as discussed above.

Other Elective Income Tax Returns

An elective return can be filed in certain cases in respect of income from an unincorporated business that was being carried on by the deceased. You can also file a separate return if the deceased had received income from someone else's estate and that estate was a "graduated rate estate" for tax purposes, as explained earlier.

Filing an elective return will almost always result in some income tax savings, because the lower graduated rates will apply to the income reported in the separate return. The less attractive alternative is to report the income in the regular final return, which results in it being taxed "on top" of the income already reported in that return, at the applicable marginal income tax rate.

As with a rights or things return, the deceased's full personal tax credits can also be claimed in the elective return.

Quebec Income Tax Return(s), If Applicable

If the deceased person was a resident of Quebec on December 31st of the previous calendar year, or at the time of death, the executor(s) may be required to file Quebec income tax returns. There may also be a Quebec filing requirement in the case of a deceased person who was a member of a partnership (e.g. a national accounting firm or law firm) that carries on its professional business in more than one province, including Quebec.

SPECIAL TAX RULES APPLICABLE TO DECEASED TAXPAYERS

Employment Income up to the Date of Death

Income from salary or wages from January 1st up to the date of death must be reported in the deceased's final income tax return. This includes any accrued employment income as well as vacation pay that may be owing to the deceased's estate or beneficiaries.

Some companies pay a gratuitous lump-sum death benefit to the surviving spouse or dependent child of a deceased employee. The first $10,000 of such a payment is tax-free. Any lump-sum death benefit in excess of $10,000 is taxed in the hands of the recipient(s), rather than in the deceased's final income return.

Pension Benefits

Pension income received by the deceased during the period January 1st to the date of death must also be reported in the deceased's final income tax return for the stub period.

If a CPP death benefit is payable as a result of the person's death, it will be paid to the estate or to the deceased's spouse, depending on the circumstances. This payment is treated as income of the recipient, and is not the type of pension income that is taxed in the deceased's final income tax return.

Accrued Income up to the Date of Death

Most kinds of accrued but unrealized income as of the date of death must be reported in the deceased's final stub period income tax return. For example, this would include any accrued interest income on government or corporate bonds owned by the deceased covering the period from when the interest was last paid on the bond, up to the date of death.

Deemed Disposition of Assets for Capital Gains Tax Purposes

As explained earlier, one of the most unusual features of the Canadian income tax system is the way in which accrued, but unrealized capital gains at the time of death are subjected to tax. Exceptions to the rule, such as where property is bequeathed to a surviving spouse, or to a qualifying spousal trust, are fully discussed in Chapter 8, "Death and Taxes."

Capital Losses

Normally, capital losses realized on the sale of investments can only be offset against capital gains. In the case of a deceased taxpayer, capital losses can be deducted from other income. However, the ability to do this may be limited, if the deceased previously claimed a lifetime capital gains exemption.

Another special rule (Section 164(6) of the *Income Tax Act*) allows capital losses realized *after* the individual's death during the first fiscal year of the estate to be *carried back* from the estate into the deceased's final income tax return. This is an important tax planning strategy in certain situations where an operating company or investment holding company is being wound up during the estate's first fiscal year, and where a capital loss is expected to arise on the winding-up.

RRSPs and RRIFs

Another way in which estate tax arises at the time of a person's death is that the full value of a person's Registered Retirement Savings Plan (RRSP) and Registered Retirement Income Fund (RRIF) investments must be reported as income in the deceased's final income tax return.

Another important exception is where the deceased is survived by a spouse or dependent children or grandchildren. Instead of the RRSP/RRIF being taxed in full in the deceased's final income return, the tax can be deferred by transferring the funds into a RRSP or RRIF for the spouse or dependent children/grandchildren.

However, in cases where the investments in a RRSP or RRIF have dropped in value after the person's death, a deduction is allowed in the final tax return. This means in effect that it is the actual (lower) value of the RRSP/RRIF investments at the time they are transferred to beneficiaries that is subject to income tax on death, which is a fair result.

If you are married, and you wish your spouse to receive all or most of your estate after your death, you should consider naming your spouse as the beneficiary of your RRSP, rather than your estate. This can save on probate fees. Also, it will streamline the spousal rollover procedure for the RRSP and may also be useful for creditor proofing, if you are worried that claims might be made against your estate after your death.

RRSP Contribution for the Year of Death

More often than not, the deceased will not have made a RRSP contribution for the current calendar year in which he or she died. Also, depending on the time of year, an RRSP contribution may not have been made for the previous calendar year.

Where the deceased's RRSP is being rolled over to a surviving spouse, it may make sense for the executor(s) to make a RRSP contribution on behalf of the deceased, thereby obtaining an income tax saving in the previous year's return or in the final stub period return.

RRSP Home Buyer's Loan

The Federal Home Buyer's Plan allows people to borrow from their RRSP in order to help finance the purchase of a home, provided that certain repayment conditions are met. Any balance of such a loan that is unpaid at the time of a person's death must be included in the deceased's income in the final return, unless a surviving spouse agrees to assume the liability.

Charitable Donations

Donations to registered charities, universities and hospitals that are made under a person's will are treated for income tax purposes as if the deceased had made such donations "immediately before death." This means that such donations qualify for a donation tax credit.

Another special rule allows any unused donations in the final income tax return to be carried back to the previous year's income tax return. (Normally, any unused charitable donations can only be carried forward, not back.) Futhermore, donations of up to 100 percent of the deceased's net income in the year of death and the preceding year can be claimed. The usual 75 percent of net income limitation does not apply.

Medical Expenses

Medical expenses incurred in the 24 months preceding the date of death may be claimed in the final income tax return, provided they have not already been claimed.

Personal Tax Credits and Exemptions

The full personal tax credits and exemptions normally claimed by the deceased can be taken in the final stub period return (and in any additional elective returns), even though the time period covered by the return(s) is less than a full year. Fortunately, there is no requirement to pro-rate the personal credits, etc. based on the number of days from January 1st to the date of death.

Disability Tax Credit or Deduction for Attendant Care

If you are the executor for someone who died after a serious or prolonged illness, it may be possible to claim a disability tax credit in the final return, and possibly in the return for one or two preceding years. To qualify for the credit, the individual's ability to perform an activity of daily living has to have been markedly restricted all or almost all of the time.

If the deceased was being looked after by an attendant or was in a nursing home, it may be better to claim a deduction for such costs as *medical expenses*, rather than to claim the disability tax credit.

Minimum Tax

The Alternative Minimum Tax (AMT) does not apply in the final income tax return of a deceased person.

This tax relief is of no relevance to most people. However, it can make an important difference in some situations (e.g. where there is a large capital gains exemption in the final income tax return, or unusually large write-offs relating to tax shelter type investments).

Income Taxes Owing on Capital Gains
Resulting from the Deemed Disposition

A large amount of income tax may be owing on the deceased's final income tax return as a result of the deemed disposition of assets owned by the deceased at the time of death. For example, the deceased may have owned shares of a private company whose fair market value was significantly greater than the adjusted cost base of such shares.

If they wish, the executors can elect to spread the resulting "capital gains tax" over a 10-year period, provided that acceptable security for the unpaid tax is posted with the CRA. This tax deferral is no bargain, because the CRA will charge interest on the unpaid portion of the income tax from year to year, and such interest is not tax deductible. However, where there is not enough cash or other liquid assets in the estate to cover the tax liability, it may be the only sensible course of action.

TAX RETURNS TO BE FILED BY THE EXECUTORS FOR THE ESTATE

T3 Trust Return for the Estate

The moment of a person's death brings into existence a new "taxpayer"—namely, the estate. An estate is treated as a *trust* for income tax purposes.

Any income that arises *after* the person's death is regarded for tax purposes as income of the estate, not the deceased's.

The executors are allowed to choose any date as the tax year-end for the estate, provided that it does not go beyond the anniversary of the date on which the person died. Most estates choose to use the anniversary of the date of death as the fiscal year (in which case, the first fiscal year of the estate will be a full twelve months). In other situations, there can be tax advantages in choosing a different date, so that the first fiscal year of the estate is less than twelve months.

The filing deadline for a T3 return is 90 days after the fiscal year-end of the estate. This means March 31st for an estate with a December 31st year-end (except in a leap year, when the deadline becomes March 30th).

The taxable income of an estate may be taxed either in the estate itself, or in the hands of one or more beneficiaries of the estate, depending on the circumstances. For the first 36 months from the date of death, an estate is entitled to use the same graduated income tax rates that apply to individuals. Therefore, there can be tax savings if income is taxed in the estate itself, rather than in the hands of beneficiaries in the top tax bracket. However, after the first 36 months, if the estate is still in existence, it is no longer considered to be a "graduated rate estate" and it is taxed at the top marginal rate.

T3 Trust Return for Any Testamentary Trusts Established Under the Will

Some people establish trusts under their wills that are to continue for many years. For example, the typical spousal trust will remain in existence for the rest of the surviving spouse's lifetime.

Strictly speaking, a separate T3 return should be filed for each trust created under a person's will, as if it were a separate taxpayer from the estate. However, the widespread and long-standing practice is for the executors/trustees to file just one T3 return that covers both the estate and the trust.

Foreign Estate Tax Return(s), if Applicable

If the deceased owned any non-Canadian assets at the time of death, there may be a liability for estate taxes in the other country. For example, Canadians who own U.S. real estate or shares of U.S. publicly-traded companies may be liable for U.S. estate tax at the time of death, depending on the value of such assets, and the overall value of the estate.

A liability for foreign estate taxes may also arise simply because of the deceased's citizenship or domicile. For example, the estate of a U.S. citizen is subject to U.S. estate tax, regardless of where the person resided at the time of death.

A Canadian resident individual serving as the executor of an estate should not take lightly the responsibility to comply with the tax laws of a foreign country, such as the United States. When it comes to paying an estate tax or inheritance tax imposed by another country, it might be tempting for an executor to adopt the position of "catch me if you can" (especially if the executor is one of the beneficiaries and wants to minimize any taxes owing by the estate). This is almost always an unwise thing to do. Canada has information-sharing and tax collection enforcement arrangements with many other countries, including the United States and the U.K. If an executor willfully evades the payment of foreign estate tax that is owing by the estate, he or she may be held personally liable for the tax, and could be subject to prosecution for tax evasion in the foreign country.

WINDING UP THE ESTATE

Final Returns and Tax Clearance Certificates

The process of filing all of the necessary tax returns in Canada (and elsewhere, if applicable) can take many months—sometimes well over a year.

The mere filing of the return(s) is not the end of the matter. The CRA must process the return(s), and they will eventually issue a Notice of Assessment. In the case of large or complex estates, this assessment process may be drawn out, and could involve the CRA asking for additional information.

Eventually, a Notice of Assessment will be issued stating the amount of income tax for the applicable year, and the balance owing (or refunded). The CRA might not agree with certain deductions claimed in the returns, or the valuations used by the executors for capital gains purposes. Therefore, the income tax liability shown on the Notice of Assessment may be significantly higher than the amount reported in the deceased's final return or in the T3 return(s) for the estate. In such an event, the executors have the right to file a Notice of Objection. This appeal procedure is going to hold up the settling of the deceased's tax affairs. In fact, because of the length of time that it can take to resolve tax disputes (especially if they are litigated through the courts), it could be years before the tax liability of the estate is settled once and for all.

Fortunately, most estates are relatively straightforward and there are no items in dispute with the CRA. Typically, the Notice of Assessment agrees with the income tax calculations in the returns that were filed. Nevertheless, the safest course of action is for the executors to request what is known as a Tax Clearance Certificate from the CRA, before making any substantial distributions out of the estate to the beneficiaries. This puts the CRA on notice that the estate is going to be wound up, and in effect asks the CRA for written confirmation that they are satisfied that all income tax liabilities of the deceased and the estate have been settled. By obtaining a Tax Clearance Certificate *before* making any distributions to the beneficiaries, the executors are relieved of any personal liability for unpaid taxes of the deceased or the deceased's estate.

The vast majority of people leave estates that are very simple and straightforward. More often than not, the person's surviving spouse or adult children are named as the executors, and they may also be the beneficiaries of the estate. In such cases, it is unusual for a Tax Clearance Certificate to be obtained before the estate is wound up.

Seeking Professional Advice

If you find yourself in the role of executor, it would be worthwhile for you to seek professional advice from a trust company, or from a Chartered Professional Accountant or lawyer who specializes in estate planning. You need to understand your obligations as an executor of the estate. Furthermore, you have a fiduciary duty to the beneficiaries of the estate to ensure that all reasonable steps are taken to keep the taxes owing by the deceased and the estate to the legal minimum. You are not expected to engage in "aggressive tax planning." However, if you fail to take advantage of an elective tax return or some other special exemption or deduction, you might be exposing yourself to a lawsuit for negligence from one or more of the beneficiaries.

PLANNING TIPS

The time and money that you spend in planning your estate will have been wasted if the various tax returns that are to be filed after your death are not completed properly and filed on time. Here are some suggestions:

- Line up an accounting firm or trust company now to handle the future preparation of your final income tax return and the required return(s) for your estate or any trusts arising under your will. Even if you currently do your income tax return yourself, it often makes sense to put the tax return preparation arrangements in place in advance.

- If your tax affairs are at all complex, prepare a memorandum (or ask your tax advisor to help) explaining your tax situation and how various matters should be handled in your final income tax return. File the memorandum with your copy of your will, so that it will be seen by your family and your executor(s) after your death.
- In your memorandum, or in your role as executor, make sure that any special elective returns are filed (e.g. a rights or things return) to take advantage of a second set of personal tax credits and graduated rates.
- If you own assets outside of Canada, if any of your beneficiaries live outside of Canada, or if you are a citizen of another country, get tax advice now to determine whether any foreign estate taxes or inheritance taxes could be payable after your death. If so, determine what tax returns might have to be filed by your executors. Also, explore ways of reducing or eliminating the foreign tax exposure (e.g. by putting your foreign assets into a Canadian holding company or trust).

WHERE TO GET MORE INFORMATION

The CRA has issued a number of Interpretation Bulletins, Information Circulars, and booklets on various topics relating to deceased taxpayers and estates, including:

- Preparing Returns for Deceased Persons—booklet
- T3 Trust Income Tax and Information—tax return and booklet
- Interpretation Bulletin IT-212R3, Income of Deceased Persons—Rights or Things
- Interpretation Bulletin IT-244R3, Gifts of Individuals of Life Insurance Policies as Charitable Donations.

Copies of these and other publications can be obtained from your local CRA office, and from their website: *www.cra.gc.ca.*

SUMMARY

In this chapter, we have described:

- the various tax returns that may have to be filed by your executor(s)
- some of the special tax rules that come into play when a final income tax return is being prepared
- the tax compliance requirements that your executors need to consider in the course of winding up your estate
- some planning ideas

This chapter, along with Chapter 8, "Death and Taxes," and Chapter 10, "Tax Planning Strategies," should give you a fairly comprehensive understanding of the tax issues, planning ideas and tax compliance requirements relating to deceased taxpayers and their estates.

❓Frequently
❗Asked Questions

1. *If I die and leave everything to my spouse, will any income tax be payable on my death?*

At the risk of generalizing too much, the answer is "no." Capital gains on any of your assets that have appreciated in value will be deferred because of the spousal rollover. However, this is a *deferral* of tax, not an absolute saving. Income tax on such gains will simply be postponed until such time that your spouse disposes of the assets during his or her lifetime. If the assets are held for the rest of your spouse's lifetime, the capital gains tax will arise at the time of your spouse's death—assuming that your spouse has not remarried and does not leave the assets to the new spouse!

Income tax on the value of your RRSP(s) and RRIF(s) at the time of your death will also be postponed, if such accounts are rolled over to an RRSP or RRIF of your surviving spouse.

In the event that all assets go to your spouse, the only income tax that is likely to be payable in your final income tax return is on income earned by you from January 1st to the date of death.

There may, however, be an exposure to provincial probate fees, if your home or other assets are owned separately by you or your spouse, rather than jointly. Speak to your lawyer about whether you and your spouse should put assets into joint name.

2. *In a situation where a person dies and leaves everything to his or her spouse, is it always necessary to file a T3 tax return for the estate?*

It depends on the kinds of assets that were owned by the deceased, and on how simple or complex the situation is. For example, a simple situation is where the deceased jointly owned a home that passed to the surviving spouse because of a right of survivorship, and the deceased owned little else except bank accounts, Canada Savings Bonds, and some publicly-traded stocks or mutual funds. In this situation, there is probably no need to file a T3 return. Instead, any income received up to the date of death would be reported in the deceased's final income tax return, and any income received after that date would be reported by the surviving spouse. In effect, the "estate" would be by-passed from a tax reporting viewpoint. The CRA is unlikely to challenge this approach, even though it is technically incorrect. Strictly speaking, a T3 return should be filed by the estate, covering the period from the date of death until the time that the deceased's investments are transferred over to the surviving spouse.

Tax Planning Strategies

"We don't pay taxes. Only the little people pay taxes."

LEONA HELMSLEY, U.S. ENTREPRENEUR, CONVICTED OF TAX EVASION

INTRODUCTION

Even if you are not a "do it yourselfer" when it comes to tax planning, it helps to have a general understanding of the various kinds of tax planning strategies that are in use today. As we have said before, this book is not going to turn you into an expert. However, the odds are that at least one of the strategies outlined in this chapter will help you minimize or postpone the future taxes that would otherwise be payable in your estate.

The topics that are covered include:

- understanding the difference between legitimate tax planning and improper tax avoidance or evasion
- identifying your primary tax planning goals
- utilizing the spousal rollover to achieve the optimum deferral of capital gains taxes
- utilizing the $800,000 plus exemption for capital gains on small business corporation shares
- utilizing the farm property rollover, if you are carrying on a farming business
- using a holding company to carry out an estate freeze
- using a family trust for income splitting and estate planning purposes

Tax Planning as Opposed to Tax Avoidance or Evasion

Tax *planning* as opposed to tax *evasion,* is perfectly legal, and has been condoned by the courts in numerous judicial decisions on income tax matters. Even the CRA has accepted the fact that the avoidance or deferral of income tax is permissible, provided that one does not cross the line into the realm of "improper" tax avoidance or tax evasion. A famous U.K. court decision, *The Duke of Westminster v. Commissioner of Inland Revenue,* contained the following passage that has often been quoted by the courts in Canada in various decisions on income tax matters:

> *Every man is entitled, if he can, to order his affairs so that the tax attaching under the appropriate acts is less than it otherwise would be. If he succeeds in ordering them so as to secure this result, then however unappreciated the Commissioners of Inland Revenue or his fellow taxpayers may be of his ingenuity, he cannot be compelled to pay an increased tax.*

Anti-avoidance Rules

We don't want to leave you with the wrong impression. Tax planning is no "piece of cake." The Canadian income tax legislation is replete with rules and regulations that are specifically designed to curtail "tax planning" activity. And as if the host of specific anti-avoidance rules is not enough, there is also a catch-all *general anti-avoidance rule* (GAAR for short) which is intended to catch "abusive" tax planning arrangements that escape the application of the more specific rules throughout the *Income Tax Act.* However, even the general anti-avoidance rule has an exception, namely, any transactions or arrangements that do not represent an "abuse" or "misuse" of the provisions of the *Income Tax Act* will not necessarily be attacked under GAAR.

The CRA has issued Information Circular IC-88-2, which outlines how they intend to apply the general anti-avoidance rule. The Circular contains the following statement:

> *A transaction will not be an avoidance transaction if the taxpayer establishes that it is undertaken primarily for a bona fide business, investment or family purpose.*

So where does this leave us? In spite of some comforting words in the *Duke of Westminster* case and in the CRA's Information Circular, it is certainly not "open season" for tax planning. There are more pitfalls and traps in our tax legislation than you can possibly imagine. Proceed with caution, and get professional tax advice before taking any action.

High Taxes Encourage Tax Planning

The prime objective of any income tax legislation is to generate tax for the government that is imposing the tax. Furthermore, studies of various tax regimes down through the ages have proven that the higher the tax, the greater the effort that will be expended in avoiding the tax. It is no wonder that tax planning is a growth industry in Canada, when you consider the fact that a high income person's marginal income tax rate can be over 50 percent, when surtaxes are taken into account, depending on your province of residence. The fact that more than half of the money you earn must be paid over as income tax is incentive enough for you to take whatever *legitimate* steps you can to minimize your tax bill, both now and in the future.

Some people have gone to almost any lengths to avoid paying taxes, and some, like Leona Helmsley and Al Capone, managed to cross the line into the realm of improper tax avoidance or tax evasion. *Tax evasion* is a criminal offence, and could land you in jail. Generally speaking, *tax avoidance* arrangements that contravene the rules in the *Income Tax Act* are not criminal offenses; however, there can be stiff penalties, plus interest on the unpaid taxes, if you get caught.

Importance of Obtaining Professional Advice

Unlike tax evasion and tax avoidance schemes, the tax planning strategies outlined in this book are "tried and true," and in many cases, specifically condoned by the CRA. However, we must emphasize the importance of your obtaining competent professional advice before you embark on any transactions. Every individual's situation is different, and what will work for one person, may not for another. Remember the example in Chapter 8, "Death and Taxes," of the two women who were each making a $25,000 gift to their daughters. Their situations were similar, but not identical. One was giving cash, and the other was going to give shares of a corporation that had risen significantly in value. The gift of the cash was tax-free, but the gift of the shares attracted $6,000 of income tax on a taxable capital gain.

All too often, people are "penny wise and pound foolish" when it comes to getting professional advice. Someone might think nothing of spending $2,500 to $7,500 on a vacation or on new furniture, but to spend that money on "intangible" professional advice seems unthinkable. Please consider the consequences of *not* getting professional advice. The actions that you take (or do not take) today could have long-term effects on your and your family's financial well-being for many years.

Balancing "Tax" Factors Against Other Considerations

When reading about the various tax planning strategies outlined in this chapter, keep in mind that you should always keep the tax issues and potential savings in perspective, and always consider whether the particular tax planning strategy fits in with your overall estate planning goals. For example, *estate freezing* is a useful technique for shifting the future growth in a family business to one or more children, or even grandchildren. It is a way of limiting the amount of capital gains tax that will be payable on the death of the present owner. However, this strategy may make no sense whatever if an individual has no intention of keeping the ownership of the company in the family, and the business will be sold in the not-too-distant future.

YOUR PRIMARY TAX PLANNING GOALS

The primary tax planning objectives that should be an integral part of your estate planning are:

Tax Deferral

It makes sense to defer (postpone) capital gains taxation for as many years as possible, by taking advantage of any *rollovers* that are available, such as the spousal rollover, or the farm property rollover.

Minimize Taxes Arising on Death

You should minimize the future capital gains taxation on death, by taking advantage of whatever exemptions are available, such as the *principal residence* exemption, and the lifetime capital gains exemption for shares of a *small business corporation.*

Minimize or Eliminate Your Exposure to Foreign Estate Taxes

If you own assets outside of Canada, or if any of your intended beneficiaries reside in a country that imposes an estate or inheritance tax, you should explore ways of reducing or eliminating the exposure to foreign estate or inheritance taxes that could be payable on your death. For example, consider setting up a Canadian investment holding company to hold your investment portfolio, if it includes U.S. stocks or bonds. See Chapter 11 for more details.

Achieve Current Income Tax Savings

You may achieve some current income tax savings at the same time as you restructure your affairs to achieve future estate planning objectives. For example, there might be some income tax savings resulting from the formation of an *income splitting* family trust that is part of your overall estate plan. Any tax savings that you realize during your lifetime should mean that you will have a larger net worth in the future, and a larger estate for your family.

Avoid Unnecessary Complexity, and Retain Flexibility

Ensure that any plans that you implement are sound from a financial and legal viewpoint, and flexible enough to be adapted to your changing circumstances and future changes in the tax laws. Don't embark on a complex tax planning strategy, unless you fully understand what is involved, and you are prepared to live with the complexity.

YOUR GENERAL ESTATE PLANNING OBJECTIVES

Before delving into tax planning objectives, keep in mind that any tax planning strategies that you may be thinking of implementing should always be tested against your more general objectives, to ensure that they are not at cross purposes.

The primary non-tax objectives of estate planning are:

1. arranging your affairs during your lifetime so as to ensure that your assets will ultimately be distributed amongst your family members and other beneficiaries according to your wishes (as opposed to dying intestate and having your estate distributed according to a statutory formula) and

2. ensuring that your spouse and other dependents will be adequately provided for and financially secure after your death.

TRANSFERRING PROPERTY TO YOUR SPOUSE

Chapter 8, "Death and Taxes," was mostly a "bad news" story of how capital gains taxation can arise under various circumstances at the time of death, or upon a transfer of assets during a person's lifetime. One of the most significant exceptions to the rule is where property is transferred to a person's spouse, either during the person's lifetime or upon death.

Spousal Rollover for Tax Purposes

Generally speaking, a *rollover* occurs when an asset that has appreciated in value is transferred to a spouse. Instead of having to calculate a capital gain as if the property had been disposed of for fair market value proceeds, a rollover transfer is considered to have taken place at the *adjusted cost base* (defined in the glossary and Chapter 8). This means that if you were to leave your assets to your surviving spouse, no capital gains tax will arise on your death. Instead, the assets will go to the spouse at your adjusted cost base.

But here's the catch. Since your spouse will take over your adjusted cost base for the various inherited assets, the accrued capital gains at the time of your death are merely deferred (postponed) until the spouse eventually disposes of the assets, or until the spouse's death, whichever occurs first. In other words, the spousal rollover is really a *tax deferral* mechanism, not an outright exemption. Nevertheless, if you can't be exempt from tax, the next best thing is to defer the payment of tax for as long as possible by taking advantage of whatever rollovers are available.

PLANNING TO PROTECT ● *Delaying the Inevitable for David and Edith*

In one of the examples in Chapter 8, we assumed that David was a widower. Let's change the facts and assume that David was married to Edith. David passes away, and under his will, everything is to go to Edith. In the previous example, approximately $55,000 of income tax would have been payable on the RRSPs and accrued capital gains as of the date of David's death. However, because David designates Edith as the beneficiary of his RRSP, and since all of the assets will go to Edith under the terms of David's will, the $55,000 tax liability can be avoided (for now at least).

As a result, Edith will eventually have to account for the capital gains tax when she disposes of the assets. If she holds on to all of the assets (other than the RRSP) for the rest of her life, there will be a deemed disposition at fair market value at the time of her death, and for capital gains tax purposes the final moment of reckoning will occur at that time.

In the case of David's unmatured RRSPs, Edith will be able to postpone the income tax, but not indefinitely. It will be necessary for her to convert the RRSP to an annuity or to a Registered Retirement Income Fund (RRIF) not later than December 31st of the year in which she turns 71 years of age. After that, the annuity or RRIF payments will be taxable in her hands.

Outright Transfers and Transfers in Trust

Careful planning is required in order to ensure the spousal rollover will be available in your estate (assuming you intend to transfer assets to your spouse in the event you pass away first). There are generally three situations where the spousal rollover is available:

1. where property is transferred *outright* to the deceased's surviving spouse pursuant to the terms of the deceased's will
2. where property is left *in trust* exclusively for the surviving spouse under certain required terms and conditions specified in the *Income Tax Act* and
3. where property is transferred by a person 65 or older to a joint partner trust and the assets ultimately go to the person's spouse.

In the case of property passing on death, one of the technicalities that must be satisfied is that the property must be transferred to the spouse (or to the spousal trust) within 36 months of the date of death. In some cases, it may take longer for the executors to effect the transfer of assets (for example, where the will is being contested). In such cases where there are "extenuating circumstances" delaying the administration of the estate, the CRA is authorized to extend the 36 month deadline if it is "reasonable under the circumstances" to do so.

Spousal Trusts

Where a person intends to leave property in trust rather than outright to a surviving spouse, it is essential that the person's will be drafted in a particular way in order to meet the following requirements for the capital gains spousal rollover:

1. The will must stipulate that under the terms of the trust, the spouse is entitled to receive all of the income of the trust for the rest of that person's lifetime; and
2. The will must also be written in such a way that it is not possible for any of the income or capital of the trust to be distributed to anyone but the spouse, during the spouse's lifetime.

There have been numerous cases of a deceased person's will being written in such a way that the trust created under the will for the benefit of the surviving spouse fails to meet the necessary conditions for the capital gains rollover. For example, a person's will might create a spousal trust under which "the income of the trust shall be payable to my wife, if she survives me, but shall cease to be payable to her in the event that she remarries." Such a provision would disqualify the trust from the capital gains rollover, because the surviving spouse's entitlement to the income of the trust is not absolute and will only continue to be paid if the spouse does not remarry.

PLANNING TO PROTECT ● *Deborah Defers Taxes and Protects Her Children's Inheritance*

Deborah and Brian recently got married in their late sixties. Each was married before, and each of them has children from the first marriage. Deborah is quite wealthy, having inherited a large portfolio of investments and real estate when her first husband died some years ago. Brian is not as well off financially as Deborah, but he has enough from his savings and a modest pension to enable him to make ends meet. Deborah wants to ensure that Brian does not have to scale back his lifestyle if she dies before him, but she doesn't feel that it would be fair to her children if she leaves her wealth outright to Brian. After all, Brian could remarry or he might even squander the assets and nothing would be left for Deborah's children.

Deborah decides to draw up a new will that will have the following features:
- $100,000 will be transferred outright to each of her three children
- the balance of her estate will be held in trust for Brian whereby all of the income that is earned on the investments will be paid to Brian each year and
- after Brian's death, the remaining capital of the trust will be divided equally among her three children.

• •

This is the type of spousal trust that enables the capital gains spousal rollover to apply on the first death. Therefore, it will not be necessary for the executors of Deborah's estate to pay income tax on whatever accrued capital gains exist at the time of her death on those assets that will be held in trust. Keep in mind that this is merely a *deferral* of tax, not an absolute saving. Under this type of trust arrangement, the trust will eventually have a deemed disposition of all of its assets in the year that Brian dies. Any accrued capital gains on the spousal trust assets will be subject to income tax at that time.

As mentioned earlier, if Deborah's will were to have said that Brian would cease to be entitled to any income in the event of his remarriage, this would disqualify the trust for purposes of the spousal rollover on Deborah's death. Therefore, any accrued capital gains on her investments would be taxed on her death. Similarly, if her will permitted any of the income of the trust to be distributed to any or all of her children during Brian's lifetime (assuming that he survives her), the trust would not meet the requirements of a qualifying spousal trust and the spousal rollover would not apply.

Chapter 6, "Understanding Trusts," contains a more detailed description of the taxation of trusts, and their uses in estate planning.

Electing Out of the Spousal Rollover

The *Income Tax Act* allows a person to opt out of the normal rollover that applies on the transfer of property to a spouse. This *election* is available for transfers during one's lifetime to a spouse. It is also available to the executors of an estate, where under the terms of the deceased's will, property is to be transferred to the surviving spouse or to a qualifying spousal trust. By electing out of the rollover treatment, the transfer of property to the spouse (or spousal trust) is considered to have taken place at the fair market value of the property, rather than at the adjusted cost base.

Why would one want to elect out of rollover treatment? One reason is that the deceased may have realized capital losses in prior years from stock transactions or other dispositions of property, and the losses could not be utilized for tax purposes because there were not enough capital gains in the earlier year. By electing out of the spouse rollover treatment on some or all of the assets that are to be transferred to the surviving spouse, capital gains can be triggered in the person's final income tax return, which will be offset by the capital loss carry-forward amounts. By doing this, the particular assets on which the rollover treatment does *not* apply will go to the surviving spouse at an adjusted cost base equal to the fair market value at the time of death, rather than at the deceased's original adjusted cost base (i.e. historical cost). Therefore, when the surviving spouse eventually disposes of those assets, only the increase in value from the time of the first death will be subject to capital gains tax in the spouse's hands.

PLANNING TO PROTECT ● *Should Peter's Executors Allow the Spousal Rollover or "Elect Out?"*

Peter died in June, and under his will, everything is to go to his wife Patty. At the time of his death, Peter owned marketable securities with a fair market value of about $300,000. The portfolio was made up of both "winners" and "losers." The "winners" had a market value of $200,000 and a cost of $150,000. The losers were worth $100,000, and had a cost to Peter of $120,000. Peter also owned a ski chalet that was worth $120,000 at the time of his death, and which had an adjusted cost base of $80,000.

Therefore, Peter had accrued capital gains totalling $90,000 ($50,000 on the securities, and $40,000 on the ski chalet), and accrued capital losses on other securities totalling $20,000.

Peter had played the market for a number of years, but without much success. He had an unused capital loss carry-forward from prior years of $60,000. (For illustration purposes, this is the "gross" amount of the unused prior year capital losses, rather than the "50 percent" amount.)

Peter's executors have some choices. They can allow the spousal rollover to apply for capital gains purposes. In that case, the various securities and the ski chalet will go to Patty at Peter's adjusted cost base for each property, and no capital gains will need to be reported in Peter's final income tax return. However, this approach would also mean that Peter's allowable capital loss carry-forward of $60,000 will simply disappear. (There is no mechanism in the *Income Tax Act* for this to be transferred to the surviving spouse.) Furthermore, Patty will have to account for capital gains tax when she eventually disposes of the securities or the ski chalet. In effect, she will end up paying income tax on the accrued gains that existed at the time of Peter's death. Not a sensible result.

A better strategy would be for the executors of Peter's estate to elect out of the spousal rollover treatment on the ski chalet (thus triggering the $40,000 capital gain) and to elect out on some of the "winners" in the investment portfolio so as to trigger $20,000 of capital gains. This will create $60,000 of capital gains in Peter's final income tax return, which will fully absorb the $60,000 capital loss carry-forward from prior years that would otherwise have gone to waste. By making these elections on specific assets, Patty will acquire the assets at a higher "cost" for capital gains tax purposes. When she eventually disposes of the assets (or at the time of her death), the capital gains tax will be much lower than would otherwise be the case.

• •

UTILIZING THE $800,000 PLUS CAPITAL GAINS EXEMPTION FOR SMALL BUSINESS CORPORATION SHARES

There is a special lifetime capital gains exemption for gains realized by a Canadian resident on the disposition of shares of a qualifying small business corporation, if certain conditions are met. The exemption has been increased a number of times with it reaching $800,000, after which point, it became indexed to inflation. For example, for 2017, the capital gains exemption is $835,714. If you own shares of any Canadian private corporations, you may be able to take advantage of this exemption and reduce the future capital gains taxes that would otherwise be payable in your estate. This exemption is discussed in more detail in Chapter 13, "The Family Business."

UTILIZING THE FARM PROPERTY ROLLOVER

If you or your immediate family are carrying on a farming business, there are some important tax issues for you to consider in your estate planning, and succession planning. Generally speaking, it is possible for a *family farm* (including a farm corporation or partnership) to be transferred from one generation to the next on a rollover basis without having to recognize any capital gain. This topic is discussed in more detail in Chapter 13, "The Family Business."

ESTATE FREEZING

Estate freezing is a tool that is used in many situations to minimize the tax cost of particular assets being transferred from one generation to the next. The term is used to describe a particular planning strategy that involves altering the form of ownership of a particular asset so that the future growth in the value of the asset is shifted to the next generation. In that way, the current owner's financial interest in the property is *frozen* at the present fair market value of the property, thereby limiting the amount of capital gains tax (or estate tax if applicable) that will arise at the time of the taxpayer's death.

By carrying out an estate freeze, the amount of tax arising on the individual's death will be based on the fair market value of the particular asset at the time that the freeze was carried out, not the value at the time of the individual's death. A fundamental assumption of estate freezing is that the *freezees* (the person or persons in whose favour the freeze was carried out) will outlive the person who carried out the freeze. Estate freezing in the context of a family business is discussed in more detail in Chapter 13, "The Family Business."

Estate freezing is also used with respect to real estate investments and other assets that are expected to be held for a long time.

PLANNING TO PROTECT ● *Alex Uses Estate Freezing to Manage His Investment*

Alex is a widower in his mid-fifties and he is quite wealthy. He acquired a commercial property 10 years ago, which has been generating rental income. He has been claiming depreciation (capital cost allowance) in his tax returns to partially offset the rental income he has been receiving.

Although the value of the property dropped quite drastically after he acquired it, the value has now recovered to approximately what he paid for the property.

Alex feels that the property is a good long-term investment, and he had intended to eventually transfer it to his two grown daughters. After talking with his friendly Chartered Professional Accountant, he is now concerned about the amount of capital gains tax that could be payable in his estate. His accountant explained that there would also be *recapture of depreciation* to report in his final income tax return, after he dies.

Alex and his accountant have worked out the following "estate freezing" strategy:

- Alex will form a new holding company: "Alex Holdings Inc."
- Alex will transfer the ownership of the real estate to the holding company in return for redeemable preferred shares.
- The shares will have a redemption price equal to the current fair market value of the real estate.
- Alex will also have the legal right to require the shares to be redeemed at any time, meaning that the shares will be "retractable" at Alex's option.
- Alex will arrange for common shares of the holding company to be issued 50/50 to his two daughters.

Alex's accountant has advised him that this arrangement must be carefully constructed in order to ensure that Alex does not have to recognize any capital gain or recapture of depreciation on the transfer of the real estate to the holding company. The transfer would be structured as a rollover using certain rules in Section 85 of the *Income Tax Act*. Among other things, it will be necessary for Alex to file an election form with the CRA setting out certain details of the transfer.

The overall tax effects of these transactions are as follows:

- Alex has frozen his investment in the real estate because he has exchanged a *growth asset* (the real estate) for an asset having a fixed value (the fixed value redeemable shares of the holding companies).
- The future growth in the value of the real estate that is now owned by the holding company, will accrue indirectly to the benefit of his two daughters, since they will now own the common shares of the company.
- No tax arose on the transfer of the property to the holding company, since Alex was able to use a rollover provision.
- When Alex eventually dies, the capital gain arising in his estate under the deemed disposition rule will be based on the fair market value of Alex's preferred shares of the holding company.

• •

As a matter of corporate law, the *shareholders' equity* value of a corporation attaches first to any *preferred shares* that have a fixed redemption amount, and which have certain *preferential rights* over the common shares. Any remaining value of the corporation attaches to the *common shares*. Thus, the growth in the value of a corporation will generally accrue to the benefit of the common shareholders. The holders of any fixed value redeemable preferred shares of a corporation can generally expect never to receive any more than the redemption amount of their shares, plus any unpaid dividends or cumulative dividends as the case may be.

Generally speaking, the CRA considers the fair market value of preferred shares such as those used in the above example to be equal to their redemption amount, provided that the shares are also retractable at the shareholder's option.

An estate freeze is a complex estate planning technique. We have oversimplified the steps involved, and it is beyond the scope of this book to explain all of the tax, legal, financial, and estate planning issues that must be considered. If you hold any property that you feel might be suitable for an estate freeze, you should talk to your accountant, lawyer and tax advisor who can advise you on the appropriate strategy. Another thing to consider is that at some point, the government of the day and/or the CRA might change its view on estate freezing and introduce new rules in the Income Tax Act or new assessing policies to make estate freezing more difficult to do, or to prevent this tax planning technique from being used at all.

USING FAMILY TRUSTS FOR INCOME SPLITTING AND ESTATE PLANNING

For several hundred years, trusts have been used extensively for estate planning purposes. Because of the importance (as well as the complexity) of using trusts in tax and estate planning, we have devoted Chapter 6, "Understanding Trusts," to this subject. In that chapter we explained what a trust is, how to form one, and the various ways that they can be used in your tax and estate planning.

PLANNING TIPS

You owe it to yourself and your family to arrange your financial affairs in such a way that the income taxes (including taxes on capital gains) arising in your estate are minimized or postponed as much as possible—provided of course that you do not "cross the line" into the realm of improper tax avoidance or tax evasion.

Here are some things to keep in mind:

- If you are married, living in a common-law arrangement, or you have a same-sex partner, write your will in such a way that you can take advantage of the spousal rollover rules. This will postpone capital gains taxes as well as income tax on RRSP or RRIF accounts until the death of the surviving spouse/partner.
- If you are very wealthy, consider creating a spousal trust under your will and leaving some of your assets in trust for your spouse/partner rather than outright. This will ensure that the assets that remain after the death of your spouse will pass to your own children (or grandchildren). Also, a trust would preserve a part of your wealth from any adverse financial consequences of your spouse remarrying after your death.
- Your executor(s) should consider electing out of the spousal rollover treatment for one or more assets on which there are accrued capital gains at the time of death. This could be

advantageous if the deceased had a carry-over of capital losses from prior taxation years that can only be utilized in the deceased's income tax returns.

- If you are a shareholder in a Canadian private company that carries on some type of active business in Canada, look into the possibility of utilizing the $800,000 plus lifetime capital gains exemption. This exemption can either be *crystallized* during your lifetime, or your estate could use it in the future (assuming that the exemption is still available, and the shares of your company still qualify for the exemption).

- If you are involved in a family farming business, make sure that your affairs are structured to take advantage of various exemptions (including an inter-generational farm property rollover) that are available for active farming businesses.

- Consider carrying out an estate freeze if you own your own business. But beware of the potential consequences! In the authors' opinion, you should not even think about an estate freeze unless your overall net worth is more than $10 million. This is a "rich man's game."

- Consider one of the tried and true income splitting strategies, in order to spread invest-ment income and capital gains amongst other members of your family who are in a lower tax bracket than you. Over a number of years, the income tax savings can be quite substan-tial. The more income tax you are able to "save" during your lifetime, the more there will be for your spouse and children after you are gone.

Where to Get More Information

Numerous books have been published on personal financial planning and tax planning. Because the focus of this book is on estate planning, we have not attempted to cover all of the possible income tax planning strategies that may be applicable in your situation.

Many large accounting firms have produced publications on personal tax planning and most of this information is available on their websites. There are also a large number of other websites that contain personal financial planning and tax planning tools, and more are crop-ping up all the time.

Summary

In this chapter, we have given you an overview of some of the major tax and estate planning tools that are commonly used in Canada. No list of planning strategies can ever be complete, because our tax laws are constantly changing, and no two people are in exactly the same posi-tion. Sometimes, the circumstances of a particular individual can lead to the creation of a unique estate planning strategy that has no relevance in any other situation. What may work for one person can have disastrous results for someone else.

We cannot stress too strongly the importance of your obtaining professional advice to guide you through the tax planning process. Chapter 16, "Selecting Professional Advisors," describes the roles of the various professional advisors who should be included in the planning process, and some of the factors to consider in selecting an advisor.

❓Frequently Asked Questions

1. *If I am survived by a common-law spouse, will tax be payable on the value of my RRSP or RRIF if I leave it to him or her?*

   Generally, common-law spouses are treated the same as legally-married spouses for income tax purposes. Therefore, income tax on the RRSP or RRIF can be postponed by rolling it over to your common-law spouse's RRSP or RRIF as the case may be.

   The same rollover rules are available for same-sex couples as well.

2. *What happens if I die without a will (i.e. intestate)? Would assets passed on under provincial legislation to my spouse be eligible for the spousal rollover?*

   The answer is "yes." Assets that pass to a deceased's spouse, whether pursuant to the person's will, by operation of law (e.g. jointly-owned property where there is an automatic right of survivorship), or by virtue of the applicable provincial intestacy laws, are all eligible for the capital gains rollover treatment.

Tax and Estate Planning If You Own U.S. Assets

"Why does a slight tax increase cost you two hundred dollars but a substantial tax cut save you thirty cents?"

PEG BRACKEN

INTRODUCTION

Are you currently a Snowbird or planning to be? Have you purchased U.S. property for recreational purposes or invested in U.S. property or companies?

If you live in the United States part-time and/or own U.S. property, income tax and estate planning can become quite complex because you could be affected by the tax laws of both Canada and the United States. In the United States, for example, you could be liable, under certain circumstances, for federal income tax, capital gains tax, estate tax, gift tax and even individual state taxes.

The following overview provides general guidelines only; obtaining current competent professional cross-border tax advice customized to your personal situation is essential. Legislation, rules and regulations are always in flux. Reporting and filing requirements can be complicated, confusing, and overwhelming to the layperson. This chapter will give you a good awareness of some of the key concepts and issues, allowing you to better communicate with your professional advisor. Topics covered include:

- determining if U.S. federal tax laws affect you
- renting U.S. property
- selling U.S. property
- U.S. gift tax

181

- paying U.S. and Canadian taxes on death
- implications of the Canada/U.S. tax treaty
- strategies for reducing taxes on U.S. vacation property
- filing deadlines with the IRS
- tax information exchange between the U.S. and Canada
- where to get tax advice and information.

DO U.S. TAX LAWS APPLY TO YOU?

Even though you are a Canadian citizen and only living in the U.S. periodically or part-time, you could still be subject to U.S. taxation or various U.S. filing requirements. The Canada/U.S. Tax Convention (treaty) includes provisions, discussed later in this chapter, that will affect you. Since changes can occur at any time, be sure to obtain current professional tax advice. If you are a U.S. citizen, the discussion in this section will not apply to you. If you have been granted lawful permanent residence in the United States by the U.S. Bureau of Citizenship and Immigration Service (BCIS) (i.e. you have a "green card"), a special set of rules may apply to you. (Please see "Residency and the Tax Treaty" later in this chapter.) If you are a citizen of a country other than Canada or the United States, or are a Canadian citizen working full-time in the United States under the *North American Free Trade Agreement* (NAFTA), or one of the other available U.S. visas, some of the following comments may apply. If you fall into any of the categories just noted, contact your tax advisor. If you are going to the United States on business or for employment, contact the CRA and obtain a copy of the pamphlet, *Canadian Residents Abroad*.

Resident Versus Non-resident Alien Tax Status

It is important to know whether you are a resident alien or a non-resident alien because substantially different U.S. tax rules apply to you in each case. For example, resident aliens are generally taxed in the United States on income from all sources world-wide, which of course would include Canadian income. Non-resident aliens are generally taxed in the United States only on income from U.S. sources and income "effectively connected" with a U.S. trade or business.

There are two different tests to determine if you are a resident or non-resident alien for U.S. federal income tax purposes:

1. The "green card" test
2. The "substantial presence" test
   (Certain individuals also can elect to be treated as a resident of the United States.)

The *green card test* is fairly straightforward: If you acquire a green card and enter the United States, you are a resident alien of the United States (see "Residency and the Tax Treaty" later in this chapter for further information).

The IRS also considers you a resident alien of the United States if you meet the *substantial presence test*. The substantial presence test uses the number of days you have spent in the United States over the last three years, that is the current and two prior years, to determine your U.S. income tax residency status. The following is a brief overview of the implications of time spent in the United States related to the substantial presence test:

- If you were in the United States for 183 days or more in the current year, you meet the substantial presence test.
- If you were in the United States for 31–182 days in the current year, you may meet the substantial presence test.
- If you were in the United States less than 31 days in the current year, you do not meet the substantial presence test.

Here is a formula to calculate whether or not you meet the substantial presence test:

Each day in the United States in the current calendar year counts
as a full day (e.g. no. of days $\times$ 1)   =_____

                                                   Plus:

Number of days in the United States in the preceding calendar year
counts as one-third of a day (e.g. no. of days $\times$ 1/3)   =_____

                                                   Plus:

Number of days in the United States in the second preceding year
counts as one-sixth of a day (e.g. no. of days $\times$ 1/6)   =_____

                                                   Equals:

Total number of days   _____

When totalling all the days for each of the above three years, remember that the days don't have to be consecutive, and a part of a day constitutes a full day (unless you are in transit through the United States). If you regularly spent over four months (122 days) a year in the United States, and you have done so for the past three years, you would meet the substantial presence test, at least in the latest year. If the total is more than 182 days, you have met the substantial presence test and are considered a resident alien for U.S. income tax purposes for the current year. However, if certain valid filings are made, the following individuals can exclude days present in the United States for the computation:

- individuals who are unable to leave due to a medical condition that arose in the United States
- certain regular commuters to employment in the United States
- certain travelers in transit
- "exempt" individuals (i.e. certain government people, certain teachers/trainees/students and certain athletes in charitable events)

If the total is 182 days or less, you do not meet the substantial presence test (please also see "Residency and the Tax Treaty" later in this chapter).

The Closer Connection Exception

If you meet the substantial presence test, you can avoid being considered a U.S. resident for tax purposes for the current calendar year if you:

- have spent less than 183 days in the United States in the current calendar year
- do not hold, or have applied for, a green card, or adjustment of status
- have a "tax home" in Canada or other foreign country
- can demonstrate a closer connection to the above "tax home" country than the United States by completing and filing the IRS Closer Connection Exception Statement for Aliens (IRS Form 8840)
- you file IRS Form 8840 by the deadline (or can demonstrate you tried to comply by the deadline).

Your "tax home" is generally where you work. If you do not work, your tax home is your "habitual abode." IRS Form 8840 requires responses to various questions intended to demonstrate whether you maintain more significant ties to Canada (or a third country) than the United States including the location of the following:

- your permanent residence
- your family
- your personal belongings, such as cars, furniture, clothing and jewelry
- your bank
- the place where you carry on business (if applicable)
- the jurisdiction where you vote
- the jurisdiction where you hold a driver's license
- where you maintain health insurance.

Filing Requirements for the
Closer Connection Exception

IRS Form 8840 (Closer Connection Exception Statement for Aliens) must be filed with the IRS by June 15th of the following year (April 15th if you had wages subject to U.S. withholding) unless you obtain an extension. Each person claiming the closer connection exception must file. You should file IRS Form 8840 by registered or certified mail (return receipt requested) as your proof of filing, because the IRS will not acknowledge receipt of your filing. *If you meet the substantial presence test and fail to file Form 8840 by the due date, you could be required to file a U.S. income tax return.* Please see "Residency and the Tax Treaty" below. To obtain Form 8840, contact your cross-border tax advisor. Another option is to obtain the form from the IRS website, which is at *www.irs.gov.* Click on "Individuals" and then "Forms and Publications" under "IRS Resources."

RESIDENCY AND THE TAX TREATY

Individuals Who Meet the Substantial Presence Test

If you are a resident alien because you meet the substantial presence test and you cannot claim the closer connection exception (or failed to file IRS Form 8840 by the due date), you may still be able to compute your U.S. income tax liability "as if" you were a non-resident alien. Article IV of the Canada/U.S. Tax Convention (the "treaty") provides residency "tie-breaker" rules that are applicable to individuals who simultaneously meet the residency rules of both Canada and the United States.

The tie-breaker rules may result in being able to compute your U.S. income tax liability on the basis that you are a non-resident alien of the United States. In this scenario, however, you still remain a resident alien of the United States for other purposes of the U.S. income tax laws. For example, you must file a U.S. income tax return to make this tax treaty claim, and you are subject to all the other U.S. income tax reporting rules to which U.S. resident aliens are subject. For instance, you must report certain types of involvement with non-U.S. financial accounts and non-U.S. corporations, partnerships and trusts. Very substantial penalties can apply for non-compliance with the income tax return filing requirement and the tax reporting requirements. For more information on Article IV of the treaty, contact your cross-border tax advisor.

Individuals Who Possess a Green Card

If you are considered a resident alien because you possess a green card, you are also potentially able to claim the benefits of Article IV of the treaty to compute your U.S. tax liability as a non-resident alien of the United States as described in "Individuals Who Meet the Substantial Presence Test" above. Of course you must meet all the requirements of Article IV to make the claim, and you are nevertheless still treated as a U.S. resident alien for all the U.S. reporting requirements applicable to resident aliens. *Please note that such a claim may endanger your possession of the green card, inasmuch as the treaty claim potentially conflicts with the basis for the issuance of the green card itself.*

Income Tax Filing Requirements for Tax Treaty Article IV Claim

To make the tax treaty Article IV claim described above, you must file a U.S. income tax return on Form 1040 NR for the year in question. The deadline is June 15th of the following year (April 15th if you had wages subject to withholding or if you are a resident alien the following year and not able to make the Article IV claim for that year). You must report all U.S. source income, and any other income "effectively connected" with a U.S. trade or business, which might include interest, dividends and rent. Obtain cross-border tax advice.

SUMMARY OF GUIDELINES REGARDING FILING A U.S. INCOME TAX RETURN

- *Resident alien.* Subject to the discussion under "Residency and the Tax Treaty" above, resident aliens generally must file a U.S. income tax return annually reporting world-wide income for the year.
- *Non-resident alien.* If you are a non-resident alien, your income that is subject to U.S. income tax is divided into two categories:
  - Income that is *effectively connected* with a trade or business in the United States, including income from the sale or exchange of U.S. real property. This income, after allowable deductions, is taxed at the same rates that apply to U.S. citizens and residents.
  - Income that is *not effectively connected* with a trade or business in the United States, but is from U.S. sources, such as dividends, pension annuities and (sometimes) rental income. This income is taxed at a flat rate of 30 percent except where the rate is reduced by the tax treaty. As a non-resident alien, you must file a U.S. income tax return if you have income that is "effectively connected," or income not effectively connected that had insufficient withholding, or overwithholding and you wish to claim a refund.

THE IRS WANTS YOUR NUMBER

If you are a non-resident alien and you are not qualified to obtain, and do not have, a U.S. social security number, there are circumstances in which you must obtain a U.S. "Individual Taxpayer Identification Number" (referred to as an "ITIN"). Among other circumstances, you are required to obtain an ITIN:

- if you are filing a U.S. income tax return for yourself. For example, if you sell U.S. real estate or you want to claim a tax refund or you have U.S. real estate rental income or U.S. business income, you must obtain an ITIN for yourself.

- if you are claiming your spouse as a dependent for deduction purposes on your U.S. income tax return, an ITIN must be obtained for your spouse, even if your spouse has no connection with the United States.
- if you are claiming children (or others) as dependents (assuming they are eligible) on your U.S. tax return, an ITIN must be obtained for each dependent. For example, if you are a non-resident alien filing a U.S. tax return for U.S. real estate rental income and you wish to claim a deduction for your children, you must obtain an ITIN for each child, even if they are all minors living in Canada. Similarly, if you are a U.S. citizen or green card holder living in Canada, the same requirement exists when you file your U.S. tax return.
- if you are the spouse of a U.S. person and you elect to file a joint U.S. tax return with that person, you must obtain an ITIN.

How to Obtain an ITIN

You apply for an ITIN on IRS Form W-7, which you must submit with Form W-7, a certified copy of your passport, and supporting documentation for the reason an ITIN is needed. The IRS will no longer issue an ITIN over the phone, and the passport must be certified by the issuing agency, a U.S. embassy or consulate, or in certain circumstances a Certifying Acceptance Agent. The IRS will not accept a passport notarized by a U.S. or foreign notary. The form is then submitted by mailing it to the IRS, ITIN Operation, P.O. Box 149342, Austin, TX 78714-9342 or by taking the form to an IRS Taxpayer Assistance Center.

IRS Shares Information with the CRA

The ability of the IRS and the CRA to exchange data on Canadian and U.S. taxpayers by computer has increased dramatically as a result of the new requirements for certain Canadians to have a U.S. taxpayer identification number (ITIN).

When you apply for your ITIN, you must provide some brief but very personal information to the IRS. This includes your name, your name at birth, if different, and your address in Canada. Post office boxes and "care of" addresses are not allowed. Your date and place of birth are asked for, along with your sex. In addition, you are asked for your passport number and U.S. visa number, if any.

You are also asked for your Canadian social insurance number. You can imagine the cooperation between the IRS and the CRA this could facilitate. The IRS potentially has a computerized cross-referencing capability between your U.S. and Canadian taxpayer numbers. Information on certain U.S. tax-related activities in which you are involved, such as the sale or rental of U.S. real estate, or your claim for a U.S. tax refund on U.S. investment or pension income, can be transmitted to the CRA by computer, giving the CRA your name, your Canadian address and your Canadian social insurance number.

THE IRS HAS YOUR NUMBER

What Does the IRS Know About You?

The IRS potentially has a wide variety of information on individuals who have U.S. income, own U.S. property or are involved in a U.S. financial transaction. For example:

- If you purchase U.S. real estate, your name and address are recorded in the local county property records. When you sell your U.S. real estate, another entry is made in the county records. Information on both of these transactions is readily available to the IRS if it wishes to obtain it.
- If you *sell* U.S. real estate, the closing agent (e.g. the lawyer, title insurance agent, etc.), must complete the required IRS form and submit it to the Internal Revenue Service along with a copy to you. This form includes your name, address and the sale price of your property. The IRS can use the form to determine if you have filed a U.S. tax return.
- If you *sell* U.S. real estate to a U.S. person and take back a mortgage, a notation of the interest paid to you must be made on the U.S. person's tax return.
- If you *rent* out your U.S. real estate, another IRS form may be generated. The rental agent is required to complete the required IRS form and submit it to the Internal Revenue Service along with a copy to you. The form lists your name, Canadian address and the rental income you received. Again, the IRS can use this form to determine if you have made the proper U.S. filing.
- If you receive certain types of interest or dividends from U.S. sources, the required IRS form is also filed with the IRS.
- If you receive pension income from U.S. sources, similar IRS forms may also be generated and sent to the IRS.

  As mentioned, all the information available to the IRS can also be given to the CRA.

Your U.S. Bank Interest Will Be Reported to the CRA

If you receive U.S. bank interest, your bank will be required to advise the IRS of your name, address and the amount of interest paid to you, even if you use a U.S. address on your account. The bank will be able to identify you as a Canadian from the required IRS form, which you must file with the bank. Normally, you must file the required IRS form at the bank when the account is opened, and every three years thereafter. If you do not do so, the bank is required to deduct U.S. withholding tax on your interest.

Tax Information Exchange Between the U.S. and Canada

The purpose of exchange of information is to ensure a correct and speedy application of domestic tax legislation, to assist in the application of tax treaties and to prevent tax avoidance and evasion. There are three main types of information exchange between countries:

1. **On request.** For example, the CRA could *request* from the IRS specific information about a U.S. real estate sale by a particular Canadian resident.
2. **Automatic.** For example, information available to the IRS on U.S. rental income received by Canadians or U.S. real estate sales by Canadians could be sent *automatically*, in bulk, to the CRA by the IRS.
3. **Spontaneous.** For example, in the course of an IRS tax audit of a Canadian for a U.S. real estate sale, the IRS might *spontaneously* decide to send the information to the CRA if it believes the information may be of interest.

Mutual Assistance in Collection Efforts

The Canada/U.S. tax treaty includes a provision that Canada and the United States will, in some cases, assist each other in collecting revenue owing for taxes, interest, penalties and costs. This makes it harder for some taxpayers to avoid collection efforts from the other country.

FATCA is an intergovernmental agreement between the U.S. and Canada by which financial institutions must report certain financial information on the other country's citizens to the other country's government.

DEADLINES FOR FILING WITH THE IRS

Here is a summary of some key deadlines of which you should be aware. Depending on your situation, there could be other forms to complete and file with the IRS.

Closer Connection Exception Statement

Form 8840 must be filed within 5½ months after the end of your tax year (3½ months if you had wages subject to U.S. withholding) unless you received an extension. Thus, it is generally due June 15th for the previous tax year. Failure to file a required Form 8840 will likely result in your being considered a U.S. resident for U.S. income purposes unless you can demonstrate that you tried to comply. (See the earlier section "Residency and the Tax Treaty.")

Qualified Domestic Trust Election

Canadian estates wishing to defer U.S. estate tax on U.S. property through the use of a qualified domestic trust must generally make an election no later than one year after the normal due date for the return (including extensions). The due date (without extensions) is normally nine months after the date of death. If the election is not made in time, the trust cannot be used in most cases, and hence the tax deferral is forfeited. We have already discussed the general concept of living (or *inter vivos*) trusts in Chapter 6.

Estate Tax Marital Tax Credit Claim

Canadian estates desiring to reduce their U.S. estate tax liability by claiming a marital tax credit under the Canada/U.S. tax treaty have an important deadline to meet. The estate will generally be disqualified from obtaining this important tax reduction if the proper waiver and claim are not made by the same deadline described above for the qualified domestic trust election.

RENTAL INCOME FROM U.S. REAL ESTATE

You may be renting out your U.S. property on a part-time or full-time basis. As a non-resident alien, you are subject to U.S. income tax on the rental income.

Tax on Gross Rental Income

Subject to the next section entitled "Net Election on Rental Income," the gross rents you receive are subject to a 30 percent withholding tax, which your tenant or property management agent is required to deduct and remit to the IRS. It doesn't matter if the tenants are Canadians or other non-residents of the United States, or if it was paid to you while you were in Canada. An exception applies if the rental income is clearly *effectively connected* with a U.S. trade or business. Your rental income may not automatically be considered to be "effectively connected" if there is only a small amount of activity.

If the proper tax was not withheld, you must file Form 1040 NR, U.S. Non-resident Alien Income Tax Return, showing the gross rental income and withholding tax. Your tenant or property management agent must withhold the tax and complete Form 1042, Annual Withholding Tax Return for U.S. Source Income of Foreign Persons, as well as Form 1042-S, Foreign Persons' U.S. Source Income Subject to Withholding. For more information, contact the IRS and request Publication 515, *Withholding of Tax on Nonresident Aliens and Foreign Entities*, and Publication 527, *Residential Rental Property*.

Net Election on Rental Income

As an alternative to paying the 30 percent tax on the gross rental income described above, you may prefer to elect to pay tax on the net income after deducting expenses. This could result in reduced tax and possibly no tax. The Internal Revenue Code permits this option if you choose to permanently treat rental income as income that is effectively connected with the conduct of a U.S. trade or business.

You can then claim expenses related to owning and operating a rental property during the rental period, including mortgage interest, property tax, utilities, insurance and maintenance.

You must also deduct an amount for depreciation on the building. However, the IRS only permits individuals to deduct the mortgage or loan interest relating to the rental property if the debt is secured by the rental property or is not secured at all. If you borrow the funds in

Canada, secured by your Canadian assets, you would not technically be able to deduct that interest on your U.S. tax return. Special rules apply to corporations. Obtain strategic tax planning advice on this issue.

After making this net election, you must file Form 1040 NR, U.S. Nonresident Alien Income Tax Return, each year you have rental income. The election involves a one-time attachment to the first tax return stating that you are making the election, and including the following information:

- a list of all of your real estate located in the United States
- the extent (percentage) of your ownership in the property
- where the property is located
- the purchase price and any major improvements in the property
- any previous applications you have made of the real estate net income election

Once you have made the election, it is valid for all subsequent years, unless approval to revoke it is requested and received from the IRS.

If you want to be exempt from the 30 percent non-resident withholding tax and are making this election, you must give your tenant or property management agent the required IRS form (Certificate of Foreign Persons Claim That Income Is Effectively Connected with the Conduct of a Trade or Business in the United States). Consult with a cross-border tax advisor.

When you file your annual return, show the income and expenses, as well as the tax withheld. If you end up with a loss, after deducting expenses from income, you would be entitled to a refund of the taxes withheld, if any. The due date of your return is June 15th of the following year (April 15th if you had wages subject to U.S. withholding). It is important to file on a timely basis. If you fail to file on the due date, individuals have 16 months thereafter to do so. If you don't do so, you will be subject to tax on the gross income basis for that year, that is, 30 percent of gross rents with no deduction for any expenses incurred, even if you made the net income election in a previous year.

PLANNING TO PROTECT ● *Don't Make the Same Mistakes as Linda and Dave!*

Linda and Dave owned a condo in Arizona. They had been using it for their own recreational purposes for many years, but due to ill health decided to rent it out full-time. They didn't realize that they had to either pay 30 percent withholding tax on the gross rents, or make the "net election" and file an annual U.S. income tax return. Nor did they realize that they also had to declare their U.S. rental income on their Canadian income tax return.

After a few years of rental, Linda and Dave decided to sell their condo. They did not realize that they needed to report this sale to the IRS and potentially pay tax on the sale, depending on the amount of the sale and other factors. In addition, they did not realize that they had to report the sale to the CRA and be subject to tax on any capital gain. Canadian residents are taxed on their world-wide income and capital gains.

You can appreciate the multiple complications, hassle and migraines that would ensue with both taxing authorities once the facts became known. In addition to taxes and penalties, there would also be retroactive interest compounded from the date the money was due. As a consequence, it is prudent to make sure that you are getting expert professional tax advice on your obligations on both sides of the border, if you own property in the United States.

● ●

SELLING YOUR U.S. REAL ESTATE

If you sell your U.S. real estate, you are subject to U.S. federal (and perhaps state) income tax on the sale. Of course any permanent improvements you made are added to your adjusted cost base to reduce the tax. After the end of your tax year, you must file a U.S. income tax return to report the sale. The sale must also be reported in Canada, but any Canadian income tax payable on the capital gain may be offset in full or in part by the U.S. tax. To help enforce compliance with this U.S. filing requirement, the IRS generally requires 15 percent of the "amount realized" at the time the sale transaction is completed to be remitted to the IRS as a prepayment of any tax you owe on the sale. This withholding is generally referred to as the "FIRPTA" withholding tax. When you file your U.S. income tax return, the *actual* U.S. tax is computed. You are given credit on the tax return for the FIRPTA tax withheld, and you either receive a refund or owe more tax depending upon the difference between the actual tax and the FIRPTA tax withheld.

To lower your Canadian tax liability, you may be able to claim the principal residence exemption (all or part) on the sale of your U.S. residential property, assuming you were eligible (i.e. the residence qualified for principal residence treatment for some or all of the years that you owned the property and you meet the other Canadian requirements).

Reduction or Waiver of FIRPTA Withholding Tax

If the 15 percent FIRPTA tax to be withheld exceeds your "maximum U.S. tax liability," you can apply to the IRS in advance to have the withholding tax reduced or eliminated. To do this you file the required IRS form to obtain a "withholding certificate" from the IRS. However, the closing agent must still collect the withholding tax and hold it in escrow until the IRS response to the required IRS form has been received. If the transaction has already closed and the 15 percent has already been sent to the IRS, you can still file the required IRS form and apply for an "early refund."

FIRPTA is now 15 percent. In certain situations FIRPTA can be reduced to 10 percent or even 0 percent. In order to reduce the FIRPTA tax, the buyer must intend to use the property at least 50 percent of the time it is occupied by any persons during the next two 12-month periods. The buyer does not have to be a U.S. citizen or resident, or use the property as a principal residence. If the buyer is able to sign an affidavit confirming the intended personal use, and the sale price is between $300,000 and $1,000,000 U.S., the FIRPTA will be reduced to 10 percent of the amount realized. If the selling price is less than $300,000, then the FIRPTA is reduced to 0 percent.

In all of the cases above you still must file a U.S. income tax return after the end of your tax year.

Filing Requirements

As indicated above, you are required to report the gain or loss on the sale of your U.S. real estate by filing the required IRS form, the U.S. Nonresident Alien Income Tax Return. If you own the real estate jointly with another person, such as your spouse, each of you must file the form.

In addition, you would have to report any capital gain on the sale of your U.S. property on your next annual tax return filing with the CRA. Remember, you have to report your worldwide income and gains and pay tax on 50 percent of any capital gain, translated to the equivalent in Canadian dollars at the time of sale.

U.S. GIFT TAX

One might think that as a non-resident alien of the United States you could give anything to your spouse, children or other family members, and the IRS would not have any jurisdiction. The laws, however, are not that simple. You may have U.S. gift tax to pay if you give U.S. "real property" (i.e. real estate) or "tangible personal property" (e.g. an automobile, antique furniture, artwork) located in the United States to another person.

There is a U.S. $14,000 annual exclusion per recipient, adjusted for inflation, meaning you can give a total of U.S. $14,000 per year to as many different people as you wish, without being subject to gift tax. If the recipient is your non-U.S. spouse, the annual exclusion is U.S. $148,000 adjusted for inflation. If the recipient spouse is a U.S. citizen, as a general rule you can give unlimited amounts without gift tax—but exceptions apply for both exclusions. Consult your tax advisor.

Traditionally, the gift tax rates have been the same as the estate tax rates, but the actual amount of the gift tax may be higher because there generally are no tax credits or deductions for gift tax purposes and the Canada/U.S. tax treaty does not provide benefits for gifts. Subject to these exclusions, the rules are as follows:

Gift of U.S. Real Estate

If you own U.S. real estate directly and give it to another person, U.S. gift tax will generally be payable, subject to the U.S. $14,000 exclusion. Alternatively, if you buy real estate jointly with another person (other than your spouse) and the two of you make unequal contributions to the purchase price, gift tax may be payable. If you made equal contributions, there would not be any gift tax payable.

If you purchase real estate jointly with your spouse and make unequal contributions, beware when you sell the property. If the sales proceeds are not distributed to the two of you in proportion to your original contributions, gift tax may apply.

Suppose, at the time of purchase, the title to the property is placed entirely in the name of your spouse (or other family member) but the funds to make the purchase come solely from you. Gift tax may apply since the IRS may consider the transaction to be tantamount to a gift of the property from you to the other person.

Gift of Personal Property

"Personal property" (as distinguished from real property such as real estate) can be classified into one of two types—tangible or intangible.

GIFT OF TANGIBLE PERSONAL PROPERTY

Tangible personal property includes things such as residence furnishings, cars, boats and jewellery.

You are subject to U.S. gift tax on your gifts of tangible personal property *located* in the United States. However, in this case, as a general rule your property is only considered located in the United States if its normal location or *domicile* is the United States. For example, if you give a car to a family member while both you and the car are in the United States, the gift tax position may depend upon whether the car was normally based in Canada or the United States.

GIFT OF INTANGIBLE PERSONAL PROPERTY

Normally, a non-resident alien is not subject to U.S. gift tax on the gift of intangible property (e.g. stocks and bonds) regardless of where the property is located. In other words, as a general rule you can give U.S. stocks or bonds to another person regardless of whether the securities are located in a U.S. or Canadian brokerage firm.

However, an exception applies if you are a "covered expatriate." (Expatriation rules apply to certain U.S. citizens renouncing U.S. citizenship and certain "long-term" residents giving up a green card). Check with your tax advisor.

POSSIBLE SIMULTANEOUS U.S. AND CANADIAN TAXES ON DEATH

If you are a resident of Canada and a non-resident alien of the United States you may be taxed at death on certain kinds of U.S. assets you own, by both U.S. and Canadian authorities. Such assets include U.S. real estate, stocks in a U.S. corporation, interests in certain partnerships and certain other U.S. assets. Of course there may be no tax in Canada if the assets pass to a surviving spouse or other qualified individual. *This occurs because the United States imposes an "estate" tax at the time of death, whereas in a deceased person's final Canadian income tax return, Canada potentially imposes a "deemed disposition" at the time of death for capital gains tax purposes.*

U.S. Estate Tax

The U.S. estate tax laws (federal and state) change frequently and by early 2017, were in a state of uncertainty due to political discussions in Washington. Please contact your tax advisor for up-to-date information. However, generally, the United States imposes a federal estate tax that is based on the fair market value of a deceased's U.S. assets on the date of death. Individual state estate taxes may apply as well, depending on the state. The estate tax applies to "U.S. situs" property as defined in the tax code. Among other items this includes U.S. real estate, U.S. stocks, equity memberships in U.S. golf clubs and *tangible* property such as cars and boats that are considered to be "domiciled" in the United States. (For further information see the section "Gift of Tangible Personal Property" under the heading "U.S. Gift Tax.")

Remember that since the definition of U.S. situs *assets includes U.S. stocks, you may be subject to U.S. estate tax on U.S. securities you own in an investment portfolio you have with a Canadian brokerage firm or investment manager, and even in your Canadian RRSP or RRIF. However, many (perhaps most) U.S. debt securities are not subject to U.S. estate tax regardless of where they are located, provided they are not effectively connected with a U.S. business in which you are involved.*

Canadian "Deemed Disposition" (Capital Gains) Tax on Death

Although Canada does not have an estate or death tax as such, there is a deemed disposition at death, in which there can be Canadian capital gains tax on the appreciation in the value of the property. This would apply to both U.S. and Canadian property. Of course, if the property passes outright or in trust to your spouse or certain other qualified individuals (e.g. a disabled child), there is generally a deferral of Canadian capital gains taxation until either the property is either sold or the party who received the property passes away. Under the Canada/U.S. tax treaty, discussed in more detail in the next section, you can potentially claim foreign tax credits in Canada for part or all of the U.S. estate tax on gains taxed in Canada that are associated with U.S. assets on which U.S. estate tax was payable.

THE CANADA/U.S. TAX TREATY

Because of certain provisions in the Canada/U.S. tax treaty, only fairly well off Canadians have any exposure to U.S. estate tax (based on the current U.S. tax legislation contained in the Internal Revenue Code) with respect to U.S. stocks, U.S. real estate, and certain other kinds of U.S. assets owned at the time of death. We will provide an overview of how U.S. estate tax is calculated under the rules that were in effect at the time of writing, and how the Canada/U.S. tax treaty comes into play in a very beneficial way to limit or even eliminate any potential U.S. estate tax for the vast majority of Canadians. However, make sure you obtain advice about the most current status and any changes from a professional tax advisor familiar with cross-border tax issues. The following discussion is intended to raise your awareness of key issues that may affect you.

U.S. Estate Tax Credit

U.S. federal tax is calculated on the gross value of the estate value at death, less any allowable deductions or credits. Credits include any state death taxes and the federal "unified tax credit." The unified tax credit is an amount that can be deducted from the "gross" estate tax to determine the net estate tax payable. The unified credit is equivalent to a particular estate value "exemption amount," which for the deaths that occurred in 2016 was $5,450,000 U.S. This means, in effect, that only a fairly small percentage of Americans have any possible liability for U.S. estate tax—that is to say, those situations where the total value of the deceased U.S. citizen's or U.S. resident's assets at the time of death was greater than the exemption amount (e.g. $5,450,000 U.S. for 2016). Fortunately for residents of Canada, the Canada/U.S. tax treaty has a provision that makes that same unified credit/exemption amount available to the estates of deceased Canadian residents on a pro-rated basis. This means that if a Canadian resident owned certain kinds of U.S. assets at the time of death, but the person's total world-wide assets were worth less than the U.S. estate tax exemption amount (e.g. $5,450,000 U.S. for the 2016 year), no U.S. estate tax would be payable on the value of the person's U.S. assets. This is because the unified credit, even though being applied on a pro-rated basis, would completely offset any U.S. estate tax otherwise payable.

In the case of a Canadian resident whose world-wide assets at the time of death exceeded the exemption amount (e.g. $5,450,000 U.S. in 2016), the unified credit/exemption is pro-rated (i.e. reduced) based on the ratio comparing the value of the deceased person's U.S. situs assets at the time of death to the total value of the person's world-wide assets at the time of death.

Thus the unified tax credit available to Canadians is:

$$\frac{\text{Gross U.S. estate}}{\text{Gross world-wide estate}} \times \text{the unified tax credit available to U.S. citizens} = \underline{\hspace{2cm}}$$

Your gross world-wide estate includes assets in the United States and Canada, including RRIFs, RRSPs, certain life insurance proceeds and certain pension income that continues to a surviving spouse.

However, as stated earlier, if the deceased Canadian's world-wide estate was *less than* the applicable unified credit/exemption amount for the year in which the person died (e.g. $5,450,000 U.S. in 2016), the calculation shown above has the effect of producing a credit that fully offsets the U.S. estate tax that would otherwise be payable.

Marital Tax Credit

If U.S. property is left to a non-U.S. citizen spouse, there is a second tax credit potentially available to Canadians under the tax treaty, referred to as the *marital tax credit*. Simplistically, if all the U.S. property subject to U.S. estate tax passes to the surviving spouse, there is a non-refundable marital tax credit equal to the unified tax credit. If all the U.S. property does not go to the surviving spouse, the marital tax credit is reduced proportionately.

STRATEGIES FOR REDUCING U.S. ESTATE TAX ON YOUR U.S. ASSETS

If the unified credit remains at a high level (e.g., U.S. $5,450,000 for 2016), this means that only those Canadians whose total worldwide assets are worth more than that at the time of death have a possible exposure to U.S. estate tax on their U.S. assets.

Joint Ownership of Property with Spouse or Family Members

When property is jointly held, the U.S. federal estate tax applies to the total fair market value of the property, except to the extent your estate can prove the surviving owners contributed to the purchase of the property including improvements and mortgage payments. Therefore, when purchasing U.S. real estate jointly, it may be helpful for each owner to pay for their share of the property with their own funds and to be able to prove it. In this case only your (the decedent's) portion of the fair market value is taxed if you die, thus reducing the tax liability.

If you now own the property jointly and you contributed all the funds for the purchase, you can examine, with your tax advisor, the practicality of formally gifting all or part of the property to the other owner(s). In contemplating such gifts you must take into consideration the U.S. gift tax rules previously explained. (See "Avoiding the U.S. Gift Tax.") In many cases this may involve a gifting program covering several years.

It is important to take into consideration Canada's income tax rules that apply to "gifts in kind" (i.e. gifts of property as opposed to cash gifts) when evaluating the practicality of such gifts. Transferring appreciated property (other than a principal residence) may trigger a "deemed disposition" of the property at fair market value for Canadian income tax purposes, thus creating a Canadian capital gains tax liability. Of course, if the gift is to your spouse or other qualified individual, there should be no taxable gain for Canadian purposes.

If you decide to sell all or part of your U.S. property to your spouse and/or other family members to avoid estate tax, you could sell the property at fair market value (less the potential gift tax exclusion if you wish). But if you want to be confident the change in ownership will be respected by the IRS for estate tax purposes, you must ensure the sale cannot be treated as a sham by the IRS, and treated as a gift instead. The IRS may consider the sale a sham if you gave all the purchase funds to the new owner(s) or if you sell the property and take back a mortgage that is unrealistic (for example, if the mortgage terms are not somewhat similar to terms you would require for a sale to an arm's length third party). Also, you are subject to U.S. tax on any gain on the sale and to the FIRPTA withholding tax rules as described earlier under the section "Selling Your U.S. Real Estate."

Again, there could be Canadian tax consequences to such a sale. However, you would obtain a full or partial tax credit in Canada for any U.S. tax payable. If you receive payment in installments, you can spread the tax liabilities in both the United States and Canada over a specified period of time. In this case you should synchronize the payment structure to ensure you obtain the best result in Canada with respect to offsetting U.S. tax.

Sale and Leaseback

If you want to avoid any estate tax but still continue living in your U.S. residence, you may be able to sell the property at fair market value and then lease it back for a certain number of years with options for renewal. This would minimize or reduce taxes, such as Canadian and U.S. capital gains tax on any profit from the sale, and U.S. estate tax on the value of any mortgage you receive from the purchaser as part of the purchase price package (assuming the mortgage is properly structured). However, you must ensure that the sale and/or any mortgage involved do not constitute a sham and that full fair market value is paid for the property. Since everyone's situation is unique, make sure you get specific tax advice from a professional tax advisor. Again, please refer to the prior section "Selling Your U.S. Real Estate."

Buying Term Life Insurance

This is an option to help pay for any future estate tax liability shortfall. For many older Canadians, however, it is not a realistic option, because it is either impossible to acquire or too expensive. Even if you could afford to acquire enough coverage, you would need to increase the face value if the property appreciates in value. You should attempt to buy a policy that enables you to increase the face value up to a certain amount, without having to undergo a medical exam each time. If you can't obtain term life insurance, you may want to consider the cheaper accidental death insurance. Refer to Chapter 15 on insurance.

Owning Your Foreign U.S. Real Estate or Investments Through a Canadian Holding Company

Provided the original purchase of U.S. real estate is made with a non-U.S. corporation and the corporation is properly structured, maintained and operated as the true owner of the property, the IRS heretofore has not levied estate tax on such indirect ownership of the real estate. However, if the real estate is a personal use residence, this is often not practical for a Canadian resident since the CRA may levy a shareholder benefit on the personal use of the property. An exception applies to certain grandfathered Canadian "single purpose" companies. However, the structure may still be practical for U.S. rental real estate and the investment in U.S. securities.

Placing a Non-recourse Mortgage on Your U.S. Real Estate

Under U.S. regulations, if your U.S. real estate is subject to a valid "non-recourse" mortgage (i.e. you have no personal liability in the event of default), then only your net equity in the real estate (not the full fair market value of the property) is subject to U.S. estate tax. However, it is often difficult to find a source for such a mortgage. You may be able to arrange such a mortgage among family members or family entities, but such a "related party" mortgage must avoid the characteristics of being a "sham." Thus it is possible that interest must be paid, which could trigger taxable income to the lender without a compensating tax deduction to the borrower.

Purchasing the Property Through an Irrevocable Non-U.S. Trust

Under this potentially controversial scenario, an irrevocable Canadian trust would be formed to purchase a U.S. personal use residence. Generally, beneficiaries and others involved with an irrevocable trust are not subject to U.S. estate tax on their death if property is owned by the trust. However, there are potential pitfalls with regard to the formation of the trust and the ultimate sale of the property by the trust. Please consult your international tax advisor before proceeding.

Purchasing the Property Through a Canadian Partnership

As indicated above, ownership of your U.S. real estate through a Canadian holding company has the potential to avoid U.S. estate tax. However, the income tax rate on corporate gains is generally higher than the income tax rate on individuals. If you own the U.S. property through a Canadian partnership and you sell the property for a gain, you will be taxed at the lower tax rate for individuals. If the partnership has a very active business in Canada and none in the

United States, it is possible (though definitely not a certainty) that there will be no estate tax on the death of a partner if the partnership does not terminate. Be sure to consult your tax advisor before proceeding.

On the other hand, if a partner dies, and the partnership has some minimal business activity, the partnership could make the U.S. "check-the-box" election to treat the partnership as a Canadian corporation for U.S. tax purposes in an attempt to avoid U.S. estate tax. This procedure is complex and has many ramifications and pitfalls—please consult your cross-border tax advisor before taking any action.

Giving the Property to Your Beneficiaries During Your Lifetime

Under this scenario the U.S. (and Canadian) gift tax rules may apply. Please see the earlier section, "U.S. Gift Tax."

Leaving Your U.S. Property to a Qualified Domestic Trust (QDOT)

The purpose of this strategy is to defer rather than eliminate estate tax until the death of the second spouse. If it is structured properly, the QDOT may also conform to Canadian tax laws in terms of being considered a qualifying spousal trust. That would mean that the CRA would not consider the transfer to be a deemed disposition and therefore charge capital gains on your death. This strategy is worth considering if there are insufficient liquid assets in your estate tax to pay the estate tax.

Investing in U.S. Securities Through Canadian Pooled Fund Corporations or Canadian Mutual Funds

Canadian mutual funds may be formed (organized) as either corporations or trusts. If you purchase a Canadian mutual fund that is organized as a corporation that invests in U.S. securities, there will generally be no U.S. estate tax on your death. However, if the mutual fund is organized as a trust, the IRS attitude is unclear. It is possible you would be subject to U.S. estate tax on the mutual fund's underlying U.S. securities. Read the fund prospectus and obtain professional tax advice in advance.

There may be other strategies that could be beneficial in your particular situation to reduce or eliminate U.S. estate taxes, which you should discuss with a tax advisor knowledgeable in U.S./Canada tax strategies.

WHERE TO GET MORE INFORMATION

There are many sources of information and assistance available to you to help you understand the tax issues and improve your decision making.

- The CRA has many free guides, pamphlets and interpretation bulletins covering a wide range of issues. They will also provide you with assistance on your tax return questions and on international tax issues. See their website at *www.cra-arc.gc.ca*.

- The U.S. Internal Revenue Service (IRS) has many free publications and a toll-free inquiry number for assistance in terms of the tax implications and filing requirements of being a Canadian non-resident alien of the United States or other category of temporary resident. See their website at *www.irs.gov*.

- Many Canadian and U.S. accountants and lawyers specialize in cross-border tax matters between Canada and the United States. Obtain two opinions from such independent professional advisors, at least one from a Canadian advisor and one from a U.S. advisor or cross-border tax agent to make sure the advice is consistent. The more extensive your investments or assets in the United States, the more important it is to satisfy yourself that the advice you are getting is consistent. If you are considering moving to the United States permanently, it is imperative that you receive opinions from international tax accountants or lawyers on both sides of the border. For suggestions on what to look for in a professional tax accountant or lawyer, refer to Chapter 16, "Selecting Professional Advisors."

- There are also a number of books that could be consulted. *The Canadian Snowbird Guide* (*Everything You Need to Know About Living Parttime in the USA or Mexico*) by Douglas Gray (published by John Wiley & Sons) provides a comprehensive overview of the key issues that any seasonal resident of the United States should know. It is available at local bookstores or online.

- Go online to view the free *Brunton's U.S. Tax Letter and Tax Alerts for Canadians*, *www.taxintl.com*. For further information, contact the Brunton-McCarthy CPA firm at 561-241-9991 or 1-800-325-2922.

- Refer to Appendix A, "Sources of Information," for contact numbers for the CRA and the IRS, as well as website addresses.

- Website: *www.snowbird.ca*.

SUMMARY

There are many issues to consider if you own U.S. assets, rent or sell U.S. property or die while owning U.S. assets anywhere.

We have provided a general overview of the U.S. laws that apply to Canadians, filing requirements with the IRS, cross-border tax issues and information on how to avoid or minimize taxation in the United States. We also discussed the Canada/U.S. tax treaty, strategies for reducing U.S. estate tax on U.S. assets and where to get more information.

It cannot be overstated how important it is to obtain skilled professional tax and legal advice from professionals in Canada and the United States or from advisors with combined cross-border experience. Advance planning is critical to minimize stress and taxes and maximize peace of mind.

❓ Frequently Asked Questions

1. *Do U.S. tax laws apply to me if I own property in the United States?*

   Yes. Whether you rent or sell your U.S. property, there are tax filing requirements with both the IRS and the CRA. Taxes could be payable in both countries. However, in general the countries allow tax paid in one country to offset tax payable, in full or in part, in the other country. The country of source of the income is usually the first country entitled to the tax.

2. *What is the tax impact if I die in the United States or die while owning U.S. assets?*

   It depends on various factors. If you are only a seasonal visitor in the United States and own no U.S. assets, then only the CRA will be involved. But please refer to the definition of U.S. assets in the section "U.S. Estate Tax," which can include U.S. stocks held in Canada. The CRA requires a deemed disposition of all your assets (e.g. any capital gain as of your date of death is taxed). An exception may apply if the property passes to your surviving spouse or other qualified individuals (e.g. minor or disabled children).

   On the other hand, if you own certain types of U.S. assets, including those located in Canada, and your total worldwide assets at the time of death exceeds the verified credit exemption amount applicable to U.S. citizens and U.S. residents (e.g., it was U.S. $5,450,000 for deaths occurring in 2016), there will likely be some U.S. estate tax payable on the U.S. situs assests held at time of death. However, Canada may allow a foreign tax credit for some or all of the U.S. estate tax paid on any U.S. assets that are subject to tax in Canada as a result of the "deemed disposition" on death.

Vacation Properties

> **"A home is not a mere transient shelter;**
> **its essence lies in the personalities of the people who live in it."**
>
> HENRY LOUIS MENCKEN

INTRODUCTION

Millions of Canadians have fond memories of spending their holidays at a family cottage. In fact, thousands of cottages, camps and chalets have been in the same family for several generations, and are the magnets that bring far-flung family members back together for family reunions. In this chapter, we will give you some "food for thought" on how you might want to deal with your vacation home under your estate plan. As well, we'll explain how the capital gains tax rules apply to second properties, and we'll discuss the following strategies that may help you reduce or postpone such taxes:

- how to utilize the *principal residence* exemption on your vacation home
- how to *double up* the exemption for properties acquired before 1982
- claiming the principal residence exemption on the property with the larger gain
- arranging the ownership so as to capitalize on another family member's unused principal residence exemption
- transferring ownership to a trust
- creating a *life interest* and a *remainder interest*.

The cottage is supposed to be the place to relax, and to forget your troubles. You might worry about the septic system getting clogged, or the property taxes being too high, and you may keep busy tinkering with the boat, repairing the dock, painting the shed or building a sleeping cabin. But aren't these worries a small price to pay for the peace and tranquillity of cottage life? Financial concerns, especially capital gains taxes, should be the furthest thing from your mind when you are sitting on the dock waiting for the fish to bite, or watching the sun set over yonder mountain.

Sadly, some of the peace and tranquillity of cottage life has been removed because of changes in the capital gains tax rules. The first attack occurred back in 1981, followed by the elimination of a $100,000 lifetime capital gain exemption in the 1992 and 1994 Federal Budgets. Cottage life is sure not what it used to be. Now everyone at the lake talks about capital gains taxes! Besides lining up repair people to help you with various cottage projects, just about every cottage owner now needs a tax specialist! This is because you, the cottage owner, will most likely face capital gains taxation when you eventually sell or transfer the ownership of your family cottage. And in many situations, the capital gains tax liability resulting from a transfer of ownership to one's children or grandchildren can be so high as to force the sale of the cottage.

If you own both a home and a vacation property, there is not much that you can do to completely avoid capital gains tax on both properties. However, we will outline in this chapter some strategies that you might be able to use to defer the tax liability for as long as possible, and to make the most of whatever tax exemptions are applicable in your situation. These strategies usually involve changing the ownership in some way, so as to shift the future growth in value to younger members of your family (such as children, or even grandchildren). Or it could mean putting the ownership into the hands of another family member who is in a position to utilize the principal residence exemption.

KEEPING THINGS IN PERSPECTIVE

Please keep in mind that there are many important personal, financial and legal factors that you need to consider before taking any action. Although achieving tax savings now or in the future is a worthwhile objective, the tax considerations should not be paramount. Your cottage or chalet is probably the most "emotionally charged" asset that you own. If it has been in your family for a long time, you, your spouse and each of your children probably have a very close attachment to the place.

We recall the comment of one cottage owner who was seeking advice on how to minimize the amount of capital gains tax arising on her death. In her own words, "the cottage is sacred ground; it is the very essence of our family." She went on to say that it was even more important to her than several of her children! (Perhaps she was getting a little carried away in the heat of the moment.) Nevertheless, we shouldn't make light of just how important a cottage can be to members of a family. But all too often, the cottage ends up causing family fights over its ownership, use and the sharing of the annual operating expenses.

Often, a parent will leave the cottage to one child, rather than leaving it to all of the children, fearing that joint ownership among siblings and their spouses will lead to family squabbles. But this approach can also cause hard feelings, because the children who are left out may feel that the parent loves the child who received the cottage more than them. This happens even in cases where the parent equalizes bequests by leaving cash, securities or other assets to the other children.

Whether you decide to do nothing or to adopt one of the tax and estate planning strategies outlined below, your decision should "withstand the test of time." Your personal circumstances will change over the years, and there is no way of knowing what your family situation will be in 5, 10 or 20 years time. Therefore, don't back yourself into a corner. If possible, adopt a plan that is flexible and that can be revised to reflect changing circumstances.

THE PRINCIPAL RESIDENCE EXEMPTION

Surprisingly, a cornerstone of the tax planning strategies for your vacation property is the *principal residence* exemption. Probably, more Canadians make use of this exemption than any other, and yet it is also the most misunderstood. The term *principal residence* implies that the particular property must be your primary, or main place of residence; in other words, the place where you make your home. However, *this is not the case.* In fact, the definition of principal residence in the *Income Tax Act* is quite broad, and will allow even a seasonal residence, a mobile home or a houseboat to be claimed as a person's principal residence if so desired.

We'll try to clear up some of the misconceptions, and outline how you may be able to maximize the tax benefit of this exemption.

Your Principal Residence Versus Your Home

If you and your spouse own more than one residential-type property (such as a house as well as a cottage), it is generally not necessary for you to decide which property is to be designated as the principal residence for capital gains tax purposes until the year that either property is sold or disposed of. The fact that you show your home address on your income tax return does not mean that you are designating your house as your principal residence.

A Seasonal Residence Can Qualify as Your Principal Residence

A principal residence, by definition, is a dwelling place that is owned by you, or in which you have a part ownership interest, and it must be *ordinarily inhabited* by you, your spouse, or a child, *during the year.* A seasonal residence that you use for weekends or vacations can therefore qualify, because you will meet the test of having occupied the property for some period or periods of time during the year. You are not required to inhabit the property throughout the year.

You Don't Have to Move to Your Vacation Property

You do not have to move to your cottage or vacation home on a permanent or year-round basis in order to qualify it for the principal residence exemption. The "183 day rule" that is sometimes used in determining whether a person is a resident of Canada has no relevance whatsoever in this context. As long as you, your spouse or at least one of your children occupy the vacation property for some period or periods of time during the year, that is enough to bring you within the principal residence definition.

When to Disclose Your Principal Residence to the CRA

Even if you have made up your mind that you will treat your vacation home as your principal residence for capital gains purposes, there is no need to disclose this when you file your income tax return. You would continue to show your home address and your mailing address of your permanent residence, if that is what you have been doing all along. As far as the CRA is concerned, you need not work through the principal residence exemption formula until the year that you dispose of a property. At that time, you can make your final decision on whether to designate the property as your principal residence for some or all of the years of ownership.

Principal Residence Exemption Is Calculated Under a Formula

It is not simply a matter of establishing a property as your principal residence at the time that you are about to sell it, in order to claim a full exemption from capital gains tax. Instead, the exemption is calculated by reference to the number of years that you owned the property, and the number of years that you are able to *designate* it as your principal residence for capital gains tax purposes. The exemption formula is as follows:

$$\frac{\text{Number of years after 1971 designated as your principal residence, } \textbf{plus "1"}}{\text{Number of years after 1971 that you owned the property}} = \text{exemption fraction}$$

The Principal Residence Exemption Formula

It is worth spending a few minutes now to understand how the exemption formula works, in order for you to be able to estimate how much tax will arise in the future. Upon an actual disposition during your lifetime, or a deemed disposition on death, you or your executor(s) would need to do the following:

1. First, calculate the capital gain in the usual way. This means taking the actual proceeds of disposition (or the fair market value in the case of a deemed disposition) and subtracting the selling expenses if any, and the adjusted cost base.
2. Next, you would apply the exemption fraction described above to determine how much of the capital gain is exempt.

3. The remainder is the capital gain that you would have to report in your tax return, and 50 percent of that amount would be included in your taxable income.

    The following case illustrates how the exemption formula works.

PLANNING TO PROTECT ● *How Karen and Ron Made the*
Most of the Exemption Formula

Karen and Ron bought a house in 1992 for $400,000. In 1995, they bought a cottage for $200,000. In 2017, they decided to sell both the house and the cottage and to move into a rental condo. The house was sold for $700,000 and the cottage for $300,000. In this simple fact situation, it doesn't take a mathematical genius to figure out that the principal residence exemption should be claimed on the house, because it has the larger gain. However, strange as it might seem, a small principal residence exemption can also be claimed on the cottage because of the "plus one" in the formula.

In order to obtain a 100 percent exemption on the house, it could be treated as Karen's and Ron's principal residence for the years 1992 to 2016 inclusive. This works out to 25 years (when you include both 1992 and 2016). The "plus one" makes the numerator equal to 26.

The denominator of the fraction is all of the years of ownership (1992 to 2017), which is 26. Therefore, the fraction is 26 over 26, which is 100 percent. This means that the $300,000 gain on the house will be tax-free.

Because of the "plus one" in the formula, it was not necessary to designate the house for the 2017 calendar year. This allows Karen and Ron to designate the cottage as their principal residence for capital gains tax purposes for the 2017 year. They can't designate any other years, since they have used them for the house. Since the cottage was purchased in 1995, there were 23 years of ownership up to, and including, the year of sale (i.e. 2017). Therefore, the principal residence exemption fraction for the cottage will be:

$$\frac{1 + 1}{23} = 8.7\%$$

Therefore, 8.7 percent of the gain realized on the sale of the cottage will be tax-free under the principal residence exemption. This isn't much, but some exemption on the $100,000 cottage capital gain is certainly better than nothing.

· ·

WILL PLANNING AND YOUR VACATION PROPERTY

It is extremely important that you take the potential capital gains tax on your vacation property into account when designing your will. Since capital gains resulting from the deemed disposition of property at the time of death will one day have to be reported in the final income tax return, your or your spouse's portion of the overall income tax bill for the final year will relate to such capital gains.

Wills are always drafted in such a way that the executors are instructed to pay the deceased's *debts*. One such debt would be the income tax for the deceased's final year. The typical will then goes on to describe the specific bequests to various beneficiaries, and what is left (the *residue*) usually goes to one person or is divided equally among various people. Because the capital gains tax on a vacation property has to be accounted for *before* the specific bequests and the distribution of the residue, inequities among beneficiaries can occur unintentionally, as revealed in the following example.

PLANNING TO PROTECT ● *Freda's Children Learn About Capital Gains Tax the Hard Way!*

Freda wants to divide her estate between her two children, Andrea and Simon. She has $800,000 in cash and securities, mostly from the sale of her Winnipeg house earlier this year. She used the principal residence exemption to exempt a large capital gain from tax. She also has a vacation chalet in Alberta that is worth about $800,000. She bought the chalet five years ago for $400,000.

She wants to make the administration of her estate as simple as possible. Therefore, she decides to leave the chalet (worth about $800,000) to Andrea, and her remaining assets (also worth about $800,000) to Simon. Thus, each will get 50 percent of the estate—or will they?

Well, if you were Andrea, it may not be a bad result! After Freda's death, she will get the chalet, and Simon will get what's left, minus the capital gains tax on the chalet that went to Andrea! Capital gains tax of about $92,000 (50 percent of $400,000 capital gain and assuming a 46 percent effective income tax rate) must be reported in Freda's final income tax return, and this tax must be paid out of the cash or securities in Freda's estate. Since her will made a *specific bequest* of the chalet to Andrea, the capital gains tax had the effect of reducing the residue, which was Simon's.

Obviously, this is not what Freda intended. Since she really wanted her estate to be divided equally between Andrea and Simon, she could have left out the specific bequest of the chalet to Andrea, and requested that the residue was to be split 50/50. She could also have stated that it was her desire that Andrea was to get the ownership of the chalet as part of her 50 percent share of the estate. Provision could also have been made in the will for the possibility that the value of the chalet might be greater than the dollar value of Andrea's 50 percent share of the estate (after deducting whatever taxes are owing). In that event, Andrea could make up the shortfall with a payment to the estate, if she really wanted the chalet. Otherwise, it could be sold by the executors, and the proceeds simply added to the other assets and be distributed 50/50 to Simon and Andrea.

• •

PLANNING STRATEGIES FOR YOUR VACATION HOME

The following tax planning strategies may help you achieve savings in the amount of capital gains tax that would otherwise be payable when you sell or transfer the ownership of your vacation home:

- Make optimum use of the principal residence exemption.
- Shift the future growth in the value of your vacation property, by:
  – a direct transfer of ownership to children or grandchildren;
  – transferring ownership to a trust; or
  – creating a life interest and a remainder interest form of ownership.

Some of these strategies may produce actual tax savings while others are intended to achieve merely a deferral of tax.

Utilize the Principal Residence Exemption

ONLY ONE PRINCIPAL RESIDENCE PER FAMILY AFTER 1981

This is now a bit of ancient history, but prior to 1981, it was possible for a married couple to "double up" on the principal residence if they owned two residential type properties, such as a house and cottage. Although the rules had always stated that an individual can only designate one property as a principal residence for a particular calendar year, there was nothing to prevent the husband from owning one property and designating it as his principal residence, and the wife owning the other property and designating it as her principal residence.

Unfortunately, this loophole was plugged in 1981 when the rules were changed so as to allow a "family unit" consisting of the taxpayer, the person's spouse, and any children under the age of 18, to be able to designate only one property for a particular calendar year. It is no longer possible for a husband and wife to obtain exemptions from capital gains taxation on *two* properties for gains accruing after 1981. Although, as outlined above, the exemption can be used on either the primary residence or a seasonal residence (or shared between them), some capital gains tax will inevitably be payable on one property or the other, if both have appreciated in value.

DOUBLING UP THE EXEMPTION FOR PROPERTIES ACQUIRED BEFORE 1982

In the case of properties that were both acquired before 1982, it has usually made sense from a tax planning viewpoint for the husband to be the sole owner of one property, and the wife to be the sole owner of the other. (This is strictly for technical reasons because of peculiarities in the principal residence definition, and in the income tax rules relating to spousal transfers.) Thus, it is only the post-1981 appreciation in the value of one of the properties that would eventually be subject to capital gains tax (assuming that the principal residence designations after 1981 are allocated entirely to one property).

JOINTLY-OWNED PROPERTIES ACQUIRED BEFORE 1982

In the case of jointly-owned properties that were both acquired before 1982, it may not be possible to *double up* on the principal residence exemption up to the end of 1981. In some cases, it may be desirable from a tax planning viewpoint, for the husband to make a gift of his half-interest in one of the properties to his wife, and for the wife to gift her half-interest in the other property to the husband. If you are in this situation, you should get professional tax advice to determine whether it is necessary to go through the red tape of creating separate ownership for each property, and whether, after all these years, the potential tax savings relating to the pre-1981 accrued gains are large enough to make it worth the trouble. You should also speak with your lawyer to find out whether there are any family law or other legal implications of making such ownership changes.

CLAIMING PRINCIPAL RESIDENCE ON THE PROPERTY
WITH THE LARGER GAIN

Some people may find themselves in the situation of owning one or more properties that are worth less than what they paid for them. Therefore, capital gains tax is not a problem—at least for the time being. Or, in the case of a property that has not been held for a long time, the current market value may not be much higher than the original cost. Also, because some locations are more desirable than others, and real estate prices across Canada do not necessarily follow the same pattern of change, the appreciation in the value of a person's house may be quite small compared to the gain on the vacation property.

Every situation is different, and we can't possibly cover all of the permutations and combinations in this chapter. The point that we are making is that you need to carefully consider how your principal residence exemption can be used in the most effective manner because one of the largest elements of the capital gains tax arising in your estate could be related to your vacation property.

USE ANOTHER FAMILY MEMBER'S PRINCIPAL RESIDENCE EXEMPTION

In some situations, it makes sense to arrange for a vacation property to be owned by a close family member who does not own any other residential property. This would allow the other person to designate the cottage as his or her principal residence for a number of years, thereby sheltering the appreciation in value from capital gains taxation.

PLANNING TO PROTECT ● *"Sheltering" Helen's Cottage from Capital Gains Taxation*

Helen is a widow in her seventies. She and her late husband Bruce bought a cottage a number of years ago for $130,000. It is currently worth about $500,000. She lives in a rental apartment and seldom goes to the cottage because of poor health. However, the cottage is used extensively by her son John and his wife Susan. Helen offered to transfer the ownership of the cottage to John as a gift, but he refused. Why?

From a capital gains tax viewpoint, John thought that it made sense to leave the ownership of the cottage in Helen's hands for the rest of her life, or until such time that she wished to sell it. John and his family could continue to have the use and enjoyment of the cottage, even though the ownership remained in his mother's hands. Meanwhile, the future appreciation in the value of the cottage would be sheltered from capital gains taxation by Helen's principal residence exemption. Even though she seldom visited the cottage, the cottage was able to satisfy the occupancy test in the principal residence definition, because of her occasional visits. In addition, a child (John) was occupying it for portions of each year.

Eventually, the ownership of the cottage would pass to John under Helen's will, and no capital gains tax would arise on Helen's death. For capital gains tax purposes, John's cost would become the fair market value of the cottage at the time of Helen's death. Thus, only the subsequent increase in value after Helen's death would be subject to capital gains taxation in John's hands, and only at such time that John eventually sells or transfers the ownership of the cottage.

If Helen had transferred the ownership to John during her lifetime, no immediate capital gains tax would have been payable by Helen, because of the principal residence exemption. However, once the property was in John's hands, any subsequent appreciation in the value of the cottage beyond the current $500,000 value would one day have attracted capital gains taxation in his hands. This is because he already owned a house and it would be better for him to earmark his own principal residence exemption for the house, rather than the cottage.

The strategy of leaving the ownership of a vacation property in the parent's hands made sense in Helen's and John's situation because he was going to be the sole beneficiary of her estate. In situations where other siblings are involved, or if there is any possibility that the parent will remarry, the potential savings in capital gains tax by leaving the cottage in the parent's name could be outweighed by other factors. For example, from a family law viewpoint, a vacation property may be subject to the "matrimonial home" rules.

● ●

Transfer the Ownership to a Child

One way of preventing a capital gain from arising on the future death of you or your spouse is to transfer the ownership *now* to one or more children. Such a transfer (either as a sale, or as a gift) would have the effect of shifting the ownership and the future growth in value to one or more of your children. Since children normally outlive their parents, such a move will generally have the effect of postponing the time at which there will be a deemed disposition at fair market value of the vacation property. However, as discussed earlier, a transfer of ownership at this time could give rise to an immediate taxable capital gain, because your deemed proceeds of disposition for capital gains purposes would be the current fair market value of the property.

Up to 1994, a straightforward transfer of ownership to a child was one way of taking advantage of a special $100,000 lifetime capital gains exemption, since such a transfer had to be recorded at fair market value for capital gains purposes. Unfortunately, this $100,000 capital gains exemption is long gone.

The prime motivating factor in transferring ownership to one or more children is that the odds are that the cottage can "stay in the family" for a much longer period of time, before capital gains tax is triggered at the time of someone's death under the deemed disposition rule. However, there are a host of personal, legal and financial factors to consider in deciding whether or not to make such a transfer. Some of the questions you should ask yourself are:

- How will you decide which child or children to transfer the property to?
- What if a child has a future marriage break-up? Will the applicable provincial family law legislation exempt the vacation home from any marriage settlement?
- Should you keep the ownership of the property as a hedge against inflation? Maybe the time will come when you would want to sell the property in order to be able to invest the sale proceeds so as to have additional investment income to live on during your retirement years?

Transfer the Ownership to a Trust

Over the past 20 to 30 years, many vacation properties were transferred into family trusts for tax and estate planning reasons. In spite of various tax changes, trusts continue to be extremely effective estate planning tools in many situations. There are several reasons for the popularity of a trust being used as a vehicle for holding the ownership of a vacation property. Many people are reluctant to transfer ownership directly to one or more children for a variety of reasons. For example, how can you know what the relationship will be like with any of your children in the future? You may not want to lose the legal control over your vacation home, as well as the legal right to use the property. A trust is a useful vehicle for dealing with some of these concerns, and for keeping the ownership of the cottage "one step removed" from the children.

In spite of the "21-year deemed disposition rule" for trusts (which is outlined in Chapter 6, "Understanding Trusts"), trusts continue to be a useful device for holding the ownership of vacation properties in many situations.

USING A FAMILY TRUST

The following example illustrates the use of a *family trust* to hold the ownership of a vacation property.

PLANNING TO PROTECT ● *Lawrence and Christina Place*
Their Cottage into a Family Trust

Lawrence and Christina bought their cottage three years ago and it has not appreciated in value. However, they are worried about the large amount of future capital gains tax that may be payable in one of their estates under the deemed disposition rule. The cottage was purchased in joint names with the right of survivorship. This means that on Christina's death, her half interest in the cottage will automatically go to Lawrence if he survives her. Similarly, Lawrence's part ownership interest will automatically go to Christina if he dies first. Christina's and Lawrence's wills both specify that if there is no "surviving spouse," the ownership of the cottage is to be transferred to their four grown children, with each getting a 25 percent ownership interest. Christina and Lawrence have talked over their plans with the children and all feel that when the time comes, they can work things out as co-owners of the property.

Lawrence believes that the cottage will double in value over the next 10 or 15 years. Having paid about $150,000 for the cottage, this means that there could be a capital gain of $150,000 or more that would have to be reported in Lawrence's or Christina's final income tax return, depending on who outlives the other. On a gain of $150,000, the taxable capital gain would be $75,000 and the income tax (assuming a 50 percent marginal rate) could be about $38,000.

Lawrence and Christina decide that it makes sense to transfer the ownership of the cottage into a trust for the benefit of the children now, rather than waiting for the inevitable to happen and letting the ownership pass on death. Since the cottage has been owned for only a short period of time, and has not gone up in value, no capital gain has to be recognized on the transfer of the cottage into the trust.

Under the terms of the trust, Lawrence and Christina are given the legal right to occupy the cottage for the rest of their lives. They are also the income beneficiaries, which means that in the event that the cottage is sold by the trust, and the sales proceeds are invested rather than used to buy another cottage, they would be entitled to receive the interest and dividend income on the investments. This gives them a measure of protection if their retirement income from other sources falls short of their future financial needs.

The capital beneficiaries of the trust will be the four children. This means that after the death of Christina and Lawrence, the trust will be dissolved and the ownership of the cottage will be transferred to them in equal shares.

Lawrence and Christina should probably make the trust discretionary so as to give the trustees of the trust the ability to transfer the ownership of the cottage to the children in unequal shares, or possibly to give the full ownership of the cottage to one of the children, to the exclusion of the others. Also, because of the "21-year deemed disposition rule" (discussed in Chapter 6, "Understanding Trusts"), such a trust should be written in such a way as to permit the cottage ownership to be transferred to one or more of the children at any time after the creation of the trust, rather than only at the time of Christina's or Lawrence's death, whichever occurs later.

By setting up such a trust in the correct way, Lawrence and Christina will shift the future growth in value of the cottage to their children. By only retaining a life interest in the trust, no capital gains tax will arise on Christina's or Lawrence's death with respect to the cottage. A life interest terminates at the time of a person's death, and has no value for capital gains tax purposes.

- -

CHOOSING THE TRUSTEES OF THE TRUST

With this type of family trust, you do not need to hire a trust company to act as the trustee. In fact, most trust companies would decline to act as a trustee for the type of discretionary trust that is so often used as a vehicle for holding the ownership of a cottage. There are too many family issues to consider and too many potential conflicts (or lawsuits!) if the trustees were to ever decide to transfer the ownership to one of the capital beneficiaries, to the exclusion of the others.

Under trust law, there is nothing to prevent the *settlors* of the trust from being the *trustees* (those who hold legal ownership of the trust). However, there may be a tax problem in doing this. Under a particular set of rules that apply to *revocable trusts*, the trust might be forced to recognize a capital gain (assuming the cottage goes up in value) if the cottage were to be transferred to any of the children during the lifetime of the settlor(s) of the trust. We mentioned earlier that the trust should be designed so that it can be terminated, if necessary, prior to its twenty-first anniversary, so as to avoid the 21-year deemed disposition rule. Ordinarily, a trust can distribute property that has appreciated in value to any capital beneficiary who resides in Canada on a rollover basis, without having to recognize the accrued gain for tax purposes. However, in the case of trusts that are subject to the revocable trust rules (Subsection 75(2) of the *Income Tax Act*), a rollover to the capital beneficiaries can generally be done only after the death of the settlor(s).

It is usually possible to prevent the application of the revocable trust rules, however it is not possible to go into the technical details. You should ensure that you fully understand all of the consequences of putting the ownership of your cottage into a trust, and be sure to get legal and tax advice from an accountant and lawyer who are familiar with the special rules relating to the taxation of trusts.

Create a Life Interest and a Remainder Interest

Another planning technique that can produce results that are similar to those achieved with the use of trust, involves the creation of a *life interest* and a *remainder interest* in your cottage. If you already own a vacation property, this would mean altering the form of ownership so that one or more of your children would be granted a remainder interest in the property. You and/or your spouse would retain a life interest.

If you are about to acquire a vacation property, you might consider arranging the purchase so that you and/or your spouse acquire the life interest in the property, and one or more of your children acquire the remainder interest. This could be a good way of deferring capital gains taxation, provided that you are absolutely certain about the full ownership ultimately passing to the particular child (or children) who hold the remainder interests, after the deaths of you and/or your spouse.

Under this form of ownership, the person who holds the life interest has the legal right to the use and enjoyment of the property for the rest of his or her life (unless something is done to intentionally terminate the life interest prior to the person's death). The person who acquires the remainder interest does obtain a type of ownership interest in the property, but there are no immediate rights to use the property. Basically, they must wait until the person who holds the life interest dies, at which time the full rights of ownership and use of the property will pass.

The life interest/remainder interest form of ownership can produce similar tax results to those that are achieved with a trust. However, you don't have as much flexibility as with a discretionary trust, because you need to decide now rather than later, who will ultimately get the ownership of the property.

On the other hand, a distinct advantage over a trust is that a vacation property that is owned by way of a life interest/remainder interest is not subject to the *21-year deemed disposition rule,* which applies to trusts. Whereas the "useful life" of most trusts is not more than 21 years because of the deemed disposition rule, you could hold a life interest in a vacation property for the rest of your life without there being any deemed disposition for capital gains tax purposes.

Why would you want to utilize this form of ownership? One reason might be that you are absolutely certain about whom the property should go to after your death. By creating the remainder interest now, rather than allowing the property to pass to the intended beneficiary under the terms of your will, no capital gains tax will arise at the time of your death. This is because the termination of your life interest does not attract capital gains taxation, under the present income tax rules.

However, there is always a catch. Unfortunately, the creation of the life interest and remainder interest is treated for capital gains purposes as a deemed disposition for proceeds equal to the fair market value of the property at that time. Therefore, if you currently own a property that has gone up in value, the creation of a remainder interest in favour of one of your children would trigger a taxable capital gain, and income tax would be payable now rather than later.

SHOULD YOU PAY TAX NOW OR LATER?

The dilemma you may be facing is whether to "bite the bullet" now and pay the capital gains tax based on today's fair market value, or leave things as they are and have your estate bear the capital gains tax burden at the time of your death, based on that fair market value.

When it comes to tax planning, a good principle to follow is that you should never trigger a tax liability any sooner than you have to. Although your arithmetic might show that it is cheaper to trigger the capital gain now and pay the applicable tax than to pay tax in the future on a much higher gain, there is still no way of knowing when the future *taxable event* (death) will occur. Therefore, it is usually wise for one to plan his or her affairs so that capital gains taxes can be postponed until the time of death, rather than triggering taxable capital gains on transfers of ownership to a child (grandchild) or trust during one's lifetime. However, it is difficult to generalize, because everyone's situation is different.

BUYING LIFE INSURANCE TO COVER FUTURE TAX LIABILITIES

We have devoted all of Chapter 15 to life insurance. However, it is worth mentioning here that in many situations, the least expensive solution to the capital gains tax problem on your vacation property may be to purchase enough life insurance to cover the future capital gains tax liability. Therefore, instead of setting up a trust (and possibly paying tax on a taxable capital gain that is triggered on the transfer into the trust), it may be better to acquire some form of permanent life insurance (such as *universal life* or *Term-to-100* insurance) to provide funds to cover the tax.

Obviously, there is a cost in taking out life insurance, and the older you are, the more expensive it is. If you are in your sixties or seventies, the premiums may be prohibitive on the amount of insurance that would fully cover the future capital gains tax liability. A further consideration is that the capital gains tax exposure on your vacation property will keep rising, if the property grows in value. Therefore, the amount of life insurance that you take out today may not be enough in 5, 10 or 20 years' time.

USING A CORPORATION TO OWN YOUR VACATION PROPERTY

It is almost always a bad idea to utilize a corporation to hold the ownership of a property that is for the personal use and enjoyment of the shareholder of the corporation or members of his or her family. Suffice to say that there can be a variety of adverse income tax implications. In particular, the shareholder may have to report a *taxable benefit* each year in his or her income tax return, based on an *imputed rent* calculation of the value of the personal use of the corporate-owned property.

For many years, one exception to the rule is where a so-called *single purpose corporation* was used to hold the ownership of a vacation property that is located in the United States. This had been a common practice for many years as a device for avoiding U.S. estate tax, and this is mentioned in Chapter 11, "Tax and Estate Planning If You Own U.S. Assets." Even this strategy is now fraught with Canadian and U.S. tax problems.

PLANNING TIPS

We have outlined the various tax and estate planning strategies that may be appropriate in your situation. Keep the following things in mind:

- If you are thinking of selling or changing the ownership of your vacation property in the near future, whatever you do, talk it over with your family before you act.
- If you are planning to leave your cottage, camp, or ski chalet to one or more children under your will, discuss your plans with all your children now. It may be better to resolve any hard feelings now, rather than causing an irreparable family rift after you have gone.
- If you are planning to leave the cottage to your children under a joint ownership arrangement, is that really such a good idea? Your hope might be that the cottage will be the "glue" that keeps the family together after you're gone. However, this might be the last thing that the children would want. And they might be unwilling to admit their true feelings about this to you or your spouse.

There are thousands of vacation properties that are jointly owned by second- and even third-generation descendants of the original owners. Everybody gets along reasonably well, and they manage to sort out the various problems of sharing the use and financial responsibilities. However, there are also many other situations where the jointly-owned vacation home has become the battleground for siblings, cousins and in-laws who can't agree on anything. Talk over your plans with your family, and speak to your tax and legal advisors to help you reach a decision.

WHERE TO GET MORE INFORMATION

If you own a cottage, ski chalet or second residence, consider subscribing to *Cottage Life* magazine. It is a constant source of useful information, and often contains articles or letters to the editor that deal with financial and tax matters.

Internet

You will find many helpful websites to assist your research including *www.homebuyer.ca* and *www.cottagelife.com*. Do Google searches under keywords such as "recreational property," "cottage property," "vacation property," etc.

Books

One of the authors, Douglas Gray, has written or co-written several relevant real estate books that could be helpful references, including the following titles:

- *The Canadian Guide to Buying and Owning Recreational Property in Canada*
- *101 Streetsmart Condo-Buying Tips for Canadians*
- *The Canadian Landlord's Guide: Expert Advice to Become a Profitable Real Estate Investor* (with Peter Mitham)
- *Making Money in Real Estate: The Canadian Guide to Profitable Investment in Residential Property*
- *Real Estate Investing for Canadians for Dummies* (with Peter Mitham)
- *The Canadian Snowbird Guide*

SUMMARY

If you did not know it before, you now realize that the capital gains tax implications of owning a cottage or second residence are rather complicated. A cottage can be your principal residence (for purposes of an exemption from capital gains taxation), even though your main residence is in the city. Options do exist for holding the ownership of the second residence, in order to reduce or postpone capital gains tax for as long as possible.

? Frequently
: Asked Questions

1. *I am planning to sell my cottage next year, which has gone way up in value. My wife and I are going to move there from our house in our city, and establish it as our principal residence. This will make the entire capital gain on the cottage tax-free—right?*

    Wrong. First, the principal residence exemption does not depend on whether your vacation home is your "main" residence, nor does it matter if you show it as the address on your T1 income tax return. Secondly, the principal residence exemption is based on a formula that takes into account the number of years of ownership, and the number of years the particular property is *designated* as your principal residence (for capital gains purposes only). Read this chapter and the examples to see how the rules and the formula work.

2. *I own a vacation property that is surrounded by 15 acres of land. Can I claim the principal residence exemption for the entire property?*

    The principal residence automatically allows one-half hectare of land to be included with the dwelling as a principal residence. This is equivalent to about 1.25 acres. The *Income Tax Act* also allows land in excess of one-half hectare to be included under the principal residence umbrella, provided that the taxpayer can demonstrate that the excess land is necessary for the person's "use and enjoyment" of the property as a principal residence.

Privately-Owned Businesses

"The final test of greatness in a CEO is how well he chooses a successor and whether he can step aside and let his successor run the company."

PETER DRUCKER

INTRODUCTION

If you are an owner or owner/manager of a privately-owned business, you already know that you face formidable challenges. Creating an effective succession/exit arrangement and estate plan are just two of them. This chapter should help you gain a better understanding of the factors that can mean success or failure for businesses such as yours, and outline some planning strategies that may enable your business to survive and prosper for many years to come.

If you are an owner in a business run by a related family member, this chapter is particularly relevant. There are more than 100,000 family businesses in Canada, and they employ more than half of the people who are working in Canada today. Such businesses also account for more than 70 percent of the Gross National Product. From Confederation to the present day, family-owned businesses have been the major driving force in building and sustaining our economy.

Throughout this chapter, we use the expression *family-owned business* in a broad way to describe any type of privately-owned company that is owned and operated by one or more individuals. One thinks of car dealerships, insurance agencies, small manufacturing companies, or even family farming businesses, to name but a few. Sometimes they are owned by one individual. In other cases, the business may be owned by a number of members of one family, or sometimes by unrelated individuals. We think of them all as "family businesses" because they are not public companies, whose shares may be purchased by anyone.

The topics covered in this chapter include:

- background information on family and privately-owned businesses in Canada
- the importance of having *a plan*

- the *planning process*, including
  - analyzing your financial situation
  - establishing your objectives
  - implementation, and
  - reviewing the plan on a regular basis
- tax planning
- shareholder agreements
- creditor-proofing your business when estate planning

Unfortunately for business owners and their families, the deck is stacked against them. Many studies and surveys have revealed that more than two-thirds of family-owned businesses do not survive through the changes of ownership and management that occur as a result of the business being handed down to the next generation. Furthermore, the instances of a family-owned business surviving through the third generation are extremely rare—perhaps only one in a hundred. Given their significance in the fabric of Canadian life, why is the failure rate so high? Competition from abroad and technological change are two factors. In fact, it may come as a surprise to learn that the prime reason for the failure of family-owned businesses is the absence of effective succession planning.

Many books and countless articles have been written about family-owned business, and much of the literature promotes the idea that every business owner's dream is to pass on the ownership of the company to his or her children. In spite of the low survival rate of family-owned businesses when ownership has passed from one generation to the next, there is a commonly-held belief that with proper and effective planning, one can "beat the odds."

While this may be true for some, in many, if not most situations, no amount of planning or expertise will make it feasible to keep the business in the family. Sometimes, success means that the value of the business gets too high, making a family succession arrangement impractical. Fortunately or unfortunately (depending on your point of view), in the real world of "family business," it often makes more sense to find an outside buyer, or to have the current owner/manager adopt an exit strategy that does not involve a family succession arrangement.

All too often, one or more of the essential ingredients for a successful transition to the next generation are missing.

PLANNING TO PROTECT ● *Bob Considers an "Interim CEO" Until His Children Can Take Over*

Bob is the owner/manager of a small tool and die company, which he started 20 years ago. The business is very successful, and he is able to take a salary and bonus each year of more than $400,000. Life is good. However, Bob is getting tired of 16-hour days. He is now in his mid-fifties, and ready to take early retirement. He loves the idea of the business staying in the family. His two children are working in the business, but they are only in their early twenties, and far too young to take on the leadership role in running the company right now. What should Bob do?

Bob could consider bringing an interim CEO on board, to run the company for the next 5 or 10 years (maximum). The new CEO would bridge the gap between Bob's retirement, and the time when one of the children is ready to take over the CEO role. In fact, one of the new CEO's main responsibilities would be to help develop the management and leadership skills of the children, and to groom one of them to take over the CEO role in due course.

• •

Sometimes, a lack of talent amongst one's children is not the problem.

PLANNING TO PROTECT ● *No Easy Answers for Catherine's Family*

Catherine is the owner/manager of a highly successful advertising agency. She has just turned 60, and is thinking about an "exit strategy." She has three extremely capable children in their thirties. Each of them is ready, willing and able to take over the management of the business. They are all MBAs. None of them lacks confidence in being able to learn the business in a flash, and run it profitably.

The trouble is, Catherine's children have never been able to get along with one another and Catherine does not want to play favourites. In her current will, she leaves the ownership of the company to all three of them in equal shares. She does not currently have enough outside wealth to be able to leave 100 percent of the company to one of the children, and assets of equal value to the other two. Deep down, Catherine knows that transferring the ownership of the business to the children (one-third each) and letting them work out who among them should become the new CEO, would be a disaster. The chances are that they would come to blows, and what's left of the family harmony among them would be destroyed. What should she do?

There are no easy answers for this one. Catherine needs to explore the alternatives that are open to her, and she should consider involving the children in the process. Possibly, the best strategy is to sell the business now, take the money, and enjoy life!

• •

Another common reason for a family succession arrangement not being feasible is that none of the children has the slightest interest in working in the company. Many articles have been written about why children of "business families" so often decide to pursue careers outside the family firm. Often the owner/manager's shining example to his children as an entrepreneur and builder is the very reason that the children want to pursue their own goals, rather than "following in Daddy's footsteps."

Having painted such gloomy pictures of family business succession planning, does this mean that you, the business owner, should simply give up? Definitely not!

You owe it to yourself and to your family to develop a succession plan or exit strategy that recognizes the realities of your business and family circumstances. You need both an emergency plan that would come into play if you died suddenly or became mentally or physically disabled, and you need a long-term plan. Perhaps a family succession arrangement is possible in your situation, with proper planning. Alternatively, some other plan, such as a sale of the company to an outsider, or a management buy-out, may be the best long-term strategy for you to pursue. Perhaps preserving the family's wealth via a sale to outsiders should be more important to you than keeping the business, whatever the financial consequences.

THE IMPORTANCE OF HAVING A PLAN

Consider some of the consequences if you were to die suddenly:

- Would anyone know what to do at the office—which customers or suppliers to call, what to say to any outside lenders?
- Is your will up to date, and does it reflect your current wishes on what you want done with the business after your death? Even if you have not decided on any long-term strategy, you should at least have an emergency plan in the event that you were to die suddenly and prematurely.
- Do you know roughly how much capital gains tax would be payable if you were to die tomorrow? Are any arrangements in place to ensure that your estate has enough liquidity to pay the taxes arising on your death?
- Have you explored various tax and estate planning strategies (e.g. an *estate freeze*) for reducing or postponing the capital gains tax that would be payable as a result of your death?
- Have you considered the use of life insurance to cover the capital gains tax arising in your estate, or as a means of funding another shareholder's purchase of your shares of the company?
- Who would take over the day-to-day management of the business? Have you been grooming a successor?
- Does your spouse or any of your children have the qualities to take on the top leadership role as CEO? Some managers are good "caretakers," but have poor leadership skills.

These are just some of the questions that should give you food for thought.

Most business owners have put in too much "blood, sweat and tears" to contemplate the possibility that the business will go down the drain after the owner's death because of a lack of planning. Where do you start?

Seeing the Big Picture and Being "Strategic" in Your Thinking

One of the hardest things for most owner/managers is to step back from the day-to-day affairs of the business and to think strategically. Looking at the big picture is not easy. It means taking off your "manager" hat, and putting on your "owner" hat. Perhaps the manager of the business (i.e. you!) is not doing such a good job anymore, and has become complacent. Perhaps it means facing the fact that your son or daughter who is working in the business does not have what it takes to assume the management of the business.

Alternatively, you may not want to admit to yourself that the business is worth a lot more today than it might be in 5 or 10 years. Therefore it may be more sensible to sell the business now, under an arrangement where you could stay on for a few years under some transition arrangement. But what do you do with your time if you sell the business? You have no hobbies, and the business has been your life!

THE PLANNING PROCESS

There is certainly no boiler-plate or off-the-shelf planning process that will work in all cases. However, here are some suggestions on how you should go about it. We have identified four phases of the planning process:
1. Analyze your financial situation.
2. Establish your objectives.
3. Implement the plan.
4. Review the plan on a regular basis.

Analyze Your Financial Situation

Start by analyzing your current financial position. Ask your accountant and tax advisor to help you determine the current *fair market value* of your business, and prepare a statement of net worth. Include an estimate of the capital gains tax that would arise on your death. For this, you need to know the *adjusted cost base* of your shares of the company, as well as the fair market value of the shares. It may be a good idea to obtain a formal independent valuation of the business. Poor decisions are often made because a business owner has grossly over-estimated, or under-estimated the value of the family business.

If you owned your company before 1972, your adjusted cost base may be the fair market value of your shares on December 31, 1971 (the so-called *valuation day* when capital gains taxation was introduced in Canada). During the 1970s, private companies were allowed to pay out special non-taxable dividends that, in some cases, reduced the adjusted cost base of the shares. Your accountant or tax advisor might need to examine old financial statements and corporate tax returns for the company to see whether this was the case.

You may also have taken advantage of the lifetime capital gains exemption for shares of a small business corporation, by "stepping up" your adjusted cost base by up to the current exemption amount, depending on your circumstances. Ask for your tax advisor's help in determining your adjusted cost base and in estimating your capital gains tax exposure on your shares of the business.

Establish Your Objectives

Establishing objectives is easier said than done, especially for a business owner who has not followed a disciplined approach in business planning, and who says: "It's all in my head."

THE "SWOT" ANALYSIS

One useful tool is the so-called *SWOT* analysis. This stands for:

- Strengths
- Weaknesses
- Opportunities
- Threats

You could hold a strategic planning workshop session for some of the key people in your business, or perhaps for your family members who are involved in the business. Put the four words on a blackboard or flip chart, and ask the participants to discuss the factors or events that could fall into each of these categories. This process may help you gain a better understanding of your business—both on the positive, as well as negative side.

Hold follow-up sessions to see how you can capitalize on the strengths of the business and exploit the opportunities. Also, look into ways of protecting you and your business on the downside. You may not be able to eliminate the threats to your business. However, what you can do is develop a defensive strategy.

LEADERSHIP TALENT EVALUATION TOOLS

You might also consider utilizing a management talent evaluation tool in order to get a better sense of the depth of management and leadership talent in your business. While this may be part of the implementation phase for some business owners, you may feel that this is a good preamble to establishing your objectives for the business. After all, what is the point of adopting an objective such as "pass down the ownership and management of the business to my eldest son," if your son is entirely lacking in the abilities needed for the role?

Information on leadership evaluation programs is available from the major accounting firms and management consulting firms, and from Canadian universities and colleges that offer business and MBA programs.

STRATEGIC PLANNING

Having used the SWOT analysis, or a management talent evaluation tool, you may now be ready to develop a strategic plan for your business. Establishing objectives for your business is really about *strategic planning*. Thousands of books are devoted to the subject. Our comments can merely scratch the surface.

However, here are a few suggestions:

- Do not look for immediate answers—this is a *process* that may take some time. It may take a while just to identify the *problems*.
- Carefully consider who should be involved in the process. Would it make sense to hire someone with strategic planning expertise to help you develop a long-term plan for the business?
- Keep an open mind, and be willing to consider all of the possible alternatives. Do not second guess or pre-empt the process by stating up front that you have already made up your mind on the course of action to follow. You would be wasting your money if you are simply hiring outside experts to validate your conclusions.

CONSIDER THE ALTERNATIVES

Consider such alternatives as:

- a family succession arrangement involving one or more of your children
- selling the business during your lifetime, perhaps to one of your competitors who would see this as an opportunity to achieve a greater market share, and obtain cost savings through economies of scale
- arranging a management buy-out, if there are key people in the business who have the talent and the financial resources to purchase the business from you on acceptable terms or
- taking the business public through an IPO (*initial public offering*), whereby your family might hold a significant stake in the company, but professional management is brought in, and control might pass to others

ESTABLISH REALISTIC GOALS

It is essential that you establish goals and objectives that are realistic and obtainable. Suppose that your two prime objectives are:

1. Position the company for a sale to an outside buyer within five years, by:
   - strengthening the management team, and grooming a successor to take over from me within five years
   - increasing the company's market share by 30 percent over the next five years

- increasing sales by 300 percent over the next five years
- improving net income before income tax by 15 percent a year

2. Implement an estate plan under which the bulk of my estate will go to my spouse, followed by an equal division of the remaining assets among our children after her death

There may be a number of different ways of achieving these goals. Perhaps over the next several years, you should send your key management people on intensive management and leadership programs, in order to prepare them for your retirement. There is also the expression: "you can't make a silk purse out of a sow's ear." Perhaps your existing management team is simply not up to the challenge. In that case, you might need to hire a recruiting firm to bring in one or more experienced managers from the outside.

From a tax and estate planning standpoint, a number of planning strategies could be considered for achieving the second objective stated above. An *estate freeze* is one of them (even though your intention is to sell the company). Spreading the ownership of the company amongst members of your family by means of an estate freeze might enable you to multiply the use of the $800,000 plus lifetime capital gains exemption when the arm's length sale eventually occurs (outlined later in this chapter).

Other things that you could do now depending on your situation, in order to lessen the capital gains tax that will arise on a future arm's length sale, include putting the ownership of the operating company underneath a family holding company. Then, substantial dividends equal to the after-tax profit of the business are paid each year to the holding company. This strategy may lessen the future capital gains tax when the holding company sells its shares of the operating subsidiary. Your tax advisor can enlighten you on the concept of *safe income* dividends, which would be relevant in this situation.

Every situation is different and you should not narrow your focus on only one or two scenarios. Your professional tax and legal advisors can help you identify and evaluate all of the alternatives, taking into account the various business, financial, taxation and personal factors.

WHO SHOULD BE INVOLVED IN HELPING YOU ESTABLISH OBJECTIVES?
The people you should involve in the objective-setting process could include:
- your spouse
- some or all of your children (and certainly any children who are involved in the business)
- your professional advisors, including your lawyer, accountant, tax advisor, insurance agent and investment advisor
- if applicable, the person who has served as your "mentor" through the years when you were building up the business

You may decide that some of the people mentioned above need not be involved at the early stages of objective-setting but rather during the implementation stage of your planning.

Implementation

All too often, the "best laid plans" of business owners fail to materialize. Lack of willpower, procrastination, or fear of what lies ahead may account for the failure to implement the objectives that have been set. In this critical stage, it is very important that someone (not necessarily yourself) play the role of "quarterback" or coordinator to ensure that everyone does what he or she is supposed to do, according to a timetable.

Consider using a "critical path planning" approach, under which the various elements of the implementation process are each given a time line and target completion date, and prime responsibility is assigned to particular individuals.

Review the Plan on a Regular Basis

All plans and strategies need to be reviewed from time to time, to ensure that they still make sense, in light of current circumstances.

Estate planning is an ongoing process. Your personal and financial circumstances will change through the years—sometimes for the better, and sometimes for the worse. Every effort should be made to ensure that the planning that you carry out today will withstand the test of time. Ideally, enough flexibility will have been built into your planning arrangements to accommodate unexpected changes in your financial or personal circumstances. This is why it is so important that you put your best effort into the planning process, and that you involve experienced outside professionals to help you decide what is best.

Many business owners follow the practice of setting aside one day a year to meet with their professional advisors (e.g. lawyer, accountant, tax advisor, investment advisor, and insurance agent). Although such a meeting can be quite expensive (most accountants and lawyers charge fees based on an hourly rate), we know from experience that the benefits of such a planning and review exercise can often far outweigh the costs, and provide you with viable options, peace of mind, and stress reduction.

TAX PLANNING IN THE FAMILY BUSINESS

One of the greatest challenges faced by business owners is finding ways to minimize the capital gains tax that will arise on a sale or other type of transfer of ownership.

As outlined in Chapter 8, "Death and Taxes," capital gains tax is imposed at the time of death because of the so-called *deemed disposition rule*. This means that if you, the business owner, decide to leave your shares of your company to your child under your will, whatever appreciation there has been in the value of your shares will be taxed as a capital gain in your final income tax return. Unfortunately, you cannot get around this rule by transferring the shares during your lifetime. As explained earlier, a gift of property including a family business is treated for capital gains purposes as if the transferor had received proceeds of disposition equal to the *fair market value* at the time of the transfer.

It is beyond the scope of this book to describe all of the strategies to reduce or defer capital gains tax on the sale or transfer of ownership of the business. However, we can alert you to a few that may be possible in your situation, and prepare you for discussions with your tax advisor(s).

$800,000 Plus Lifetime Capital Gains Exemption

The *Income Tax Act* provides a special exemption of over $800,000 of the capital gain arising on the disposition of shares of a *small business corporation* (e.g., for dispositions occurring in 2017, the gains exemption is $835,716). In order to qualify for the exemption, your business must:

- carry on an *active business* primarily in Canada
- at least 90 percent of the assets of the company must be used in the active business (meaning that investment holding companies generally do not qualify)

If you think this capital gains exemption may apply to your business (its use is limited where a person has a cumulative net investment loss), refer to Chapter 9 and speak to your tax advisor to see how you may be able to utilize it.

Estate Freezing

Estate freezing is a tax planning strategy that has the effect of freezing the value of a person's ownership interest in a private company to limit the amount of capital gains tax that will be imposed on the death of the individual, to the tax that relates to today's value of the business.

Typically, a freeze involves the current owner of the business exchanging his or her common shares for special, redeemable preferred shares that have a fixed redemption amount. Such a share exchange qualifies as a rollover for Canadian tax purposes, thereby avoiding any immediate capital gains tax. Any unrealized capital gain that is currently reflected in the owner's common shares (i.e. the excess of the current fair market value over the adjusted cost base) is merely shifted to the new preferred shares.

When a freeze is carried out, it is customary for new common shares of the business to be issued to the chosen successor(s) of the business. Sometimes, a discretionary family trust is utilized, if the business owner has not yet made up his or her mind as to which child or children should take over the business. Under the new share ownership structure after the freeze, future growth in the value of the business will accrue to the benefit of the common shareholders (e.g. one or more children). This could be as a result of them having direct ownership of the common shares, or by virtue of them being named as beneficiaries of a trust that owns the common shares. In either case, when the current owner dies, only the freeze shares will attract capital gains tax in his or her final income tax return.

This planning strategy is based on the assumption that the new common shareholder (i.e. the child) will outlive the parent. However, sometimes estate freezes "backfire" because the child who acquired the growth shares dies before the parent who froze his shares. Capital gains tax then becomes payable on the child's common shares of the business (assuming they have gone up in value since the estate freeze). Estate freezes are also discussed in Chapter 10.

Utilizing the Spousal Rollover

One of the most obvious ways of postponing capital gains tax on your death would be to leave your shares in the family business either outright, or in trust for your spouse. If you pass away before your spouse, no capital gains tax on your shares of the business would arise on your death, but would be postponed until the death of your spouse or until the business is sold after your death.

Family Farming Business

In Chapter 8, "Death and Taxes," we explained that a transfer of property between family members is generally treated for capital gains tax purposes as if the transfer had been made at fair market value. In the case of appreciated assets, this means triggering a capital gain on which income tax is payable.

Farming businesses are afforded different and far more generous treatment. For example:

- If property that is used in an active farming business (e.g. the farm land itself) is transferred to a spouse, child, grandchild, or great-grandchild of the person carrying on the business, the transfer is generally considered to take place at cost, not fair market value. Thus, no capital gain has to be reported.
- Farming businesses are also eligible for the $800,000 plus lifetime capital gains exemption similar to the one that applies for small business corporations. This exemption will save capital gains tax if the family farm business is being sold to a non-family member, where the above-mentioned *intergenerational exemption* does not apply.

Talk to a tax advisor who specializes in estate planning strategies that are unique to family farm businesses to explore which of them may be applicable in your case.

SHAREHOLDER AGREEMENTS

Potential Conflicts If There Is More Than One Shareholder

Many family businesses have a number of shareholders. Some businesses are essentially partnerships that are owned 50/50 by unrelated individuals. Second- and third-generation family businesses are often owned by a number of brothers, sisters and cousins. Sometimes they own equal shares in the business, even though only one of them is actively involved in running the company. This often leads to serious conflicts, for example, those who are not actively involved in the business may want the company to pay out all profits in the form of dividends each year. The family member who is running the company may feel that the company's profits are better utilized within the business (e.g. to reduce loans, or to acquire equipment). The remuneration level of family members who are employed in the business is also a bone of contention in many situations.

Utilizing a Buy/Sell Agreement

Where there is more than one shareholder of a private corporation, it is extremely useful for all of the parties to enter into a comprehensive shareholders' agreement. Such an agreement can deal with issues such as:

- the policy regarding the reinvestment of annual earnings in the business, or the payment of dividends
- the remuneration levels of officers and directors
- what happens if an owner/manager becomes seriously ill or permanently disabled
- what happens after the death of the shareholder to his or her shares in the company

Some shareholder agreements deal primarily with the last point, and are referred to as "buy/sell agreements." The typical buy/sell agreement sets out the terms and conditions under which the surviving shareholder, or the company itself, is to acquire the deceased's shares. This type of agreement is especially useful in situations where conflicts are likely to arise after the death of a shareholder. By hammering out the terms of the buy/sell transaction in advance, it is hoped that future problems or disputes will be averted.

Some buy/sell agreements call for a compulsory purchase by the surviving shareholder(s). The purchase price may be stated in the agreement itself (and revised from time to time by means of an Addendum to the agreement). Another approach is to set a formula for determining the purchase price (e.g. a formula based on a certain multiple of earnings or book value). Alternatively, the buy/sell agreement may require an independent third-party valuation of the company to be carried out by a major accounting firm or firm that specializes in business valuations.

If you are not the sole owner of the business, a shareholder agreement is a must, regardless of what approach you decide to take regarding the determination of the purchase sale price after a shareholder's death. The absence of a buy/sell agreement only leads to problems and conflicts, in many situations.

A shareholder agreement is almost as important as your will. One major advantage of having a shareholder agreement is that it could impose a binding legal obligation on the survivor(s) to acquire your shares from your estate. In that way, your spouse or children would not find themselves in the position after your death, where they cannot find any interested third-party buyer. Furthermore, in the absence of a binding buy/sell agreement, the other surviving shareholder(s) might be content to carry on with your spouse or children as their fellow shareholders. This might not be what you had in mind. It is one thing for you to own shares of a private company when you are actively involved in its management; your spouse or children might be in an entirely different position, and resent the imposition.

Funding a Buy/Sell Agreement with Life Insurance

If you already have a buy/sell agreement, or are thinking about putting one in place, consider how the purchase of shares after a shareholder's death will be funded. Will the surviving shareholder(s) have to obtain a bank loan to finance the purchase? What if the person has trouble obtaining a loan? Alternatively, should the company itself buy back the shares from your estate, using excess cash? What if the company is not in a financial position to do this, and is also unable to borrow any additional money from its banker? Are there other sources of funds (e.g. selling off part of the business)?

Of all the funding alternatives, life insurance usually makes the most sense. In fact, there can be significant income tax advantages in utilizing corporate-owned life insurance to provide the funding for buying back a deceased's shareholder's stake in the company. Talk to an experienced life insurance agent to explore the possibilities.

Here is a summary of the common methods of insurance funding options:

CORPORATE-OWNED INSURANCE

The corporation insures the lives of the shareholders and receives the insurance proceeds on their deaths. These funds are then used by the corporation to buy the deceased's shares, either from the estate of the deceased shareholder or from the surviving spouse.

CRISS-CROSS INSURANCE

With this type of policy, each shareholder of a corporation acquires a life insurance policy on each other's life. When one shareholder dies, the surviving shareholders receive the tax-free proceeds of the policy, then used to purchase the shares of the deceased from his or her beneficiaries or estate. The disadvantage of this type of structure is that the insurance cost on each shareholder can vary considerably depending on their health and age.

SPLIT-DOLLAR INSURANCE

This is a hybrid version of corporate and criss-cross insurance. In this example, each shareholder purchases a whole-life type of policy on the other shareholder. The cash value of the policy is assigned to the company, which the company receives when a shareholder dies. The surviving shareholders receive the face value of the policy minus the cash value. These funds are then used to purchase the shares. Most, if not all, of the premiums are paid for by the company.

KEY PERSON INSURANCE

In addition to buy/sell insurance, you should also consider disability and key person insurance. Disability insurance is covered in Chapter 15, "Life, Health and Disability Insurance." Although key person insurance is not directly related to a buy/sell agreement, you should be aware of this insurance option. Basically, it means that the key person or persons in the company are insured, usually the general manager or a managing partner. The purpose of the coverage is to provide funding for the company to weather the transition of a person who is integral to the operation of the business. This could include paying for temporary consulting expertise or hiring a replacement with extensive experience—anything to ensure that the company survives the loss of the key person.

CREDITOR-PROOFING YOUR BUSINESS

What if you are still running your business at the time you suddenly die? Maybe you are the key element to the business success, whether it is a family business or not. What would be the impact on the business and your estate? The business could cease to function after your death. If the business goes under, the creditors will start looking for assets. If you are liable under a personal guarantee of a corporation, or as a director, or if you are operating an unincorporated business, the assets of your estate could be at risk.

Here are some options to consider and discuss with your professional advisors to minimize the risk of eroding your estate before you die, or having your business creditors make a claim on your estate after your death. Make sure you obtain advice from your lawyer and accountant in advance.

Incorporate Your Business

The problem with a partnership or proprietorship type of business is that, in law, you and your business are deemed to be one and the same. This means a creditor can go after your personal assets.

The alternative is to incorporate your business. In law, you and your incorporated business are deemed to be separate legal entities. To get maximum protection from your corporation, always sign all documents in the corporate name, as an "authorized signatory."

Never Have Oral Agreements

Always make sure your business dealings are clear and put into writing to eliminate the risk of uncertainty. For example, if you died or were incapacitated, how would anyone know the details of the deal? Over time, people can innocently and honestly forget the details. Others could exploit the lack of paperwork for their own interests. If a lawsuit occurred, it is almost impossible to reconstruct and prove the facts, when there are differing and sometimes self-serving recollections of the bargain. This type of uncertainty puts your business in jeopardy and wastes a lot of time, energy and money, and creates a great deal of stress.

Don't Sign or Limit Personal Guarantees

There is no point in going to the effort of incorporating a company, if you nullify the personal protection by signing a personal guarantee of the corporate debts. Don't sign personal guarantees at all, for example, to suppliers, trade creditors, landlords, etc. Alternatively, only do so for a bank if absolutely necessary, and then limit the amount of liability. Get legal advice before you sign any guarantee or other security to a lender. Remember that the marketplace is competitive. Use that knowledge as leverage when negotiating with one creditor over another.

Don't Pledge Personal Security

Adopt a policy of not pledging any personal security, for example, your personal care, house or life insurance policy.

Transfer Property and Other Assets to Your Spouse

You can transfer the ownership of your home and other personal assets, such as your car, to your spouse. Obtain strategic legal advice in advance. That way, assets are not in your personal name. In the event of a marital breakup, the matrimonial home is deemed to be owned 50/50 in most situations anyway. Also, under the family relations legislation of most provinces, family assets are combined for calculation purposes and then divided in half in most cases.

Be Aware of Director Liability

If you are a director of a corporation, you do have potential liability risk particularly under government legislation, e.g. workers' compensation, employment standards, builder's lien, HST, GST, provincial sales tax, corporate income tax, employee deductions for EI/CPP, income tax, etc. Therefore, if you intend to be a director, re-think that option, or consider not owning any personal assets of consequence, in order to limit the personal risk.

Don't Have Your Spouse as Guarantor or Director

To limit the family's risk, you don't want to ask your spouse to act as a director, officer, or personal guarantor of your company debt. If your spouse is potentially legally exposed, it could create a lot of family and relationship stress.

Don't Have Joint Business Accounts

If you have a joint business account, and a creditor garnishes your bank account, they will seize all the funds in that account. By having separate accounts, you separate that risk.

Consider Spousal RRSPs

If your spouse is earning less than you are, you may wish to contribute to his or her RRSP, as a spousal RRSP. You get the RRSP tax deduction, but your spouse gets the money in his or her RRSP account. Therefore, if a creditor tries to collect on your RRSP with a court judgment, there will be less money available.

Consider RRSPs with Insurance Companies

If you have an RRSP, RRIF or non-registered investments with an insurance company, under certain circumstances, creditors are not able to collect on the RRSP. Check with your financial and legal advisor.

Consider Allocating CPP Primarily in Spouse's Name

Another income splitting option, which also has the effect of putting more money in your spouse's hands, is to ask the CPP to do a 50/50 split of your CPP pension with your spouse. You are entitled to start taking out your CPP at age 60, at a reduced amount. This approach means there is less money available for creditors from your personal income.

Lend Money to Your Corporation and Become a Secured Creditor

You could lend money as a creditor to the company, e.g. shareholder's loan, and take back security, like any other creditor could, such as a mortgage on the company property or General Security Agreement on the assets of the business.

If your company wants to borrow money from a lender, and the lender does not want to be secured behind your security, then you can subordinate or postpone your claim to that of the secured creditor. However, your security document remains registered. In addition, you can also have umbrella security from the company that covers you for any future loans that you give the company, under the same security document that you have registered. Therefore, you don't need to keep registering security each time you advance a loan.

Shareholder's Agreement with Buy/Sell Clause Covered by Insurance

Basically, this means that the company has insurance on your life. In the event of your death, the company has the financial resources to pay your estate the value of your shares, based on a formula set out in the shareholder's agreement.

Designate Beneficiaries of Your Insurance Policies

By designating beneficiaries of your insurance policies, the money bypasses the will completely and is therefore not part of your estate. It goes directly to your designated beneficiaries tax-free. Your personal or business creditors can only claim from assets in your estate.

Designate Beneficiaries of Your Investments

By designating a beneficiary for your RRSPs, RRIFs, TFSAs, and other registered retirement plans, you bypass your will and your estate. The money goes directly to the beneficiary and is unavailable to creditors.

Consider the Use of Trusts

Refer to Chapter 6, "Understanding Trusts." Basically, if you set up a *living trust* while you are alive (*inter vivos* trust) or an alter-ego trust, it bypasses your will and therefore your estate on your death. However, this technique will not work as a means of avoiding debts that you already owe. In such cases, the provincial "fraudulent preferences," "fradulent conveyances" legislation, or federal bankruptcy legislation would likely come into play, and allow the courts to reverse your attempt to divert assets that would otherwise be used to pay off your creditors. Speak to your legal advisor.

In summary, creditors can only make a claim to the assets that are in your estate at the time of your death. By utilizing strategic legal and tax planning in advance, you can minimize the value of the assets in the estate available to creditors.

Planning Tips

Here are some suggestions to help make the planning process as effective as possible:

- Set aside time each week to read material on the Internet, books and periodicals about family or small businesses. The better informed you are, the more effective the planning process will be.
- Make sure that you assemble a competent team to work with you on the planning process, and be sure that each person knows what is expected of him or her. Encourage frank discussion, and don't come down hard on those who disagree with you.
- Advise your existing professionals of your plans. They know you best.
- Don't "reach for the sky" when you set your goals and objectives. Be realistic. If the objectives seem unattainable, you may have difficulty getting anyone else in the business or your family to become committed to your plans.
- Consider hiring an outside consultant to spearhead the planning process. You might also want to hire someone to serve as a "facilitator" at planning meetings (especially if you are a domineering type, who tends to stifle frank and open discussion).

- Consider holding structured "family meetings" with your spouse and grown children to discuss your vision for the family business, your thoughts about retirement and succession, their views about being involved in the business, and the possible alternatives.
- If relations are strained between two or more of your children or other family members who are involved in some way in the business, consider hiring a family therapist to work with the family individually and as a group.
- Effective tax planning is one of the keys to the ongoing success of most family-owned businesses. Make sure that the CPA, lawyer, insurance agent and other professional advisors that you use have prior experience in dealing with privately-owned businesses.

WHERE TO GET MORE INFORMATION

Books and Periodicals

- A visit to your local business reference library could be fruitful. Quite a number of books have been written on family business and related topics. There are also a number of periodicals and newsletters from organizations serving the needs of privately-owned businesses.
- Many CPA firms have produced various booklets and checklists on family business succession planning. Check the Internet or contact one of their offices to see if you can obtain copies.

One of the co-authors, Douglas Gray, has written several business books that could be helpful references, including the following:

- *The Complete Canadian Small Business Guide* (with Diana Gray)
- *Start and Run a Consulting Business*
- *Marketing Your Product* (with Donald Cyr)

The Internet

If you search the Internet using the key words "family business" or "small business," you will find a large number of interesting and extremely useful sites. Also refer to the website: *www.smallbiz.ca*.

Courses and Seminars

Several Canadian universities have established "Centres for Family Business" (e.g. York University, University of Calgary and University of Waterloo) that offer courses and seminars for business owners and their families on topics relating to succession planning.

Business and Family Business Organizations

- The **Canadian Federation of Independent Business** (CFIB) has branches in each province. A membership organization providing lobbying governments, business support, and benefits.

CFIB	Tel: (416) 222-8022
401–4141 Yonge Street	Website: *www.cfib.ca*
Toronto, ON M2P 2A6	

- The **Family Enterprise Xchange** (FEX) has chapters in a number of centres in Canada. They hold regular local meetings and seminars, as well as a national annual conference. You should consider joining FEX, especially if you are seriously considering a family succession arrangement. For more information, contact:

Family Enterprise Xchange	Tel: (866) 849-0099
National Office	Website: *www.cafenational.org*
690 Darval Drive, Suite 135	
Oakville, ON L6K 3W7	

- In the United States, there are a number of family business organizations, such as the **Family Firm Institute** (FFI). This organization is for professionals such as accountants, lawyers, insurance agents, and family business counsellors, who serve as advisors to family businesses.

FFI	Tel: (617) 482-3045
200 Lincoln Street, #201	Fax: (617) 482-3049
Boston, MA 02111	Website: *www.ffi.org*

SUMMARY

This chapter was one of the more difficult ones to write for this book, because there is so much that can be said about a privately-owned business. You should now have a good sense of the issues that you, the business owner, need to face. And the sooner you do this, the better. For some business owners, the various issues and problems relating to management succession, ownership, maintaining family harmony, treating all of the children fairly (or equally), etc., seem to be overwhelming. Since there does not seem to be any light at the end of the tunnel, too often nothing is done. Creating a plan, and using our strategies to tackle the planning process, will serve as a catalyst for you to start the process.

? Frequently
: Asked Questions

1. *I am the owner of a small business, and I have heard about estate freezing. How wealthy do I need to be in order to consider this estate planning strategy?*

   Since an estate freeze would shift some or all of the future growth in the value of your business to one or more of your children, you must ensure that you leave yourself well enough off to protect yourself against inflation for the rest of your life. As we said earlier, this is a "rich man's game." The purchasing power of the dollar is likely to erode significantly over the next 20, 30 or 40 years. If you were to freeze your ownership interest in the business and take back $3 million worth of dividend-paying preferred shares (with a fixed redemption price), this may seem to be a lot of money today. However, in 20, 30 or 40 years the redemption amount of $3 million, and the annual dividends on the shares, might not be nearly enough to maintain your desired standard of living.

   Opinions vary amongst tax and estate professionals about the level of wealth at which an estate freeze may make sense. It really does depend on the circumstances. For example, do you have most of your wealth tied up in your business, or do you also have other significant assets (e.g. rental real estate properties or a sizeable investment portfolio)? Again, you really need to obtain customized tax and legal advice.

2. *I am thinking of transferring 50 percent of the ownership of my business to my daughter. She has been working in the business for a number of years, and I have been grooming her as my successor. She is about to get married. Is there anything to worry about if her marriage breaks down in the future, regarding her ownership stake in the business?*

   Family law varies from province to province. However, a common theme is that assets owned by the husband and wife at the time of the marriage are valued, and any subsequent appreciation in the value of such assets is subject to a 50/50 split, in the event of a marriage break-up. Generally, cash and other assets received by way of gift *when a person is already married* are excluded from the 50/50 equalization calculation if the marriage subsequently ends.

   With this in mind, you might consider delaying your gift of the shares of your business to your daughter until *after* she gets married. If you go ahead with the gift now, it is possible that one-half of the increase in the value of her interest in the business will be part of a settlement, if her marriage breaks up in the future. You should also encourage her to enter into a prenuptial contract.

   As we have cautioned throughout, we are only providing general guidelines. You always need to consult professionals to obtain customized advice in your particular circumstances.

Charitable Giving and Philanthropy

"We make a living by what we get, but we make a life by what we give."

WINSTON S. CHURCHILL

INTRODUCTION

No book on estate planning would be complete without a discussion of charitable giving and philanthropy. In this chapter, we will outline:

- the tax benefits of making charitable donations during your lifetime, or at the time of your death
- the various ways that charitable donations can be made, including:
  - cash gifts
  - gifts in kind
  - donating assets and retaining a life interest
  - life insurance and life annuities
- the use of a private charitable foundation as a vehicle for supporting your favourite charitable activities

Over the past century, hundreds of millions of dollars have been donated by Canadians under their wills to support various charities, universities, hospitals, art galleries, and museums. Many of the greatest works of art that are on display in the public art galleries and museums in Canada are there for all of us to enjoy because of Canadian generosity. Similarly, many Canadian universities have received substantial endowments from the estates of their alumni. Such gifts have been used to construct university buildings as well as to support educational and research programs.

In your will, you have "one last chance" to be benevolent by directing gifts to be made out of your estate to one or more charities of your choice. One need not be wealthy to consider a charitable donation bequest under one's will. Every year, thousands of testamentary gifts ranging from a few hundred dollars to millions of dollars, are received by charitable organizations because of the foresight and generosity of ordinary Canadians who took the trouble to write one or more charitable bequests into their wills. Large charitable donations can also bring a form of "immortality." Just think of the hospitals, university buildings, athletic facilities and cultural centres that have been named after their largest benefactors.

TAX INCENTIVES FOR CHARITABLE GIFTS

Individuals who make charitable donations are entitled to a tax credit in calculating their federal and provincial income tax. Charitable donations will also reduce an individual's federal and provincial surtaxes, if applicable. Donations by corporations also receive income tax relief, in the form of a deduction in arriving at the taxable income amount on which corporate income tax is calculated.

Donations Made by Individuals

Charitable donations by an individual are eligible for a federal tax credit of 15 percent on the first $200 donated, and 29 percent on any donations made in excess of $200 in the particular year. There is also a provincial income tax saving, since provincial income taxes in all of the provinces (except Quebec) are calculated as a percentage of basic federal income tax.

Once provincial income taxes are taken into account, and if an individual's charitable donations are more than $200 in a particular year, the effective rate of tax savings on charitable donations made by a high income individual is about 40 to 50 percent. In other words, for every $100 of donations made in excess of $200 each year, the tax saving will be about $40 to $50. Because the rates of provincial income tax vary from province to province, the effective rate of tax savings applicable to charitable donations varies.

Annual Limitations on Amount Eligible for Donation Tax Credit

Claims for charitable donations are generally limited to 75 percent of the *net income* that is reported in your income tax return. If donations in a particular year are more than the allowable amount, the excess can be carried forward for up to five years. There is no carryback of unused donations, except in the year of death.

Donations Made Under a Will

Charitable donations that you specify in your will are eligible for the donation tax credit in your final income tax return that will be filed by your executor(s). Such *testamentary* gifts may be deducted from up to 100 percent of the net income amount reported in a deceased's final income tax return. Thus, a large gift or gifts under a person's will may have the effect of eliminating the income taxes that would otherwise be payable for the year of death.

In some situations, the donations reported in a deceased's final income tax return may be more than the net income reported therein. In that event, the executors are allowed to carry the excess back to the deceased's previous year's income tax return, and to have the CRA open up the return to process the extra tax credit (resulting in a tax refund). The normal limit of 75 percent of net income on donations qualifying for the donation tax credit has also been removed for the year preceding the year of death. Executors also have some flexibility in the claiming of donations in the year of death by being able to claim them against the income of the estate instead of the deceased's income tax returns. Consult the CPA's web site for details of the circumstances when this can be done.

TYPES OF DONATIONS

Cash Donations

There are various ways of making a donation under your will. A cash gift is the simplest and the most obvious. However, if the gift is large, you need to make sure that there will be enough liquid assets in your estate to enable your executors to carry out your wishes. For example, if you decided to leave $100,000 to your favourite charity, but at the time of your death, your estate consisted only of cash and term deposits amounting to $50,000, plus various parcels of real estate, your executors might have to sell one of the properties in order to raise the funds necessary to fulfill the donation bequest. This may not be what you had in mind.

Gifts in Kind

Instead of a cash gift under your will, you could provide for a gift of tangible property (referred to as a *gift in kind*) to be made to one or more charities. For example, you might consider donating valuable paintings to a public art gallery; a donation of scenic real estate to a provincial conservation authority; or perhaps donating a car to a hospital foundation for its use in transporting patients.

Most gifts in kind are eligible for the same donation tax credit as a cash gift, but with a few notable exceptions as outlined below. In the case of a gift in kind, the donation tax credit is based on the fair market value of the property that is donated. Normally, it is necessary to obtain an independent appraisal in order to substantiate the fair market value of such a gift, so as to enable the charitable organization to issue an official donation receipt. With a gift of publicly-traded securities, the fair market value is readily available from stock market quotations on the date the gift was received by the charity.

There are also capital gains tax implications of making a gift in kind. As outlined in Chapter 8, Death and Taxes, when any property is disposed of by way of gift, the donor is considered (for income tax purposes) to have received notional sale proceeds equal to the fair market value of the property. In the case of property that is donated to charity under the terms of a person's will, one needs to look at the combined effect of the usual deemed disposition of the property at the time of death for capital gains tax purposes, as well as the donation tax credit that may be claimed based on the fair market value of the property.

SPECIAL TAX TREATMENT FOR GIFTS OF QUALIFYING PUBLICLY-TRADED SECURITIES

There is also a special rule that provides a tax incentive for making a gift of publicly-traded securities rather than the cash equivalent. Individuals and corporations who donate securities that are traded on a "prescribed" stock exchange (e.g. the recognized Canadian stock exchanges) are not required to include any of the capital gain in income, versus the usual 50 percent of the gain (as explained in Chapter 8, Death and Taxes). This also applies to gifts of Canadian mutual funds and segregated funds of life insurance companies.

This special rule means that the donation tax credit itself is based on the full market value of the securities that are donated to the charity, but the taxable capital gain that would normally be included in the donor's taxable income is eliminated.

PLANNING TO PROTECT ● *Ward's Executors Make Use of Special Tax Treatment of Securities*

Ward died on August 1, 2017. Ward's investment portfolio included 1,000 shares of TV Inc., a public company, which he purchased in 2001 for $10,000. At the time of his death, the shares had a market value of $50,000.

Under his will, he bequeathed $50,000 to the Toronto Hospital. His will said that the executors of the estate could make the *gift in kind* rather than in cash, if they thought it wise to do so. Ward's wife June died some years ago, so there is no spousal rollover on Ward's death for capital gains purposes.

Ward's executors have prepared his final personal income tax return covering the period January 1 to August 1, 2017. The return shows net income of more than $200,000.

As outlined in Chapter 8, Death and Taxes, there is a deemed disposition for capital gains tax purposes of all of Ward's assets at their fair market value at the time of his death. Therefore, there would normally be a $40,000 capital gain on his TV Inc. shares, which would have to be reported by the executor(s) of Ward's estate in his final income tax return.

The executors have two options. The most obvious thing is for them to write a cheque for $50,000. However, there is an alternative, which is to transfer all of the TV Inc. shares (worth $50,000) to the hospital in satisfaction of the bequest under Ward's will. Which is better?

Whether the gift is made in cash or in shares makes no difference as far as the donation tax credit is concerned. The tax credit will be the same (i.e. $50,000). Therefore, the income tax saving applicable to the donation tax credit in Ward's final tax return will be about $25,000 in either case.

However, from a capital gains tax viewpoint, it makes more sense for the executors to make the donation in the form of $50,000 worth of TV Inc. shares, rather than cash. This is because the *taxable* portion of the capital gain in Ward's final income tax return would be zero, rather than 50 percent of the gain.

By transferring the shares rather than cash to the hospital, the executors can eliminate the capital gains tax arising on Ward's death with respect to his TV Inc. shares.

• •

Gifts of Certified Cultural Property

There are also special tax incentives for gifts in kind that fit the description of *certified cultural property*. A certified cultural property is a national treasure with cultural significance in Canada, for which a certificate has been issued by the Canadian Cultural Property Export Review Board. An individual who makes a donation of certified cultural property to a designated cultural institution is entitled to a donation tax credit based on the fair market value of the property. However, whereas ordinary gifts in kind can result in the donor having to recognize a taxable capital gain, a gift of certified cultural property is exempt from capital gains taxation. Furthermore, if the value of the property is less than the donor's cost, the donor is allowed to claim a capital loss (within the normal limits).

The CRA has issued an Interpretation Bulletin (IT-407R) which sets out the requirements for a donation to qualify as certified cultural property. The *Cultural Property Export and Import Act* (CPEIA) contains provisions to encourage the retention of national treasures (Canadian cultural property) within Canada. The exemption from capital gains taxation is intended to encourage residents of Canada to donate such property to institutions or public authorities in Canada which are designated under the CPEIA. In order to obtain favourable tax treatment, the donor must obtain a certificate from the Canadian Cultural Property Export Review Board. Contact the Canadian Cultural Property Export Review Board for more information. See the end of this chapter for contact particulars.

Because no capital gain has to be recognized on the donation of certified cultural property to a designated institution or public authority (such as the National Gallery, or the Royal

Ontario Museum), there may be substantial tax savings in donating such property if it has been held by the donor for a long time, and there has been a large appreciation in value. A sale of the property or even a transfer of the property from one generation to the next, may give rise to a capital gain, 50 percent of which is subject to income tax. On the other hand, a donation of the property to a designated institution will result in a donation tax credit at the top marginal tax rate, and no taxable capital gain.

From a financial standpoint, a person would still be further ahead by selling the property, paying the capital gains tax, and keeping the after-tax proceeds, rather than donating such property to a designated institution. However, the favourable tax treatment for gifts of certified cultural property does provide a significant incentive for wealthy Canadians to donate such property to Canadian cultural institutions, as does the opportunity to preserve our cultural history and artifacts.

Anyone contemplating making a gift under their will of valuable paintings, works of art, or other items that might qualify as certified cultural property would be well-advised to determine the status of the property in advance, rather than leaving it for the executors of the estate to sort out. The income tax effects of the property qualifying or not qualifying could be quite significant, especially if the property has been held for a long time and there has been a large appreciation in value in the donor's hands. You should also consider discussing your proposed gift with the curator of the institution to which the gift will be made.

Using Life Insurance for Charitable Purposes

Some people are worth "more dead than alive" to the charities they support, because they have obtained additional life insurance and designated the charity as the beneficiary. If you were to take out a life insurance policy and *irrevocably* designate a charity as the beneficiary of the policy, the insurance premiums paid on the policy would be viewed as charitable donations for income tax purposes, and would be eligible for the donation tax credit. However, you should realize that an irrevocable beneficiary designation means that the charity cannot be removed as the beneficiary under any circumstances.

Another approach is for you to earmark an insurance policy for a particular charity, without actually designating the charity as the beneficiary under the policy. Instead, the named beneficiary would be your estate, and your will would contain a clause directing the death benefit (proceeds) from the insurance policy to be paid to the charity after your death. Under this scenario, the insurance premiums paid by you during your lifetime would *not* qualify as a charitable donation. However, the entire amount of the insurance policy death benefit that is payable to the charity after your death would qualify as a *testamentary donation* and be eligible for the donation tax credit in your final income tax return. The same can be accomplished by designating a charity as a beneficiary of the policy (it is deemed to be a testamentary gift, even if not included in the will). This would have the added benefit of not having to pay probate fees on the proceeds of the insurance policy if the beneficiary is your estate.

Whether or not your estate would realize the full benefit of the donation tax credit would depend on your income level, the value of any RRSPs or RRIFs at the time of death if there is no spousal rollover, and any taxable capital gains in your final income tax return. If the insurance donation exceeded the "net income" amount in your final tax return, your executors could carry back the excess to the prior year's income tax return. In that case, the CRA would be required to allow an additional donation tax credit for that year (provided that the donations do not exceed the prior year's net income). If the charitable donation under your will is still too large to be fully utilized in your final income tax return, and the return for the year preceding death, the executors may be able to claim the donation tax credit against the income of the estate itself.

There are also other ways of utilizing life insurance and annuities for charitable giving and estate planning purposes. You should talk to an insurance agent who has expertise in this area to determine whether any of these techniques may be appropriate in your situation. The input of a financial planner may also be useful.

Charitable Gift Annuities

Another donation technique involves making a cash donation to a charity, in return for a *life annuity*. Perhaps you have your mind made up that you want a capital sum to go to a specific charity after your death. You cannot make the donation now because you need to keep the funds invested to provide you with interest or dividend income to live on.

A gift to a charity during your lifetime in return for a life annuity would produce tax savings, but the tax results are somewhat unusual. Ask the charity in which you are interested about their "planned giving" programs.

Typically, an individual contributes capital to a registered charity in exchange for guaranteed specified payments for some period of time, frequently the individual's lifetime. For income tax purposes, such an arrangement is treated as the purchase of an annuity by the individual from the registered charity and gives rise to certain tax consequences. The annuity payments to the individual are based on the person's life expectancy. Generally, the annuitants are required to include only a portion of the annuity payments in their income for tax purposes. A formula in Part III of the *Income Tax Act* and *Regulations* is used to calculate the *return of capital* element of the annuity payments that can be excluded from income for tax purposes.

The CRA points out in the Bulletin that an individual will sometimes pay more to the charity for an annuity than the total amount that the individual can expect to receive from the charity as annuity payments. They will generally accept that the excess of the purchase price over the amount expected to be received as annuity payments is a *gift*, and the individual is entitled to a donation tax credit provided that an official receipt is submitted. Furthermore, in such circumstances, the CRA is willing to exempt all the future annuity payments from income tax.

Charitable Remainder Trusts

In some situations a trust can be used to make a donation of property to a charity. A *charitable remainder trust* involves the creation of a trust under the terms of which a particular charity is named as the *capital beneficiary* and the donor is named as the *income beneficiary*. The donor would then transfer one or more assets to the trust. The trustees of the trust would hold the legal title to the property under the terms and conditions spelled out in a written trust agreement. As income beneficiary of the trust, the donor could be entitled to all of the income that is earned on the funds that are invested within the trust. The trust agreement would specify that upon the donor's death, the trust's assets are to be transferred to the capital beneficiary charity.

Alternatively, such a trust might be used to hold real estate that is intended to be donated to the charity after the death of the donor. Under the terms of the trust agreement, the donor might retain the exclusive use of the property during his or her lifetime.

The CRA's Interpretation Bulletin 226R contains a highly technical discussion of the tax treatment of *residual interests in real property* and *remainder interests in trusts*. In most situations, a donation tax credit is allowed at the time that the property is transferred to the trust, provided that the trust agreement contains certain terms and conditions. However, the amount that is eligible for the donation tax credit is not the full value of the property transferred into the trust. Instead, the donation amount is a reduced amount that must be calculated by an actuary, based on the donor's life expectancy. In effect, the donation amount is the value of the property transferred to the trust, minus the actuarial value of the donor's "life interest."

A *charitable remainder trust* may be of interest to you if you are contemplating making a charitable donation of a valuable art collection or other property. However, rather than giving up the asset entirely, you would retain a legal *life interest*. This would allow you to retain possession and continue to have the use and enjoyment of the property during your lifetime. This is a somewhat complex estate planning technique. You should not undertake it without first obtaining professional tax and legal advice.

PRIVATE FOUNDATIONS

Many of Canada's wealthiest families, and some not-so-wealthy families, have established *private charitable foundations* as a vehicle for carrying out their philanthropic activities. A private foundation must be *registered* with the CRA in order to obtain its status as a charitable organization, and it must comply with a host of rules and regulations. In the case of a private foundation, the requirements are that:

- it must be constituted and operated exclusively for charitable purposes
- it must not carry on any business
- it cannot hold a controlling interest in any corporation
- it must annually expend its disbursement quota (a predetermined amount each year) for charitable purposes.

In addition, the foundation must file an annual information return with the CRA, as well as financial statements.

There are complex tax rules if shares or debt of a private corporation are being donated to a private foundation. You should certainly obtain professional advice if you are considering such a step.

Various pamphlets, bulletins and circulars written in relatively non-technical language outlining what is involved in creating and running a private charitable foundation can be obtained from the Charitable and Non-Profit Organizations Section of the CRA in Ottawa. See the end of this chapter for contact particulars.

PLANNING TIPS

If you are thinking about including a charitable donation bequest in your will, here are some pointers:

- While philanthropy is a noble cause, your family comes first. Make sure that your spouse and other dependents will be adequately provided for after your death, and in accordance with your wishes.
- Ensure that your estate will have sufficient liquid assets to cover the donation under your will, without forcing your executors to liquidate other assets in order to raise the cash.
- Make sure that you identify the desired charity by its precise full legal name and include the charity's address and phone number. There have been many legal battles over the years where more than one charity with the same or similar name has laid claim to a donation mentioned in a deceased person's will, where the address of the charity was not stated.
- Ensure that the tax consequences of any donations under your will are well thought out in advance. For example, if you own any Canadian "Group of Seven" paintings or other assets that you think might qualify as certified cultural property, you may want to clarify the tax status of such assets during your lifetime and obtain the necessary certification from the CRA.
- If you intend to make a substantial donation to one or more charities upon your death, explore the idea of making gifts during your lifetime under a planned giving program, which might produce better overall tax results than if the donations only took effect after your death.
- Keep in mind that legislation varies from province to province on issues relating to wills and donations to private foundations. For example, in British Columbia, there is legisla-

tion to apply to the court during the probate process, to ask to vary a will following the death of the person involved. In this scenario, the claimant could feel that the distribution of assets was not fair or equitable in the circumstances, and wishes to challenge the will distribution. In some provinces there is legislation giving the right for someone claiming to be a dependent to challenge the will during the probate process, on the basis that the distribution of assets of the deceased did not adequately or equitably account for the needs of the dependent person.

PITALLS TO AVOID AND TIPS TO CONSIDER WHEN CHARITABLE GIVING

Here are some scenarios and issues that those in the charitable sector have encountered and that may be relevant for individual donors to consider.

There are benefits and consequences of charitable giving, other than the "feel good, do good."

Always seek independent professional legal and tax advice prior to making any charitable donation.

Mismatch Between Charitable Credits and Tax Liability

One of the biggest issues that can arise for the individual donor is the mismatch between the charitable donation tax credits and the tax liability, such as between the individual's and the estate tax return. Similarly, charitable tax credit may not be available at all if the donation is made through a trust where the document identifies the charity as a beneficiary (rather than providing the trustee with the discretion to make a charitable gift).

Not Communicating Estate Plans to Family While Donor Is Still Alive

The use of certain planning structures may also give rise to difficulties if the donor does not discuss philanthropic plans with his or her family while still alive. Specifically, in some situations, a donor may intentionally choose a less beneficial tax consequence because making a gift via a trust provides other benefits that are more important to the donor (e.g. to safeguard the donation from a will's variation challenge). Such decisions are based purely on the donor's personal considerations and knowledge of the specific issues in his or her family. Even if the donor works with an independent legal or financial advisor to implement the donor's wishes, after the donor's passing, the family may still question the arrangement on the basis that it does not provide the most beneficial tax result for the donor's estate, and the assumption that an individual will always choose to maximize tax benefits to the exclusion of all other considerations.

Not Communicating with the Intended Charitable Beneficiary

Another issue arising with respect to charitable giving in general, and especially relevant for testamentary gifts, is ensuring that the name of the charitable beneficiary included in the testamentary document is the organization's correct legal name. In addition, if tax benefits are desired, the donor should also ensure that the charity is a registered charity and that the charity's charitable business registration number is included in the gift documents.

A donor should also contact the charity to ensure that the proposed purpose for the gift can be met by the charity. Charities can only expend their funds for the purposes included in their constituting documents and in the most prudent way given the circumstances at the time when the gift is received. Especially for testamentary gifts that may not be realized for many years, individuals may want to consider not designating a particular purpose for their donation. This will allow the charity to use the donations for the areas of greatest need or greater promise at the time when the gift is received.

Changing the Purpose of a Gift

Another issue that arises quite often is that most individuals do not appear to be aware of the fact that once a gift has been made to charity and the corresponding tax receipt has been issued, the donor does not have the legal right to subsequently direct or compel the charity to change the purpose for which the gift is used, or to compel the charity to provide the gift to another charity. Although the donor can provide recommendations on the use of the gift, if the gift document so specifies, it is the charity that must make the final determination in respect of the gift, in accordance with the gift document and its policies.

Legislative Changes

Federal and/or potential legislation, rules and regulations can change at any time that could affect how to effectively structure your donation to meet your needs. That is why we have consistently recommended throughout this guide how important it is to obtain current and customized expert legal, tax, insurance and financial advice in an integrated, rather than ad hoc, fashion, to fully meet your needs and expectations.

Gifts in Kind (E.g. Car, Paintings, Etc.)

- Not all charities can accept all types of gifts in kind due to liquidity and/or valuation issues.
- A charity's primary objective is to obtain funds that can be applied to its purposes. If donated property cannot be easily or quickly sold to realize proceeds that can be used for programs, this will present a problem for the charity, in addition to the fact that other costs may need to be incurred for insuring or maintaining the property until such time as it is sold.

- With respect to valuation, most donors do not appear to be aware of the fact that a charity cannot simply accept the donor's estimate of what the gift "is worth" and issue a receipt for that amount. Some donors do not appear to know that the charity is required to take reasonable steps to determine the fair market value (FMV) of the gift in accordance with CRA guidelines.
- Related to this issue is the fact that if the FMV of the gift cannot be determined, a charitable gift receipt cannot be issued. Lastly, donors also do not appear to have given thought to the fact that any negative consequences arising from an improperly issued tax receipt will affect both the individual and the charity.

Endowments

The following are some of the issues that could be of interest to donors considering establishing an endowment:

- When considering whether to establish an endowment, consider what income the endowed amount will be able to provide for the charity's programs. Given the relatively low return rates in recent years, an endowment may only provide a small amount to programs.
- Related to the above, sudden and persistent stock market declines can significantly reduce the value of endowment funds and therefore further reduce the amount of income available for charitable programs.
- Although the notion of perpetuity appeals to donors, forever is a very long time. In practice, restrictions placed on the use of contributions to perpetual endowment funds can severely restrict the charity's ability to respond to changing circumstances over time and therefore limit the charity's ability to make a difference to the very cause that the donors originally wanted to support. Ultimately, the donors may wish to consider what is most important to them and whether they are prepared to move away from the traditional concept of an endowment in order to provide the charity with the ability to make a bigger difference to the cause that is important to them.
- Examples of concepts that donors may wish to consider supporting in order to accomplish this: move away from using interest only in favor of a total-return model that allows for some use of capital, include a "right to vary" clause in the endowment agreement which enables the charity to redirect the use of the annual payout if the original purpose is no longer relevant, and include time limits and sunset clauses.

Life Insurance

The issues that arise most often with respect to donating using life insurance policies include:

- For policies with an investment component, the estimate provided to potential donors by their life insurance agent for how long the policy would remain in force is based on certain assumptions regarding the interest/income to be obtained from the investment component.

- Quite often, donors subsequently do not remember that the return rate was only an assumption, and when the actual interest rate is lower and the investment component does not grow at the required rate to allow for payment of premiums and maintaining the policy in force for life, this can come as a surprise to the donor. The gift that the donor intended to make may not come to fruition if the donor (or the charity) is not able to make additional cash contributions to the investment account.

- Because the premium payments are lower for term policies, donors sometimes choose to donate this type of policy. However, because premium payments must be continued for life, and because the donor's life or financial circumstances can change given such a potentially long period of time, the situation can arise when a donor is no longer able (or willing) to continue to pay the premiums. As a result, unless the charity is able to continue the premium payments (which may not be the case), the policy will lapse and no gift will be made to the charity despite premiums having been paid by the donor over many years.

- This is a less than ideal result for both the donor and the charity. For this reason, donors may wish to give significant thought to donating only policies that can be paid up within 5–10 years rather than policies that require premium payments for life (or to age 100).

- That said, there can be significant tax advantages in donating certain types of insurance policies to charity (e.g. Term 100) if your particular policy has a fair market value, notwithstanding the fact that it may not have any cash surrender value. This situation is explained in Chapter 15 in the section "Think Twice Before Cancelling a Term 100 Policy."

WHERE TO GET MORE INFORMATION

The CRA has issued a number of Interpretation Bulletins, Information Circulars, and brochures dealing with charities, foundations, and charitable giving, including:

- P113 Gifts and Income Tax Guide
- Interpretation Bulletin IT-110R3
- Interpretation Bulletin 226R

Additional information on charity registration requirements and private charitable foundations can be obtained from:

Charities Directorate
Canada Revenue Agency
Ottawa, ON K1A 0L5

Tel: (613) 954-0410
or 1-800-267-2384

Information concerning gifts of certified cultural property can be obtained from:

The Canadian Cultural Property Export Review Board
25 Eddy Street
9th Floor   Telephone: (819) 997-7761
Gatineau, QC   or (866) 811-0055 (toll free)
K1A 0M5   Website: *www.canada.pch.gc.ca*

SUMMARY

In this chapter, we have explained the various ways that you can include charitable giving in your overall estate plan; different ways that a gift can be made and the tax consequences of making cash gifts; gifts in kind; and gifts of life insurance. We also touched on the use of a private foundation.

You need to obtain skilled professional tax and legal advice to make sure your charitable donations are made in the most tax-effective manner.

? Frequently
: Asked Questions

1. *If I make specific bequests in my will to favourite charities, can my executors claim an income tax deduction or credit?*

   The answer is "yes." The donation tax credit would be claimed in your final income tax return that your executors would be filing with the CRA. If you did not have enough taxable income to absorb the full donation tax credit, the excess donations can then be carried back and claimed in an amended tax return for the calendar year preceding the year of death. Also, in circumstances where a donation tax credit can be claimed against the income of the estate, consult with the CRA website for details.

2. *Are donations to charitable organizations outside of Canada eligible for the same tax relief as donations to eligible Canadian charities?*

   It depends on the circumstances. Certain universities outside of Canada are eligible for the Canadian donation tax credit/deduction, because they are listed in the *Income Tax Act* and *Regulations*. Furthermore, Canada has entered into tax treaties with a number of countries (including the United States and the United Kingdom) that contain provisions allowing Canadian tax relief for donations to qualifying charitable organizations within the foreign country. In some cases, the amount of the donation tax credit or deduction may be limited to a certain percentage of the taxpayer's income or capital gains from sources within the foreign country.

If you are thinking of making a large donation under your will to an educational or charitable organization outside of Canada, speak to a tax professional to determine whether or not the desired Canadian tax benefit will be available upon your death.

Life, Health and Disability Insurance

**"It's not that I'm afraid to die,
I just don't want to be there when it happens."**

WOODY ALLEN

INTRODUCTION

Life insurance can play an important role in your estate planning. This chapter will give you a general understanding of the various kinds of life insurance and their uses, in order to help you determine your own insurance needs. However, as we have said many times before, you should "talk to the experts" because of the variety of choices that are available. Also included will be an overview of some health and disability insurance options. These all have a financial risk management implication, in terms of protecting the potential value of your estate.

In this chapter, we will discuss:

- identifying the need for life insurance in estate planning
- the different types of life insurance
- choosing an insurance agent
- factors to consider in choosing a life insurance company
- group insurance versus individual insurance
- the income tax treatment of life insurance
- various planning strategies involving life insurance
- types of health and disability insurance.

IDENTIFYING THE NEED FOR LIFE INSURANCE

Life insurance can serve a number of purposes, whether a person dies at a ripe old age, or has the misfortune to die prematurely because of an illness or an accident.

Factors to Consider and Questions to Ask

These are some of the questions to ask yourself and factors to consider in determining whether life insurance has a role to play in your estate planning:

- Do you have a spouse or any dependent children?
- Do you have an elderly parent or any other relatives who are dependent on you for support, or who are likely to become financially dependent on you in the future?
- Would their "financial health" and lifestyle be affected in the event of your sudden death?
- After your death, will your spouse be able to generate sufficient income to maintain the lifestyle to which both of you have become accustomed? If necessary, would your spouse be able to take on full- or part-time work in order to supplement any pension income and investment income? How do you feel about your spouse being forced to work after you are gone in order to supplement his or her income?
- If you have children, will there be enough money to enable them to attend college or university, if you are no longer around to provide financial support?
- What investments do you own and how much investment income can be generated each year to support your family in the event of your death?
- Do you own any "non-essential" assets, such as a vacation property, that could be sold in the event of your death, so that the sale proceeds could be invested to generate additional income for your spouse and family? How do you feel about your spouse or children being forced to sell such assets in order to raise cash?
- Will any income taxes become payable in the event of your death under the capital gains deemed disposition rule? If so, will there be enough liquidity in your estate to cover such taxes?
- Do you still have a mortgage on your house or any other debts that you would not want your family to be burdened with after your death?
- Do you own a business which you want to pass down to one or more of your children? Your estate might be faced with a large taxable capital gain and a significant income tax liability if your shares of the company have appreciated in value.

How Much Insurance Is Enough?

Life insurance can be used to address any of the situations mentioned above. But how much insurance should you have? The truth of the matter is that the cost of insurance must be weighed against the degree of risk that you are prepared to accept. If you are single, you have no one who is financially dependent on you for support, and there are no charities that you have any interest in supporting, you probably do not need life insurance. However, if you answered "yes" to some of the earlier questions, you may have a need for life insurance. Most of us are not well enough off financially to leave behind sufficient capital to enable our spouse or children to maintain their current lifestyle in the event of our death. Generally speaking, the cost of life insurance to provide a measure of financial protection is a relatively small price to pay in relation to the immediate "peace of mind" and the potential future benefits.

The Use of Life Insurance by Wealthy Individuals

Surprisingly, some of the largest life insurance policies are taken out each year by wealthy people whom you might think "don't need life insurance." Although wealthy people may not need life insurance for the same reasons as a young married couple with young children, life insurance is sometimes a necessity for individuals who own a business or other assets that they wish to pass down from one generation to the next.

As outlined in Chapter 8, "Death and Taxes," Canada imposes "estate taxes" by requiring all accrued capital gains at the time of death to be subject to income tax in the deceased's final tax return. In many cases, the capital gains taxes on the shares of a business that are being left to a son or daughter can be in the millions of dollars. Many business owners have the majority of their wealth tied up in the business. At the time of death, there may not be enough cash or marketable securities on hand to cover the capital gains taxes on the business shares. Business owners who anticipate this being the case often take out life insurance to provide the funds needed to cover the income taxes or other taxes arising in the estate.

TYPES OF LIFE INSURANCE

Life insurance is essentially a financial contract between an individual and a life insurance company, under which the *face amount* of the policy will be paid by the insurance company to the named beneficiary upon the death of the person whose life is insured. Of course, there is a cost. In return for this *promise to pay*, the owner of the policy must pay *premiums* to the insurance company.

There are two basic forms of life insurance: *term insurance* and *permanent insurance*. Under each of the broad categories of insurance—term and permanent—there are a variety of choices. Many of the life insurance companies have their own brand names to describe their various kinds of policies. This can make it difficult for a buyer to distinguish between term and permanent. In fact, some policies are a hybrid of the two—such as Term to 100. There are also a bewildering array of options, special features, and "bells and whistles" that can be added to a life insurance policy. The wide variety of choices makes it difficult for one to comparison shop, which is why it is so important to sit down with an experienced life insurance agent.

Term Insurance

Term life insurance is what its name implies—it provides coverage for a specific number of years, or until a certain age is reached. Generally, a death benefit is payable by the insurance company only after the death of the insured person has occurred, and only if the death has occurred within the time period covered by the policy.

Typically, the premiums paid under a term policy are low (compared to permanent insurance) in the early years, and the premiums rise each year or in stages as you get older.

NO CASH SURRENDER VALUE

Term insurance generally does not have any *cash surrender value*. This means that you cannot withdraw cash from the policy (as in the case of permanent insurance), nor will the insurance company give you a policy loan against a term policy. If you stop paying the premiums under a term policy, the coverage will end. Most policies do not allow the coverage to be reinstated if you decide at a later date that you would like to resume paying the premiums.

LOWER PREMIUMS THAN FOR PERMANENT INSURANCE

Term insurance is more popular with young people than permanent insurance, because the premiums are so much lower. However, to compare term with permanent is like comparing apples and oranges—they have some things in common, but there are also major differences.

Term insurance may be ideal for providing a large amount of insurance coverage at the least cost in situations where the insurance is needed for a limited period of time.

PLANNING TO PROTECT ● *Cam and Mary Opt for Term Insurance*

Cam and Mary are in their thirties, and have three young children. Cam is a chartered professional accountant, and Mary is an architect. They both work outside the home, and they depend on their combined incomes to cover the family's living expenses and to pay the mortgage on their newly purchased house. They are managing to make their maximum RRSP contributions each year, but they have not been able to spare any additional funds for savings outside the RRSP.

Cam and Mary are concerned that if either of them were to die prematurely, either because of illness or in an accident, the family's financial health would be jeopardized. Therefore, they have decided that each of them will take out $2 million of term life insurance. They recognize that there will not be any cash value to the policies, the premiums will rise as they get older, and the coverage will terminate at a certain age (probably age 80). However, in spite of these drawbacks compared to permanent insurance, they feel that term insurance gives them the maximum protection that they can afford for the next 15 to 20 years that the children will be financially dependent on them.

Cam decided to purchase the maximum available amount of insurance through his province's CPA Group Plan, because the premium cost was significantly lower than for the term policies that he could have obtained privately. Mary is considering whether to buy some of her insurance through her architects' association group plan, and to make up the difference by taking out a term policy on her own. Although the premiums seem to be lower under the group plan, she feels that the additional features offered under the private coverage (such as the ability to convert the policy into permanent insurance) outweigh the premium savings.

· ·

CONVERTIBLE TERM INSURANCE

One of the many options that are open to you when taking out term insurance is that you can pay an additional premium for the right to convert the policy to permanent insurance, without having to pass a medical examination. If you are in good health now, but you are not willing to take the chance that you will still be in good enough health in the future, this might be worth considering, especially in light of the relatively small extra cost for the convertible feature.

DECREASING TERM INSURANCE

Instead of term insurance where the coverage remains level and the premiums increase over time, you might want to consider obtaining *decreasing term* insurance, where the premiums remain level. If you are concerned that you will not be able to afford the premiums in 5, 10, or 15 years, but you still want to have as much term insurance as you can afford, a decreasing term policy may be the answer. However, this may not be a wise thing to do from a long-term estate planning viewpoint. Your family's need for insurance coverage on your life will not necessarily end after your children are grown up and supporting themselves.

Permanent Insurance

There are several kinds of permanent insurance, such as:

- whole life
- universal life
- variable life

What all types of permanent insurance have in common is that they will remain in force for your entire life—provided of course, that you have paid the required premiums! Permanent insurance differs from term insurance in another important way. A permanent insurance policy has a savings element or so-called cash value. In simple terms, the savings component of permanent insurance will grow larger the longer the policy remains in force. Most permanent policies allow the policyholder to withdraw some or all of the cash value of the policy during the policyholder's lifetime. (With term insurance, you have to die before any payment will generally be made.) Also, permanent insurance policies usually give the policyholder the ability to obtain a loan from the insurance company up to the cash surrender value of the policy.

When you purchase permanent insurance instead of term, your premiums are higher because part of the premium is to cover the pure insurance risk, and part is for the so-called savings or investment component of the policy.

WHOLE LIFE INSURANCE

Whole life is the traditional type of permanent insurance where the premiums you pay, some of the cash values of the policy and the future death benefit are all predetermined at the time that you acquire the policy and are guaranteed by the insurance company. Policyholders will typically receive *dividends* on the policy, which will vary according to the actual investment performance, "mortality experience" and expenses. Generally, the investment component of a whole life policy is similar to a diversified bond fund, and is risk averse over the long run.

UNIVERSAL LIFE

Universal life has two components: the pure *life insurance* coverage, and the *investment* component. These policies offer the policyholder more flexibility over the years. For example, you can choose (within certain parameters) the type of investment for the savings component of the policy (e.g. a particular stock market or bond index). Also, you can switch investment strategies from time to time according to changing economic conditions and the degree of investment risk you are prepared to take. Unlike the traditional whole life policy, the rate of return on the investment component of the policy is not predetermined, nor is it guaranteed by the insurance company. Both universal life and whole life policies offer the policyholder flexibility over the years. For example, universal life can allow for variable premium deposits or death benefit options.

Many people choose universal life type policies over the more traditional type of permanent insurance in order to reduce their premiums or to achieve a faster build-up in the investment component of the policy. However, if investment rates of return fall, it may be necessary to make additional "deposits" to the policy, because the rate of return on the investment component is no longer large enough to create the required reserve to cover the insurance risk under the policy. If you are considering some form of permanent insurance, ask your agent to what extent, if any, the investment returns reflected in the projections that were given to you are guaranteed by the insurance company and get their response in writing.

Term to 100

A *Term to 100* is a hybrid of term and permanent insurance. Unlike ordinary term insurance, which expires at a certain age (usually age 80), Term to 100 policies continue in force until the insured person reaches age 100. The reason for the extended coverage is that the premiums in the early years of the policy are higher than what is required to cover the insurance risk on ordinary term insurance, which expires at a certain age. The higher premiums enable the insurance company to build up a reserve to fund the future death benefit payment.

Another major difference between Term to 100 and other forms of permanent insurance is that there is no cash surrender value to a Term to 100 policy.

Premiums under a Term to 100 policy usually remain level throughout the period of time the policy is in force. Furthermore, if you stop paying the premiums, the policy will lapse. Refer to Appendix C for the pros and cons of different types of life insurance.

THINK TWICE BEFORE CANCELLING A TERM 100 POLICY

If you have a Term 100 policy that you took out some years ago, and you feel that your family circumstances and needs have changed so that you no longer really need this coverage, whatever you do, don't cancel the policy before speaking to an insurance agent who is familiar with charitable giving strategies involving life insurance. Even though Term 100 policies do not have any cash surrender value, your particular policy might still be worth something in an economic sense and have a *fair market value*. An actuary who is experienced in the valuation of life insurance policies would be able to determine the fair market value, if any, based on your age, life expectancy, the death benefit amount of the policy, the annual premium amount, and certain other factors. Thus, if your particular policy does have a significant fair market value, you might be able to donate the policy (i.e. transfer its ownership) to a particular charity or hospital that is important to you. This would result in you receiving a charitable donation tax receipt for the fair market value amount, which you could claim in your income tax return for the year in which you donated the policy.

By doing this, the particular charity would become the legal owner of the policy, and provided that the premiums are paid each year to keep the policy in force, the charity would receive the insurance policy death benefit when you die. With such arrangements, the donor and the charity would enter into a binding legal agreement, and the insurance company would also be involved in order to put the change of ownership into effect. The charity might also request that you make an additional lump-sum charitable donation to the charity in cash to cover the future premiums for a few years, or make ongoing cash donations monthly or annually for several years in order to cover the future premiums payable by the charity. If applicable, once you are no longer covering the charity's premium payment obligations with cash donations, it would then be up to the charity to decide whether or not to continue paying the premiums to keep the policy on your life in force— but most likely it would want to do this, by covering the future premiums out of its own financial resources.

This is a fairly complex and sophisticated area of philanthropy that requires the expertise of an insurance advisor who has experience in this particular area. Also, you should obtain legal and tax advice if you are considering such a strategy.

Second-to-Die Policies

You might decide that life insurance is the best way to provide the funds to cover capital gains taxes that will arise when a family business or real estate passes down to your children or grandchildren. In that case, a *second-to-die* type coverage on you and your spouse is something to consider. This would involve both you and your spouse being jointly insured under one policy. The face amount of the policy (the death benefit) would be paid by the insurance company only after *both* you and your spouse have died, in other words, on the second death.

Why would one want to do this? There are several reasons. First, the premiums will be substantially lower than if separate policies were to be taken out by you or your spouse. From an actuarial viewpoint, the mortality risk can be calculated by the insurance company based on the combined life expectancy of both people. Therefore, this type of coverage can work to your advantage if either you or your spouse happens to have any medical condition that could affect your insurability—if one of you is a smoker, or if one is much older than the other. However, even in situations where both husband and wife are non-smokers and in good health, a second-to-die policy will always mean lower premiums than if separate policies were to be taken out.

Frankly, the most important reason for considering this type of coverage is that you may not need the insurance money when the first spouse dies, but only on the second death. This fits well with the estate planning strategy of postponing the deemed disposition problem until the death of the surviving spouse. However, this means arranging your wills so that any property which is owned by you or your spouse (such as your family cottage) will pass either outright (or in trust) to the surviving spouse after the first death, rather than going directly to one or more children.

PLANNING TO PROTECT ● *If You're Lucky Enough to Own Two Vacation Properties...*

Josephine, who is 58 years of age, and her husband Frank, who is age 60, jointly own their home in Toronto. Josephine also owns a ski chalet that she bought some years ago with money she saved from her part-time job as an interior decorator. And Frank owns a summer cottage up north, which he inherited from his parents more than 20 years ago. Both vacation properties have gone up substantially in value. Josephine and Frank eventually want to transfer the cottage to their son Louis, and the ski chalet to their daughter Joan.

They figure that about $50,000 of additional income tax would become payable if either property were to be transferred now. (As outlined in Chapter 9, a transfer of property by way of gift to someone other than one's spouse, is treated for income tax purposes as a sale at fair market value for capital gains purposes.)

Josephine's current will stipulates that the ski chalet is to go to Joan, and the remainder of her estate is to go to Frank, if he survives her. Otherwise, the residue of her estate is to be divided equally between her two children. Frank's current will is similar to Josephine's, in that it states that the cottage is to go to Louis, after Frank's death, and the residue of the estate is to go to Josephine, if she survives him. Otherwise, the residue of Frank's estate is to be divided equally between the two children.

The way things stand at the moment, a capital gain will arise on either Josephine's or Frank's death because their wills each provide for the particular person's vacation property to be left directly to one of the children, rather than going *first* to the surviving spouse. Thus, there will not be a spousal rollover, and the deemed disposition for capital gains purposes will apply. Josephine and Frank are concerned that from an estate planning viewpoint, there may not be enough cash on hand or liquid assets in their estates to cover the taxes, and they fear that one of the properties might eventually have to be sold to raise the required funds.

What do you think they should do?

First, Josephine and Frank should consider revising their wills so that the vacation property is left initially to the surviving spouse. This would prevent the capital gain from arising on the first death. Alternatively, instead of leaving the property outright to the surviving spouse, their wills could stipulate that the property is to be held *in trust* for the surviving spouse, with the spouse having the exclusive legal right to use the property for the rest of his or her life. Provided that the trust provisions of their wills meet certain conditions set out in the *Income Tax Act*, the spousal rollover will apply, and the deemed realization for capital gains purposes can be postponed until the death of the surviving spouse. Taxes will then arise on the second death, not the first, which is a far more palatable result.

Now what? Where will the money come from to pay the tax on the capital gains arising on the second death? This is the type of situation where a second-to-die type of insurance coverage could be used. Since Josephine is younger than Frank and has a longer life expectancy because she is a woman, the premium on a second-to-die policy would be considerably lower than if each of them took out separate insurance policies to cover the capital gains tax.

If you think that a second-to-die type of coverage might be useful in your situation, it is essential for the insurance coverage to dovetail with your and your spouse's wills. In the above example, a second-to-die policy for Frank and Josephine would not do them much good if they don't revise their wills so that the capital gains spousal rollover will be applicable to each vacation property, thereby postponing the moment of reckoning until the second death.

CHOOSING AN INSURANCE AGENT

It is becoming increasingly common for life insurance to be mass marketed and to be sold directly to the consumer without the involvement of an agent. Computer programs and statistical analyses are used to determine a person's financial profile and the level of insurance coverage needed. Some insurance companies are marketing their insurance products both through their existing network of life insurance agents, and also by means of direct selling techniques. Because the commission-based agent is being bypassed, the marketing and distribution costs may be lower. This may result in a lower insurance cost (premiums) compared to a policy bought through an agent.

Some people decide to be "their own insurance advisor" by purchasing the insurance directly from one of the insurance companies or financial institutions that are authorized to sell life insurance. However, if you decide to "buy direct," how will you know if the policy is the right type (for example, term versus permanent insurance)? Can you be sure that you will have taken all of the relevant financial and personal factors into account in deciding on the amount and type of insurance? Product and cost comparisons are often difficult to make, because of the multitude of life insurance product features and options.

Role of a Life Insurance Agent

An experienced life insurance agent can help you in a number of ways, including:

- assessing your life insurance needs
- determining the type of policy
- recommending the amount of coverage that you should have
- obtaining competitive quotes from more than one insurance company, preparing a comparative analysis, and making a recommendation on which insurance company you should go with
- helping you with the policy application and arranging for any medical examinations that may be required
- providing ongoing advice and reviewing your insurance needs with you on a regular basis

Agents' Qualifications

Insurance agents are licensed and regulated by the provincial governments. Some agents are tied to a particular insurance company, and will generally sell only the insurance products offered by that company. However, it has become far more common for life insurance agents to operate as *brokers* and to deal with any number of insurance companies, even though they may be officially licensed by one particular insurance company.

Agents who hold the designation "Chartered Life Underwriter" (C.L.U.) have completed a course of study over several years in various areas of insurance and personal financial planning. There are also other professional designations, such as Chartered Financial Consultant (CH.F.C.) and Certified Financial Planner (C.F.P.), which may attest to the agent's level of knowledge and experience.

Factors to Consider in Choosing an Agent

- In deciding which agent to deal with, ask your business associates and friends if they have someone they would strongly recommend.
- The agent you choose should be someone you can trust, and who will take the time to listen to you and understand your needs.
- You should ask the agent how long he or she has been in the business, and you might consider asking for references from one of the agent's other clients.
- Ask the agent if he/she is a member of the Society for Trust and Estate Planning Practitioners (STEP) and holds the TEP designation.
- If your financial situation is complex or if you own a family business, you should inquire whether the agent has any experience in dealing with business owners and their estate planning needs. As discussed in more detail in Chapter 13, "Privately-Owned Businesses," there are a number of ways that life insurance can be used in the business succession planning context. For example, it can be used to provide funding for a shareholder buy-out arrangement, or to provide funds to cover capital gains taxes arising on death.
- Your insurance agent should be willing to work with your accountant, lawyer, investment advisor and tax advisor in order to develop the optimum estate planning strategy to ensure the survival of your privately-owned business.

The factors to consider in choosing a life insurance agent are discussed more fully in Chapter 16, Selecting Professional Advisors. Talk to and compare two or three insurance agents before deciding which one, if any, you want to rely on for advice. You need that benchmark for comparison and to accelerate your learning curve on the issues important to your situation.

Agents Earn Commissions

Most life insurance agents earn their income in the form of commissions on the life insurance policies they sell. The commissions on permanent insurance tend to be greater than on term insurance products. Commission rates vary from company to company, and from one life insurance product to another. Because insurance agents' incomes depend on the volume of insurance they sell, one might think that their recommendations on the need for, and the amount of, life insurance that is required in a situation are "product and sales driven." In the writers' experience, this is not the case. Good insurance agents are "planning driven," and they will recommend what they believe is best for you and your family.

People should not dismiss the recommendations of an insurance agent, because they perceive the agent to have a strong bias, due to the fact that he or she stands to earn a commission from a sale of life insurance. The vast majority of life insurance agents are people of integrity who will not recommend the purchase of life insurance unless it is clearly warranted under the circumstances. They know that their recommendations must be able to withstand scrutiny by the client's accountant or financial advisor, and their reputations are at stake. Life insurance agents have a valuable role to play in the estate planning process.

CHOOSING A LIFE INSURANCE COMPANY

Historically, life insurance companies have been among the strongest financial institutions in the country. Insurance companies are subject to strict federal and provincial regulatory requirements, and must meet various solvency tests in order to maintain their licences to operate.

Is Your Insurance Policy "Guaranteed"?

A life insurance policy is not protected in the same way as a deposit with a bank or trust company. If you have funds on deposit with a Canadian chartered bank or trust company, your deposit is guaranteed by the federal government (up to $100,000 through CDIC) in the event of the financial collapse of the particular bank or trust company. Such protection is not provided in the case of life insurance companies. However, all life insurance companies that carry on business in Canada belong to the Canadian Life and Health Insurance Compensation Corporation, and contribute to a fund (Assuris) that is to be used to compensate policyholders in the event of the failure of a particular insurance company. For more information on insurance protection, refer to Chapter 2, "What Assets Will You Have?"

Although many years ago, bondholders and shareholders of several failed companies such as Confederation Life took huge financial losses, the life insurance policies issued by such companies were taken over by other companies. As a result, the policyholders were not "left out in the cold." It is our understanding that no one to date has lost their life insurance coverage as a result of the financial collapse of a Canadian life insurance company. Whether this continues to be the case in the years ahead remains to be seen. Since insurance companies are subject to very stringent regulatory requirements and because of close scrutiny of their financial affairs both by government authorities and the public, one hopes that there will not be any more failures.

Your choice of which life insurance company to go with is one of the most important financial decisions of your life. You will be making a financial contract with the insurance company whereby, in return for the payment of premiums over time, the insurance company guarantees that it will pay the stated benefits under the policy in the future. You must be confident that the insurance company is financially sound, and will be able to honour its financial promise when the time comes.

Rating of Insurance Companies

Your insurance agent can help you decide which company you should use in addition to various reports that rate the financial condition of Canadian life insurance companies. Your insurance agent should be able to give you an analysis showing how various companies have been rated. You may find useful the reports issued by rating agencies such as Standard and Poor's, Moody's, or Fitch, to name but a few.

COMPARISON OF GROUP INSURANCE OVER INDIVIDUAL INSURANCE

Group insurance is a method of buying a range of types of insurance at a reduced premium price. Because of economies of scale and risk averaging, these discounted packages can be offered.

The bulk of group insurance is obtained by employers for their full-time employees. Generally, group benefits are only available while employed. Other major suppliers of group insurance are trade and professional associations for their members.

Although there could be some premium cost saving to group insurance, there could also be disadvantages. Premium rates could go up every year, depending on the claims history of the group. The policy is probably not portable, meaning that if you leave the association or employer, you can no longer continue the policy group coverage. The problem then is that you may not be medically insurable for a variety of reasons when you apply for individual coverage through a different insurer. Maybe you would be considered higher risk, with higher premiums and reduced or limited coverage.

After reviewing the pros and cons, depending on your situation, you may want to consider the benefits of having some of both types of coverage.

INCOME TAX TREATMENT OF LIFE INSURANCE

Life insurance policies have long received very favourable treatment under the Canadian income tax system. Life insurance is treated favourably for tax purposes in two ways:

- The *death benefit* payment of the face amount of the policy following the death of the insured person is completely tax-free.
- The annual cash build-up in the investment component of a permanent insurance policy (such as traditional whole life or universal life) is exempt from income tax in the policyholder's hands, while the policy remains in force.

Death Benefit Is Tax-Free

In the United States life insurance proceeds that are payable upon the death of the insured person are generally included in the total estate value for U.S. estate tax purposes. However, this is not the case in Canada, since we no longer have any estate tax or succession duties. (As outlined in Chapter 8, "Death and Taxes," the federal estate tax was abolished at the end of 1971 at the time that capital gains taxation was introduced. All of the provinces had abandoned gift taxes and succession duties by the late 1970s.)

Proceeds from Cancellation of a Permanent Insurance Policy

If you cancel a permanent insurance policy and receive the *cash surrender value* of the policy, you may be subject to income tax on a portion of the proceeds. To the extent that there has been a tax-free build-up in the cash value of the policy during the time the policy was in force, the policyholder may be required to include an amount in his or her taxable income if the policy is cancelled. In such cases, the insurance company will advise the policyholder of the taxable amount.

Tax-Free Accumulation of the Investment Component

Virtually any income-earning investment that you make will result in your having to report income in your tax return each year, whether it be interest income on a term deposit, dividends on publicly-traded shares, or capital gains realized on the sale of securities. One of the major exceptions is your Registered Retirement Savings Plan (RRSP) in which income or capital gains are *tax sheltered* from year to year.

A permanent insurance policy that has an investment component is in some ways similar to an RRSP, because the annual build-up in the cash value is not subject to income tax in the policyholder's hands on a year-by-year basis. This could be merely a deferral of income tax, if the policy were to be cancelled during the person's lifetime and the person received the cash surrender value (a portion of the proceeds may be taxable). However, if such a policy is left in force until after the insured person dies and the face amount of the policy is paid out, the year-by-year increase in the investment component of the policy may ultimately become part of the tax-free death benefit payment. This can represent a permanent tax saving on the investment component of the policy, not merely a tax deferral.

Policy Must Be an Exempt Policy for Income Tax Purposes

In order for the investment component of a policy not to be subject to income tax in the policyholder's hands each year, the policy itself must qualify for income tax purposes as an exempt policy, and comply with certain tests set out in the *Income Tax Act* and *Regulations*. Canadian life insurance companies are well aware of the rules, and design their policies to fit these tax requirements.

If you were to purchase a policy from a life insurance company outside of Canada, it is possible that the policy does not meet the exempt policy tests in the *Income Tax Act* and *Regulations* (unless it was specifically designed to meet this test). You might find yourself in the unfortunate position of having to report some amount each year in your income tax return, representing the annual increase in the investment component of the policy. In addition to this adverse tax effect, you might also be taking a significant financial risk in purchasing a life insurance policy from a foreign insurance company. It might be subject to little if any government regulation in the country in which it is based.

Insurance Company's Taxes Affect the Rate of Return

It should be noted that life insurance companies that operate in Canada are themselves subject to income taxes, as well as to various capital taxes. These taxes indirectly affect the rate of return that they can offer on the investment component of a permanent insurance policy. However, the somewhat lower rate of return on the savings component of a permanent insurance policy must be weighed against the favourable income tax effects outlined above.

Policy Loan

If you have some type of permanent life insurance policy with a cash value, a situation might arise where you have a need for funds, but you don't want to cancel the policy. You may be able to obtain a loan from the insurance company for an amount up to the cash surrender value of the policy. In certain situations, a portion of such a loan may be subject to income tax in your hands.

If you were to use a policy loan to acquire investments or use the borrowed funds in a business you are carrying on, the interest on the loan may be tax deductible by you. You should speak with your accountant or tax advisor before entering into such a transaction, in order to ensure that your borrowings obtain the optimum tax results.

HEALTH AND DISABILITY INSURANCE

Although life insurance is a key type of insurance to have, you should also be aware of other types of insurance, particularly health and disability. Disability and poor health could seriously erode your assets resulting in less available for your estate, let alone your quality of life in the meantime. Here is a brief overview of some of the insurance options to consider, including disability, critical illness, long-term care and out-of-country emergency medical insurance.

Disability

Good health is by far our greatest asset. With it, we can acquire other assets and improve our financial net worth. Without it, only liabilities.

The chances of becoming disabled are sobering. Statistics show that the chance of becoming disabled between 40–65 years of age for a minimum of three months is almost 40 percent. It is equally disturbing to know that almost one-half of those still disabled after six months will continue to be disabled at the end of five years.

Depending on the nature of the disability, you might be covered by Workers' Compensation benefits, CPP benefits or Employment Insurance disability benefits. Possibly you have coverage under group disability plan insurance benefits or personal disability insurance plan coverage. Group and individual plans will only cover a portion of your gross earnings.

It is important to review exactly what protection you currently have, if any, and the nature of that protection. You can then make appropriate plans to increase your protection on your lifestyle and financial needs. Basically, *disability* is defined as the inability, due to illness or injury, to continue to work. Disability insurance is designed to compensate the insured for a portion of the income that is lost due to the disabling injury or illness.

Definitions of disability vary from insurance company contract to contract. Whether or not your policy will pay you benefits may well depend on how the company defines disability. Most contracts define disability according to one of four types. Carefully read the wording of your contract, as some are so restrictive it might be almost impossible to be eligible for a claim. Here is an overview, from the least to the most restrictive.

OWN OCCUPATION

Disability is defined as inability to work in your own occupation only. Prove that you are disabled from doing your own job and are under the care of a doctor, and you qualify for benefits. Even if you went to work in another occupation, you may still qualify for benefits. Individual insurance contracts may offer an "own occupation" clause to age 65.

REGULAR OCCUPATION

This type would provide coverage in the event that you are disabled and unable to work in your own occupation, provided that you choose not to work in an alternative occupation.

ANY OCCUPATION

This would cover disability from any suitable occupation, based on your education, training and/or experience. Most, but not all, group insurance contracts specify an "any occupation" disability after the first two years of disability.

TOTAL AND PERMANENT

Some insurance contracts require that you not only be totally disabled from working, but also that your disability must be permanent.

Critical Illness

Although life insurance protects your dependent(s) in the event of your death and disability insurance replaces a portion of your earnings if you are unable to work, there could be a lot of additional expenses that might occur as a result of your disability. Recovering from a major illness could rapidly diminish your savings and ability to obtain credit.

The main purpose of *critical illness insurance* is to provide you with a lump-sum benefit, which is generally tax-free, if you conform to the policy requirements. You can then use these funds to enhance your quality of life and reduce financial stress. For example, you could pay off any outstanding debts including the mortgage, pay for any necessary home renovations to make your daily living needs easier or pay for specialized medical treatment not covered by your provincial health insurance. The lump-sum benefit could also be used to travel to other countries to seek alternative therapies or facilitate recuperation.

There are no restrictions on what you can do with the lump-sum benefit. It is not based on your ability to work and you are entitled to the full benefit, even if you subsequently make a full recovery.

The policy coverage normally requires that you have been diagnosed with, or have surgery for, a critical illness specified in the policy. In addition, you need to survive for at least 30 days. The types of illness include: stroke; heart attack, including coronary bypass surgery; terminal cancer; blindness; paralysis; or kidney failure. In many cases, those who have received organ transplants are also covered. If you are interested in this type of coverage, check with various insurance companies to obtain competitive quotes. Premiums, coverage and eligibility can vary.

Long-Term Care Insurance

This type of coverage will pay for the cost of long-term care if you develop a disabling condition or chronic illness. For example, maybe you require being relocated to a long-term care facility or require in-home caregiver assistance.

Normally, this type of insurance pays a fixed amount each day, for example, $100 for long-term care or other care. The payments are free from tax. Naturally, premiums will vary depending on the amount of daily coverage that you want.

Out-of-Country Emergency Medical Insurance

Statistics show that more Canadians per capita travel outside the country than any other country. Are you one of those looking forward to travelling somewhere warm or exciting in the near future? If so, make sure that you are protected by out-of-country insurance. The potential financial risk exists whether you leave the country for an hour, a day or a month. You could be travelling anywhere in the world, but the country with the most expensive medical system is the U.S.

If you have a serious injury or illness in the United States and require emergency medical attention, you will be financially devastated unless you have out-of-country medical insurance. The need for this extra insurance protection is simple. Provincial health insurance plans vary by province, but each provides you with the necessary protection when travelling within Canada. Coverage by provincial plans for hospital care outside Canada is nominal, e.g. $75 to $500+ Canadian funds per day, depending on your province. This is very low compared to medical costs in the U.S. It may only cover 5 percent, if that, of your total outlay.

The problem is that health care in the U.S. is very different from the Medicare coverage we are accustomed to in Canada. We are not accustomed to being personally billed, so we don't fully appreciate the real cost of treatment. In the U.S. system, private hospitals and doctors operate in a profit-oriented environment, and costs are much greater. In the U.S., the average hospital stay often exceeds $1,500 U.S. a day, and can run as high as $10,000 U.S. a day or more for intensive care. Certain emergency surgical operations can cost $250,000 U.S. or more. So who pays the shortfall if you have a medical emergency in the U.S.? You do. Unless, of course, you have wisely purchased supplemental medical insurance *before* you leave Canada, for the duration of your U.S. stay, be it a day or six months. Keep in mind this supplemental insurance covers emergency non-elective treatment for injury or illness only. It does not cover non-emergency treatment or services. It is not a substitute for Canadian Medicare.

You can get extended stay coverage (e.g. for Snowbirds) or a multi-trip plan. This latter type of plan allows you to travel outside Canada for as many times as you like within the one-year period of the plan up to a certain number of days at a time. You select the number of days, for example, 10, 20, 30 days, etc. Premium rates vary greatly between insurers depending on factors such as the nature of coverage, your age and pre-existing medical condition, policy exclusions and limitations, the deductible portion of policy, whether you have a preferred (for healthy people) or standard rate plan, and the duration of your stay in the U.S. Do not choose a plan based on price alone but consider such factors as benefits, limitations, exclusions, and deductibles. Remember to claim your insurance premiums for a tax credit on your income tax return under "medical expenses."

Check out as many insurance programs as you can that offer the type of coverage you are seeking. You need a full range of comparisons to evaluate the relative strengths and weaknesses of the various plans, to make your final decision much less stressful. To eliminate misunder-standing, get confirmation in writing of any representations or responses to requests made by you to your insurance company. Keep copies of all correspondence between you and your insurance company, as well as any receipts for items to be claimed for reimbursement.

Here is a brief overview of the three common types of insurance plan options.

EXTENDED STAY INSURANCE

This coverage is intended to protect you for the whole duration of your travel or Snowbird stay in the U.S., Mexico or elsewhere, for a continuous period. The premium is based on the duration of your stay, for example, up to six months. You pay for the exact number of days you need.

MULTI-TRIP INSURANCE

This plan is designed for shorter-term stay coverage outside Canada. You arrange coverage for a packaged number of days, e.g. a maximum single duration stay not exceeding 15, 30, 45, 90 days, etc. This means you can travel outside Canada as many times as you like within the length of your policy coverage, as long as any one trip does not exceed your maximum number of days per trip (e.g. 15, 30–90, etc.). As soon as you return to Canada for at least a day, the cycle starts again.

These multi-trip plans are usually based on an annual premium, for example covering a calendar year period or 12 months from the time you take it out. One of the key benefits of a multi-trip plan is that it is available for spontaneous trips any time you cross the Canada-U.S. border. You can obtain multi-trip plans through travel agents, auto associations, banks and some credit card companies or insurers directly.

TOP-UP INSURANCE

This plan provides additional supplemental emergency medical coverage to *top-up* an existing out-of-country medical plan. This existing plan could be coverage as a retiree from a govern-ment, other employer, union or association plan or credit card plan. There are risks, however, with this top-up approach. Some plans don't permit top-ups. There can be great differences between different plan policies. There is a risk that there could be a lapse in time periods between coverage, or disputes between different insurers as to the issue of coverage. For example, if your basic medical plan coverage has a ceiling cap of say $50,000, and lasts for a maximum number of days, and your top-up plan kicks in at the end of that time period, what happens if you have a catastrophic injury just before the first plan lapses? You are only covered for $50,000. Your expenses could be $200,000. You would be out the difference. Another problem could arise if the top-up company deems your illness was pre-existing, if you make a claim with your first insurer first. An alternative is to co-ordinate a basic plan and top-up plan from the same insurer.

The other reality is that generally it is less expensive and less risky to have just one plan over everything. It certainly eliminates the uncertainty and saves the inconvenience and frustration of having to deal with two different claims procedures.

If you take insurance with one insurer and they find out that you have existing out-of-country insurance coverage of some form through an employer, pension health plan or other carrier, they can make a claim against that plan up to the limit of the plan, a process called *subrogation*. You may not want that to happen if it dilutes your fixed health benefits under your pension plan coverage. However, if your main out-of-country insurance company is a member of the Canadian Life and Health Insurance Association (CLHIA) they will not look to your pension plan coverage for the first $50,000. Contact the CLHIA for their current policy and member companies (contact information is provided later in this chapter).

BUSINESS-RELATED INSURANCE

If you have a business involving partners, you should seriously consider the need for, and benefits of, buy/sell insurance, as well as key person insurance. Refer to the discussion of those options in Chapter 13, "Privately-Owned Businesses."

PLANNING TIPS

There are a variety of ways that life, health, and disability insurance can be used as part of your overall estate planning strategy, such as:

- to create additional capital after your death to be used to generate investment income for your spouse or family
- to provide funds to pay off the mortgage on your home
- to cover various expenses arising upon death, such as funeral costs
- to provide the funds needed to cover capital gains taxes arising on death on property transferred to someone other than your spouse
- to provide the financing for the purchase of shares of a closely-held corporation, as a result of the death of one of the shareholders.

WHERE TO GET MORE INFORMATION

- A life insurance agent is a good source of information on the kinds of insurance policies that are available and their uses. Refer to the discussion on selecting an agent earlier in this chapter. Look on the Internet using search engines such as Google for Insurance Agents and Brokers. Read Chapter 16, "Selecting Professional Advisors."

- The Canadian Life and Health Insurance Association Inc. (CLHIA) has published a useful booklet entitled *A Guide to Life Insurance*, which can be downloaded from the "Consumer Assistance" section of their website. The booklet provides a very useful overview of the various kinds and uses of life insurance, and offers some helpful planning tips. In addition, CLHIA have published other information booklets. Refer to Appendix A, "Sources of Information." Copies of any booklets can also be obtained from:

  The Information Centre
  Canadian Life and Health Insurance Association Inc.
  1 Queen Street East, Suite 1700
  Toronto, Ontario M5C 2X9
  Tel: (416) 777-2344 or 1-800-268-8099
  Website: *www.clhia.ca*

- For an in-depth discussion of life insurance, read *Estate Planning with Life Insurance* (6th edition) by Glenn R. Stephens, available from Wolters Kluwer (formerly CCH Canada).

- Refer to Appendix C for charts relating to life insurance needs and comparison of different types of insurance.

- Refer to *The Canadian Snowbird Guide: Everything You Need to Know About Living Part-Time in the USA and Mexico* (4th edition) by Douglas Gray (published by John Wiley & Sons Canada Ltd.), for an extensive discussion about out-of-country emergency supplemental medical insurance.

- Refer to websites: *www.estateplanning.ca*, *www.snowbird.ca*, *www.smallbiz.ca*, and *www.homebuyer.ca*.

SUMMARY

There are many issues to consider when reviewing the benefits of life, health and disability insurance. We have discussed ways of identifying the need for life insurance and determining the desirable amount, outlined the types of life insurance and given guidelines on choosing an insurance agent and company. Also covered were the tax implications of using life insurance, comparison of group over individual insurance, the key types of health and disability insurance and where to get more information.

? Frequently
: **Asked Questions**

1. *Is life insurance subject to income tax or capital gains tax, when paid to a person's estate, or to one or more named beneficiaries, after the insured person's death?*

   No. The "death benefit" payable under a life insurance policy (usually the "face amount" of the policy) is received tax-free by the deceased's estate, or by one or more named beneficiaries. Furthermore, since Canada does not have an "estate tax" as such, life insurance proceeds that are payable as a result of a person's death are not subject to such a tax.

2. *Which is better—term insurance or permanent insurance (e.g. universal life)?*

   There are pros and cons to each type of insurance. Many factors must be considered in deciding which type of insurance should be used in a particular situation, including:
   - the annual premium—term insurance is cheaper now, but the premiums will rise in the future, and the coverage may cease upon reaching a certain age
   - the number of years for which life insurance coverage is required
   - the reason(s) for life insurance being used
   - the age and health of the person whose life is to be insured

Selecting
Professional Advisors

"A prudent person benefits from personal experience, a wise one from the experience of others."

JOSEPH COLLINS

INTRODUCTION

Professional advisors are essential to protect your tax and estate planning interests. They can provide knowledge, expertise and objective advice in areas in which you have little experience. They can also make sure that you maximize the amount of your estate and minimize the amount of tax paid on your death.

It is important to recognize when it is necessary to call in an expert to assist you. Because of the costs associated with hiring a lawyer, accountant, or financial planner, some people are inclined to try the do-it-yourself approach. This can be a short-sighted detrimental approach. For instance, the person who processes his or her own income tax return (even using one of the popular tax return programs) rather than hiring a professional tax accountant may miss out on tax exemptions that could save much more than the cost of the accountant's time. A possible saving grace, however, is that a missed deduction or exemption on a tax return is often caught by the CRA when they process your tax return. There is no such "safety net" for your will or power of attorney. A person who does his or her own will or power of attorney could end up having the document(s) deemed invalid due to a technicality and cost the estate many thousands of dollars.

Although you would be utilizing the services of various advisors for specific tasks, you may also want to consider the benefits of having a trusted advisor who provides a long-term professional role of coordinating an appropriate team of experts to meet your ongoing needs. In other words, such a coordinator can provide a holistic approach to the stewardship of wealth, financial management and estate planning to preserve your wealth and ensure that your post-demise wishes are fully met.

These types of advisors provide hands-on service and relate to their clients on various levels, such as physical, emotional, financial and spiritual wellness. Next to personal health, financial health is the second most common concern that people have. As financial reversals have a direct effect on your personal health, selecting the right team of advisors is essential to your overall personal well being and quality of life.

This chapter will include the following topics:
- general selection factors to consider
- selecting a lawyer
- selecting an accountant
- selecting a financial planner
- selecting other financial and investment advisors
- where to get more information

GENERAL FACTORS TO CONSIDER WHEN SELECTING AN ADVISOR

There are many factors you should consider when selecting professional advisors including the person's professional qualifications, experience in your specific area of need, and their fee for services. It is helpful to prepare a list of such questions, plus others relating to your specific needs, and pose these to each of the prospective advisors. Prioritize the questions in case you run out of time scheduled for the meeting. That way your meeting will be more productive. You can always set a subsequent meeting. You also want to see if the advisor is pro-active, that is, asks you questions; rather than being strictly reactive and expecting you to ask all the questions. Some people may feel awkward discussing fees and areas of expertise, but it is important to establish these matters before you make a decision to use that person's services. Some of the most common general selection criteria include:

Qualifications

Before you entrust an advisor with your affairs, you will want to know that he or she has the appropriate qualifications to do the job. This may include a lawyer's or accountant's professional degree, or if an investment advisor or a financial planner, professional training accreditation and experience relative to their professed area of expertise. The fact that the person is an active member of a professional association or institute usually means an ongoing interest in seminars and courses to keep his or her professional training current.

Experience

It is very important to take a look at the advisor's experience in the area in which you need assistance. Such factors as the degree of expertise, the number of years' experience as an advisor, and percentage of time spent practising in that area are critically important. For example, the fact that a lawyer has been practising law for 10 years does not necessarily mean that the lawyer has a high degree of expertise in the area on which you are seeking advice, for example, will preparation and estate planning. Perhaps only 10 percent of the practice has been spent in that specific area. An accountant who has had 15 years' experience in small business bookkeeping may not have expertise to provide advice on tax and estate planning strategies. In addition, you may require specialized expertise on Canada–U.S. cross-border tax and estate planning, if you have assets in the U.S. It cannot be overemphasized how important it is to inquire as to the expertise and length of experience in your specific need area. If you don't ask the question, you won't be given the answer that will make a difference between the right and wrong advisor selection.

Society for Trust and Estate Practitioners

The Society for Trust and Estate Practitioners (STEP) is the leading international organization for trust and estate professionals, and there are several thousand members in Canada. Many lawyers, CPAs, life insurance agents, trust officers with banks and trust companies, and other professionals who work in the wills, trusts and estates area in Canada belong to STEP and hold the Trust and Estate Practitioner (TEP) designation, having met STEP's membership requirements. Also, they attend various STEP conferences and seminars on a regular basis in order to keep up to date and expand their knowledge. When you are in the process of interviewing possible professional advisors, you should enquire if the particular professional is a member of STEP and holds the TEP designation, which would show that he or she has both knowledge and experience in the wills, trusts and estates area.

Compatible Personality

When deciding on an advisor, make certain that you feel comfortable with the individual's personality. If you are going to have an ongoing relationship with the advisor, his or her attitude, sincere approach, and commitment to meet your needs is important. A healthy respect and rapport will increase your comfort level when discussing your needs, and thereby further enhance understanding of the issues. If you don't feel that there is "good chemistry," don't continue the relationship. It is only human nature that if you don't like someone, you resist contacting them, thereby compromising your best interests.

Good Communication Skills

You want an advisor who is a good listener, who elicits your responses and provides feedback in understandable layperson's terms. You want any issues and options fully disclosed, with pros and cons and recommendations.

You also want an advisor who is responsive to your communication needs, in terms of returning your e-mails and phone calls promptly, and keeping you informed on a regular basis in writing of matters dealing with your affairs. Some people and situations require more frequent communication than others do.

Accessibility

It is important to have an advisor who is accessible to you when you need them. If they become too busy for you, re-consider the relationship. You want to feel that your needs are a priority. You also want to have loyalty and not be shifted to another or junior advisor, because your original advisor is culling their clientele to concentrate on more lucrative clients.

Objectivity

This is an essential quality for a professional advisor. If advice were tainted in any way by bias or personal financial benefit, obviously it would be unreliable. That is why you want to get two or three opinions on your personal situation from each type of advisor, before carefully deciding which professionals to select.

Trust

Trust is a vital trait in the person you select to advise you. Whether the person is a lawyer, accountant, financial planner or other investment advisor, if you don't intuitively trust the advice as being solely in your best interests, never use them again. You have far too much to lose, in terms of your financial security and peace of mind, to have any doubts whatsoever. You cannot risk the chance that advice is governed primarily by the financial self-interest of the advisor, with your interests as a secondary consideration.

Integrity

This concept involves a number of traits, such as ethics, morality, honesty and credibility. You want an advisor with a high standard of personal and professional integrity. The advisor's reputation with other professional colleagues is one reference point. Keeping confidential information confidential is another trait. Depending on the nature of the advisory relationship, you may be disclosing many of your personal needs, hopes and dreams, as well as concerns. This puts you in a potentially vulnerable position.

Confidence

You must have confidence in your advisor if you are going to rely on the advice to enhance the quality of your decision making and minimize your risk. After considering the person's qualifications, experience, personality and style, you may feel a strong degree of confidence and trust in the individual that they will be totally objective. If you do not, don't use the person as an advisor; seek someone else as soon as possible.

Fees

It is important to feel comfortable with the fee being charged, and the payment terms. Is it fair, competitive, and affordable? Does it match the person's qualifications and experience? The saying "you get what you pay for" can be true of fees charged by lawyers, accountants, financial planners and other professionals. For instance, if you need a good tax accountant to advise you on minimizing taxes, you may have to pay a high hourly rate for the quality of advice that will save you thousands of dollars. On the other hand, if you only require bookkeeping services, then perhaps a junior accountant can do the job competently at a more affordable rate. Be certain the rate is within your budget, or you may not fully use the advisor effectively because of the expense factor.

Quite often, an initial meeting with a lawyer, accountant or financial planner is free or with a nominal fee. Ask about this when booking the appointment. An initial "no-fee" meeting provides an opportunity for both parties to see if the advisory relationship would be a good fit.

References

This is an important sourcing criterion, in addition to word-of-mouth referrals. This approach is particularly important for any advisor who would be playing an overall holistic role in your financial and estate planning affairs. Ask what other professional colleagues they deal with on a regular basis (e.g. lawyer, accountant, etc.) that would be familiar with their work. Then contact those professionals and ask about their strengths and weaknesses. In addition, ask how long they have been dealing with them. Don't feel embarrassed to ask the tough questions. You have far too much to lose by taking professional competence for granted and you need candid feedback.

Don't ask for, or expect an advisor to provide you with a list of clients. That would normally breach confidentiality. It would also not be fruitful, as the advisor is naturally only going to give names of clients whose positive assessment could be predicted.

An additional technique is to ask other professional advisors who you are dealing with, who they would recommend and why. You want to know what professionals are part of their network, in terms of who they enjoy working with and respect.

Comparison

Do not make a decision as to which advisor to use without first seeing a minimum of three advisors. You need that qualitative comparison to know which one, if any, you want to rely on. Seeing how they each respond to your questions will be an effective benchmark. The more exacting you are in your selection criteria, the more likely that a good match is made, and the more beneficial that advisor will be for you. As mentioned, you will probably use different advisors for different purposes.

SELECTING A LAWYER

There are many situations where you will require a lawyer, for example, to do a will, living will, power of attorney, trust, estate planning, buying or selling of real estate, leases, contracts, insurance or accident claims or legal disputes. If you have a business, you will need a lawyer to assist you. Every business decision involves a legal implication.

Although your lawyer is trained to give you legal advice as to your rights, remedies and options, it is you who must decide on the action to be taken.

Qualifications

Lawyers generally have a Bachelor of Laws degree (LL.B.) or Juris Doctor (J.D.) degree from a recognized Canadian university, and have to be licensed by the provincial law society in the province where they are practising. A lawyer in Canada is called both a barrister and a solicitor, but depending upon the preference of the lawyer, the lawyer may act as a barrister or solicitor or both. A *barrister* is a lawyer who practises courtroom law and deals in civil and/or criminal legal matters. A *solicitor* generally does not attend court, and performs specialized services such as drafting or reviewing legal agreements, including wills, leases, mortgages or contracts, estate or trust matters, or real estate conveyancing.

How to Find a Lawyer

There are many methods of finding lawyers.

LAWYER REFERRAL SERVICES

Most provinces have a lawyer referral program, which is usually coordinated through the Canadian Bar Association. Do a Google search for "Lawyer Referral Service" or contact the provincial Law Society or Canadian Bar Association branch in your province.

When you call, explain briefly the specific problem you have, or the type of law on which you want a lawyer's opinion, for example, real estate conveyancing, mortgages, wills, trusts, leases, contracts, tax, etc. The lawyer referral service will give you the name of a lawyer in your geographic area, and you can set up an appointment. A lawyer will give you an interview of up to 30 minutes for free or at a nominal fee, which may vary depending upon the province. At the end of the interview the lawyer will tell you what it would cost to provide a legal service to you and how long it would take. Then, if you and the lawyer agree to proceed, you may hire the lawyer to help you further at a negotiated fee.

Most lawyer referral services programs will only give you one lawyer's name per day, so keep phoning back to get two or three additional names for comparison purposes. However, be careful when using the above search technique. Lawyers usually have their names on up to three or more different areas of law, e.g. family, real estate, criminal, etc. You want to ask what percentage of time is spent in your area of interest. As a guideline, use a minimum of 50 percent. There is a direct correlation between the percentage of time spent in a particular field and the quality of expertise, interest and related advice.

REFERRAL BY FRIENDS, BANKER, ACCOUNTANT OR OTHER PROFESSIONAL ADVISOR

Ask these reference sources if they can recommend a lawyer who would be appropriate for your needs. A friend or relative might suggest a lawyer, for example, whose law speciality has nothing to do with wills, and who would be impractical for you to use. If someone recommends a specific lawyer, or a number of lawyers, ask the reason why he or she feels the person would be helpful for your needs, and what their personal experience has been with that lawyer. Maybe the person is just their next door neighbour or friend. Word-of-mouth referral from a trusted advisor is helpful, but still do your own comparison.

INTERNET SEARCH

If you use a search engine like Google, and type in "Lawyers" and the town or city where you live, a number of directories and lists will come up. Note that firms pay to be included in some or all such lists and directories, so some firms' names may not be shown. Still, there are a lot of names from which to choose, making it difficult. It can be a case of "too much information," which is all the more reason to get a few recommendations from people you know and trust.

Preparing for the Meeting

Since you are buying your lawyer's time, the less you use, the less it will cost. On the other hand, it is important that you clearly understand the advice that is given and what options are available to you.

Before going to see your lawyer, make sure that you get all your papers and documents together and put them in order—assuming that you wish to get advice on existing facts. Then, write out all the issues that you want advice on, and all the questions you want to ask. Arrange the sequence of your questions so that the critical matters are dealt with first. It may be helpful to give a copy of your questions to the lawyer, who could use that as an agenda for covering the various issues. Thinking about your questions will force you to focus on the reasons for seeing the lawyer. You will be satisfied that the meeting was productive when all questions are answered by the end of the interview.

When you talk to the lawyer, stick to the facts and make sure you tell your lawyer all the facts, good and bad. Ask questions if you don't understand the advice you are given, and ask what you can do to minimize costs. Request that the lawyer keep you regularly informed of developments if you are retaining the lawyer on an ongoing basis.

Understanding Fees and Costs

Here are the most common fee arrangements and the types of costs you might encounter.

HOURLY FEE

A lawyer bills out on a fixed rate per hour for all work done. The fee could range between $200 and $500 or more per hour, depending on your geographic area, specialized area of expertise, or amount of experience.

FIXED FEE

If you hire a lawyer to provide a routine service such as a conveyance (transfer of property to your name), or a will, the lawyer may be able to quote a flat fee, regardless of how much work might be involved. A lawyer may use this method when the time required can be calculated fairly accurately. For example, a simple will may cost from $300 to $750. A more complex will and related estate plan will obviously cost more.

PERCENTAGE FEE

Sometimes fees are calculated as a percentage of the value of the subject matter. This approach is often used when probating an estate. Most provinces have legislation that limits the maximum percentage that can be charged, regardless of the time spent.

CONTINGENCY FEE

Many provinces allow lawyers to charge on a contingency fee basis, that is, for a percentage of the total amount awarded if the case is won. Check the legislation in your province. For example, let's say that you have a fairly strong case, as a consequence of a personal injury due to a car accident, but do not have the funds to pay your lawyer at the outset or for ongoing work on the case. Your lawyer may agree to act for you and charge a percentage of the amount that you may eventually receive, either at trial or on a negotiated settlement prior to trial. If you win, the lawyer receives the fee; if you lose or the matter is not settled the lawyer gets nothing for the time spent. You would be responsible for paying the lawyer's disbursements and costs, however.

RESOLVING DISPUTES

Misunderstandings on fees or other matters should be immediately clarified to avoid having them mount into serious problems. If the relationship does not appear to be a beneficial one, you may decide at any time to use the services of another lawyer, and have the working file transferred to the new lawyer. If you seriously question a lawyer's invoice, you can have it "taxed," "assessed" or reviewed by a Court registrar or master. This procedure results in the fee being upheld or reduced. Your local court office will be able to provide further information on the procedure.

In the event that you feel that the lawyer acted improperly or incompetently, you have other forms of recourse. All provincial law societies require their members to have a certain minimum coverage for professional liability insurance for negligent or incompetent advice. Individual law firms could have additional coverage. If trust funds are missing, the Law Society allocates funds to cover that situation. Suing a lawyer is an option, but certainly the last resort for obvious reasons.

If you have complaints over issues such as possible conflict of interest, poor advice or other forms of professional misconduct or incompetence, you can make a formal complaint to the law society in your province. The complaints committee has many forms of discipline. If any money held in trust with the lawyer is missing, each provincial law society has an insurance fund to protect client losses in that type of situation.

SELECTING AN ACCOUNTANT

You should speak with a professionally qualified tax accountant to advise you on matters dealing with tax and estate planning, including the possible use of trusts, in order to minimize taxes during your life and tax consequences on your death. Depending on the size and nature of your estate, there could be considerable tax issues and consequences involved.

Many accountants are generalists who can provide basic advice on tax and estate planning issues. Others have branched out into financial planning, and have obtained their C.F.P. (Certified Financial Planner) designation. They would therefore be able to develop a full financial plan and organize a team of other experts to assist you in implementing it. Many Chartered Professional Accountants specialize in areas such as international tax and estate planning, either through specialty firms or large international chartered accountancy firms, with offices and expertise throughout the world.

Qualifications

Anyone can call himself or herself an accountant. One can also adopt the title "public accountant" without any qualifications, experience, regulations, or accountability to a professional association. That is why you have to be very careful when selecting the appropriate accountant for your needs. Chartered Professional Accountant is the main designation of qualified professional accountants in Canada who provide tax and estate planning advice. You may have heard of another professional accounting designation called a Certified Management Accountant (C.M.A.). However, as the designation implies, this type of accountant does not normally get involved in individual tax or estate planning. Provincial statutes govern accountants with the above designations.

How to Find an Accountant

One of the key services provided by an accountant is strategic tax and estate planning customized to your needs. Seek advice from a professional accountant, who specializes in tax matters exclusively, for your tax and estate strategic planning, as this is a highly specialized area. Consider speaking to two or three different tax experts, and make your choice based on which individual or firm is likely to do the best job for you.

When you are phoning an accounting firm, ask which accountant specializes in tax and estate planning matters. Sometimes, initial meetings are free, without any further obligation. Clarify this in advance. Keep in mind that all professional tax experts do not have the same mindset. Some enjoy the professional and intellectual challenge of knowing where the fine line is, and adopt an aggressive approach to tax planning strategies. Others are more reluctant to do this. In all instances, we are talking about using accredited professional accountants. They have too much to lose, in terms of their career and reputation, to advise you improperly. But you will definitely find a difference in style and attitude. The quality and nature of the advice could make a profound difference in the tax and estate savings you enjoy. That is why you need to compare accountants by exploring the following avenues.

PROFESSIONAL ASSOCIATIONS

The professional institute or association that governs CPAs may be a source of leads. You can e-mail, telephone or write the institute or association with a request for the names of three accountants who provide public accounting services relating to tax and estate planning within your geographic area.

REFERRAL BY FRIENDS, BANKER, LAWYER OR OTHER FINANCIAL ADVISOR

Friends or a banker, lawyer or financial advisor may be able to give you names of people they personally deal with or know.

INTERNET SEARCH

You can use an Internet search engine such as Google, and type in "accountants" or "chartered accounts" and narrow your search by specifying your town or city.

Preparing for the Meeting

Prior to a meeting with your accountant, make a list of your questions and concerns. Put them in writing and list them in order of priority in case you run out of time. As noted earlier, you will want to know the person's qualifications and areas of expertise.

Understanding Fees and Costs

Accountants' fees vary depending upon experience, speciality, type of service provided, size of firm and other considerations. The fee can range between $150 and $500 or more per hour for specialized tax and estate planning advice.

PLANNING TO PROTECT ● *Susan and Duane Switch Accountants and It's Worth Their While!*

Susan and Duane were financially independent entrepreneurs. They had established successful careers as professional golfers, but were frustrated at the amount of tax that they were paying. They had been using the services of a relative for tax advice, but were starting to lose confidence in the quality of the advice. They did not want to hurt family feelings, but felt that their best interests were not being served. They decided to seek out the services of a professional accountant with tax expertise and short-listed three prospective accountants. After meetings with all three accountants, they felt they had the benchmark comparison to make an informed decision.

The accountant they selected reviewed the tax strategies available and the tax paid unnecessarily in the past. She came to the conclusion that many legitimate expenses had not been fully used to offset income. In addition, many tax planning strategies were never utilized. As a result, the previous three years of tax returns were amended and a different approach adopted for the current year. This change of advisor resulted in a tax rebate of $15,000 and tax savings of approximately 20 percent in the current year.

Resolving Disputes

If you have complaints about fees, service or conduct, attempt to resolve the dispute directly with the accountant concerned. If that doesn't work, complain to the manager of the firm. Depending on the issues involved, you have other options, such as complaining to the provincial professional accounting association of which the accountant is a member. The association can investigate and discipline members. In addition, these provincial professional associations will have a basic insurance package to cover professional liability for negligence or incompetence, as well as missing trust funds. Individual accounting firms may have supplemental professional liability insurance coverage.

SELECTING A FINANCIAL PLANNER

Financial Planning is very individual and personal. The process should take into account all the psychological and financial factors that may have an impact on your financial goals and objectives. In short, comprehensive financial planning provides you with a foundation, a strategic plan, and should provide peace of mind. The plan should include all aspects of your tax, insurance and estate planning needs.

Some financial planners act as a liaison with other professionals to make sure that the overall plan is integrated, rather than ad hoc. This role would include coordinating advice and an action plan with professional accountants and lawyers.

Qualifications

Once you've determined that you need a financial planner, look into the different professionals who label themselves as such. Anyone can call himself or herself a planner; no federal, provincial, state or local laws require certain qualifications (except Quebec), such as those imposed upon other professionals such as lawyers. So, you have to be extremely selective. However, several associations and organizations grant credentials that signify a planner's level of education. As criteria can change from time to time, check with the association involved. Some of the most commonly recognized designations follow.

CERTIFIED FINANCIAL PLANNER (C.F.P.)

C.F.P. is an internationally recognized designation used in the U.S., United Kingdom, Australia, New Zealand and Japan. It was first introduced into Canada in November, 1995 by the Financial Planners Standards Council of Canada (FPSCC), a non-profit organization with the objective to increase consumer understanding and enhance the reputation of the financial planning industry.

To obtain a C.F.P., one must take various financial planning programs and pass exams. Candidates must also satisfy a work requirement of at least two years in the industry. After the license is granted, it is renewed annually, as long as the planner follows the code of ethics and completes the required number of hours of continuing education each year. If complaints are received by the FPSCC about a planner, and if they prove to be valid and serious, FPSCC has the authority to revoke the C.F.P. designation.

CHARTERED FINANCIAL CONSULTANT (CH.F.C.)

The CH.F.C. designation is conferred by the Life Underwriters Association of Canada (LUAC). The LUAC deals with life and health insurance agents and sets standards of conduct, ethics and professional development. CH.F.C.s deal with issues such as wealth accumulation and retirement planning, and may sell mutual fund products and segregated funds. To earn the designation, the financial planner must pass various courses on all major topics of personal finance, possess industry experience and adhere to strict ethical standards. These individuals may also have a C.L.U., or Chartered Life Underwriter designation, also awarded by the LUAC. This latter designation deals primarily with life and disability insurance products and group benefits for employees.

CHARTERED FINANCIAL ANALYST (C.F.A.)

This designation is awarded to those who pass exams administered by the Financial Analysts Federation and demonstrate expertise in investing in mutual funds, stocks, bonds and other investments. Many C.F.A.s have also branched out into full-service financial planning as investment counsellors. C.F.A.s would normally be used if you have a lot of money to invest and require the assistance of an investment professional. They frequently use a team approach with other professionals such as a lawyer, tax accountant and insurance broker to coordinate and integrate information and strategies.

How to Find a Financial Planner

There are several ways of locating a financial planner, as follows.

REFERRAL BY FRIEND, ACCOUNTANT OR LAWYER

Word-of-mouth referral is an effective reference source. You want to ask however, why a particular name is being recommended. Are they currently using the services of the planner? On what other basis are they making the reference? How long have they known the person professionally?

PROFESSIONAL ASSOCIATIONS

There is one national professional association in Canada, the Financial Advisors Assocation of Canada. You can go to their website and get details about member names in your area, and their credentials, means of remuneration and areas of expertise. There is also extensive consumer information, including articles and questions to ask when selecting an advisor.

Financial Advisors Association of Canada
Toronto, ON

Website: *www.advocis.ca*
Tel: 1-800-563-5822

Financial Planners Standards Council of Canada (FPSCC)
Toronto, ON   Website: *www.fpsc.ca*
                                               Tel: 1-800-305-9886

FPSCC is a non-profit organization that provides consumer information on financial plan-ning standards. In addition, it administers the ongoing continuing educational requirement of those who have been awarded the C.F.P. designation. The FPSCC has the authority to revoke a C.F.P. designation if complaints about a planner are proved to be valid and serious. Check out their site for consumer information, names of planners and any complaints about planners.

INTERNET

You can obtain names of qualified financial planners through the Internet search engines in your geographic area, by simply typing in the relevant keywords.

However, as reinforced throughout this book, you need to filter and screen the prospective advisor thoroughly. In the case of financial advice, you need to vet the prospective advisor through both the Financial Planners Association of Canada and the Financial Planners Standards Council of Canada.

How to Select a Financial Planner

Once you've made the decision to seek the services of a financial planner, you may have many more questions: Which professional is right for me? How do I identify a competent financial planner who can coordinate all aspects of my financial life? Just as you select a lawyer or accountant, you should base your decision on a number of factors: education, qualifications, experience and reputation.

When selecting your financial planner, choose one you can work with confidently. You are asking this person to help shape your financial future and you are paying him or her to do so. It is your responsibility and right to inquire about the practitioner's background, numbers of years in practice, credentials, client references and other relevant information.

Call the practitioner and ask for a meeting. Use this opportunity to determine compati-bility and to discover exactly how the practitioner will work with you. Ask questions about financial planning that will give you a basis for comparison with other practitioners you have contacted. In short, get the information you need to feel confident that this person is right for you and your needs.

Research shows that consumers rate "trust" and "ethics" as the most important elements in their relationship with financial advisors. In fact, survey respondents gave this response twice as often as they mentioned good advice and expertise.

As mentioned earlier, it is recommended that you meet with at least three planners before you make your final selection. To work effectively with a planner, you will need to reveal your personal financial information, so it's important to find someone with whom you feel completely comfortable.

By asking the following questions, you should get the information you need to make your decision on which financial planner to hire. As you think of others, add them to your list. Keep in mind how the answers fit your personal needs.

- How long has the planner been working with clients in the comprehensive financial planning process?
- What did the planner do before becoming a financial planner? Most planners come from fields related to financial services. If he or she started out as a lawyer, accountant, insurance agent or other specialist, it will most likely affect the advice the planner gives.
- What are the planner's areas of expertise? Ideally, these should include investments, insurance, estate planning, retirement planning, and/or tax strategies.
- What services do they provide? Most planners will help you assemble a comprehensive plan, while others specialize in particular areas of finance. The services you should expect include cash management and budgeting; estate planning; investment review and planning; life, health and property/casualty insurance review; retirement planning; goal and objective setting; and tax planning. Ask about each service specifically.
- Who will you deal with on a regular basis? You might see the planner only at the beginning and end of the planning process and work with associates otherwise. Ask if this will be the case, and ask to meet the personnel involved. Also enquire about their qualifications.
- What type of clientele do they serve? Some planners specialize by age, income category or professional group.
- Will they show you a sample financial plan they have done? The planner should be pleased to show you the kind of plan you can expect when the data-gathering and planning process is complete. Naturally, any plan they show you would not reveal client names or confidential information.
- Do they have access to other professionals if the planning process requires expertise beyond the scope of the planner? Most financial planners are generalists, and frequently consult with other professionals from related fields for added expertise in specialty areas. A good planner has a network of lawyers, accountants, investment professionals and insurance specialists to consult if questions arise. A team approach is adopted.
- Do they just give financial advice, or do they also fulfill the advice by selling financial products? As discussed earlier, there are several different types of advisors.
- Will their advice include only generic product categories or specific product recommendations? Some planners will name a particular mutual fund or stock, for example. Others will advise that you keep a certain percentage of your assets in stocks, bonds and cash, leaving you to assess which bonds, stocks, and money market funds are appropriate.

- Will they spend the time to explain their reasons for recommending a specific product and how it suits your goals, tolerance for risk and circumstances? Ask how they plan to monitor a recommended mutual fund or investment product once you've bought it. You should feel comfortable that the planner will take the time to make sure that you understand the strategy and products that are recommended.
- Will the planner do independent analysis on the products, or become dependent on another company's research? Does the practitioner have any vested interest in the products recommended?
- How will you follow up after the plan is completed to ensure that it is implemented? A good planner makes sure that you take steps to follow your plan. The plan should be reviewed and revised as conditions in your life, tax laws or the investment environment changes.
- How do they get compensated? Some planners charge for the advice they give. Others charge on a fee-based percentage of the amount they are managing. Still others collect commissions from the sale of products they recommend. Some charge both a planning fee and receive a sales commission. Make sure that you receive a written estimate of any fees you must pay. An explanation of compensation is covered in the next point of this chapter.
- Will they have direct access to your money? Some planners want discretionary control of their clients' funds, which permits the planner to invest at their discretion. You have to be extremely careful, as there is a high degree of potential risk. If you do agree to it, make sure that the planner has an impeccable track record and is bonded by insurance and is covered by professional liability insurance. Also limit the amount to ensure you stay within your financial comfort zone and request regular written reporting.
- Are there any potential conflicts of interest in the investments they recommend? A planner must advise you, for example, if he or she or the planner's firm earns fees as a general partner in a limited partnership that the planner recommends. You will want to know if the planner receives some form of payment, frequently called a referral fee, when they refer you to someone else.
- What professional licenses and designations have they earned? Inquire whether the planner holds a C.F.P., CH.F.C., CPA, T.E.P., or C.F.A. Also find out the planner's educational background.
- Have they ever been cited by a professional or governmental organization for disciplinary reasons? Even if the planner says that he or she has an impeccable professional track record, you can check with the provincial securities office and the provincial or financial planning associations.
- Are they covered by professional liability insurance? Ask what amount of coverage and request a copy of the policy. The policy is only as good as the "fine print," e.g. limitations,

exclusions and deductibles. If you are dealing with a financial advisor who has a C.F.P. designation, that person should be covered for a minimum of $1 million. Verify this yourself.

How a Financial Planner Is Compensated

It is important to understand, and be comfortable with, the way your financial planner gets paid. Generally, financial advisors are compensated in one of four ways: solely by fees, a combination of fees and commissions, solely by commissions, or through a salary paid by an organization that receives fees. In some cases, financial advisors may offer more than one payment option. Here's how these different methods work:

FEE-ONLY

Many financial planners charge an hourly rate, and your fee will depend on how much time the advisor spends on your situation, including time in research, reviewing the plan with you, and discussing implementation options. Others just charge a flat amount. Such planners usually offer a no-cost, no-obligation initial consultation to explore your financial needs. Some will do a computerized profile and assessment of your situation and options for a nominal fee that can range from $200 to $1,000 or more. You would complete a detailed questionnaire.

Fee-only financial advisors typically advise you on investments, insurance and other financial vehicles, but do not benefit from commissions if you take their suggestions. The advantage of this type of arrangement is that the planner has no vested interest in having you buy one product over another. Some fee-only financial planners will help you follow through on their recommendations using mutual funds and other investments, if you so wish. Otherwise, you will have to take your own initiative.

COMMISSION-ONLY

Some financial advisors charge no fee for a consultation, but are compensated solely by commissions earned by selling investments and insurance. A commission-only advisor will develop recommendations for your situation and goals, review the recommendations with you and discuss ways to implement these recommendations.

In some cases, the commissions are clearly disclosed, for example, a percentage front-end load (an upfront charge) commission on a mutual fund. In other cases, the fees are lumped into the general expenses of the product, as with life insurance, so you won't know how much your planner makes unless you ask him or her. You want confirmation in writing in advance in terms of what you will be paying. When you interview such a planner, ask him or her approximately what percentage of his or her firm's commission revenue comes from annuities, insurance products, mutual funds, stocks and bonds and other products. The planner's answers will give you a sense of the advice his firm usually gives in terms of their historical product priorities.

You pay fees not only in the form of an upfront charge, but could also pay ongoing charges as long as you hold an investment. For example, some insurance companies pay planners trailer fees for each year a client pays the premiums on an insurance policy. In addition, some mutual funds levy fees, which are annual charges based on your assets designed to reward brokers and financial planners for keeping clients in a fund. These can range from 1 percent to 5 percent or more.

In other situations, you must pay a fee if you sell a product before a particular amount of time has elapsed. If you want to cash in an annuity or insurance policy early, you must pay surrender charges of a certain percentage of your investment, part of which reimburses the insurer for the commissions it has paid your planner. If you sell certain mutual funds within a certain time frame of buying them, you might have to pay a back-end load, which allows the fund company to recover the upfront sales load it paid your planner. Such back-end loads usually are applied on a sliding scale, that is, diminishing year by year. At the end of the time period, for example, six years, you will not be charged a back-end fee. This acts as an incentive to keep the product for an extended time. However, you may have taken out no load or front-end load mutual funds.

Some companies entice commission-motivated planners with prizes of free travel or merchandise if their sales of a particular product reach a target level. Other arrangements award planners who attain certain target sales goals with incentives such as investment research.

Your planner might not like your questioning his or her cash payment and other perks. However, it is your right to know whether the products you buy generate direct fees and indirect benefits for the planner. By knowing the full extent of your planner's compensation, you will be better able to decide whether his or her advice is self-serving or objective.

FEE-PLUS-COMMISSION

Some planners charge a fee for assessing your financial situation and making recommendations, and may help you implement their recommendations by offering certain investments or insurance for sale, for which they typically earn a commission.

In some cases, planners are captives of one company, so they recommend only its product line. Other planners are independent and therefore recommend the mutual funds or insurance policies of any company with which they affiliate.

As with fee-only planners, fee-plus-commission advisors may charge a flat fee or bill you based on the amount of time they spend on your situation. Others use a fee scale, varying their fees according to the complexity of your financial situation.

Another form of compensation is called *fee offset*, meaning that any commission revenue your planner earns from selling you products reduces his or her fee for planning. If you buy so many products that your entire fee is covered, you should request a refund of the fee you paid for your basic plan.

SALARY

Many banks, trust companies, credit unions and other companies offer financial planning services. In most instances, staff financial advisors are paid by salary, and earn neither fees nor commissions. Of course, there could be other monetary incentives or bonuses based on the volume and value of the business done. Alternatively, there could be quotas to be met. Career advancement could be tied to sales performance. The companies are compensated through revenue and profit margins generated by the sale of investments and/or services.

Management and Transaction Fees May Be Additional Charges

You have options for implementing the strategies recommended by your financial advisor through the purchase of investments or insurance. However, if an advisor helps you select and monitor those purchases, there will be some cost to you and/or payment to the advisor. This could be in the form of a commission, redemption fees, trailer fees, or asset management fees.

Additionally, many investments have associated annual management and transaction fees. For example, if you open an RRSP, the company that serves as trustee may charge an annual custodial fee for the service. You can frequently obtain weekly comparisons of the management expense ratios of various funds from various national publications such as the *Globe and Mail*. These costs will be in addition to a fee you pay to the financial planner for advice.

What You Need to Know About a Financial Planner

Keep in mind that compensation is just one among many important elements that should figure into your decision about hiring a financial advisor.

Foremost, be sure that the planner you choose uses the financial planning process. It includes addressing the current situation, setting goals, identifying alternatives, selecting and implementing a course of action, and periodically reviewing. It is a client-centred process, with a commitment by the advisor to put the client's interest first.

All four compensation methods, discussed in the previous section, have their advantages. You must choose the method which, combined with the other qualities of the advisor you select, best meets your needs. If you don't understand how your financial advisor is compensated, question your financial advisor in as much detail as necessary until you are clear. As a smart consumer, you want to know what you're buying and how much you're paying for it and you're entitled to that information.

Resolving Disputes

If you have any complaints about fees, service or conduct, first attempt to deal with the issues directly with the person concerned. If that does not resolve the matter, you can complain to the management, the professional association that the advisor may belong to, the national industry association, the provincial regulatory association and the provincial securities commission with which the advisor is registered. If your advisor's employer is a member of an organization that offers mediation services, that is an option, but be aware of your rights and obligations before you agree. Depending on the nature of the issue, you could have a claim against the Canadian Investor Protection Fund if the company is covered by that fund, in case of insolvency or bankruptcy. Litigation tends to be the last resort, as the process is lengthy, expensive and results unpredictable. You want to avoid potential advisory problems by pre-empting them in advance by careful selection.

OTHER FINANCIAL AND INVESTMENT ADVISORS

As discussed earlier, having an objective financial planner assess your current financial situation and needs, and give advice on fulfilling your long-term objectives with an integrated and comprehensive financial plan, is your first step. You don't want to make financial or investment decisions in a vacuum. There is too much to lose.

There are many other people in the financial and investment area, however, that you might have dealings with at some point. Here is a brief summary.

Investment Counsellors

This type of financial advisor generally only deals with wealthy clients wishing to invest a minimum of from $250,000 to $1 million. This is due to the time involved to customize and monitor an investment portfolio. The counsellor's only business is to manage portfolios and advise individual clients. The management fee is generally a percentage, normally 1 to 2 percent, of the value of the assets in the portfolio. If his or her management skill results in an increase in value of the client's portfolio, the fee obtained increases accordingly.

Many counsellors have a Chartered Financial Analyst (C.F.A.) designation. There are several dozen firms offering these types of professional services, sometimes as part of a team approach within the firm of associated professionals, such as Chartered Professional Accountants and lawyers with expertise in various fields. Tax and estate planning and wealth preservation are also commonly part of the services offered.

Generally, the investor's accounts are separately managed and monitored by a specific money manager. The account is customized to meet the client's current and changing needs. Once the account is established, the money manager usually has the discretion to manage the assets within the parameters established by the investor.

All of the major banks in Canada have developed a special service for high net worth individuals, frequently referred to as "Private Client Services." There are also a number of partner-owned investment firms that cater to the affluent market. The purpose is to provide customized and personalized service on an individual basis. Very often, the minimum investment required is $500,000 to $1 million.

Retirement Counsellors

These people specialize in clients who are generally over 50 years of age, that is, nearing retirement or actually retired. Types of investments sold include RRSPs, Registered Retirement Income Funds (RRIFs), Life Investment Fund (LIF) annuities, GICs and mutual funds. The main thrust should be preservation of capital and low- or moderate-risk investment objectives, depending on your age, needs, assets, and risk tolerance comfort zone.

Company Human Resources Personnel

If you have a pension plan from your employer, you should ask the people administering the plan to provide you with details of it. Also ask them to assist you in projecting the income you will receive from the plan, and after you retire, what additional benefits, other than pension income, you will be entitled to. Ask if these benefits are guaranteed or if the employer can withdraw them at any time.

Bank, Trust Company and Credit Union Personnel

These financial institutions have an extensive range of investment products available in the area of mutual funds, GICs, term deposits, etc. In terms of mutual funds, there is generally a wide selection of money market, growth, income funds and balanced funds to accommodate people's investment needs and risk tolerance.

The range of training and expertise of bank, trust company or credit union personnel can vary. Advice by staff licensed to sell mutual funds can be very helpful in terms of the nature and benefits of their particular products. Expect to get general advice, however, not comprehensive advice or planning to deal with all your present and future needs. Many of these institutions have instructive pamphlets to give you a better understanding of general money management strategies.

Many of the major financial institutions in Canada are expanding into collateral financial services beyond their traditional scope. This is being done through subsidiary companies, in areas such as discount stock brokerages, investment portfolio management, estate planning, trusts, and insurance. The strategy is to present themselves as a one-stop service centre meeting all the client needs. Some very careful analysis of the pros and cons of doing all your financial business with a bank should be considered before making a decision.

There is a trend for bank employees to obtain various credentials, such as C.F.P. designations.

Insurance Agents or Brokers

The primary goal of these advisors is to sell life insurance and other insurance company products such as annuities or segregated mutual funds. As a consequence you may be limited to building a financial plan around an insurance policy. If he or she is an independent insurance broker, there could be a wide range of insurance-related products available from different companies but some agents are restricted to one company. As mentioned earlier, many insurance agents also have CH.F.C. or C.L.U. professional designations. Refer to Chapter 15, "Life, Health and Disability Insurance," for a full discussion of this topic.

Mutual Fund Agents or Brokers

As in insurance, an agent is a person who generally only sells the products of one company, whereas a broker can sell the products of any company. Because all sales are commission-based, you have to satisfy yourself that it is the right type of product and the best choice of that product for your needs. A high degree of trust is necessary, as you don't want to feel a broker's recommendation is based on the size of the commission or other special incentives to sell you a fund from a particular fund company. Be cautious, as a broker may only have a mutual fund license but promote himself or herself as a professional financial planner. To obtain a basic mutual fund selling license is relatively easy.

Stockbrokers

Sometimes stockbrokers refer to themselves as "investment advisors." Although the advice may be free, the client pays for it usually through commissions that his or her accounts generate. Many full-service brokers offer investment advice on a broad range of financial products, such as stocks, bonds, mutual funds and mortgage-backed securities. Some stockbrokers don't want to deal actively with small investor accounts, due to the time involved, but instead would probably recommend mutual funds and pooled funds to serve your needs.

Some stockbrokers and investment advisors also have obtained the FCSI (Fellow of the Canadian Securities Institute) designation through the Canadian Securities Institute. This is a demanding program with tough entry standards.

Many brokerage firms offer *managed* accounts, referred to as *wrap* accounts in the industry. In this instance, your money is invested in several pooled portfolios, depending on your risk profile, and managed generally by an outside money manager, rather than a broker. You normally pay a fixed annual fee, based on a percentage of the value of the money invested.

Discount Brokers

Although these brokers charge significantly lower commissions than do full-service stock brokers, they only buy and sell. They do not give advice. Using discount brokers is only a realistic investment option if you know the stock and bond market thoroughly, and can regularly take the time to make prudent decisions by researching the market.

Deposit Brokers

These individuals generally sell term deposits, GICs, annuities, RRIFs and in some cases, are licensed to sell mutual funds.

Where to Get More Information

- For lawyers, use the Internet. Also contact your local or provincial lawyer referral service. The initial consultation may be free or at a nominal fee. Ask your professional accountant who they would recommend and why.
- For professional accountants, such as a Chartered Professional Accountant (CPA), contact their provincial association for names of accountants with various speciality areas. Do an Internet search. An initial consultation may be free, but make sure you ask that question in advance. Also ask your lawyer who they would recommend and why.

For financial advisors, contact the following organizations:

Financial Advisors Association of Canada
390 Queens Quay West, Suite 209   Tel: (416) 444-5251
Toronto, ON M5V 3A2   or 1-800-563-5822
Website: *www.advocis.ca*

Look for the section on the site called "Consumer Info."

Financial Planners Standards Council of Canada
375 University Avenue   Tel: (416) 593-8587
Toronto, ON M5G 2J5   or 1-800-305-9886
Website: *www.fpsc.ca*

Look for the section on the site called "Find a Planner."

Summary

As you can see, there are many issues and options to consider when selecting the professional advisors you need to meet your present, future and estate planning needs in a competent fashion.

We gave an overview of the general factors to consider; how to select a lawyer, accountant and financial planner; and how to deal with disputes. We also covered the other types of financial and investment advisors that you might be dealing with, and gave an outline of where to get more information.

It is important to see a minimum of three of each type of professional advisor you might use, before you make a final decision. You require that benchmark for comparison to optimize the odds of making the right choice for your needs.

❓Frequently
❗Asked Questions

1. *What general factors should I consider when selecting an advisor?*

There are certain qualities and attributes that you should be looking for, including trust, integrity, objectivity, professionalism, membership in professional organizations and professional credentials. In addition, you should look for good chemistry, excellent communication skills and experience. Word of mouth recommendations from those you know or other professional advisors is a good sign. To obtain a comparative benchmark, obtain initial consultations from at least three potential advisors.

2. *How do lawyers charge for their services?*

The most common way is based on an hourly rate. The next most common way is a flat rate for specific tasks performed, e.g. transferring a house or putting a mortgage on the house or preparing a will. There are other ways that lawyers bill out as well, such as on a contingency fee basis. This happens most frequently with personal injury situations. In this case, a lawyer will take a percentage of the final award or settlement for his or her fees, e.g. 35 percent. In this situation, you would normally be responsible for paying all the out-of-pocket disbursements.

3. *What if I have a dispute over my lawyer's fees?*

The first thing to do is to attempt to resolve the issue with the lawyer concerned. If this does not resolve the problem, you could speak to the managing partner in the firm, assuming it is a large enough firm. Ideally, put your concerns in writing and ask for a written response. Your next step would be to challenge the lawyer's fees in court. This is called "taxing" or reviewing the lawyer's account and is an inexpensive process. You can find out more information from your local courthouse.

4. *How do I maximize the benefit of my meeting with my lawyer or accountant?*

Being prepared and focused is critical to get the most productivity and value out of any meeting. Avoid going off on tangents not relevant to the matters you have come to discuss. Time is money. Put your questions in writing and prioritize them in case you run out of time. That way you can control the agenda and pace of the meeting.

5. *How do I find a financial planner who I can trust to advise me objectively?*

You need to be very cautious. The guidelines outlined in the first question above should be followed. In addition, make sure that the advisor has professional credentials, such as a Certified Financial Planner (C.F.P.) designation. Check to see if the advisor is a member of the Financial Advisors Association of Canada (*www.advocis.ca*). Ask about minimum coverage protection for professional liability insurance. This is in case you receive bad advice that causes you to suffer financially. Make sure you verify this coverage yourself. Check with the Financial Planners Standards Council of Canada (*www.fpsc.ca*) to see if the advisor has had any complaints or disciplinary actions.

Selecting
Retirement Residences
and Care Facilities

"Without a sense of caring, there can be no sense of community."

ANTHONY D'ANGELO

INTRODUCTION

At some point in your later years, you will probably be faced with the decision of moving into a retirement residence or care facility. Some people live in their house or condominium until they die or go to hospital. However, many people, by choice or circumstance, go into a private retirement residence or public care facility.

As part of your retirement planning, you should look at the effect a retirement residence or care facility would have on your finances. Your savings and health will dictate which option you choose. Also, if you plan ahead and consider long-term care insurance and critical illness insurance, it could provide you with that extra financial protection if your savings are insufficient. These two types of insurance products are discussed in the chapter on life, health and disability insurance. The implication on estate planning is that the more money you spend before you die, the less that will be available to your estate. This may or may not be an issue for you.

This chapter will provide information and suggestions that can help you make decisions wisely and with confidence. It will cover the following topics:

- Where do I start?
- What is a retirement residence?
- Why live in a retirement residence?
- How much does a retirement residence cost?

- How to find a retirement residence
- How to select a retirement residence
- What is a care facility?
- Types of care facilities
- How to apply
- What is the cost?
- Selecting a care facility
- Visiting a care facility
- Investigating the care facility
- Regulations, licensing and accreditation
- Where to get further information

WHERE DO I START?

The first step is to assess your health and assistance needs. If you need to have assistance in many of your daily needs, then you would be looking at a care facility. If you are capable of independent living, then you would be considering a retirement residence.

WHAT IS A RETIREMENT RESIDENCE?

Retirement residences are private pay facilities that offer a flexible lifestyle option for seniors who are active and independent and who want to make their own choices. These types of residences generally have a wide range of organized activities. Suites are generally unfurnished and large enough that you can bring your own furniture. They frequently have kitchens or kitchenettes. In some cases, a retirement residence also has a care wing, in case a guest needs more assistance at some point, but still wants to remain in the overall complex, where friendships have been established and there is a sense of community.

Why Live in a Retirement Residence?

There are many reasons why people choose a retirement residence. Once a decision is made to move out of a home, condominium or apartment, either because you no longer want the commitment, or possibly your spouse has died, then a viable option is a retirement residence. These types of residences generally have a central dining room, and a highly sociable, stimulating and relaxing environment. Many people do not want to cook for themselves any more, so having an interesting menu selection is an attractive option.

Other attractive reasons are peace of mind, that is, not having to look after your home and having others around in case you are ill. Companionship is another factor—living with others to share memories and activities. A feeling of fulfillment in terms of participating in a range of interesting scheduled activities is a motivation. Privacy is another factor. Some people prefer to entertain in their own suite, while others prefer to join a group for an outing.

How Much Does a Retirement Residence Cost?

Retirement residence rates can vary depending on the location, degree of quality, room size, and nature of amenities and services provided. Prices can range from $1,500 a month to $7,000 a month or more. Some residences are modest, while others are like a cruise ship on land.

How to Find a Retirement Residence

There are no government agencies established to help you find a residence that meets your budget and your needs. However, there are some private agencies that perform this service. You can find them by doing a Google search for "Retirement Communities and Homes." Refer to the section at the end of this chapter on "Where to Get Further Information" to get other contact information and refer to Appendix A.

How to Select a Retirement Residence

It is important to have a family member and friend attend with you when visiting the residence. You don't want to make a hasty decision. You want to short list and then comparison shop. You also need to consider your wishes before you start the process. Make sure you do a list of your needs and wants. Obtain information by mail from the various prospective residences and then start the selection process in a methodical way.

Call ahead and schedule a tour. In some cases, a residence will let you stay a night to get an impression. In any event, you want to visit it a number of times, preferably at different times of the day, evening and weekend. Talk to residents and staff. You may also wish to attend a few activities and try a meal or two. Ask for copies of any paperwork required for admission, along with samples of activity calendars, newsletters and menus. Refer to the Retirement Residence Comparison Checklist 9 in Appendix D. It will provide you with an excellent guide.

PLANNING TO PROTECT ● *Joe Encourages His Mother to Move into a Retirement Residence*

Joe's mother is a recent widow. She is 79 years of age and lives in her townhouse on her own. Joe has been concerned that she is feeling lonely and isolated. He is also worried about her health and safety living alone. When Joe discussed with his mother the idea of moving into a retirement residence, she resisted the idea. She felt she was OK where she was.

After extensive research, Joe decided it was time to approach his mother again, and encourage her to at least go with him to check out three retirement residences he had seen and shortlisted. They were all within easy driving distance of his home. He showed his mother the brochures for them first and she was impressed. Joe arranged to have a guided tour and meal at each place. His mother particularly liked one of them, the friendly staff and residents, as well as the activities, entertainment and meals. She really liked the comfortable suite. Two weeks later she made her decision, which was to sell her townhouse and move into the retirement residence. She has lived there for almost a year and loves it. Her energy, enthusiasm and joy of life has returned and she has made many new friends.

• •

WHAT IS A CARE FACILITY?

A care facility is one that looks after people who need medical care or assistance, who would otherwise have difficulty living independently. The terminology is generally referred to as long-term care or extended care. There could be various classifications, such as intermediate care level 1, 2 and 3. Level 1 tends to be just above independent living; level 3 is almost long-term care. The difference being the number of hours in a day that the person needs assistance. For example, getting in and of bed, dressing, bathing, eating, moving, taking medications, etc. Basically, a sliding scale from total independence to total dependence.

Types of Care Facilities

Care facilities provide care for people with diverse needs. Some people require assistance with activities of daily living such as taking their medication, bathing and dressing. Other people require considerable assistance, including professional services, such as nursing, 24 hours a day.

Care facilities can be a mixture of private sector facilities, public sector facilities, or facilities operated by religious, charitable or ethnic organizations.

Some care facilities are large and have hundreds of residents. Others are small and provide care to as few as three or four people.

- **Community care facilities.** These provide care to people who have been assessed as being able to function at a personal or intermediate level of care. These facilities tend to provide care to small groups of people, e.g. three or four.
- **Family care homes.** These are single family homes that provide assistance, care and supervision to one or two persons only. These homes tend to be found in more rural areas.
- **Extended care facilities.** These provide care to persons who have been assessed as needing extended or long-term care.

- **Multi-level care facilities.** These provide care to people who are assessed at various levels of care.
- **Private hospitals.** These can also provide care to people who are assessed at any level of care.

How to Apply

Contact your community or provincial health care department.

What Is the Cost?

It depends on the nature of the facility, whether it is public or privately operated and, in many cases, your income. In a funded facility, a portion of the monthly charges for your accommodation and care will be provincially subsidized according to your annual net income. In a non-funded facility, you will be responsible for paying the full cost of your accommodation and care. These facilities are sometimes referred to as "private pay" facilities.

If you are considering a funded facility, the specific policies could vary from province to province and region to region. In general terms:

- **Admission.** Once you are notified a room is available, you may have to accept that room within 48 hours. You will therefore have to pay accommodation in two places during the transition period, that is, your home and the facility.
- **Subsidized rate.** The subsidized payment generally provides you with accommodation, meals, laundry, care and supervision consistent with the level of care you require. Generally, when you are admitted to a care facility, you continue receiving any government income supplements you are currently receiving.
- **Extra charges.** In some facilities, there could be a differential higher rate for single or double rooms of superior quality. In most cases, you have to pay extra for magazines or newspapers, dry cleaning, telephone and cable. You are also responsible, in most cases, to buy or lease any special equipment required for your own use, such as wheelchairs and walkers.
- **Time spent away from facility.** In most cases you can be away for a maximum of 30 days with the government continuing to pay the subsidized amount. You would be responsible for continuing to pay the daily user rate.
- **Hospitalization.** If your room is held during hospitalization, you are generally required to continue to pay the daily accommodation rate.

Selecting a Care Facility

You want to select a care facility that best matches your needs and lifestyle preferences. You need to comparison shop. Although you may be able to have your name on the waiting list for several facilities, you will probably need to accept the first one that comes up. You can obtain further information from your provincial industry association or provincial government health department. Refer to the section near the end of this chapter "Where to Get Further Information" and Appendix A. Also refer to Appendix D for a comparison checklist.

VISITING A CARE FACILITY

It is important to personally visit the location, preferably with a relative or friend. If you like it, visit it a number of times to satisfy yourself that you like it. For your protection, you need to have a checklist for comparison and to make sure you have not forgotten anything. Refer to the Care Facility Comparison Checklist 10 in Appendix D.

INVESTIGATING A CARE FACILITY

In addition to touring a care facility, comparison shopping, and getting independent feedback from friends and family, you also should do background checks on the facility. Your local health authority office could supply you with information regarding a particular facility, including answering your questions and concerns. To locate the local Health Authority in your area, do a Google search for your local government. You could also contact your provincial government enquiry line (see Appendix A). Provincial long-term care associations could also provide you with background information. Refer to the section "Where to Get Further Information."

The types of questions for which you want answers include the following:

- Has the facility ever been cited for health and safety violations?
- Have there been any reported abuses of residents by staff or other residents?
- Has there been any accidental deaths caused by negligence on the part of staff?

REGULATIONS, LICENSING AND ACCREDITATION

Depending on the province and the type of facility, there could be provincial regulations involved. In some cases, the province regulates the care facility. In other cases, the provincial industry association regulates in a self-governing fashion. In almost all cases, there is provincial legislation governing care facility operation. This would include matters such as: health and safety, building requirements, staffing, food service, administration of medicines and resident care. Make enquiries.

WHERE TO GET FURTHER INFORMATION

There are several options:

- Speak with your family and doctor first to discuss your needs and wants, concerns and wishes. Also, contact your provincial and local health departments. Refer to Appendix A for a list of provincial enquiry centres to get contact numbers for health and continuing care, long-term care and related government departments.

- Contact various industry associations for names of private retirement residences or public care facilities in your geographic area. If you can't locate one in your area, you could contact your provincial enquiry centre for a government health department. Refer to Appendix A for a list of associations and websites.
- Do a Google search for listings under various categories, such as: Retirement Communities and Homes, Community Care Facilities, Nursing Homes, Home Support Services and Senior Citizen's Services and Centres.
- Visit various private and public retirement and care facilities to get your own impressions by short listing and then comparing the options. Visit the facilities with family members and friends to get their objective assessments.
- Refer to Appendix D, Checklists, for questions to ask when objectively and subjectively comparing private retirement residences (Checklist 9) or public and private care facilities (Checklist 10).
- Refer to the book by Douglas Gray, *Risk-Free Retirement*.
- Refer to the website: *www.retirementplanning.ca* and *www.estateplanning.ca*.

SUMMARY

In this chapter, we have covered the differences between retirement residences and care facilities, the financial costs involved, how to find and select the right facility for your needs, visiting the facilities, making the move, investigating the care facility and regulations and licensing.

As you can see, there are many issues to consider when making your selection. The right decision will immeasurably enhance your quality of life, and mental, emotional and physical health.

❓Frequently
∶ Asked Questions

1. *How do I find the right retirement residence?*

It is a three-part process—research, referrals and testimonials. Obtain a list of private retirement residences in the geographic area that interests you. Refer to Appendix A. Most private residences are for people who want independent living, that is, do not require care. Get information sent to you, then shortlist them and check out your top three choices thoroughly, including having a tour and a meal. Have a family member and/or a good friend go with you. Ask your doctor for recommendations and why they were recommended. Also, speak to other residents when you are visiting the residences. Go back at several different times of the day and week to get further impressions. Be very observant. Check out some activities and ask for a copy of the monthly bulletin. Use the checklist in Appendix D as an objective benchmark for comparison.

2. *How do I find the right care facility?*

You need to be very careful when making this selection, as you are dependent on some form of care. Follow the procedures outlined in the previous question. Speak to the community health personnel in your area and get candid feedback. Also, speak with your doctor to get recommendations. There can be considerable differences between facilities. Ask about the range of care required, and whether medications or restraints are used for patients who require a lot of care. This is a key issue to consider. As mentioned, you need to be very cautious and selective. Refer to Appendix A for a list of associations. Use the checklist in Appendix D when visiting the facilities that interest you.

Planning Your Funeral

"It matters not how a man dies, but how he lives.
The act of dying is not of importance, it lasts so short a time."

SAMUEL JOHNSON

INTRODUCTION

Most people find it difficult to think or talk about death at any time. However, it is inevitable that everyone will experience the death of a close family member or friend at some point. In the midst of the grief and sorrow of losing a loved one, decisions have to be made and responsibilities have to be faced. In spite of the great sense of loss, important decisions must be made consistent with the philosophical and spiritual beliefs of the deceased. Planning can help.

This chapter will provide information and suggestions that can help you make decisions wisely and with confidence. It will cover the following topics:

- the funeral process
- pre-arranged funeral services
- using a funeral home or doing it yourself
- funeral costs
- the funeral service
- how to make your funeral or memorial service more memorable
- burial and cremation options
- possible sources of financial assistance
- organ donations
- where to get more information

WHAT IS A FUNERAL?

A funeral commemorates in praise and gratitude the life of one who has died. The funeral is a ceremony of proven worth and value for those who mourn. It provides an opportunity for the survivors to express their love, respect and grief, thereby meeting the religious, social and psychological needs of the mourners. In arranging a funeral, the feelings and needs of others that shared in, or benefitted from, the life of the deceased should be considered in order to be of real value.

Public Funeral

A public funeral is one of the few personal events and ceremonies to which none are invited but all may attend. It gives the community a chance to offer its support and share the sorrow of the immediate family of the deceased.

Private Funeral

A private funeral normally is not restricted to family members, but could be invitation only. For example, friends and colleagues might also be given the opportunity to share in the grief.

ARRANGING YOUR FUNERAL SERVICES IN ADVANCE

A pre-arranged funeral is a practical way of making final arrangements before they are needed, sometimes years before the death occurs. Details such as the type of service preferred, music, clergy, casket and final disposition can all be discussed and arranged with the funeral director. When making your plans for your funeral arrangements, consider the feelings of your family members. Imposing certain restrictions in your pre-arrangements, such as "no service by request," could cause hardships on the survivors who may feel the need for some form of ceremony. You should leave your requests flexible enough to allow survivors to make appropriate arrangements for the fulfillment of their own emotional needs. Consideration in death is a reflection of your caring in life.

A reputable funeral home will assist you in completing pre-arrangement forms. You can either meet with the funeral director or pick up a form and study the options. Whatever decisions you make can be recorded and kept on file at the funeral home—with copies for your family members and executor. It is important to inform family, friends and your physician if you have made pre-arrangements with a specified funeral home. It is not wise to solely record your wishes in your will as this is not usually accessible at the time of death.

Pre-arrangement can be made in a number of ways:

- You can pre-arrange your funeral through a funeral home and pay in advance.
- You can pre-arrange your funeral through a funeral home and pay by installments.

- You can ask a funeral home or a memorial society to keep a list of your wishes on file for quick reference at the time of your death. This service may be performed free-of-charge or you may be charged a small registration fee. It should be noted that at the time of death any pre-arrangements can be altered by the next of kin or executor.
- You can set out your wishes in a letter of instruction to your next of kin to follow after your death. You may wish to set aside money at a financial institution or elect to have the costs paid by your estate or next of kin.

Benefits of a Pre-arranged Funeral

Some benefits to pre-arranging are as follows:

ALLEVIATES THE BURDEN PLACED ON FAMILY AND FRIENDS

By pre-arranging your funeral and cemetery services, you will make your wishes known to your family and friends and provide direction to the executor of your estate.

ALLOWS YOU TO MAKE A MEANINGFUL DECISION

Planning ahead enables you to make a meaningful and informed decision about your funeral and cemetery services and the form of memorial you may prefer, with no sense of urgency. Decisions made in advance of need can be made with less haste and without the anxiety which accompanies a death, when newspaper advertisement decisions, transportation, and other last-minute decisions have to be made and carried out. In addition, you can make rational financial decisions about your choices. In this context, it is helpful to have your spouse, a trusted family member and executor attend with you when you make a decision. Some of the points you can consider are:

- how much of your estate you want to go towards paying your funeral and cemetery expenses
- if you prefer a traditional funeral or a simple, less lavish service
- if you want to be cremated, interred in the ground or entombed in a mausoleum

PROTECTS YOU FROM INFLATION

The full sum can be deposited or payments can be made by installments. Prepayment offers the advantage of setting aside funds with a funeral home that accrue interest to offset any increased costs of services and products. Your money is kept in a trust account that is governed by provincial legislation. Pre-arranging allows you to purchase your services at today's prices, without having to be concerned about the effects of inflation. You will gain peace of mind knowing that your family will be relieved of the financial burden often associated with making funeral arrangements.

SAVES MONEY

If you don't pre-arrange a funeral, those who are making the decision for you at the time of death could end up feeling obliged to spend more money than necessary. An emotional atmosphere is not a conducive environment for sound financial decision-making. In the pressure of the moment, there is little time for investigation of, and comparison between, funeral providers. You really should compare a minimum of three funeral providers to have the benefit of comparison of prices, services, facilities and attitude.

The Contractual Agreement

Every province has legislation dealing with prepaid funerals. Any funds paid are held "in trust" by the funeral home or a provincial organization. The funds should bear interest to your credit or the credit of your estate. Make sure the contract doesn't simply state that the funds to be held in trust by the funeral home will only be applied towards the actual cost of the funeral. Otherwise, the unwritten implication is that the deceased's family or the estate will pay any additional amounts owing at the time of the funeral.

The contract should contain the following provisions:

1. If the funeral costs are less than the funds held "in trust" any surplus plus accrued interest, will be returned to the estate, and

2. If the funeral services are not carried out by the funeral home, the funds held "in trust" plus accrued interest, will be returned to the estate. There are provisions in some provinces for the funeral home to hold back a portion of the funds paid as a fee.

PLANNING TO PROTECT ● *The Advantages of Prepayment*

Kieran arranged to prepay $5,000 for funeral services and ensured that his contract guaranteed that the pre-arranged services were paid in full. In this scenario, because the funds he paid the funeral home earned interest of $650 over a period of time, the total amount in trust would be $5,650. Assuming the actual cost of the funeral is only $5,300, his estate should receive a refund of $350. However, if the actual cost of the funeral exceeds the amount "in trust," the difference should be paid by the funeral home. His family or estate should not be called upon to make up the difference.

• •

If you prepay a contract with a purchase price of less than $15,000 (which is a lot more than the cost of the average funeral), any interest earned on the funds is generally tax-free. The exception is unless it is not ultimately used for the funeral services specified in the contract.

Some points to consider before signing any agreement are:

• Can you obtain a full refund if you don't require the services or change your mind?

- Can you obtain a partial refund if you decide to have a memorial service or cremation, rather than a formal funeral?
- Is there a holdback by the funeral home permitted by your province, in the event that you cancel, and how much is that holdback?
- What happens if you move away from the area?
- What happens if the funeral home ceases to operate?
- Can you obtain a full refund if you cancel the contract within 30 days of signing?

Check the applicable provincial regulations with respect to rights of cancellation. For example, one province might have a prepaid plan that can be cancelled at any time but the funeral home is entitled to withhold 20 percent of the funds. In another province, the funeral home may deduct up to 10 percent of the prepaid funds, up to a maximum of $200. It can vary between provinces and change at any time.

In some provinces, funeral homes operate independently from cemeteries and crematoriums so you may have to make separate arrangements for the purchase of a burial plot or cremation of the body.

MAKE YOUR FUNERAL OR MEMORIAL SERVICE MORE MEMORABLE

In order to put your imprint on your final service and make it more memorable to those attending, there are various options you may wish to consider in advance. The more you prepare in advance, the easier it is for your wishes to be met on your death, and the less decision-making and stress for those arranging your service. It also ensures that your wishes are fully met. Otherwise, those looking after the service might not know your wishes. If you use a memorial or funeral service, the staff could assist you with some of the suggestions below and further ideas. Also, you would probably like to discuss some of the ideas below with your close family members.

Make sure you put your instructions in a safe place at your home, do a copy of your wishes, and give them to your executor and a close family member. Remember to review your instructions annually in case you have any changes you want to make.

- ***Poems, Songs, Hymns and Psalms.*** Select what you would like to be played, sung or read at your service. In fact, you can do up the sample service outline.
- ***Favourite Photos on Display.*** Select the photos that you would like to be displayed at the service, e.g. in a stand on the altar, or at the table where the guest book is located, if you wish to have a guest book.
- ***Prepare a Photo Album.*** You could do up a photo album with your favourite pictures that reflect the highlights of your life. This could be displayed on a table at the service, as well as at any post-service reception.

- **Funeral or Memorial Cards.** You may wish to have a card prepared that has your colour photo on the front, and some favourite poems or psalms inside. These would be distributed at the service and sent to those who were unable to attend. As they sit like a note card, they could be kept by those who care.
- **Religious Service Brochure Handout.** If a religious service is involved, there is normally a four-sided brochure prepared. To customize it with your personality, you may wish to include the psalms or poems inside, along with preparing a personalized bio of your life in your own words. That way, at least you ensure that the highlights are covered as you wish!
- **Have a Package of Your Favourite Perennial Flower Seeds Distributed.** The above idea ensures that your thoughtfulness, spirit and love of nature will continue to be remembered as the flowers blossom year after year.
- **Have Distinctive Book Marks Distributed.** You may wish to have some unique bookmarks with the message or photo that you like. Again, this enables those who are remembering your life to recall your thoughtfulness.
- **Have Individual Flowers Distributed as People Leave the Service.** It is a nice touch to have some family members handing out a favourite flower to each person as a memory, as people leave the service.
- **Prepare Your Own Obituary Notice.** To make sure that the facts and information are set out as you wish, prepare your own obituary.

Request People Remember Your Favourite Charity

In your obituary notice, memorial brochure hand-out and memorial card, you may wish to encourage people to give a donation in your memory to your favourite charity or the reader's favourite charity. Alternatively, if you would like a little bit of posterity, you may wish to set up an endowment fund for the charity or university of your choice and ask people to donate to that fund if they wish. If it is a registered charity, it is a tax-deductible donation.

For example, you may wish to set up a perpetual annual scholarship or bursary at your local university for undergraduate or graduate students in the area of your interest. The memorial scholarship could bear your name. Most institutions require a minimum, for example, $20,000 to fund an endowed scholarship bearing your name. Normally, it is structured so that the money is put into an interest-bearing account with the interest going towards the annual scholarship, e.g. $500. Refer to Chapter 14 regarding charitable giving.

PLANNING TO PROTECT ● *If Only They'd Known...*

Rupert was suddenly faced with the death of his mother who had lived in Calgary. It was not expected and no prior plans had ever been discussed or wishes made known. Rupert lived and worked in Halifax and had to fly out to Calgary to make funeral arrangements.

In addition to the stress and trauma of losing his mother, he had to make numerous decisions in a compressed time period. Funeral arrangements were planned in haste, difficult and emotional decisions were made about the type of funeral and whether to opt for cremation or a traditional casket burial. In addition, last minute details caused further anxiety along with uncertainty about cost issues to do with the funeral. Balancing the expectations and opinions of others added to Rupert's stress.

Most of Rupert's stress could have been alleviated with advance planning by his mother. If Rupert had taken the initiative years earlier, he could have been a catalyst to assist his mother in dealing with these issues in a relaxed and stress-free atmosphere. It would also have saved a lot of money, given an opportunity for input from family members and provided peace of mind for all concerned.

EXPRESSIONS OF SYMPATHY

People want to express their love, care and respect in different forms. Here are some issues to consider.

Flowers

You may consider requesting that no flowers be sent or restrict floral tributes to those from your immediate family. Before making a final decision, you should consider that the presence of flowers can be a source of comfort for your family and friends. When placed in the funeral home or church they add warmth, colour, beauty and life to the visitation and the service itself. The emotional and psychological benefit of flowers often remains for days or even weeks after the ceremony when they are enjoyed in someone's home. You may also wish to consider a potted plant or memorial tree.

Memorial Donations

If you decide to request that flowers not be sent, you may wish to specify a cause or charity to which donations can be sent. If you do not have a specific cause or charity that you wish to designate, the funeral director can provide you with information on a large number of memorial funds. Keep in mind the interests of the deceased—did he or she care particularly for animals or children? Perhaps a donation to the local humane society or the Kids Helpline would be appropriate.

Requests for memorial donations should be handled tactfully. Sometimes requests for donations can be misinterpreted as dictating to friends the manner in which they should express their sympathy or appear to demand that some expression of sympathy be made.

Your funeral director can assist you with appropriate wording that can be used in a newspaper notice that will express your preferences without appearing to be restrictive.

WHEN DEATH REQUIRES AN AUTOPSY

If the death is sudden, unexpected, unexplained or of unnatural causes, an autopsy or post-mortem examination may be carried out to try and determine the exact cause of death. This is a medical examination, which is usually carried out at the hospital by a doctor who is a specialist in pathology.

Either the attending physician or the family may request an autopsy. However, an autopsy may also be requested by the Medical Examiner who has the authority to order this procedure without the consent of the next of kin.

Only family members can obtain the autopsy results and information about the cause of death. As it is considered confidential, family members must contact the doctor or Medical Examiner to obtain it. A full autopsy report usually takes about six weeks.

The attending physician supplies the funeral director with a Medical Certificate of Death, which includes the cause of death. However, legislation in most provinces usually prohibits the funeral director from disclosing any information contained in this confidential certificate. The funeral director submits this document to the district registrar who will officially register the death and issue a burial permit.

DOCUMENTS AND PERMITS

Your funeral director will obtain and complete documents to expedite dealings with official departments at the time of your death. He or she will also take care of the appropriate forms with regard to cremation and/or burial. The following are the common types of forms. These can vary in type and terminology depending on the province:

- funeral director's Statement of Death
- provincial government Death Registration Form
- Medical Certificate of Death from the attending physician, or Medical Certificate of Death from the medical examiner if the death has been investigated by the Medical Examiner's office
- Burial Permit
- cremation authorization (if applicable)
- out-of-province transportation authorization (if applicable)

SUPPORT SERVICES

There are many supportive services available to help people cope with the issues of death, grief and the loss of someone close to them. Your funeral director, clergy or physician can refer your loved ones to some of the support groups that exist in the community. They can provide support for you, your family and your friends before, during and after death.

MAKING THE ARRANGEMENTS YOURSELF

In most provinces, it is perfectly legal to prepare a body, arrange for burial and cremation, and hold a service without hiring a funeral provider. However, it is illegal to bury or cremate human remains unless you have a Burial Permit issued under provincial legislation. Carrying out these tasks is not a simple procedure and one that most people would rather avoid. Complications can arise that are difficult to deal with at such an emotional and stressful time. Information and assistance on making your own arrangements can be obtained from:

- provincial government Vital Statistics Registry
- local hospitals
- the medical examiner or a representative (ask your local hospital for more information).

Each of these sources should be able to provide more information about the following steps. The documents and required steps can vary from province to province, so this is a general overview:

1. Start by obtaining a Medical Certificate of Death from the attending physician. If the death has been investigated by the Medical Examiner's office, a Medical Certificate of Death must be obtained from the attending medical examiner.
2. Decide upon burial, cremation, or if the body is to be donated to medical science.
3. Arrange transportation. Check with a funeral director to see if there are any provincial regulations about the kind of vehicle that must be used. If so, you may require a transportation permit.
4. If the body is to be transferred outside the province a medical examiner must examine the body and the Certificate of Death and provide a form to authorize transportation outside of the province. A Burial Permit will also be required.
5. For a burial—Obtain a Death Registration Form from the provincial Vital Statistics Registry or the local Hospital Registrar. The personal information of the deceased is required for this form. You can then obtain a burial certificate.

   For a cremation—Contact the medical examiner, who will examine the body and give you the required form. If everything is in order, the medical examiner will issue a form that provides written authority to proceed with the cremation.

6. If the burial or cremation is to take place more than 24 hours after death, arrangements will have to be made to store the body. A hospital might hold the body for a short period if it has the necessary refrigeration facilities. The hospital may charge for this service.

7. Obtain a casket or a shroud that will meet the requirements of the cemetery or crematorium.

8. Make arrangements for burial or cremation.

9. Arrange a funeral or memorial service, if desired.

10. Prepare an obituary for the newspaper, if desired.

You can see why most people would prefer to hire a funeral provider to deal with these procedural steps.

SELECTING A FUNERAL PROVIDER

A funeral provider or undertaker is licensed to own and operate a funeral home and to provide funeral services. "Full-service" funeral providers have complete facilities for funeral services. "Satellite" funeral providers are branch offices affiliated with full-service funeral homes and must be operated in conjunction with a full-service funeral provider. When choosing a funeral home or memorial society, the following guidelines will assist in your decision-making.

- How long have they been servicing their community?
- Do you know their personal and professional reputation?
- Does the funeral home and funeral director hold a valid local and provincial license, as applicable?
- Are they a member in good standing of their provincial Funeral Service Association?
- Is the funeral home a full-service facility capable of handling all your needs (chapel, visitation room, reception area, provincially licensed personnel on staff)?
- Is the funeral home a member of the local Better Business Bureau and what is their track record in terms of any complaints?

The Role of the Funeral Director

A funeral director can perform up to 100 different duties in the provision of a funeral service. Consequently, it stands to reason that the funeral director is an important part of pre-planning and the choice of funeral director should be known in advance of need. When death occurs there is little time for investigation or comparison.

A funeral director can be selected in the same manner as you would select any other professional or business person. Seek out someone who is competent, courteous and empathetic, and has a good reputation in the community. Their establishment, equipment and vehicles should be in pristine condition.

Visit several funeral homes, ideally a minimum of three. You need that benchmark for comparison, as you are going through a learning curve. Collect their information and price lists. Most funeral homes prefer that you visit them personally to discuss your funeral requirements without obligation or sales pressure.

As mentioned earlier, it is prudent to take a close family member, your executor and your spouse with you if possible. That way, issues and options can be explored logically and rationally. You also want to make a decision after some reflection, discussion with others close to you, and comparison. You don't want to make a decision in haste.

Memorial Societies

A memorial society is in the business of selling memberships. Becoming a member of a memorial society generally means that a fixed price has been negotiated between the society and a designated funeral home, generally for cremation services.

Understanding Funeral Costs

Very few people want to think of money at the stressful and emotional time of a funeral. Unfortunately, from a practical standpoint, it is necessary to deal with the issue, as funerals can be expensive. Costs can range from around $1,000 to over $15,000 or more depending on a number of factors. They may be simple, elaborate, private or public. The cost of a funeral should reflect the style of life the deceased lived. A life is not enhanced or diminished by the amount of money spent on a funeral. The services provided and the merchandise selected will determine the cost of the funeral. All funeral providers are required by law to display a current list of the services and products they offer. They are also required by law to have a book or brochure available illustrating all products for sale. Prices for funeral services are not regulated and can vary widely.

The funeral may be held in a church, a funeral chapel or a funeral home. Your options may be limited if you live in a small community, but by pre-planning you can save your family from unnecessary expense and stress. The price for funeral services does not include the sale of a cemetery lot, a grave, crypt or niche, or the sale of a memorial marker, a headstone, tombstone, monument or plaque. A cemetery operator sells lots and a memorial dealer sells markers.

According to one provincial funeral service association, a traditional formal funeral service averages about $4,500, and includes:

- transporting the body to the funeral home
- using the facilities of the funeral home
- embalming and cosmetic application
- the casket
- using a funeral limousine for transportation to the cemetery or crematorium

- arranging religious services
- registering the death and obtaining the Burial Permit
- preparing and running death notices for the newspaper
- arranging and preparing for flowers
- funeral stationery

Methods of Payment

Some funeral homes accept credit cards for payment. Discussions about payment should be held with the funeral director at the time funeral arrangements are being made.

Advance Payment

Some of the following items may have to be paid for before the service can take place:

- a portion of, if not the full price of the internment rights (i.e. grave, lot, crypt, niche, urn space)
- the internment, entombment or cremation fee
- late or Saturday charges—i.e. most internment or entombment services taking place in the late afternoon or on a Saturday incur additional charges
- fees for additional cemetery services, if any
- chapel rental, if any
- all or part of the funeral home or transfer service bill
- the casket, if not included in the above
- the clergy, organist and soloist, if not covered in any of the above

Selecting a Casket

To prevent a health hazard, the body of the deceased must be placed in a rigid container or casket that is capable of holding and transporting the body. The casket or container holding the body is also buried or cremated. If a rental casket is used, only the inner container is buried or cremated. The choice of casket can add considerably to the overall costs. Prices can range from a few hundred dollars to several thousand dollars depending on whether you select a plywood, cloth covered, hardwood or metal casket. Typically, the less expensive models are not on display and you may have to ask about their availability. If you wish to reduce costs you should consider renting a casket. You can also use a casket that is home-made.

Choosing a Cemetery

Most communities have at least one cemetery. These include municipal or church cemeteries plus those that are privately owned. As with funeral services, the costs of a cemetery lot and other goods and services can vary widely.

For earth burial, other considerations will have to be made in addition to the purchase of a lot such as: the opening and closing of the grave, a cement liner to protect the casket (if required by the cemetery), and the installation of a marker. When you purchase a lot, crypt or niche in a commercial or municipal cemetery, the cemetery operator is required by law to invest a portion of the purchase price in a care fund for the perpetual maintenance of the cemetery. Before you enter into an agreement to purchase a lot, ask for a written statement listing all costs including:

- **Plot Prices.** The price of a grave will vary depending on the cemetery and the location of the grave within the cemetery.
- **Veteran's Rates.** Some cemeteries offer reduced rates to veterans although they might not provide adjacent space for spouses.
- **Grave Markers.** Some cemeteries limit the style of grave markers and may restrict you to their approved list of suppliers. There may be an additional installation charge.
- **Permanent Care Costs.** There may be fees for services such as lawn maintenance.
- **Vault or Rough Box Requirements.** Does the casket have to be enclosed in a vault or box in the ground?
- **Double Occupancy.** Some cemeteries permit two burials in one lot, one deep and one shallow. If so, the upper casket is usually required to be three feet below the surface.
- **Grave Opening and Closing.** There may be an additional fee for opening and closing the grave.
- **Non-Resident Surcharge.** A surcharge may be applied if the deceased lived outside of the area.

THE FUNERAL SERVICE

Depending on your needs, there are various options you may wish to consider.

The Traditional Funeral Service

The traditional funeral service is a ceremony held in a church or funeral home chapel with the body present, followed by burial or cremation. The family or funeral director consults with a member of the clergy who conducts the service. A non-religious service may be held where a family member, close friend, or business associate speaks.

No two funerals are alike. The service may include a eulogy by a friend or family member, special music, songs, poems, or passages from scripture that were meaningful to the deceased. The traditional funeral usually includes viewing of the deceased, although this should not be forced on the family. When death is sudden or unexpected, an open casket can help reinforce the finality. If the deceased had a lingering illness, it is often helpful to see that the suffering is over.

This type of funeral involves the staff, facilities and equipment of a funeral home for an average of three to four days. The staff will transport the deceased from the place of death, file and secure necessary government documents and permits, arrange for desired services, embalm and prepare the deceased, provide the casket and funeral vehicles, and arrange for the flowers and acknowledgement cards.

Embalming

Embalming is a surgical technique used to disinfect, preserve and restore the human body to an acceptable physical appearance. The primary reason for embalming is the protection of health as untreated remains can pose serious health problems. Restoration is not intended to make the deceased look like they did during life, but rather to enhance the appearance of the deceased to allow for viewing.

In most cases the law does not require embalming. However, if more than 72 hours have elapsed since death and the body is being transported by train, plane or other public transportation, the body must be embalmed or placed in a sealed metal-lined container. Embalming is not necessary if the body is transported in a private vehicle or a vehicle owned by the funeral home. The body may decompose if it is not refrigerated. The law does not permit embalming if the person dies of a specified communicable disease. It requires that that body be put into a sealed metal-lined container.

You should consider the benefits of embalming and the feelings of your family when making a decision. The general consensus amongst experts on bereavement is that viewing the deceased confirms the reality of death and helps survivors take an important step towards recovering from their loss. Unless you give the funeral home instructions to the contrary, they may go ahead with this procedure and charge the costs to your estate or family.

Immediate Disposition

Any funeral home will arrange immediate disposition if requested. Membership in a memorial organization or society is not required. Immediate disposition includes transferring the deceased from the place of death, placing the deceased in a casket or appropriate container, obtaining registration of death and burial permit, securing all necessary documentation, providing a Funeral Director's Statement of Death, and arranging for a casket and the use of facilities and vehicles. Transportation to the cemetery and/or crematorium charges are the responsibility of the executor of the estate.

Military or Fraternal Services

Any veteran or serving member of Canada's armed forces is entitled to military honours. Services can include covering the casket with the Canadian flag, Red Ensign, or Union Jack, and a bugler sounding the last post. Veteran's organizations such as the Royal Canadian Legion and Army, Navy and Comrades-in-Arms, may provide pallbearers and a guard of honour if requested. The funeral director will contact such organizations if you request, and make the necessary arrangements.

Some cemeteries have a Field of Honour and Cross of Sacrifice. Veterans or members of Canadian Armed Forces can be interred in this section with permission. Recent changes to federal legislation permit past members of the Canadian Armed Forces be interred in the Field of Honour owned or controlled by the Department of Veterans' Affairs. A separate headstone marks the grave.

Memorial Service

A memorial service is usually held when the body is not present, for example, if the death occurred in a different country, the body was cremated, or donated for medical research.

Usually, a memorial service is held within a few days or weeks of the death. Like a funeral service, memorial services can be large or small. They can be held in a church, funeral home chapel, the family home, or some other location that may hold a special meaning for the deceased, and/or the family.

BURIAL OR CREMATION?

The majority of people still select burial as the chosen means of disposition, however, cremation is gradually becoming more accepted and popular. Deciding between burial and cremation will depend on a number of factors, including personal values, religious beliefs and financial resources. Cremation may be more expensive in some rural areas because of the additional cost of transporting the body to a crematorium usually located in a larger centre.

The Burial Option

Bodies must be buried in approved cemeteries. There are two ways to achieve this:

TRADITIONAL

The traditional earth burial where the casket is lowered into the ground.

ENTOMBMENT

Entombment is the internment of human remains in a tomb or crypt, usually referred to as above-ground internment. Entombment involves placing a casket or cremation urn in a crypt or niche (an individual compartment within a mausoleum or columbarium), which is then sealed. There are various options:

Community Mausoleum

A community mausoleum is simply a large building designed to provide above-ground internment, or entombment for a number of unrelated people. Sharing the costs of the mausoleum with other individuals makes it more affordable.

Crypts

Crypts are designed to hold casketed remains. Following a casket entombment, the crypt is sealed and a granite or marble front is attached.

Niches

Niches will accommodate urns containing cremated remains. Following an urn internment, a niche front of granite, marble, bronze, wood or glass is attached.

Columbarium

A columbarium, often located within a mausoleum or chapel, although sometimes free-standing, either indoor or outdoor, is constructed of numerous small compartments (niches) designed to hold urns containing cremated remains.

As mausoleum crypts are clean and dry, they offer a viable alternative for those people who have an aversion to being interred in the ground. With the growing shortage of land available for cemetery use, mausolea allow for a maximum number of entombments in a minimum amount of space. In most cases, mausoleum entombment is comparable to the cost of internment in a lot with an upright monument.

The Cremation Option

Any decisions about cremation should be educated decisions. Pre-arranging your funeral allows you time to make an informed decision in this area. In fact, cremation is only one process in a series of events that will take place. Cremation is where the body is actually prepared for final disposition. Over a period of two to three hours the body is transformed by intense heat (1600 to 2000 degrees Fahrenheit) to a state of small skeletal fragments and not fine ash as some people believe.

After the cremation process is complete, the cremated remains are removed from the cremation chamber and placed in a tray for cooling. The remains are then processed to their final consistency. The processed cremated remains are usually placed in a small cardboard box or a temporary urn at the crematorium. Before the cremated returns are returned to the family, they may be placed in an urn designed to hold cremated remains permanently. Urns are constructed from a variety of materials such as hardwoods, metals, ceramic or stone. Most cremated remains weigh between four to eight pounds. These materials are pure and do not present any health risk. You can decide what you want done with the remains. They may be disposed of by the crematorium or retained in a container that is given to the next of kin.

SCATTERING THE ASHES

You may consider having your remains scattered. However, there are several important issues to consider before you make a decision in this regard. Families have scattered remains and regretted it later. Scattering is permanent and once done cannot be reversed. You may wish to have your remains scattered on your own property. Over time, however, it may make it much more difficult for your family to sell that property. You may be considering a park or lake as an area in which to scatter your ashes. However, it may be in contravention of a local by-law or provincial law to scatter the remains in a public place. There is also no guarantee that the setting you choose will be as beautiful in the future.

Some families decide to take the urn home, because they feel that as long as they have the urn, the deceased is with them. Taking the urn home is usually a temporary measure until a decision can be made as to its final resting place. It may be more appropriate for you to make the decision in advance, thereby saving your family from having to make a decision.

Cemetery facilities for receiving cremated remains vary. It is best to check with the individual cemetery. They may have a columbarium, an urn garden where cremation lots are available for burial of an urn, or a common scattering garden where permanent records are kept and a memorial may be erected.

Burial at Sea

If your wish is to have your body buried at sea you must adhere to federal government law. There are strict regulations and guidelines that make a burial at sea virtually impossible. A permit application must be made at least eight weeks in advance and a notice of intent must be placed in a local newspaper. Proof of the notice must be sent to Environment Canada together with an application fee. Other stringent regulations include ensuring that the burial site is a minimum number of nautical miles from land, and adhering to particular casket specifications. It is recommended that alternative arrangements be considered. The regulations involved and costs incurred with a burial at sea make this choice almost prohibitive. There are no restrictions relating to releasing your cremated remains at sea.

Monuments and Markers

Ground level markers and upright monuments can be purchased from monument dealers, but are also available through some cemeteries and funeral homes. Cemeteries generally have regulations regarding the actual size and types of monuments and markers that can be used. Costs of bronze markers or stone monuments vary depending upon size, material, design and craftsmanship.

THE AVAILABILITY OF FINANCIAL BENEFITS AND ASSISTANCE

There are a number of financial resources available to your family at the time of your death. Funeral directors should have information about benefits and grants that may be available. Following is a list of some of the financial resources that may be available:

Life Insurance

Life insurance companies pay out policies at the time of death if the deceased had a valid policy. The funeral director or the life insurance agent will assist with claim forms and provide the necessary information. Alternatively, your family may wish to do this on their own. Insurance companies require a Proof of Death Certificate to complete the insurance claim. The Proof of Death Certificate can be provided by the funeral director and on occasion, from the medical practitioner. Some doctors charge for completing the physician's statements that are sometimes required by the insurer.

Accidental Death Insurance

You may not realize it, but you could have automatic accidental death coverage under your automobile association membership. In addition, you may have automatic accidental death coverage for any common carrier (e.g. plane, train, boat, bus) that you were on when you were killed. In this scenario, you would be covered by the credit or charge card company insurance policy benefits for cardholders. The normal pre-condition for coverage is that you charged the cost of the common carrier on your card. Fringe benefit coverages should be clarified and noted in your personal information record (refer to Appendix D, Checklist 1).

Canada Pension Plan

If you have contributed to Canada Pension Plan for the minimum qualifying period, the Plan makes a lump-sum payment to your legal representative or to the person who paid for the funeral. A monthly pension may also be available to your spouse or any dependent children. An application for the benefit may be made at any Canada Pension Plan district office. The funeral director can provide more information and some of the forms necessary to make a claim.

Veterans' Allowance

VETERANS' AFFAIRS CANADA

Burial, pension and other benefits are available to veterans of Canada's armed forces and their dependents. Veterans in receipt of a war pension or a veteran's allowance are eligible for receipt of a benefit. Other veterans are not entitled to a benefit. This grant is means tested, and estate and spousal assets must be declared on the form provided. In some cases, depending on the assets declared, a partial grant might be awarded. Funeral benefits from Veterans' Affairs Canada are subject to change. Obtain the latest information. You can locate the closest office by going to *www.veterans.gc.ca*.

LAST POST FUND FOR VETERANS

This society was organized to provide a dignified funeral, internment and marker for honourably discharged veterans without sufficient funds. An application for burial assistance has to be completed by the next of kin prior to the finalization of funeral and burial expenses. Financial eligibility must be determined. Contact your Veterans' Affairs Canada district office, located in all major cities, for further details or application forms, or go to *www.canada.ca*. Your funeral director can also contact the veterans' organizations or your local representative.

Company and Union Benefits

Contact your employer for information about the benefits that are available.

Compassionate Travel Policy

Many airlines provide compensation in the form of a partial rebate or discounted fare for bereaved passengers who have to make last-minute travel arrangements. The policy applies when death has occurred or the death of a relative is imminent, and applies to travel in Canada or overseas. Payment of the full fare is usually required at the time of travel and a rebate may be claimed within six months. However, some airlines offer the discounts before travel. Travel must originate in North America and be round-trip or as defined by the airline.

Check the airline's current definition as it applies to the discount for family members and relatives. Policies vary from airline to airline. Discounts are usually only available on Economy Class fares and do not apply to First Class or Business Class fares. In the case where death has already occurred, the airline will require a funeral director's Statement of Death if available, or the names of the funeral home and funeral director. The type of verification required may vary from airline to airline.

If you are outside the country it is important to obtain out-of-country emergency medical coverage to supplement Canadian Medicare if you are injured or ill—for example, if you are a Snowbird residing part-time in the U.S. or Mexico. Check the policy coverage, as many insurance companies include "repatriation." This means that in the event of your death outside of Canada, the insurance company will cover the cost, up to a maximum amount, to have your body returned to Canada for cremation or burial.

Some hotels provide discounted room rates for those travelling a distance.

Fraternal or Association Benefits

Associations you are affiliated with may provide financial assistance.

Monthly Income Cheques

Cheques that were received as income for the month in which the death occurred become the property of your estate. These can include Canada Pension, Old Age Security, supplemental benefits, company pension, veterans' benefits and most other provincial and federal benefit cheques.

Motor Vehicle Accident Insurance

If applicable, information can be obtained from the nearest office of your insurance agent.

Public Trustee

If the Public Trustee is looking after your affairs at the time of death, their office must be contacted before arrangements are made for the funeral. The Public Trustee may authorize an allowance for funeral and burial costs.

Supplemental Benefits

Canadian citizens over 65 years old whose spouses have died and who live in Canada and meet the financial criteria of a low net income, may apply for a Guaranteed Income Supplement. Check with the provincial government department for seniors. Refer to Appendix A. If widowed, an individual 60 to 65 may qualify for a Widowed Spouse's Allowance. It is necessary to supply proof of income from the last year's income tax return along with appropriate documents for Canada Pension Survivor's Benefits. Check with your closest Canada Pension Plan office or go to *www.canada.ca*. Refer to Appendix A for federal government contact numbers.

Workers' Compensation Board

If the cause of death is related to the workplace, funds may be made available to spouses, children and other dependents.

ORGAN DONATIONS AND MEDICAL RESEARCH

You may wish to give your organs or your body for transplant and/or research purposes. If so, it is very important that you make your doctor and family aware of your wishes in advance. The added stress of dealing with an unexpected request of this nature at the time of death may cause confusion among distraught family and friends. This can be easily avoided by prior planning and communication with those closest to you.

There is a tremendous need for organ donations in Canada. Your decision to provide your organs to others could provide new life or certainly an enhanced quality of life to the grateful recipient. For more information, refer to Appendix A for the provincial organ donation contact numbers. More and more people are requesting that their organs be donated.

An organ donation does not preclude a traditional funeral but it may delay it. A whole body donation would of course preclude a traditional family funeral. However, in that situation, a memorial service would enable friends and family to participate.

WHERE TO GET MORE INFORMATION

- Refer to Appendix A, "Sources of Information," for a list of provincial funeral home associations, provincial government licensing departments for funeral services and provincial organ donation agencies. Ask for further consumer information to be sent to you.
- Contact your local better business bureau to see if there have been any complaints about the funeral services company that you may be considering.
- Make sure that you have a comparison of at least three funeral homes or memorial service companies, before deciding which one is the best for your needs and budget.
- Check out the various forms of financial assistance that you might be able to obtain. Refer to the section on the availability of financial benefits and assistance, discussed earlier in this chapter as well as the list of website addresses in Appendix A for further information.
- Refer to the website: *www.estateplanning.ca*.

SUMMARY

Although some people may find it uncomfortable dealing with the funeral aspects of death, it is an essential stage of life planning. Having direct input in the decision-making of your advance funeral arrangements provides peace of mind for yourself and those closest to you. It saves a great deal of stress and money in the long run.

We have covered in this chapter pre-arranged funerals, documents required, support services, selecting a funeral home and understanding funeral costs. We also discussed the funeral or memorial service, burial or cremation options and types of financial assistance. The importance of considering organ donation was also mentioned, along with where to get more information.

? Frequently
Asked Questions

1. What are the benefits of a pre-arranged funeral?

There are a number of benefits. One key benefit is that you are making decisions about your funeral in advance so that you control the cost and nature of funeral services. If your spouse or family undertakes this process at the time of death during an emotional state, decisions could be made that result in higher funeral costs than if you had previously arranged it yourself. It also adds an extra element of stressful decision-making to the process for your family members. In addition, you might prefer to have had a cremation and a memorial service instead of a traditional funeral. These types of decisions can be dealt with during your life. There are considerable cost differences between the two options.

2. Are there any financial assistance programs available for funeral costs?

Yes, there are numerous potential sources of assistance. If you have contributed to the Canada Pension Plan, your estate would be eligible for death benefits. If you are a veteran, Veteran's Affairs Canada has assistance. Workers' Compensation will provide financial assistance if the death was work-related. In addition, check with your company, union, association or fraternal group for possible assistance. Your estate could also receive an advance to cover funeral costs from any life or accidental death insurance coverage that you might have.

3. How do I become an organ donor?

Thousands of lives are lost every year because there are not enough donors. Recent sophisticated advances in medical science have made the success rate in transplantations very high. Each organ donor can help improve the lives of as many as 13 people, sometimes making the critical difference between life and death. The main organs that you may wish to donate are heart, lungs, kidney, liver, pancreas, cornea, bone and skin.

Current provincial legislation allows any person of legal age to be an organ donor. All that is required is a signed and witnessed organ donor card, or other provincial registration procedure, and family permission. You should tell your family of course, so that they know your wishes, as well your family doctor. Keep your organ donor card in your wallet or purse, unless there is a provincial registration system in place in your province.

There is no point in outlining your wishes in your will. By the time your will is read, it would be too late for an organ donation.

Sources of Information

One of the challenges of researching information is to know where to start. This Appendix should save you a great deal of time, energy, money and hassle by providing you with the key contact numbers.

1. FEDERAL GOVERNMENT

If you can't locate the phone number for a federal or provincial government office in Canada, phone the Government of Canada information line at 1-800-O-Canada (1-800-622-6232), or *www.canada.ca*. They are very helpful and resourceful in providing information.

2. PROVINCIAL GOVERNMENT ENQUIRY CENTRES

Contact these provincial enquiry numbers if you want contact information for any government departments—for example, health departments, departments of vital statistics and offices of the public trustee.

BRITISH COLUMBIA
Website: *www.gov.bc.ca*

ALBERTA
Website: *www.alberta.ca*

MANITOBA
Website: *www.gov.mb.ca*

ONTARIO
Website: *www.ontario.ca*

QUEBEC
Website: *www.gouv.qc.ca*

NEW BRUNSWICK
Website: *www.gnb.ca*

NOVA SCOTIA
Website: *www.gov.ns.ca*

NEWFOUNDLAND
Website: *www.gov.nf.ca*

PRINCE EDWARD ISLAND
Website: *www.gov.pe.ca*

NUNAVUT
Website: *www.gov.nu.ca*

YUKON
Website: *www.gov.yk.ca*

SASKATCHEWAN
Website: *www.gov.sk.ca*

3. PROVINCIAL GOVERNMENT LICENSING DEPARTMENT FOR FUNERAL SERVICES

BRITISH COLUMBIA

Consumer Services Division
Website: *www.consumerprotectionbc.ca*

ALBERTA

Alberta Funeral Services Regulatory Board
Website: *www.afsrb.ab.ca*

SASKATCHEWAN

**Saskatchewan Prepaid Funeral
    Services Council (Funeral and Crematory
    Services Council of Saskatchewan)**
Website: *www.fcscs.ca*

MANITOBA

**Public Utilities Board Department of
    Consumer and Corporate Affairs**
Website: *www.pub.gov.mb.ca*

ONTARIO

Board of Funeral Services
Website: *www.funeralboard.com*

NEW BRUNSWICK

**Consumer Affairs Branch
Department of Justice**
Website: *www.gov.nb.ca*

NOVA SCOTIA

**Consumer and Commercial Relations
    Division**
Website: *www.gov.ns.ca*

PRINCE EDWARD ISLAND

Department of Justice and Public Safety
Website: *www.gov.pe.ca/attorneygeneral*

NEWFOUNDLAND

**Trade Practices and Licensing Division
Department of Government Services and
    Lands**
Website: *www.gov.nf.ca*

YUKON

**Consumer Services
Department of Justice**
Website: *www.community.gov.yk.ca*

NORTHWEST TERRITORIES

**Consumer Services Branch
Municipal and Community Affairs**
Website: *www.maca.gov.nt.ca*

4. Provincial Funeral Service Associations

British Columbia

Funeral Service Association of BC
Website: *www.bcfunerals.com*

Alberta

Alberta Funeral Service Association
Website: *www.afsa.ab.ca*

Saskatchewan

Funeral and Cremation Services Council of
    Saskatchewan
Website: *www.fcscs.ca*

Manitoba

Manitoba Funeral Service Association
Website: *www.mfsa.mb.ca*

Ontario

Ontario Funeral Service Association
Website: *www.ofsa.org*

Québec

Corporation des Thanatologues du QC
Website: *www.domainefuneraire.com*

New Brunswick

New Brunswick Funeral Directors and
    Embalmers Association
Website: *www.nbfuneraldirectors.ca*

Nova Scotia

Funeral Service Association of Nova Scotia
Website: *www.fsans.com*

Prince Edward Island

Prince Edward Island Funeral Services and
    Professions Board
Website: *www.princeedwardisland.ca*

Newfoundland

Newfoundland & Labrador Funeral Services
    Association
Website: *www.nlfuneralboard.ca*

5. PROVINCIAL ORGANIZATIONS FOR INFORMATION ON ADVANCE DIRECTIVES

The organizations listed below have pamphlets, forms and booklets on advance directives, or they will refer you to places where you can obtain such information. Some of these organizations may provide support and information concerning end of life issues to seniors and their families through caregiver resource centres, support groups or counseling. Of course, also speak to your lawyer about advance directives.

BRITISH COLUMBIA

The People's Law School
Website: *www.publiclegaled.bc.ca*

ALBERTA

John Dossetor Health Ethics Centre
Website: *www.ualberta.ca*

SASKATCHEWAN

Saskatchewan Seniors Mechanism
Website: *www.skseniorsmechanism.ca*

MANITOBA

Seniors Resource Network
Website: *www.seniors.clmnet.ca*

ONTARIO

Joint Centre for Bioethics
Website: *www.jointcentreforbioethics.ca*

QUEBEC

Public Curator Offices
Le Curateur public du Québec
Website: *www.curateur.gouv.qc.ca*

NEW BRUNSWICK

The Third Age Centre
St. Thomas University
Website: *www.stthomasu.ca*

NOVA SCOTIA

Legal Information Society of Nova Scotia
Website: *www.legalinfo.org*

PRINCE EDWARD ISLAND

Community Legal Information Association
    of Prince Edward Island
Website: *www.cliapei.ca*

NEWFOUNDLAND AND LABRADOR

St. John's Seniors Resource Centre
Website: *www.seniorsresource.ca*

YUKON

Yukon Council on Aging
Website: *www.yukon-seniors-and-elders.org*

6. Organ Donation Agencies

Canadian Society of Transplantation
Website: *www.transplant.ca*

Click on "Transplant Programs and Donor Organizations" at the side of the home page for links to transplant societies and hospitals in various provinces.

There are numerous hospitals in Canada that carry out organ transplants, and the list is growing.

7. Provincial Contacts for Long-Term Care Facilities

Here are some phone numbers and websites that can direct you to the regional long-term care coordinator serving your community.

British Columbia

Enquiry BC
Website: *www.seniorsbc.ca*

Alberta

**Government of Alberta Seniors &
    Community Supports**
Website: *www.seniors.alberta.ca*

Saskatchewan

Saskatchewan Social Services
Website: *www.socialservices.gov.sk.ca*

Manitoba

Manitoba Seniors Directorate
Website: *www.gov.mb.ca*

Ontario

Health INFOline, Ministry of Health
Website: *www.health.gov.on.ca*

Quebec

Local Community Health Centre
Website: *www.msss.gouv.qc.ca*

New Brunswick

**Department of Health and Community
    Services**
Website: *www.gnb.ca*

Nova Scotia

Office for Seniors
Website: *www.gov.ns.ca*

Prince Edward Island

**Department of Health
Acute, Medical and Continuing Care Division**
Website: *www.gov.pe.ca*

Newfoundland

**Department of Health
Continuing Care Division**
Website: *www.health.gov.nl.ca*

Yukon

**Yukon Government
Homecare Coordinator**
Website: *www.hss.gov.yk.ca*

Northwest Territories

**Department of Health and Social Services
    Residential Care**
Website: *www.hss.gov.nt.ca*

8. CANADIAN LIFE AND HEALTH INSURANCE ASSOCIATION (CLHIA)

The CLHIA represents over 100 life and health insurance companies in Canada. They also provide consumer publications and information services relating to life and health insurance or pensions.

Contact the CLHIA at:

Website: *www.clhia.ca*

The CLHIA produces a number of consumer brochures, workbooks and information sheets you may find of interest, which can be downloaded from their website, including:

- A guide to life insurance
- A guide to disability insurance
- A guide to coordination of benefits
- A guide to supplementary health insurance
- A guide to travel health insurance
- Key facts about segregated fund contracts
- Consumer tips: RRSPs with life insurance companies

9. HELPFUL WEBSITES

Information for Seniors

Canadian Association of Retired Persons	*www.carp.ca*
American Association of Retired Persons	*www.aarp.org*
Canadian Retirement Planning Institute Inc.	*www.retirementplanning.ca*

Financial Planning

Advocis (Financial Advisors Association of Canada)	*www.advocis.ca*
Financial Planners Standards Council of Canada	*www.fpsccanada.org*
Canadian Snowbird Institute Inc.	*www.snowbird.ca*
Canadian Estate Planning Institute Inc.	*www.estateplanning.ca*

Estate Planning

Canadian Snowbird Institute Inc.	*www.snowbird.ca*
Canadian Estate Planning Institute Inc.	*www.estateplanning.ca*

Life and Health Insurance

Canadian Life and Health Insurance Association	*www.clhia.ca*

Charitable Giving

Imagine Canada (formerly Canadian Centre for Philanthropy)	*www.imaginecanada.ca*

Family Business

Family Firm Institute	*www.ffi.org*
Family Enterprise Xchange	*www.familyenterprise-xchange.com*
National Small Business Institute Inc.	*www.smallbiz.ca*

Samples

I. A SAMPLE WILL

(Sample for illustration only. Do not use. Given the importance of a will, it is necessary that you obtain customized legal advice on the correct and current format and content applicable to your province and your needs.)

THIS IS THE LAST WILL of me, **JANE DOE**, of the City of X, in the Province of Y.

REVOCATION

I.   I REVOKE all former wills and other testamentary dispositions made by me.

EXECUTORS

II.   I APPOINT my husband, JOHN DOE (hereinafter referred to as "John") to be the Executor and Trustee of this my Will, provided that if John shall have predeceased me or shall survive me but die before the trusts hereof shall have terminated or shall refuse or be unable to act or to continue to act as such Executor and Trustee, then I appoint JAMES BRIAN and JANE SMITH, or the survivor of them to be the Executors and Trustees or Executor and Trustee of this my Will in the place and stead of my said husband. References to "my Trustees" in my Will shall include each Executrix, Executor and Trustee of my Will, my estate, or portion thereof, who may be acting as such from time to time whether original or substituted and whether one or more.

PROPERTY TO TRUSTEES

III. I GIVE all my property wheresoever situate, including any property over which I may have a general power of appointment, to my Trustees upon the following trusts, namely:

Household and Personal Effects

(a)   To deliver to my sister, NANCY DAVIS, if she survives me, my Peruvian sapphire broach.

(b)   To deliver to my sister, RUTH HILL, if she survives me, my diamond earrings.

(c)   To deliver to my sister, DORIS MILLER, if she survives me, my baby grand piano.

(d) To deliver to my sister, HELEN MCGINNIS, if she survives me, my signed Karsh photo of "Cats on a hot tin roof."

(e) To deliver to my husband, JOHN, if he survives me for a period of thirty (30) days, all remaining articles of personal, domestic and household use or ornament belonging to me at my death, including works of art, consumable stores and all automobiles and accessories thereto then owned by me.

Debts and Taxes

(f) To pay out of and charge to the capital of my general estate my just debts, funeral and testamentary expenses.

Legacies

(g) To pay to my friend, PAM ANDERSON, if she survives me, the sum of Two Thousand Dollars ($2,000.00).

(h) To pay to my friend, ALICE COOPER, if she survives me, the sum of One Thousand Dollars ($1,000.00).

Residue

(i) If my husband, JOHN, survives me for a period of thirty (30) days, to pay, transfer and assign the residue of my estate to him for his own use absolutely.

(j) If JOHN predeceases me or survives me but dies within a period of thirty (30) days of the date of my death, to divide the residue of my estate in equal shares per stirpes among my issue living at the death of the survivor of JOHN and me; provided that the share of each child of mine who shall then be living but who shall not have attained the age of twenty-five (25) years shall be set aside and my Trustees shall hold in trust and keep such share invested and, subject as hereinafter provided, from time to time until such child becomes absolutely entitled to all the capital of such share, may pay to or apply for the benefit of such child the whole or such part of the net income derived from such share or from the part thereof from time to time remaining in trust and such part or parts of the capital thereof as my Trustees in their absolute and uncontrolled discretion deem advisable. If in any year that my Trustees hold such share or any part thereof, any portion of the said net income is not paid to or applied for the benefit of such child, such portion shall be accumulated by my Trustees and shall be added to the capital of such share to be administered as if an original part thereof. Upon such child attaining the age of twenty-one (21) years, the net income of such share shall be paid to such child until he or she attains the age of twenty-five (25) years when the capital of such share shall be paid or transferred to him or her. If such child should die before receiving the whole of his or her share, such share or the part thereof remaining shall be divided among the issue of such child who survive him or her in equal shares per stirpes or, if such child should leave no issue him or her surviving, among my issue who shall be living at the death of such child in equal shares per stirpes, provided that if any child of mine shall thereby become entitled to any part of such share before attaining the age of twenty-five (25) years, such child's part shall be added to the capital of the share of my estate hereinbefore directed to be held in trust for such child and shall be administered as part thereof.

PAYMENTS FOR MINORS

IV.   I AUTHORIZE my Trustees to make any payments for any person under the age of majority or under other legal disability, to a parent or guardian of such person or to any other person my Trustees in their uncontrolled discretion deem it advisable, the receipt for any such payment shall be a full and sufficient discharge to my Trustees.

HOLDING FOR MINORS

V.   SUBJECT AS IS SPECIFICALLY provided herein, if any person should become entitled to any share in my estate before attaining the age of majority the share of such person shall be held and kept invested by my Trustees and the income and capital or so much thereof as my Trustees in their absolute discretion consider necessary or advisable shall be used for the benefit of such person until he or she attains the age of majority.

POWER TO SELL OR HOLD

VI.   I AUTHORIZE my Trustees to use their discretion in the realization of my estate, with power to sell, call in and convert into money any part of my estate not consisting of money at such time or times, in such manner and upon such terms, and either for cash or credit or for part cash and part credit as they may in their absolute discretion decide upon, or to postpone such conversion of my estate or any part or parts thereof for such length of time as they may think best. My Trustees shall have a separate and substantive power to retain any of my investments or assets in the form existing at the date of my death at their absolute discretion without responsibility for loss to the intent that investments or assets so retained shall be deemed to be authorized investments for all purposes of this my Will. No reversionary or future interest shall be sold prior to falling into possession and no such interest not actually producing income shall be treated as producing income.

INVESTMENTS

VII.   WHENEVER it becomes necessary for my Trustees to invest any moneys held in connection with my estate I will and declare that my Trustees in making such investment shall not be limited to investments authorized by law for trustees but may invest in any investment that in my Trustees' discretion my Trustees consider advisable and my Trustees shall not be held responsible for any loss that may be occasioned by any such investment made by Trustees in good faith. Without limitation, mutual funds, whether shares or units of a mutual fund corporation or trust, and shares or units of any pooled fund, including pooled funds held by XYZ Trust Company, shall constitute authorized investments for my estate.

DISTRIBUTION IN KIND

VIII.   MY TRUSTEES may make any division of my estate or set aside or pay any share or interest therein either wholly or in part in the assets forming my estate at the time of my death or at the time of such division, setting aside or payment, and I expressly will and declare that my Trustees shall in their absolute discretion fix the value of my estate or any part thereof for the purpose of making any such division, setting aside or payment and the decision of my Trustees shall be final and binding upon all persons concerned.

REAL ESTATE

IX.   I AUTHORIZE my Trustees to sell, partition, exchange or otherwise dispose of the whole or any part of my real property in such manner at such time and upon such terms as to credit or otherwise as they in their discretion consider advisable, with power to accept purchase money, mortgage or mortgages for any part of the purchase or exchange price; also to mortgage, lease for any terms of years, alter, repair, improve or rebuild the same as my Trustees may deem expedient. I also give to my Trustees power to execute and deliver such deeds, mortgages, leases or other instruments as may be necessary to effect such a sale, mortgage, lease or other disposition. The power of sale herein is discretionary and not mandatory.

SETTLEMENT OF CLAIMS

X.   I AUTHORIZE AND EMPOWER my Trustees to compromise, settle, waive or pay any claim or claims at any time owing by my estate or which my estate may have against others for such consideration or no consideration and upon such terms and conditions as my Trustees may deem advisable and to refer to arbitration all such claims if my Trustees deem same advisable.

DEALING WITH SECURITIES

XI.   IF AT ANY TIME my Trustees hold in my estate any investment in or in connection with any company or corporation or partnership or limited partnership, I authorize and empower my Trustees to join in or take any action in connection with such investment or to exercise any rights, powers and privileges which at any time may exist or arise in connection with any such investment to the same extent and as fully as I could if I were alive and the sole owner of such investment. I also authorize my Trustees to retain as an investment of my estate for such length of time as in their discretion they deem advisable any asset or other interest whatsoever acquired by them through the exercise of the powers hereinbefore given to them.

PROFESSIONAL ADVISORS

XII. I AUTHORIZE my Trustees to employ and pay out of my estate such professional advisors as my Trustees may deem necessary in the discharge of their duties and to act upon such advice and opinions as they may receive from any such professional so employed and my Trustees shall not be liable or responsible for any loss that may be occasioned to my estate by reason of their so doing.

AGENCY CLAUSE

XIII. MY TRUSTEES may appoint a person or corporation to act as my Trustees' agent for the management of my estate and from time to time may terminate such appointment and/or make another. My Trustees are authorized to fix the remuneration to be paid to any such person or corporation and such remuneration is to be charged upon my estate and payable out of the capital and/or income thereof in such proportions as my Trustees from time to time decide. In making any such arrangement as aforesaid, my Trustees may place the investments comprising my estate, or any of them, in the custody of such person or corporation and may transfer such investments, or any of them, into the name of such person or corporation, or any nominee thereof. Without limitation, my Trustees may delegate my Trustees' investment authority to investment counsel provided my Trustees set investment guidelines; and my Trustees may delegate their investment authority in the course of or as a result of the investment in, or the purchase or holding of, shares or units of mutual fund corporations or trusts or shares or units of pooled funds.

EXONERATION

XIV. I HEREBY DECLARE that my Trustees shall not be liable for any loss that may happen to my estate or to any beneficiary hereunder resulting from the exercise by my Trustees in good faith of any discretion given them in this my Will.

LIMITING INTERESTS OF SPOUSES OF BENEFICIARIES

XV. I DECLARE that no gift, or the income therefrom, under this my Will shall be assigned or antic-ipated, or fall into any community of property, partnership or other form of sharing or division of property which may exist between any beneficiary and his or her spouse, and every gift together with the income therefrom shall remain the separate property of a beneficiary here-under, free from all matrimonial rights or controls by his or her spouse. Without limiting the generality of the foregoing, I direct that all of the gifts and other benefits granted by me under this my Will and all the income derived therefrom shall be excluded from net family property of a beneficiary and the value thereof shall not be subject to division between a beneficiary and his or her spouse pursuant to the *Family Law Act* of my province, or any successor legislation thereto. All references to income contained in this clause of this my Will are intended by me and shall be deemed to include capital gains as well as any other accretions to capital arising from a gift or benefit hereunder.

TRUSTEES' COMPENSATION TAKEN IN ADVANCE

XVI. I AUTHORIZE my Trustees to take and transfer to themselves at reasonable intervals from the income and/or capital of my estate amounts on account of compensation which my Trustees reasonably anticipate will be requested at the end of the accounting period in progress, either upon the audit of the estate accounts or on approval by the beneficiaries of my estate. Provided, however, that if the amount subsequently awarded on Court audit or agreed to by the beneficia-ries is less than the amount so pretaken, the difference shall be repaid forthwith to the estate without interest. The preparations of estate accounts and tax returns shall be proper expense of my estate and shall not reduce the amount of compensation to which my Trustees would other-wise be entitled. Any Trustee of my Will who is a professional person shall be entitled to executor's or trustee's compensation in addition to reasonable fees for professional services rendered by such Trustee or by any partner, associate or employee of such Trustee or by any company of which such Trustee is an employee.

GUARDIAN

XVII. IN THE EVENT that my husband, JOHN predeceases me and if I die before any child of mine has attained the age of majority, I appoint SUSAN JONES to have custody of such child and act as the guardian of the property of such child. It is my wish that before the expiration of ninety (90) days from the date of my death, SUSAN JONES apply to have custody if such child and act as the guardian of the property of such child pursuant to the provisions of the Ontario *Children's Law Reform Act* of my province, as from time to time amended.

HEADINGS

XXV. THE PARAGRAPH HEADINGS in my Will are for convenience only and shall not be construed to affect the meaning of the paragraphs so headed.

IN WITNESS WHEREOF I have to this my Last Will, written upon this and nine (9) preceding pages, subscribed my name this   day of   , 20 .

SIGNED by the above named testatrix, **JANE DOE** as her last Will, in the presence of us, both present at the same time, who at her request, in his presence and in the presence of each other have hereunto subscribed our names as witnesses.

WITNESS:_____   WITNESS:_____

Name:_____   Name:_____

Address:_____   Address:_____

_____   _____

Occupation:_____   Occupation_____

2. A SAMPLE CODICIL TO A WILL

(Sample for illustration only. Do not use. Given the importance of a will, it is necessary that you obtain customized legal advice on the correct and current format and content applicable to your province and your needs.)

THIS IS THE FIRST CODICIL to the Will of me John Doe, of the City of X, in the Province of Y, which Will is dated the 1st day of May, 2002.

1. I revoke the appointment of Alice Cooper as set out in paragraph 2(a) of my Will, and I appoint Mary Collins in her place as executor and trustee.

2. In paragraph 3(c) of my Will. I have provided a legacy $2,000 to Nancy Miller. I now increase this amount to $5,000.

3. In all other respects, I confirm my Will.

IN TESTIMONY HEREOF I have to this First Codicil to my Will, written upon this page and the preceding page of paper, subscribed my name this 10th day of June, 2000.

SIGNED, by the above-named Testator, John Doe,   )
as a First Codicil to his Will, in the presence of us   )
both, present at the same time, who at his request,   ) _____
in his presence and in the presence of each other,   ) **JOHN DOE**
have subscribed our names at witnesses.   ) *(Signature of Testator)*
)
)

WITNESS:_____   WITNESS:_____

Name:_____   Name:_____

Address:_____   Address:_____

_____   _____

Occupation:_____   Occupation:_____

3. A Sample Continuing Power of Attorney (Property)

(Sample for illustration only. Do not use. Make sure you obtain professional advice on the correct and current format and content applicable to your province and your needs.)

1. I, _____ revoke any previous continuing power
               (Print or type your full name here)

    of attorney for property made by me and APPOINT:_____

    _____

    _____

         (Print or type the name of the person or persons you appoint here)

    to be my attorney(s) for property.

2. If you have named more than one attorney and you want them to have the authority to act separately, insert the words "jointly and severally" here:

(This may be left blank)

3. If the person(s) I have appointed, or any one of them, cannot or will not be my attorney because of refusal, resignation, death, mental incapacity, or removal by the court, I SUBSTITUTE:

(This may be left blank)

to act as my attorney for property with the same authority as the person he or she is replacing.

4. I AUTHORIZE my attorney(s) for property to do on my behalf, anything that I can lawfully do by an attorney, and specifically anything in respect of property that I could do if capable of managing property, except make a Will, subject to the law and to any conditions or restrictions contained in this document.

    In accordance with the current legislation of my province, I declare that this power of attorney may be exercised during any subsequent legal incapacity on my part. This indicates my intention that this document will be a continuing power of attorney for property under the current provincial legislation in my province, and may be used during my incapacity to manage property.

    In accordance with the applicable legislation in my province, I declare that, after due consideration, I am satisfied that the authority conferred on the attorney(s) named in this power of attorney is adequate to provide for the competent and effectual management of all my estate in case I should become a patient in a psychiatric facility and be certified as not competent to manage my estate under the current legislation in my province. I therefore direct that in that event, the attorney(s) named in this power of attorney may retain this power of attorney for the management of my estate by complying with current legislation in my province and in that case the Provincial Public Trustee shall not become committee of my estate as might otherwise be the case under the provincial legislation of my province.

    NOTE: *Other clauses to consider after discussion with your lawyer:*

    - *consent to sale of matrimonial home*
    - *gifts to family and charities*
    - *loans to family members*
    - *support of dependents*
    - *power to act as donor's litigation guardian*

5. **CONDITIONS AND RESTRICTIONS** Attach, sign and date additional pages if required. *(This may be left blank.)*

6. **DATE OF EFFECTIVENESS**
    Unless otherwise stated in this document, this continuing power of attorney will come into effect on the date it is signed and witnessed.

7. **COMPENSATION**
    Unless otherwise stated in this document, I authorize my attorney(s) to take annual compensation from my property in accordance with the fee scale prescribed by regulation for the compensation of guardians of property made pursuant to the current legislation of my province.

8. **SIGNATURE:** _____ Date: _____

   (Sign your name in the presence of two witnesses)

9. **WITNESS STATEMENT AND SIGNATURE**

   [Note: The following people cannot be witnesses: the attorney or his or her spouse or partner; the spouse, partner, or child of the person making the document, or someone that the person treats as his or her child; a person whose property is under guardianship or who has a guardian of the person; a person under the age of 18.]

   We have no reason to believe that the grantor is incapable of giving a continuing power of attorney for property. We have signed this power of attorney in the presence of the person whose name appears above and in the presence of each other.

   Witness #1: Signature: _____ Print Name:_____

   Address: _____ Date:_____

   Witness #2: Signature: _____ Print Name:_____

   Address: _____ Date:_____

4. A SAMPLE POWER OF ATTORNEY (PERSONAL CARE)

(Sample for illustration only. Do not use. Make sure that you obtain professional advice on the correct and current format and content applicable to your province and your needs.)

1. I, _____revoke any previous power of attorney for

   (Print or type your full name here)

   personal care made by me and APPOINT: _____

   _____

   _____

   (Print or type the name of the person or persons you appoint here)

   [Note: A person who provides health care, residential, social, training, advocacy, or support services to the person giving this power of attorney for compensation may not act as his or her attorney unless that person is also his or her spouse, partner or relative.]

2. If you have named more than one attorney and you want them to have the authority to act separately, insert the works "jointly and severally" here:

   _____

   (This may be left blank)

3. If the person(s) I have appointed, or any one of them, cannot or will not be my attorney because of refusal, resignation, death, mental incapacity, or removal by the court, I SUBSTITUTE:

_____

(This may be left blank)

to act as my attorney for personal care in the same manner and subject to the same authority as the person he or she is replacing.

4. I give my attorney(s) the AUTHORITY to make any personal care decision for me that I am mentally incapable of making for myself, including the giving or refusing of consent to treatment to which current legislation in my province applies subject to any instructions, conditions or restrictions contained in this form.

5. **INSTRUCTIONS, CONDITIONS AND RESTRICTIONS**
Attach, sign, and date additional pages if required. *(This part may be left blank.)*

6. **SIGNATURE:** _____ DATE:_____
(Sign your name in the presence of two witnesses)

7. **WITNESS STATEMENT AND SIGNATURE**
[Note: The following people cannot be witnesses: the attorney or his or her spouse or partner; the spouse, partner or child of the person making this document, or someone that the person treats as his or her child; a person whose property is under guardianship or who has a guardian of the person; a person under the age of 18.]

We have no reason to believe that the grantor is incapable of giving a power of attorney for personal care or making decisions in respect of which instructions are contained in this power of attorney. We have signed this power of attorney in the presence of the person whose name appears above and in the presence of each other.

Witness #1:   Signature: _____ Print Name:_____

Address: _____ Date:_____

Witness #2:   Signature: _____ Print Name:_____

Address: _____ Date:_____

5. Living Will

A "living will" is sometimes referred to by other names such as advance directive, health care directive, etc. Contact the Joint Centre for Bioethics, University of Toronto, for further information and sample formats on living wills. Refer to the end of Chapter 5 for a discussion of living wills and contact information.

(Sample for illustration only. Do not use. Given the importance of a Living Will, it is wise to obtain customized legal advice on the correct and current format and content applicable to your province and your needs.)

I, JOHN DOE, of 370 Sunnyhill Lane, Pleasantville, in the Province of *X*, Canada, designate my friend, LOIS LANE, of 210 Fourth Avenue, Pleasantville, in the Province of *X*, Canada, to be my Health Care Proxy and to act for me and in my name, place and stead, with regard to my treatment and care.

Upon the death of LOIS LANE or her becoming incapable or unwilling to act as my Health Care Proxy, I designate my friend, JIM JAMES, of #101–1070 Main Street, Pleasantville, in the Province of *X*, Canada, to be my Alternate Health Care Proxy in her stead.

I DECLARE that this Health Care Directive takes effect upon any mental infirmity on my part, or upon any incapacity on my part — that is, upon my failure, due to deteriorating physical or mental health, to be able to make informed decisions regarding the course of my medical treatment, or my failure, due to deteriorating physical or mental health, to be able to sign any documents or perform any acts necessary to decisions regarding the course of my medical treatment.

I GRANT to my Health Care Proxy full power and authority to make health care decisions for me to the same extent that I could make such decisions for myself if I had the capacity to do so. This Health Care Directive includes, but is not limited to, the following powers:

Powers of Next of Kin
1. To exercise all the authority and powers that are exercisable by my next of kin with respect to my treatment and care, such authority and powers to be limited only by the terms of this Health Care Directive. The decisions of my Health Care Proxy take priority over any wishes of my next of kin.

Visiting Priority
2. To be given priority in visiting me and in determining who shall be allowed to visit me and upon what terms and conditions those visits shall occur should I be a patient, in any hospital, health care facility, or institution including, but not limited to, any intensive care or coronary care units of any medical facility, and should I be unable to express a preference on account of any illness or disability.

Employment of Health Care Personnel
3. To employ any physicians, dentists, nurses, therapists, and other professionals or non-professionals, as my Health Care Proxy considers necessary or appropriate for my physical or mental well being; and to pay from my funds reasonable compensation for all services performed by those persons.

Gain Access to Medical and Other Personal Information
4. To request, review, and receive any information, verbal or written, regarding my personal affairs or my physical or mental health, including medical and hospital records, and to execute any releases or other documents that may be required in order to obtain this information.

5. Guided by what I have told my Health Care Proxy about my wishes about any medical care, to give or withhold consent to medical care on my behalf, including:
    (a) to give or withhold consent to medical care, surgery or any other medical procedures or tests;
    (b) to arrange for hospitalization, convalescence care or home care;
    (c) to revoke or change any consent to (a) or (b) above;
    (d) to seek or choose not to seek emergency care including paramedics, as she sees fit in light of my wishes and my medical status at the time of the decision;

(e) to sign on my behalf any document called, or purporting to be, "Refusal to Permit Treatment" and "Leaving the Hospital Against Medical Advice," and any necessary waivers or releases of liability required by a hospital or physician to carry out my wishes about medical treatment or non-treatment.

Refuse Life-Prolonging Treatment or Procedures

6. To request that aggressive medical therapy not be instituted or be discontinued, including (but not limited to) cardiopulmonary resuscitation, the implantation of cardiac pacemaker, renal dialysis, parenteral feeding, the use of respirators or ventilator, nasogastric tube use, endotrachael tube use, and organ transplants. My Health Care Proxy should try to discuss the specifics of any such decision with me if I am able to communicate in any manner. If I am unconscious, comatose, senile or otherwise cannot be communicated with, my Health Care Proxy should make this decision guided by any preference which I may have previously expressed and the information given by the physicians treating me as to my diagnosis and prognosis. My Health Care Proxy may specifically request and concur with the writing of a "no-code" (do not resuscitate) order by the attending or treating physician.

Provide Relief from Pain

7. To consent and arrange for the administration of pain-relieving drugs of any type, or other surgical or medical procedures calculated to relieve any pain even though their use may lead to permanent physical damage, addition, or even hasten the moment of (but not intentionally cause) my death. My Health Care Proxy may also consent to and arrange for unconventional pain-relief therapies such as biofeedback, relaxation therapy, acupuncture, skin stimulation, cutaneous stimulation, and other therapies which I or my Health Care Proxy believes may be helpful to me.

Protect My Right of Privacy

8. To exercise my right of privacy to make decisions regarding any medical treatment and my right to be left alone even though the exercise of that right may hasten death or be against conventional medical advice. My Health Care Proxy may take appropriate legal action, if necessary in her judgment, to enforce my right in this regard.

Execute Documents and Contracts

9. To sign, execute, deliver, acknowledge, and make declarations in any document that may be necessary or proper in order to exercise any of the powers described in this document, to enter into contracts and to pay reasonable compensation or costs in the exercise of such powers.

Take Legal Action

10. To join in, defend, dispute, answer or take any legal action or court proceeding in connection with the powers and authority conferred by this Health Care Directive and to exercise any rights, powers and privileges in connection with this Health Care Directive as fully as I could do if I were not infirm or incapable.

In accordance with the above, I HEREBY DIRECT that the costs to my Health Care Proxy in defending any action taken against her shall be borne by my estate AND I FURTHER DIRECT that should any judgment be registered against my Health Care Proxy, she be indemnified and saved harmless out of the proceeds of my estate.

IN WITNESS WHEREOF I set my hand and seal this _____ day of _____, 20 _____.

SIGNED, SEALED AND DELIVERED by JOHN DOE, in the presence of us, both present at the same time, who at his request, and in his presence, and in the presence of each other, have subscribed our names as witnesses:

)
)
)
) **JOHN DOE** _____
)

_____)
Signature of Witness)
)
_____)
Street Address)
)
_____)
City)
)
_____)
Occupation

_____)
Signature of Witness)
)
_____)
Street Address)
)
_____)
City)
)
_____)
Occupation

Accepted and Signed by Proxy:

_____)
Lois Lane)
)
_____)
Address)
)
_____)
City)

Accepted and Signed by Alternate Proxy:

_____)
Jim James   )
)
_____)
Street Address   )
)
_____)
City   )

C

Charts

TABLE 1: How Your Assets Are Distributed If You Die Without a Will

Province	Spouse Only	Spouse, Relative(s) but No Children	Child or Children Only	Spouse and One Child	Spouse and Children	No Spouse or Children
British Columbia	All to spouse	All to spouse	All to children[1]	First $300,000 to spouse;[3] rest split equally[1]	First $300,000 to spouse;[1] 1/3 rest to spouse; 2/3 to children	All to closest next of kin; in this order: parents; if neither survives, brothers/sisters;[8] if none survive, nephews/nieces; if none survive, next of kin. If there is no traceable next of kin, it all goes to the government.
Alberta	All to spouse	All to spouse	All to children[1]	All to spouse[1]	All to spouse[1]	Same as above
Saskatchewan	All to spouse	All to spouse	All to children[1]	First $100,000 to spouse; rest split equally[1]	First $100,000 to spouse; 1/3 rest to spouse; 2/3 to children	Same as above
Manitoba	All to spouse	All to spouse	All to children[1]	Either all to spouse;[5] or greater of $50,000 or 1/2 rest of estate to spouse;[10] 1/2 rest to spouse; 1/2 to children[6]	Either all to spouse;[5] or greater of $50,000 or 1/2 of estate to spouse;[3] 1/2 rest to spouse; 1/2 to children[6]	Same as above

...continued on next page

TABLE 1: How Your Assets Are Distributed If You Die Without a Will
(*continued from previous page*)

Province	Spouse Only	Spouse, Relative(s) but No Children	Child or Children Only	Spouse and One Child	Spouse and Children	No Spouse or Children
Ontario	All to spouse	All to spouse	All to children[1]	First $200,000 to spouse; rest split equally[1, 4]	First $200,000 to spouse; 1/3 rest to spouse; 2/3 to children[1, 4]	Same as above
Quebec	All to spouse	1/3 or 1/2 to spouse; rest to parents and/ or brothers and sisters[9]	All to children[1]	1/3 to spouse;[7] 2/3 to child[1]	1/3 to spouse;[7] 2/3 to children[1]	Same as above
New Brunswick	All to spouse	All to spouse	All to children[1]	Marital property to spouse; rest split equally[1]	Marital property to spouse; 1/3 rest to spouse; 2/3 to children[1]	Same as above
Nova Scotia	All to spouse	All to spouse	All to children[1]	First $50,000 to spouse;[2] rest split equally[1]	1st $50,000 to spouse;[2] 1/3 rest to spouse; 2/3 to children[1]	Same as above
Prince Edward Island	All to spouse	All to spouse	All to children[1]	Split equally[1]	1/3 to spouse; 2/3 to children[1]	Same as above
Newfoundland	All to spouse	All to spouse	All to children[1]	Split equally[1]	1/3 to spouse; 2/3 to children[1]	Same as above
Northwest Territories	All to spouse	All to spouse	All to children[1]	First $50,000 to spouse;[2] rest split equally[1]	First $50,000 to spouse;[2] 1/3 rest to spouse; 2/3 to children[1]	Same as above

TABLE 1: *How Your Assets Are Distributed If You Die Without a Will*

(continued from previous page)

Province	Spouse Only	Spouse, Relative(s) but No Children	Child or Children Only	Spouse and One Child	Spouse and Children	No Spouse or Children
Nunavut	All to spouse	All to spouse	All to children[1]	First $50,000 to spouse[2]; rest split equally[1]	First $50,000 to spouse[2]; 1/3 rest to spouse; 2/3 to children[1,]	Same as above
Yukon	All to spouse	All to spouse	All to children[1]	First $75,000 to spouse[3]; rest split equally[1]	First $50,000 to spouse[2]; 1/3 rest to spouse; 2/3 to children[1]	Same as above

NOTES:

- In the absence of a will, provincial or territorial legislation relating to wills provides for the distribution of assets as shown in this table.
- As laws are constantly changing, make sure you obtain a current review of legislation in your province or territory from your lawyer and/or trust company.
- In some cases, provincial or territorial legislation can override these distribution formulas.
- Distributions shown may also be subject to an election entitlement by the surviving spouse under certain acts enacted by provincial or territorial legislation.

FOOTNOTES:

1. Children of a deceased child (grandchildren, great grandchildren) take that child's share.
2. Spouse may elect to receive house and contents in lieu of $50,000.
3. Plus household furniture and life interest in family home.
4. Subject to possible equalization claim under provincial or territorial legislation.
5. If all the children are also children of surviving spouse.
6. If any of the children are *not* also children of surviving spouse. Children of deceased child (grandchildren) share in the estate.
7. Subject to provincial or territorial legislation.
8. Children of deceased brothers and sisters share their parents' share.
9. Depends on who the other survivors are.
10. Life interest in the home plus a possible equalization payment under provincial or territorial legislation.

TABLE 2: Provincial and Territorial Government Probate Fees*

Province	Probate Fees	Maximum
British Columbia	• No fee for estates under $25,000 • $200, plus $6 for every $1,000 or part of $1,000 between $25,000 and $50,000 • $350, plus $14 for every $1,000 or part of $1,000 over $50,000	None
Alberta	• $35 for estates under $10,000 • $135 for estates between $10,000 and $24,999 • $275 for estates between $25,000 and $124,999 • $400 for estates between $125,000 and $249,999 • $525 for estates of $250,000 and over	$525
Saskatchewan	• $7 on each $1,000	None
Manitoba	• $70 for the first $10,000, plus $7 on each $1,000 over $10,000	None
Ontario	• $5 on each $1,000 for the first $50,000 and $15 on each $1,000 over $50,000	None
Quebec	• Nominal fee for non-notarial Will • Nominal fee for notarial Will (notarial Wills do not need to be probated)	Nominal fee (non-notarial Will)
New Brunswick	• For the first $5,000: $25 • $5,001 to $10,000: $50 • $10,001 to $15,000: $75 • $15,001 to $20,000: $100 • $5 on each $1,000 over $20,000	None
Nova Scotia	• $85 for estates not exceeding $10,000 • $212.50 for estates exceeding $10,000 but not exceeding $25,000 • $358.15 for estates exceeding $25,000 but not exceeding $50,000 • $1,002.65 for estates exceeding $50,000 but not exceeding $100,000 • $1,002.65 for estates exceeding $100,000, plus $16.95 for each additonal $1,000 or fraction thereof over $100,000	None
Prince Edward Island	• Up to $10,000: $50 • $10,001 to $25,000: $100 • $25,001 to $50,000: $200 • $50,001 to $100,000: $400 • $100,000+: $400 + $4 for each individual $1,000	None

TABLE 2: Provincial and Territorial Government Probate Fees*

(continued from previous page)

Province	Probate Fees	Maximum
Newfoundland and Labrador	• $60 for the first $1,000; $60 plus $5 for each additional $1,000	None
Northwest Territories and Nunavut	• $10,000 or under: $25 • More than $10,000 but not more than $25,000: $100 • More than $25,000 but not more than $125,000: $200 • More than $125,000 but not more than $250,000: $300 • More than $250,000: $400	$400
Yukon	• No fee for estates under $25,000 in value; flat fee of $140 for estates exceeding $25,000	$140

*Fees can change at any time, so get a current update from your province or territory.

TABLE 3: Comparisons of Types of Life Insurance

Policy Type	Permanent			Term to 100	Term
	Whole Life	Universal Life			
Period of Coverage	Life	Life		To age 100 or life, depending on contract.	Depends on term in contract. Often renewable for additional terms but usually not past age 70 or 75.
Premiums	Guaranteed. Usually remain level.	Flexible. Can be increased or decreased by policyholder within certain limits.		Guaranteed. Usually remain level.	Guaranteed and remain level for term of policy (e.g., 1 year, 5 years, 10 years, etc.). Increase with each new term.
Death Benefits	Guaranteed in contract. Remain level. Dividends may be used to enhance death benefits in participating policies.	Flexible. May increase or decrease according to fluctuations in cash value fund.		Guaranteed in contract. Remain level.	Guaranteed in contract.
Cash Values	Guaranteed in contract.	Flexible. May increase or decrease according to investment returns and level of policyholder deposits.		Usually none. (Some policies have a small cash value or other non-forfeiture value after a long period, say 20 years.)	Usually none. (Some long term policies have a small cash value or other non-forfeiture value.)
Other Non-forfeiture Options	Guaranteed in contract.	Guaranteed in contract.		See above.	See above.
Dividends	Payable on "participating" policies. Not guaranteed.	Most policies are "non-participating" and do not pay dividends.		Most policies are "non-participating" and do not pay dividends.	Most policies are "non-participating" and do not pay dividends.

TABLE 3: *Comparisons of Types of Life Insurance*

(*continued from previous page*)

Policy Type	Permanent — Whole Life	Permanent — Universal Life	Term to 100	Term
Advantages	• Provides protection for your entire lifetime—if kept in force. • Premium cost usually stays level, regardless of age or health problems. • Has cash values that can be borrowed, used to continue protection if premiums are missed, or withdrawn if the policy is no longer required. • Other non-forfeiture options allow the policyholder various possibilities of continuing coverage if premiums are missed or discontinued. • If the policy is participating, it receives dividends that can be taken in cash, left to accumulate at interest, or used to purchase additional insurance.		• Provides protection to age 100—if kept in force. • Premium cost usually stays level, regardless of age or health problems. • Premium cost is lower relative to traditional permanent policies.	• Suitable for short-term insurance needs, or specific liabilities like a mortgage. • Provides more immediate protection because, initially, it is less expensive than permanent insurance. • Can be converted to permanent insurance without medical evidence (if it has a convertibility option), often up to ages 65 or 70.
Dis-advantages	• Initial cost may be too high for a sufficient amount of protection for your current needs. • May not be an efficient means of covering short-term needs. You have to hold the policy for a long time, say over 10 years, before the cash values become sizeable.		• Usually no cash values and no or limited non-forfeiture values.	• If renewed, premiums increase with age and at some point higher premium costs may make it difficult or impossible to continue coverage. • Renewability of coverage will terminate at some point, commonly age 65 or age 75. • If premium is not paid, the policy terminates after 31 days and may not be reinstated if health is poor. • Usually no cash values and no non-forfeiture options

Reprinted with the permission of the Canadian Life and Health Insurance Association Inc. from *A Guide to Buying Life Insurance*, 1996 ed. For further educational information contact the CLHIA Consumer Assistance Centre at 1-800-268-8099 or (416) 777-2344.

Checklists

I. PERSONAL INFORMATION RECORD

By completing this extensive checklist, you will be focusing on key points and issues as well as assembling information, all of which will assist you in developing an estate and financial plan. It will help clarify your wishes when discussing your needs with your lawyer, tax accountant, financial planner or financial institution. It will also enhance your peace of mind to know your affairs are in order. This checklist should be dated, reviewed and updated annually. Keep a copy in your safety deposit box. Some items may not apply to everyone. Although this checklist highlights many key areas, your advisors can suggest additional issues for you to detail in your specific situation. Ideally, print your responses so that the information is legible to others.

Date: _____

1.

	You	**Your Spouse**
Name (full)	_____	_____
Legal Name (if different)	_____	_____
Address	_____	_____
City/Province	_____	_____
Postal Code	_____	_____
Phone Numbers: residence	_____	_____
work	_____	_____
Fax Numbers: residence	_____	_____
work	_____	_____
E-mail Numbers: residence	_____	_____
work	_____	_____
Date of Birth	_____	_____

Personal Information Record (continued)

	You	Your Spouse
Place of Birth		
Citizenship		
Social Insurance Number		
Occupation		
Employer or Self Employed Name		
Business Address		
Place of Marriage		
Marital Status (married, common-law, divorced, widowed, single)		
Full Name of Father		
Father's Place of Birth		
Full Maiden Name of Mother		
Mother's Place of Birth		
Name of Doctor		
Date Personal Information Record Completed		
Date Personal Information Record Updated		
Date Personal Information Record Updated		
Date Personal Information Record Updated		

2. Children (indicate if by present or previous marriage of you or your spouse, adopted or born in a common-law relationship, and if they are dependent on you).

Name	Date of Birth	Married	Telephone	Dependent On You

3. Grandchildren

Name	Date of Birth	Name	Date of Birth

4. Other Dependents

Name	Date of Birth	Telephone	Relationship To You

5. Have you entered into a pre-marriage or other marriage contract with your spouse? If so, outline a summary of the contract's terms. Where are the documents located?

6. If you or your spouse have been previously married, describe any remaining financial obligations (e.g. child support, alimony, etc.)

Obligations	You	Your Spouse
Name of former spouse		
Address		
City/Province/State		
Postal Code/Zip Code		
Phone Numbers: residence		
work		
Social Insurance Number		

7. If you or your spouse have any prospective inheritances, detail sources, approximate amounts, and possible dates of receipt.

8. Explain any present or potential special support needs (e.g. for a disabled child, spouse or parent).

9. Location of Documents and Other Information

Item	Location
1. Birth Certificate	_____
2. Marriage Certificate	_____
3. Children's Birth Certificates	_____
4. Pre-marriage Agreements or Marriage Contracts	_____
5. Social Insurance Card	_____
6. Maintenance, alimony, or custody orders	_____
7. Husband's latest will and any codicils	_____
8. Wife's latest will and any codicils	_____
9. Wills of family members, if pertinent	_____
10. Power of Attorney for financial matters	_____
11. Power of Attorney for personal care proxy	_____
12. Advance medical directive	_____
13. Living Will	_____
14. Organ donation records	_____
15. Passports	_____
16. Citizenship papers	_____
17. Cemetery or mausoleum deeds	_____
18. Directions regarding prepaid funeral arrangement	_____
19. Divorce decrees or separation	_____
20. List of heirs	_____
21. Medical Records	_____
22. War Veteran records	_____
23. Insurance Policies	
– Life	_____
– Disability	_____
– Property	_____
– Automobile	_____

Item	Location
– Home	_____
– Other	_____
24. Stocks	_____
25. Bonds (corporate)	_____
26. Bonds (government)	_____
27. Mutual funds	_____
28. Term deposits	_____
29. Investment certificates	_____
30. Notes or mortgages receivable	_____
31. Tax shelter investments	_____
32. Annuities	_____
33. Precious metals (gold, silver, etc.)	_____
34. Real estate documents/deeds	_____
35. Leases	_____
36. Inventory of assets of estate	_____
37. Appraisals	_____
38. Bank books	_____
39. Financial records	_____
40. Income tax returns (personal)	_____
41. Income tax returns (business)	_____
42. Valuation day documents	_____
43. If you own a business, balance sheets and profit/loss statements for last five years	_____
44. Business agreements	_____
45. Business records	_____
46. Employment contracts	_____
47. Employee benefit plan documents	_____
48. Buy/sell agreements if a shareholder in a business	_____

Item	Location
49. Partnership or shareholder agreements if in a business	_____
50. Trust agreements	_____
51. Promissory notes	_____
52. Loan documents	_____
53. Automobile ownership documents	_____
54. RRSP/RRIF/TFSA records	_____
55. Pension Plan documentation (Government and/or employer)	_____
56. Bank account records	_____
57. Credit card/charge account records	_____
58. Safety deposit box	_____
59. Digital assets	_____
60. Miscellaneous documents	_____

10. Professionals or Advisors

Lawyer	Name	_____
	Address	_____
	Phone	_____
Accountant	Name	_____
	Address	_____
	Phone	_____
Family Doctor	Name	_____
	Address	_____
	Phone	_____
Dentist	Name	_____
	Address	_____
	Phone	_____
Financial Planner	Name	_____
	Address	_____
	Phone	_____

Insurance Agent	Name	_____
	Address	_____
	Phone	_____
Trust Company	Name	_____
	Address	_____
	Phone	_____
Banker	Name	_____
	Address	_____
	Phone	_____
Investment Dealer/Advisor	Name	_____
	Address	_____
	Phone	_____
Funeral Home	Name	_____
	Address	_____
	Phone	_____
Clergy (Minister, Priest, Rabbi, etc.)	Name	_____
	Address	_____
	Phone	_____
Other	Name	_____
_____	Address	_____
	Phone	_____

11. Banking Information

1. Bank Accounts (trust company or credit union)

Bank	Type and # of Account	Balance in Account		
		You	Your Spouse	Joint
_____	_____	$_____	$_____	$_____
_____	_____	_____	_____	_____
_____	_____	_____	_____	_____
_____	_____	_____	_____	_____

2. Term Deposits

Bank	Terms	You	Balance in Account Your Spouse	Joint
_____	_____	_____	_____	_____
_____	_____	_____	_____	_____
_____	_____	_____	_____	_____
_____	_____	_____	_____	_____

3. Bank Loans

Bank	Use of Funds	Terms: Payments, Interest rate, Due Date	Security	Balance Owing by		
				You $	Your Spouse $	Joint $

4. Loan Guarantees

Provide details of any guarantees you or your spouse have issued for the debts of other people or companies.

Nature of Debt	Relationship to Debtor	Degree of Risk	Amount of Guarantee $	Person who signed guarantee		
				You $	Your Spouse $	Joint $

12. Real Estate

Property #1

Date Acquired   _____

Address   _____

Registered Owner(s)   _____

    _____

Joint Tenants or Tenants in Common   _____

    _____

    _____

    Primary Residence   Yes _____   No _____

    Vacation Property   Yes _____   No _____

    Rental Property   Yes _____   No _____

Date purchased   _____

Insurance Company   _____

Policy Number   _____

Amount of Coverage

    Original Cost $_____

    Cost of additions $_____

    $_____

    Current value $_____

    Less mortgages $_____

    Equity $_____

Has the property been appraised?

    When: _____

    Value: $_____

Terms of Mortgage

    Monthly payments: $_____

    Length of mortgage term: _____

Location of Deed (if applicable)_____

Property #2

Date Acquired
_____

Address
_____

Registered Owner(s)
_____

_____

Joint Tenants or Tenants in Common
_____

_____

_____

Primary Residence   Yes _____   No _____

Vacation Property   Yes _____   No _____

Rental Property   Yes _____   No _____

Date purchased
_____

Insurance Company
_____

Policy Number
_____

Amount of Coverage

Original Cost $_____

Cost of additions $_____

$_____

Current value $_____

Less mortgages $_____

Equity $_____

Has the property been appraised?

When: _____

Value: $_____

Terms of Mortgage

Monthly payments: $_____

Length of mortgage term: _____

Location of Deed (if applicable)_____

Property #3

Date Acquired   _____

Address   _____

Registered Owner(s)   _____

                                                     _____

Joint Tenants or Tenants in Common   _____

    Primary Residence   Yes _____   No _____

    Vacation Property   Yes _____   No _____

    Rental Property   Yes _____   No _____

Date purchased   _____

Insurance Company   _____

Policy Number   _____

Amount of Coverage

    Original Cost $_____

    Cost of additions $_____

                                   $_____

    Current value $_____

    Less mortgages $_____

    Equity $_____

Has the property been appraised?

    When: _____

    Value: $_____

Terms of Mortgage

    Monthly payments: $_____

    Length of mortgage term: _____

Location of Deed (if applicable)_____

13. Personal Property

	Current Value		
	You $	Your Spouse $	Joint $
a) Household furnishings	_____	_____	_____
b) Automobiles	_____	_____	_____
c) Trailers	_____	_____	_____
d) Jewelry	_____	_____	_____
e) Boats	_____	_____	_____
f) Coin collection	_____	_____	_____
g) Stamp collection	_____	_____	_____
h) Paintings, prints, sculptures	_____	_____	_____
i) Antiques	_____	_____	_____
j) Other	_____	_____	_____
k) Location of Assets	_____	_____	_____

14. Investment Portfolio
    1. Stocks (List)

Description	V-Day value if applicable $	Cost $	Current Value by Ownership		
			You $	Your Spouse $	Joint $
		TOTAL	$	$	$

2. Bonds (List)

Description	V-Day value if applicable $	Cost $	Current Value by Ownership		
			You $	Your Spouse $	Joint $
		TOTAL	$	$	$

TOTAL STOCKS AND BONDS	$	$	$

3. Mutual Funds and Pooled Investments

Description	V-Day value if applicable $	Original Cost $	Current Value by Ownership		
			You $	Your Spouse $	Joint $
		TOTAL	$	$	$

4. Mortgages and Loans Owing to You
   Short Term

Description	V-Day value if applicable $	Original Cost $	Current Value by Ownership		
			You $	Your Spouse $	Joint $
		TOTAL	$	$	$

Long Term

Description	V-Day value if applicable $	Original Cost $	Current Value by Ownership		
			You $	Your Spouse $	Joint $
		TOTAL	$	$	$

15. Tax Shelters

Brief Description	Current Market Value			Cost		
	You $	Your Spouse $	Joint $	You $	Your Spouse $	Joint $
TOTAL	$	$	$	$	$	$

16. Investments/Ownerships in Business

   1. Where You Are The Investor

	Business		
	1	2	3
Name of business	_____	_____	_____
Nature of business	_____	_____	_____
Address of business	_____	_____	_____
Your % equity interest in business	_____	_____	_____
Approximate fair market value of your business interest	_____	_____	_____
Business structure (proprietorship, partnership or corporation)	_____	_____	_____
If a partnership or corporation, is there a:			
a) Partnership agreement/ Shareholders agreement?	_____	_____	_____
b) Buy/Sell agreement?	_____	_____	_____
Names of partners and directors and phone numbers	_____	_____	_____
Location of business records	_____	_____	_____
Name of business lawyer and phone numbers	_____	_____	_____
Name of business accountant and phone numbers	_____	_____	_____

2. Where Your Spouse is the Investor

	Business		
	1	2	3
Name of business	_____	_____	_____
Nature of business	_____	_____	_____
Address of business	_____	_____	_____
Your % equity interest in business	_____	_____	_____
Approximate fair market value of your business interest	_____	_____	_____
Business structure (proprietorship, partnership or corporation)	_____	_____	_____
If a partnership or corporation, is there a:			
a) Partnership agreement/ Shareholders agreement?	_____	_____	_____
b) Buy/Sell agreement?	_____	_____	_____
Names of partners and directors and phone numbers	_____	_____	_____
	_____	_____	_____
	_____	_____	_____
	_____	_____	_____
Location of business records	_____	_____	_____
Name of business lawyer and phone numbers	_____	_____	_____
Name of business accountant and phone numbers	_____	_____	_____

17. Insurance

1. Life Insurance Coverage

	Policies where you are the insured			
	1	2	3	Total
Company	_____	_____	_____	
Face Value	$_____	$_____	$_____	$_____
Date of Policy	_____	_____		

Type of Policy   _____   _____   _____

Cash surrender value
(if applicable) $_____ $_____ $_____ $_____

**Policies where you
are the insured**

	1	2	3	Total

Policy number   _____   _____   _____

Loan balances (if any)$_____ $_____ $_____ $_____

Premium (Annual)   _____   _____   _____

Beneficiary   _____   _____   _____

Location of policies   _____   _____   _____

**Policies where your
spouse is the insured**

	1	2	3	Total

Company   _____   _____   _____

Face Value $_____ $_____ $_____ $_____

Date of Policy   _____   _____   _____

Type of Policy   _____   _____   _____

Cash surrender value
(if applicable) $_____ $_____ $_____ $_____

Policy number   _____   _____   _____

Loan balances (if any)$_____ $_____ $_____ $_____

Premium (Annual)   _____   _____   _____

Beneficiary   _____   _____   _____

Location of policies   _____   _____   _____

2. Disability Insurance Coverage (Private or Group)

		Annual Payment		Length of Coverage	Other Terms
Company	Policy	You $	Your Spouse $		
1.					
2.					
3.					
TOTAL		$	$		

Location of policies: _____

_____

3. Personal Property Insurance

Company	Policy #	Type of Coverage	Property Coverage	Amount of Coverage $
1.				
2.				
3.				
			TOTAL	$

Location of policies: _____

_____

4. Automobile Insurance Coverage

Company	Policy #	Amount of Coverage $
1.		
2.		
3.		

5. When did you and your spouse last review and, if necessary, update your insurance coverage?

Type	Date	You	Your Spouse
Life	_____	_____	_____
Disability	_____	_____	_____
Personal property	_____	_____	_____
Other	_____	_____	_____

18. Funeral Information

Funeral home to be (church or funeral home) _____

Funeral services to be held in _____

If church, please provide name _____

Name of clergy requested _____

It is my wish my body be (buried or cremated) _____

If burial, name cemetery and location _____

I have prepaid for and have title to the cemetery
   plot or mausoleum   Yes__ No__

Location of deed (if applicable) _____

If cremation, disposition of cremains (interred in
   cemetery, given to relative or scattered) _____

I have or have not made pre-arrangements
   regarding my funeral with a funeral home   Yes___ No___

If the answer to above is yes, list funeral home address and phone number

_____

I have prepaid for the funeral   Yes___ No___

I wish to have a memorial service   Yes___ No___

Location of memorial service _____

I wish the following hymns or music at my funeral _____

_____

I wish the following readings to be read at my funeral_____

_____

Active pallbearers to be (if applicable)_____

_____

Honorary pallbearers to be (if applicable)

I prefer   – a casket   Yes___ No___

         – urn   Yes___ No___

         – monument or marker   Yes___ No___

         – organ/body donation   Yes___ No___

I wish to be remembered in the following ways

   Visitation period   Yes___ No___

   Flowers   Yes___ No___

   Donations to Charities   Yes___ No___

   Any preferences with regards to participants   Yes___ No___

Details of the above _____

_____

Special Instructions _____

_____

If I should die outside Canada, my wishes are _____

_____

Other instructions/wishes _____

_____

2. CURRENT FINANCIAL NET WORTH

Liquid Assets	You	Your Spouse
(Can be relatively quickly converted into cash)		
Term deposits/GICs	$_____	$_____
Chequing accounts	_____	_____
Savings accounts	_____	_____
Tax-free savings accounts (TFSAs)	_____	_____
Stocks	_____	_____
Bonds	_____	_____

Liquid Assets	You	Your Spouse
Mutual funds & pooled investments	$_____	$_____
Term deposits (savings)	_____	_____
Pensions (government employer)	_____	_____
Annuities	_____	_____
RRSPs / RRIFs	_____	_____
Life insurance cash surrender value	_____	_____
Demand loans		
– family	_____	_____
– other	_____	_____
Automobile	_____	_____
Tax installments made/withheld	_____	_____
Other (specify)	_____	_____
Subtotal	$_____	$_____

Non-Liquid Assets	You	Your Spouse
(Takes longer to convert into cash or accrue total financial benefit)		
Business interests	$_____	$_____
Long-term receivables, loans	_____	_____
Deferred income plans	_____	_____
Interest in trusts	_____	_____
Tax shelters	_____	_____
Primary residence	_____	_____

Other real estate (e.g. second home, revenue
 or investment property)   _____   _____

U.S./foreign assets   _____   _____

Personal property   _____   _____

Valuable assets (e.g. art, antiques, jewelry, etc.)   _____   _____

Other (specify)   _____   _____

Subtotal $_____ $_____

TOTAL ASSETS (A) $_____ $_____

Current Liabilities	**You**	**Your Spouse**

(Currently due within a year or on demand)

Bank loans $_____ $_____

(currently due or within a year,
 or a demand line of credit)   _____   _____

Credit cards   _____   _____

Income tax owing   _____   _____

Alimony   _____   _____

Child support   _____   _____

Monthly rent   _____   _____

Other   _____   _____

Subtotal $_____ $_____

Long-Term Liabilities	**You**	**Your Spouse**

(Generally not due for over 1 year)

Term loans $_____ $_____

Mortgages

– primary residence   _____   _____

– other (investment revenue
 recreational or commercial)   _____   _____

– reverse mortgage   _____   _____

Other   _____   _____

Subtotal $_____ $_____

TOTAL LIABILITIES (B) $_____ $_____

	You	Your Spouse
Net worth—before tax (A-B)	$	$
Tax Cost if assets liquidated (if any)		
Net Worth—after tax		

3. CURRENT AND PROJECTED RETIREMENT MONTHLY INCOME AND EXPENSES

	Current	Projected at Retirement
I. Income (Average monthly income, actual or estimated)		
Salary, bonuses, and commissions	$	$
Dividends		
Interest income		
Pension income		
Other		
TOTAL MONTHLY INCOME	$ (A)	$ (B)
II. Expenses		
Regular Monthly Payments:		
Rent or mortgage payments	$	$
Automobile(s)		
Appliances/TV		
Home improvement loan		
Credit card payments (not covered elsewhere)		$
Personal loan		
Medical plan		
Installment and other loans		
Life insurance premiums		
House insurance		
Other insurance premiums (auto, extended medical, etc.)		

	Current	Projected at Retirement
RRSP deductions	_____	_____
Pension fund (employer)	_____	_____
Investment plan(s)	_____	_____
Miscellaneous	_____	_____
Other	_____	_____
TOTAL REGULAR MONTHLY PAYMENTS	$_____	$_____

Household Operating Expenses:

	Current	Projected at Retirement
Telephone	$_____	$_____
Gas and electricity	_____	_____
Heat	_____	_____
Water and garbage	_____	_____
Other household expenses (repairs, maintenance, etc.)	_____	_____
Other	_____	_____
TOTAL HOUSEHOLD EXPENSES	$_____	$_____

Food Expenses:

	Current	Projected at Retirement
At home	$_____	$_____
Away from home	_____	_____
TOTAL FOOD EXPENSES	$_____	$_____

Personal Expenses:

	Current	Projected at Retirement
Clothing, cleaning, laundry	$_____	$_____
Drugs	_____	_____
Transportation (other than auto)	_____	_____
Medical/dental	_____	_____
Day care	_____	_____
Education (self)	_____	_____
Education (children)	_____	_____
Dues	_____	_____
Gifts, donations, and dues	_____	_____

	Current	Projected at Retirement
Travel		
Recreation		
Newspapers, magazines, books		
Automobile maintenance, gas, and parking		
Spending money, allowances		
Other		
TOTAL PERSONAL EXPENSES	$	$

Tax Expenses:

	Current	Projected at Retirement
Federal and provincial income taxes	$	$
Home property taxes		
Other		
TOTAL TAX EXPENSES	$	$

III. **Summary of Expenses**

	Current		Projected at Retirement	
Regular monthly payments	$		$	
Household operating expenses	$		$	
Food expenses	$		$	
Personal expenses	$		$	
Tax expenses	$		$	
TOTAL MONTHLY EXPENSES	$	(A)	$	(Y)
TOTAL MONTHLY DISPOSABLE INCOME AVAILABLE	$	(A–B)	$	(Y)

(subtract total monthly expenses from total monthly income)

TOTAL ANNUAL DISPOSABLE INCOME AVAILABLE (multiply x 12)	$	$

4. Projected Financial Needs

1. At what age do you plan to retire? _____

2. At what age does your spouse plan to retire? _____

3. Are you a citizen, or a resident, of another country?
   Yes _____ No _____ What country? _____

4. Do you or your spouse plan on becoming a non-resident of Canada?
   Yes _____ No _____ When? _____

5. Are you planning to or currently residing 3-6 months a year in the United States?
   Yes _____ No _____ Other country? _____

6. Have you thoroughly checked out the implications on your Pension Plan or Health Plan eligibility by being away an extended period?
   Yes _____ No _____

7. Do you or your spouse expect to receive any lump-sum retirement benefits?
   Yes _____ No _____
   If so, how much?

You	Your Spouse
$_____	$_____

   From what source? _____

8. Do you or your spouse anticipate any employment after retirement (part-time or full-time) or income from part-time or full-time self-employment in a home-based or small business?
   Estimated annual earnings $ _____ $ _____

9. Do you or your spouse anticipate any major changes in your financial situation in the:
   – short term (0-2 years)?   Yes _____ No _____
   – medium term (2-5 years)? Yes _____ No _____
   – long term (5-15 years)?   Yes _____ No _____

10. What combined level of income will you require in retirement (current year dollars)?

11. How many years of retirement have you projected?

12. If you or your spouse died or became disabled, what income would be required to maintain your family's current standard of living (current dollars)?

	You	Your Spouse
Until youngest child no longer financially dependent	$_____	$_____
Until age 60	_____	_____
Until age 65	_____	_____
Over age 65	_____	_____

13. What level of inflation do you anticipate will prevail during the above time periods? Have you factored that inflation factor into your projected future financial needs?

5. WHERE YOUR RETIREMENT INCOME WILL COME FROM

Monthly Income	Estimated Retirement	
	You	**Your Spouse**
Employer's pension plan	$_____	$_____
Union pension plan	_____	_____
Canada Pension Plan	_____	_____
Veteran's Pension	_____	_____
Old Age Security	_____	_____
Guaranteed Income Supplement	_____	_____
RRSP/RRIF retirement income	_____	_____
Other retirement income	_____	_____
Annuity income	_____	_____
Profit-sharing fund payout	_____	_____
Salary expected from any earned income in retirement	_____	_____
Any other fees, payments for services	_____	_____
Disability insurance payments	_____	_____
Income expected from a business (part-time or full-time, home-based or small business)	_____	_____
Income expected from real estate investments or revenue property	_____	_____
Income from renting out part of the house (e.g. basement suite/boarders)	_____	_____
Savings account interest (credit union, bank, trust company, other)	_____	_____
Canada Savings Bond interest, term deposit interest, guaranteed investment certificate interest, other	_____	_____
Other investments: stocks, bonds, mutual funds, etc.	_____	_____
Investment income from any expected inheritance	_____	_____
Other investments which you expect to create income	_____	_____
Other income sources: alimony, social welfare, UIC	_____	_____
Total Expected Monthly Income:	$_____	$_____
Total of Annual Income of you and your spouse (multiply x 12)	$_____	$_____

6. WILL PREPARATION CHECKLIST

Prior to seeing your lawyer to have a will prepared or revised, check off that you have the following information. Refer to Checklist 1 (Personal Information Record) for further questions to complete.

A. Personal information about both you and your spouse

___ Full legal names

___ Other names that you go by

___ Address and telephone numbers

___ Occupations

___ Date and place of births

___ Full names and date of births of all your children

___ Information about your children: are they adopted, infirm, born out of wedlock or are your children from a previous relationship?

B. Information about your marital status

___ Date and place of current marriage

    ___ Do you have a marriage contract?

___ Information about previous marriages

    ___ Any children of previous marriage?

    ___ Is prior spouse still alive?

    ___ Are there any existing separation agreements?

C. Summary of your assets

___ Cash and bank accounts, where located, and account number

___ Life insurance policies

    ___ With who, for what amount, and who is the beneficiary (e.g. to one or more designated individuals, or to your estate)?

___ Any securities, pension plans, annuities, RRSPs, RRIFs, or TFSAs?

    ___ With who, what amount, and is there a designated beneficiary?

___ Your primary residence (home)

    ___ Type of ownership: sole, joint tenants or tenants-in-common

    ___ Current market value, amount of your equity and mortgages

___ Similar information on any other real estate

___ Information on businesses owned: proprietorships, partnerships or private companies you have an interest in

___ Any inheritance expected or other money or assets you are expecting?

___ Your personal effects

    ___ Make a list of household furnishings, cars, boats, jewellery and other personal belongings of sentimental value

___ Location of safety deposit box and important papers

___ Location of a list of your digital assets

D. Summary of your debts

____ List any debts, such as loans, mortgages, guarantees, promissory notes, and amount owed and to whom

E. Outline of beneficiaries

____ Who do you want cash requests to go to and the amounts of each request? (e.g. spouse, children, former spouse, children by former spouse, family relatives, friends, business associates, charitable organizations, educational or other institutions)

____ In the event that you and your spouse are killed in a common disaster (e.g. auto or plane crash), how do you want your estate to be distributed?

____ Who do you want specific personal possessions to go to (describe the asset in detail)?

____ Do you have alternative beneficiaries in case designated beneficiaries predecease you?

____ Have you considered setting up a testamentary trust to have some or all of your assets in your estate managed on your death on behalf of your spouse or children?

____ Do you have minor children or disabled children? At what age do you want your children to have access to their bequest?

____ Do you want your executor/trustee to have the power to manage the investments to maximize returns, rather than immediately liquidating them and paying cash to the beneficiaries?

____ Have you considered the benefits of a trust company to manage the trust?

F. Names of people in your will who will represent your interests

____ The names of your executor, trustee, lawyer and guardian for infant children

____ Have they agreed to do this job?

____ What skills, attibutes or resources do they have that make them appropriate for the job?

____ What is their relationship to you?

____ What are their full names and addresses?

____ Do they know the location of your will?

____ Do they know the location of your safety deposit box?

____ Have you selected alternatives?

____ Have you researched the benefits of using a trust company and/or lawyer?

____ Have you completed the personal information record in the Appendix (Checklist 1) and put a copy in your safety deposit box?

G. Other information to obtain

____ Other Responsibilities

____ Are you the executor/trustee of anyone's will? For whom?

____ Do you hold any Power of Attorney or Appointment? For whom?

____ Names and addresses of financial or personal/business advisors

____ Names and addresses of your lawyer and/or trust company

____ Where do you want to leave the original copy of your will? (safety deposit box, or with your lawyer or trust company?)

___ Have you had a previous will, when was it signed, where is it located, and when was it last reviewed?

___ Does your spouse have a will, when was it signed, where is it located, and when was it last reviewed?

___ Were both wills (of you and your spouse) reviewed in conjunction with each other?

___ Have you had both wills (if applicable) recently reviewed by your lawyer and/or trust company? (Should be reviewed annually.)

___ Have you discussed your will with a tax accountant and financial planner to make sure you have taken advantage of all the tax and estate planning strategies available?

___ Do you or your spouse wish to change any provisions in your wills?

___ Have you considered being an organ donor on your death, and have you discussed this wish with your spouse? Have you completed the appropriate forms? Contact your provincial organ donor registry for information and/or the national association dealing with specific organs (e.g. heart, kidney, eyes, etc.).

___ Have you considered having a "living will" (not enforceable in many cases, but a reflection of your wishes in the case of a terminal or serious illness)?

___ Have you considered giving an enduring Power of Attorney to someone over your affairs in certain situations (financial or health related)?

___ Details on burial wishes and funeral service instructions

___ Historical information for obituary purposes

___ Names and addresses of family, relatives, and friends for notification purposes

___ Do you have a power of attorney?

___ Do you have a "living will"?

7. DUTIES AND RESPONSIBILITIES OF THE EXECUTOR

After you review these various steps, you will better appreciate the potentially extensive time involvement, degree or responsibility and diversified skills frequently required when acting as an executor. This will enhance your decision-making when selecting an executor to fulfill your wishes under your will. As mentioned in the book executors can be held legally liable to your estate for their actions or lack of actions.

A. Preliminary steps

___ Locate and review the will

    ___ Apply to the Wills Registry in your province for a wills search in all possible names the deceased may have used (the location of the will should be registered)

    ___ Look through important papers kept by the deceased at home or at a place of business

    ___ Check the safety deposit box of the deceased or contact any trust companies the deceased may have dealt with, to locate the will

___ Apply for a death certificate

___ Make funeral arrangements if necessary, and arrange for the disposition of deceased's body

___ Meet with family members and other interested parties and beneficiaries to discuss the provisions of the will (an on-going procedure)

___ Verify short-term cash needs of family or beneficiaries

___ Confer with solicitor or trust company where necessary

B. Protection of estate assets

___ Take custody of all assets including digital assets

___ Possibly change the locks on any residences if there are concerns about anyone with a key removing items without consent

___ Investigate private and business interests, and take necessary protective measures

___ Arrange for safe custody of personal valuables and important documents of the deceased

___ Consult with deceased's financial institutions holding cash and securities

___ Write to banks, trust companies, credit unions, stock brokerage firms and other financial institutions the deceased may have dealt with for information on accounts

___ Arrange to take an inventory of the safety deposit box

___ Check for any insurance policies, RRSPs, RRIFs and other investments

___ Contact pension offices for estimate of pension benefits and apply for Canada Pension Plan death, survivor's or orphan's benefits, if eligible

___ Search through all personal papers of the deceased to find any real estate or business interests and obtain current valuations

___ List and value all household goods and furnishings

___ List and value all personal effects, including cars, boats, jewellery, etc.

___ Check with the deceased's employer for any money owing to the deceased including any death benefits, if applicable

___ Check for any other debts owed to the deceased

___ Review all financial records and statements

___ Ensure adequacy of various insurance policies to protect assets

___ Notify life insurance companies of death, complete and submit claim forms

___ Notify pension offices, banks, and employer

___ Review and cancel club memberships, health insurance, subscriptions, credit cards, etc.

___ Provide for supervision of vacant real estate

___ Take valuables into custody or obtain secured storage

C. Assemble, inventory and value the estate assets

___ Arrange comprehensive listing and valuation of deceased's household goods, furniture, objects of art, collections, jewellery, automobiles and other personal effects

___ Determine benefits due under insurance policies and pension plans

___ Obtain details of employee benefits: group insurance, stock options, profit sharing and outstanding salary

___ Arrange for inspection and valuation of real estate, including summer residence, farm and income-producing property

___ Ascertain property management is in place

___ Investigate deceased's interest in estates and trusts

___ Open estate account

___ Prepare detailed inventory of assets

D. Determine all liabilities of the deceased

___ List funeral and burial expenses and any outstanding medical expenses

___ Check all on-going accounts such as charge accounts and utility bills

___ Review real estate holdings for any mortgages

___ Check with banks, trust companies and any other financial institutions the deceased may have dealt with for any loans

___ Prepare detailed list of liabilities

E. Assessment of tax situation and implications

___ Locate and review prior year's tax returns

___ Assume responsibility for all estate tax matters

___ Calculate capital gains as at date of death

___ If assets are held in other provinces or countries (e.g. U.S.), confer with relevant jurisdictions

___ Determine whether estate will adopt a calendar or fiscal year accounting period

___ Analyze various elections permitted under the federal *Income Tax Act* and provincial laws, where applicable

___ Consider advantages of filing Rights and Things Return

___ File income tax returns for the estate during the period of administration, including the year of death and any previous years

___ Prepare and file necessary returns for foreign assets (e.g. U.S. property) and pay balance owing to other government jurisdictions

___ Prepare and file final returns and request clearance certificates

Note: With sizeable estates and in complex situations, it is prudent for the executor(s) to obtain professional tax advice from a chartered accountant or lawyer, who specialize in tax and estate planning. Not only are there various "elections" and alternative methods for computing the taxes arising on death, there are sometimes planning strategies that can be used by the estate to reduce or defer the taxes that would otherwise be payable.

F. Administration and distribution

___ Arrange for probate of will, if necessary

___ Report to beneficiaries on progress of estate administration

___ Apply for benefits and transfer property into your name

___ Apply to Canada Post for redirection of the deceased's mail to the executor

___ Submit all claims for proceeds of life insurance or other insurance policies

___ Apply for eligible Canada Pension Plan death, survivor's or orphan's benefits

___ Apply for proceeds from RRSPs or other private pension plans

___ Apply for Civil Service, Union or Veteran's benefits, if applicable

___ Transfer ownership title to all registered property, such as real estate, into your name

___ Add your name to the house and car insurance and all other property insurance

___ Settle all claims and debts

___ Close bank accounts and transfer balance to estate account

___ Invest surplus cash until monies are needed

___ Review portfolio of investments and provide continuous investment management of balance of estate investments, ensure adequate liquidity for payment of income tax and other liabilities

___ Deliver personal possessions that have been bequeathed, and obtain receipts

___ Arrange for balance of household and personal goods to be sold at auction

___ Advertise for creditors, and make payment to valid claims

___ Discharge any bank or private loans, mortgages or business liabilities

___ Pay funeral expenses and all taxes payable, such as income tax or municipal taxes

___ Pay all legal and accounting fees and other expenses in administering the estate

___ Reimburse yourself for reasonable out-of-pocket expenses and pay your fee as executor (The amount of this fee is governed by provincial legislation and supplemented by any additional fees authorized pursuant to the will.)

___ Pay any other outstanding debts of the deceased

___ Sell assets to obtain sufficient cash for payments

___ Pay cash legacies and other bequests

___ Make interim distribution of bulk of assets to beneficiaries

___ Prepare and submit full accounting of estate administration to beneficiaries

___ Effect final distribution of estate assets

8. RETIREMENT RESIDENCE COMPARISON

	Residence 1		Residence 2		Residence 3	
	Yes	No	Yes	No	Yes	No
Services Available						
Maintenance	☐	☐	☐	☐	☐	☐
Daily Housekeeping	☐	☐	☐	☐	☐	☐
Weekly Housekeeping	☐	☐	☐	☐	☐	☐
Linen Laundry	☐	☐	☐	☐	☐	☐
Towel Laundry	☐	☐	☐	☐	☐	☐

	Residence 1		Residence 2		Residence 3	
	Yes	No	Yes	No	Yes	No
Personal Laundry	☐	☐	☐	☐	☐	☐
Entertainment	☐	☐	☐	☐	☐	☐
Recreation Program	☐	☐	☐	☐	☐	☐
Transportation						
• For Residence Outings	☐	☐	☐	☐	☐	☐
• Personal	☐	☐	☐	☐	☐	☐
Health Care Services						
Coordination of Health Care Concerns/ Consultation with Registered Staff	☐	☐	☐	☐	☐	☐
Respite/Convalescent Care	☐	☐	☐	☐	☐	☐
24 Hour Nursing (RN/RPN) Staff	☐	☐	☐	☐	☐	☐
Medication Supervision	☐	☐	☐	☐	☐	☐
Medication Administration	☐	☐	☐	☐	☐	☐
Liaison with Medical Services	☐	☐	☐	☐	☐	☐
In-house Scheduled Physician	☐	☐	☐	☐	☐	☐
Option to Retain Outside Physician	☐	☐	☐	☐	☐	☐
Physician On-call	☐	☐	☐	☐	☐	☐
Assisted Daily Living Services Available	☐	☐	☐	☐	☐	☐
Visiting Dental Service	☐	☐	☐	☐	☐	☐
Visiting Lab Service	☐	☐	☐	☐	☐	☐
Visiting Physiotherapist	☐	☐	☐	☐	☐	☐
Visiting Occupational Therapist	☐	☐	☐	☐	☐	☐
Visiting Eye Clinic	☐	☐	☐	☐	☐	☐
Visiting Podiatry Service	☐	☐	☐	☐	☐	☐
Visiting Hearing Clinic	☐	☐	☐	☐	☐	☐
Pharmacy Services	☐	☐	☐	☐	☐	☐
Agency Nursing Care: Arranged If Necessary	☐	☐	☐	☐	☐	☐
Vitals Monitoring	☐	☐	☐	☐	☐	☐
Dementia Unit	☐	☐	☐	☐	☐	☐
Dining Service						
Meals Included in Fee	☐	☐	☐	☐	☐	☐
Tray Service to Suites	☐	☐	☐	☐	☐	☐
Optional Meal Plan	☐	☐	☐	☐	☐	☐
Guest Meals	☐	☐	☐	☐	☐	☐
Reduced Fee For 2 Meals A Day	☐	☐	☐	☐	☐	☐
Special Diet Menus	☐	☐	☐	☐	☐	☐
Excellent Quality of Food	☐	☐	☐	☐	☐	☐
Attractive Dining Room	☐	☐	☐	☐	☐	☐
Full Table Service	☐	☐	☐	☐	☐	☐
Choice of Menu	☐	☐	☐	☐	☐	☐
Afternoon Refreshment	☐	☐	☐	☐	☐	☐
Evening Refreshment	☐	☐	☐	☐	☐	☐
Suite Amenities						
Variety of Suite Sizes and Layouts Available	☐	☐	☐	☐	☐	☐
Attractive Natural Décor	☐	☐	☐	☐	☐	☐

	Residence 1		Residence 2		Residence 3	
	Yes	No	Yes	No	Yes	No
• Residents can bring own furniture	☐	☐	☐	☐	☐	☐
• Residents can decorate suite with pictures	☐	☐	☐	☐	☐	☐
Kitchens/Kitchenettes	☐	☐	☐	☐	☐	☐
Bright and Warm Feeling	☐	☐	☐	☐	☐	☐
Carpet	☐	☐	☐	☐	☐	☐
Draperies	☐	☐	☐	☐	☐	☐
Patio or Balcony	☐	☐	☐	☐	☐	☐
Private Bath	☐	☐	☐	☐	☐	☐
Adequate Shelf, Counter and Closet Space	☐	☐	☐	☐	☐	☐
Well-Lit Hallways	☐	☐	☐	☐	☐	☐
Privacy/Security Features	☐	☐	☐	☐	☐	☐
• Deadbolt Lock	☐	☐	☐	☐	☐	☐
• Door Peephole	☐	☐	☐	☐	☐	☐
• Emergency Call System	☐	☐	☐	☐	☐	☐
• Fire and/or Smoke Alarm	☐	☐	☐	☐	☐	☐
• Sprinklers in Suite	☐	☐	☐	☐	☐	☐
Quiet Environment	☐	☐	☐	☐	☐	☐
Convenient Electrical Outlet Locations	☐	☐	☐	☐	☐	☐
Individually Controlled Heating	☐	☐	☐	☐	☐	☐
Individually Controlled Air-Conditioning	☐	☐	☐	☐	☐	☐
Are the Following Utilities Included in the Fee?	☐	☐	☐	☐	☐	☐
• Electricity	☐	☐	☐	☐	☐	☐
• Heat	☐	☐	☐	☐	☐	☐
• Water	☐	☐	☐	☐	☐	☐
• Telephone	☐	☐	☐	☐	☐	☐
• Cable TV	☐	☐	☐	☐	☐	☐
Smoking Permitted in Suite	☐	☐	☐	☐	☐	☐
Smoking Permitted in Common Areas	☐	☐	☐	☐	☐	☐
Building Amenities						
Pleasant Surroundings	☐	☐	☐	☐	☐	☐
Parking	☐	☐	☐	☐	☐	☐
• Indoor	☐	☐	☐	☐	☐	☐
• Outdoor	☐	☐	☐	☐	☐	☐
• Visitors	☐	☐	☐	☐	☐	☐
Library	☐	☐	☐	☐	☐	☐
Tuck Shop	☐	☐	☐	☐	☐	☐
Banking On-Premises	☐	☐	☐	☐	☐	☐
Elevator Easily Accessible	☐	☐	☐	☐	☐	☐
Barber/Beauty Shop	☐	☐	☐	☐	☐	☐
Resident Activities	☐	☐	☐	☐	☐	☐
Lounges	☐	☐	☐	☐	☐	☐
Guest/Vacation Suites	☐	☐	☐	☐	☐	☐
Resident Storage	☐	☐	☐	☐	☐	☐
Are Religious Services Provided on Site?	☐	☐	☐	☐	☐	☐

	Residence 1		Residence 2		Residence 3	
	Yes	No	Yes	No	Yes	No
Does Residence Have a Van or Bus to Transport Residents to Outings?	☐	☐	☐	☐	☐	☐
Personal Laundry Facilities	☐	☐	☐	☐	☐	☐
Dry-Cleaning and/or Alterations Available	☐	☐	☐	☐	☐	☐
Any Odour In Common Areas	☐	☐	☐	☐	☐	☐
Meeting Rooms	☐	☐	☐	☐	☐	☐
Quiet Environment	☐	☐	☐	☐	☐	☐
Newspaper Delivery	☐	☐	☐	☐	☐	☐
Mail Pick-up	☐	☐	☐	☐	☐	☐
Private Mail Box	☐	☐	☐	☐	☐	☐
Central Dining Room	☐	☐	☐	☐	☐	☐
Private Dining Room/Area	☐	☐	☐	☐	☐	☐
Pool Table/Billiards	☐	☐	☐	☐	☐	☐
Air-Conditioned Common Areas	☐	☐	☐	☐	☐	☐
Chapel	☐	☐	☐	☐	☐	☐
Parking	☐	☐	☐	☐	☐	☐
Wheel Chair Accessible	☐	☐	☐	☐	☐	☐
Fire and Smoke Alarms in Common Areas	☐	☐	☐	☐	☐	☐
Sprinkler System in Common Areas	☐	☐	☐	☐	☐	☐
Swimming Pool/Hydro Therapy Pool in Common Area	☐	☐	☐	☐	☐	☐
Resident Newsletter	☐	☐	☐	☐	☐	☐
Resident Petty Cash Account with Separate Accounting	☐	☐	☐	☐	☐	☐
Shuffle Board	☐	☐	☐	☐	☐	☐
Volunteer Opportunities	☐	☐	☐	☐	☐	☐
Exercise Equipment	☐	☐	☐	☐	☐	☐
Crafts Room	☐	☐	☐	☐	☐	☐
Religious Services	☐	☐	☐	☐	☐	☐
Card Room	☐	☐	☐	☐	☐	☐
24-Hour Security	☐	☐	☐	☐	☐	☐
Doorman/Concierge/Reception	☐	☐	☐	☐	☐	☐
Greenhouse or Horticulture Area	☐	☐	☐	☐	☐	☐
Patio and/or Gardens	☐	☐	☐	☐	☐	☐
Gardens for Resident Use	☐	☐	☐	☐	☐	☐
Wheelchairs Accepted	☐	☐	☐	☐	☐	☐
Walkers Accepted	☐	☐	☐	☐	☐	☐
Scooters Accepted	☐	☐	☐	☐	☐	☐
Oxygen Therapy Allowed	☐	☐	☐	☐	☐	☐
Residence Information						
Well-Established	☐	☐	☐	☐	☐	☐
Centrally-Located	☐	☐	☐	☐	☐	☐
Complaint Procedures in Place	☐	☐	☐	☐	☐	☐
Visitors Policy and Hours in Place	☐	☐	☐	☐	☐	☐
Residents Can Come and Go as They Please	☐	☐	☐	☐	☐	☐

Sign Out Policy	☐	☐	☐	☐	☐	☐
Close to Shopping	☐	☐	☐	☐	☐	☐
Close to Places of Worship	☐	☐	☐	☐	☐	☐
Close to Health Services	☐	☐	☐	☐	☐	☐
Close to Community and Seniors' Centres	☐	☐	☐	☐	☐	☐
Close to Parks	☐	☐	☐	☐	☐	☐
Close to Hospital	☐	☐	☐	☐	☐	☐
Well Served by Public Transit	☐	☐	☐	☐	☐	☐
Transit Service for the Disabled	☐	☐	☐	☐	☐	☐
Friendly Residents	☐	☐	☐	☐	☐	☐
Volunteers Available for Visiting	☐	☐	☐	☐	☐	☐
Resident Association/Council	☐	☐	☐	☐	☐	☐
Waiting List	☐	☐	☐	☐	☐	☐
Opportunity to Stay for a Short Trial Period	☐	☐	☐	☐	☐	☐
Does Residence Have a Care Wing You Can Move into if Required?	☐	☐	☐	☐	☐	☐
Health Assessment Required	☐	☐	☐	☐	☐	☐
Date Opened						
Number of Units						
Languages Spoken By Staff (If Relevant)						
Ownership						
Management						
Notice Period Required to Leave						
How Often Are Rates for Accommodation and/or Services Increased and by What Percentage and When?						
What Has Been the Average Annual Rate of Increase Over the Past Few Years?						
Policy if Your Health Deteriorates						
Pricing						
Good Value	☐	☐	☐	☐	☐	☐
Agreeable Terms	☐	☐	☐	☐	☐	☐
Cost of Suite	$_____		$_____		$_____	
Cost of Any Taxes	$_____		$_____		$_____	
Cost of Extra Services You Require:						
_____	$_____		$_____		$_____	
_____	$_____		$_____		$_____	
_____	$_____		$_____		$_____	
	$_____		$_____		$_____	
TOTAL COST:	$_____		$_____		$_____	

10. CARE FACILITY COMPARISON

	Care Facility 1		Care Facility 2		Care Facility 3	
	Yes	No	Yes	No	Yes	No
First Impressions						
Is the facility clean and tidy?	☐	☐	☐	☐	☐	☐
Does the facility have a pleasant atmosphere? (For example, pictures on walls, plants, open areas, gardens)	☐	☐	☐	☐	☐	☐
Are residents clean and well groomed?	☐	☐	☐	☐	☐	☐
Are they properly dressed?	☐	☐	☐	☐	☐	☐
Is the facility free of any offensive odours?	☐	☐	☐	☐	☐	☐
Do residents appear comfortable and at home with their surroundings?	☐	☐	☐	☐	☐	☐
Is there convenient access to public transportation, stores, banks, restaurants, library, family and friends?	☐	☐	☐	☐	☐	☐
Will family and friends be welcome at any time?	☐	☐	☐	☐	☐	☐
If the facility has a reception desk, is it staffed during the evening and on weekends?	☐	☐	☐	☐	☐	☐
Is your language spoken? If not, how will the staff communicate with you?	☐	☐	☐	☐	☐	☐
Licensing						
Is the facility licensed under provincial legislation?	☐	☐	☐	☐	☐	☐
Can you see a copy of the latest licensing inspection report?	☐	☐	☐	☐	☐	☐
Is the facility accredited?	☐	☐	☐	☐	☐	☐
Can you see a copy of the latest accreditation report?	☐	☐	☐	☐	☐	☐
Does the facility have a quality improvement plan?	☐	☐	☐	☐	☐	☐
Are residents and their families involved in accreditation and quality improvement activities?	☐	☐	☐	☐	☐	☐
Resident Rooms						
Will you have a private room?	☐	☐	☐	☐	☐	☐
Are the rooms fully or partially furnished?	☐	☐	☐	☐	☐	☐
If there are double rooms, can you choose your roommate?	☐	☐	☐	☐	☐	☐
If there are some double bedrooms, is there a waiting list for single rooms?	☐	☐	☐	☐	☐	☐
Are the rooms bright and cheery?	☐	☐	☐	☐	☐	☐
Is there adequate storage and closet space?	☐	☐	☐	☐	☐	☐
Is there a lockable cupboard or drawer?	☐	☐	☐	☐	☐	☐
Can you bring some of your own possessions (for example, pictures, furniture, television)?	☐	☐	☐	☐	☐	☐
Can you have a small appliance in your room (electric blanket, kettle, mini-fridge, toaster, microwave, etc.)?	☐	☐	☐	☐	☐	☐
Is there room for a wheelchair or walker in the bedroom and washroom areas?	☐	☐	☐	☐	☐	☐

	Care Facility 1		Care Facility 2		Care Facility 3	
	Yes	No	Yes	No	Yes	No
Is a phone available for you to use that is private and accessible?	☐	☐	☐	☐	☐	☐
Can you have a phone in your room?	☐	☐	☐	☐	☐	☐
Can you have food or alcohol in your bedroom?	☐	☐	☐	☐	☐	☐
Dining Arrangements						
Is there a central dining room?	☐	☐	☐	☐	☐	☐
Is the dining room within easy walking distance from residents' room?	☐	☐	☐	☐	☐	☐
Can you choose where you will sit in the dining room?	☐	☐	☐	☐	☐	☐
Is the menu displayed?	☐	☐	☐	☐	☐	☐
Is there a choice of menu items?	☐	☐	☐	☐	☐	☐
Can the facility provide meals that are compatible with your special diet, cultural or religious background?	☐	☐	☐	☐	☐	☐
Will healthy snacks be provided?	☐	☐	☐	☐	☐	☐
Are dietary supplements provided if your doctor/health care provider orders them?	☐	☐	☐	☐	☐	☐
Are supplements covered?	☐	☐	☐	☐	☐	☐
If you have trouble eating, will staff be able to help you?	☐	☐	☐	☐	☐	☐
Can you invite guests to a meal?	☐	☐	☐	☐	☐	☐
Is the guest meal cost affordable and easily arranged?	☐	☐	☐	☐	☐	☐
Is there an area where you or your family can make a cup of coffee, tea, or a snack?	☐	☐	☐	☐	☐	☐
Resident Care						
Can your own doctor/health care provider continue to care for you in this home?	☐	☐	☐	☐	☐	☐
Will you be able to stay at this facility if your care needs increase?	☐	☐	☐	☐	☐	☐
Are rehabilitation services such as physiotherapy or occupational therapy available?	☐	☐	☐	☐	☐	☐
Will the facility help you with daily care of your teeth or dentures? (flossing, cleaning, etc.)	☐	☐	☐	☐	☐	☐
Does a dental hygienist, denturist, or dentist visit the facility? If so, who arranges and pays for these services?	☐	☐	☐	☐	☐	☐
Are hairdressing and barber services available?	☐	☐	☐	☐	☐	☐
Does a podiatrist (foot doctor) visit?	☐	☐	☐	☐	☐	☐
Will you and/or family be involved in planning and regular reviews of your care?	☐	☐	☐	☐	☐	☐
Special Care Programming						
Is there a separate care area for persons with dementia/Alzheimer Disease?	☐	☐	☐	☐	☐	☐

	Care Facility 1		Care Facility 2		Care Facility 3	
	Yes	No	Yes	No	Yes	No
Is there an eating area specifically for persons with dementia/Alzheimer Disease?	☐	☐	☐	☐	☐	☐
Are there special or integrated social and recreational activities for persons with dementia/Alzheimer Disease?	☐	☐	☐	☐	☐	☐
Are safe indoor and outdoor walking areas provided?	☐	☐	☐	☐	☐	☐
Can you have a bath or shower when you wish?	☐	☐	☐	☐	☐	☐
Bathing						
Is there any special equipment available, such as lift equipment or wheelchair showers?	☐	☐	☐	☐	☐	☐
Can you use your own soap and shampoo?	☐	☐	☐	☐	☐	☐
Is privacy assured during bathing?	☐	☐	☐	☐	☐	☐
Lounges, Activity Areas, Outdoor Areas						
Is there a lounge where you can socialize or entertain visitors?	☐	☐	☐	☐	☐	☐
Is there a space for you to have private conversations with family and friends?	☐	☐	☐	☐	☐	☐
Is there an area or special room for crafts and other activities?	☐	☐	☐	☐	☐	☐
Is there a garden or patio?	☐	☐	☐	☐	☐	☐
Can you go outside when you wish?	☐	☐	☐	☐	☐	☐
Social and Recreational Activities						
Does the facility have an activity director?	☐	☐	☐	☐	☐	☐
Are activities, musical programs, entertainment, outings, and crafts available?	☐	☐	☐	☐	☐	☐
Is the schedule of activities, programs, and outings clearly communicated to residents?	☐	☐	☐	☐	☐	☐
Are there a variety of craft activities?	☐	☐	☐	☐	☐	☐
Are there extra charges for craft materials?	☐	☐	☐	☐	☐	☐
Will you be able to pursue your own hobbies? (gardening, bridge, etc.)	☐	☐	☐	☐	☐	☐
Are activities scheduled during evenings and on weekends?	☐	☐	☐	☐	☐	☐
Does the facility have a pet?	☐	☐	☐	☐	☐	☐
Can you bring your pet to the facility?	☐	☐	☐	☐	☐	☐
Does the facility have a wheelchair-accessible van or bus to transport residents to outings?	☐	☐	☐	☐	☐	☐
Are religious or cultural holidays celebrated?	☐	☐	☐	☐	☐	☐
Are religious services or pastoral care available?	☐	☐	☐	☐	☐	☐
Laundry						
Are these laundry facilities available to do some of your own laundry if you want?	☐	☐	☐	☐	☐	☐
Are there restrictions on the types of personal clothing that may be sent to the laundry?	☐	☐	☐	☐	☐	☐

	Care Facility 1		Care Facility 2		Care Facility 3	
	Yes	No	Yes	No	Yes	No
Will the facility mend your personal clothing?	☐	☐	☐	☐	☐	☐
Does all clothing need to be labeled?	☐	☐	☐	☐	☐	☐
If you have a lot of laundry will there be any extra charges?	☐	☐	☐	☐	☐	☐
Incontinence Supplies						
Does the facility provide incontinence supplies without charge?	☐	☐	☐	☐	☐	☐
Are the incontinence supplies provided sufficient?	☐	☐	☐	☐	☐	☐
Is there a policy if you prefer to use a type of incontinence supply that differs from the type provided by the facility?	☐	☐	☐	☐	☐	☐
Pharmacy Services						
Is the facility responsible for administering medication?	☐	☐	☐	☐	☐	☐
Is medication paid for in non-subsidized facilities?	☐	☐	☐	☐	☐	☐
Is there a policy if you want to give yourself your own medication?	☐	☐	☐	☐	☐	☐
Is there a policy regarding the use and storage of non-prescription medication?	☐	☐	☐	☐	☐	☐
Policies of Facility						
Are visitors welcome at any time?	☐	☐	☐	☐	☐	☐
Is there a resident council, family council, or a family support group established? If so, what is its role?	☐	☐	☐	☐	☐	☐
Is there a specific person to contact if you or your family wants information and/or problem solving?	☐	☐	☐	☐	☐	☐
Is there a complaint procedure for you and your family?	☐	☐	☐	☐	☐	☐
Does the facility have a resident bill of rights?	☐	☐	☐	☐	☐	☐
Do you need to sign out if you leave the facility?	☐	☐	☐	☐	☐	☐
Are there facility policies regarding advanced directives (types of medical intervention you may agree to if you become incapacitated) and "do-not-resuscitate orders" (DNR)?	☐	☐	☐	☐	☐	☐
Are there facility policies regarding the use of restraints?	☐	☐	☐	☐	☐	☐
Are there facility policies regarding smoking?	☐	☐	☐	☐	☐	☐
Staffing						
Do staff appear to be happy, responsive and caring?	☐	☐	☐	☐	☐	☐
Do they have a sense of humour?	☐	☐	☐	☐	☐	☐
Are there adequate staff on duty during the day, evening, and at night and are they qualified?	☐	☐	☐	☐	☐	☐
Do staff treat residents respectfully? (For example, do they address residents by name? Do they knock before entering rooms?)	☐	☐	☐	☐	☐	☐

	Care Facility 1		Care Facility 2		Care Facility 3	
	Yes	No	Yes	No	Yes	No
Does the person giving you a tour take the time to say hello to residents and staff?	☐	☐	☐	☐	☐	☐
Financial Arrangements						
If the facility is private pay, is the daily rate affordable?	☐	☐	☐	☐	☐	☐
Are there extra charges in addition to the daily accommodation rate? (For example, private phone, cable hook-up, newspaper, special supplies?)	☐	☐	☐	☐	☐	☐
Are there policies regarding money and valuables?	☐	☐	☐	☐	☐	☐
Can you do your own banking? If not, will the facility take care of your spending money?	☐	☐	☐	☐	☐	☐
Is there a refund policy if you move out before the end of a month?	☐	☐	☐	☐	☐	☐
Are you satisfied with the notice requirement?	☐	☐	☐	☐	☐	☐
Do you continue to pay if you are away from the facility on vacation or in hospital?	☐	☐	☐	☐	☐	☐
Security						
Can you lock your bedroom door if you wish?	☐	☐	☐	☐	☐	☐
Is the facility responsible if any of your valuables disappear or are broken?	☐	☐	☐	☐	☐	☐
Emergency Management						
Are there policies and plans in place to handle emergencies such as earthquakes, fires, snowstorms, etc?	☐	☐	☐	☐	☐	☐
Does the facility have a sprinkler system for fire safety?	☐	☐	☐	☐	☐	☐
Does the facility have regular fire drills?	☐	☐	☐	☐	☐	☐
Are there smoke alarms in every room?	☐	☐	☐	☐	☐	☐
Are emergency exits well marked?	☐	☐	☐	☐	☐	☐
Does the facility have a policy on contacting families in the event of an emergency or illness?	☐	☐	☐	☐	☐	☐

Glossary

Adjustable Life Insurance Policy: Allows the policyholder to alter the policy's plan by changing the amount of the coverage or premium.

Adjusted Cost Base: The cost of a capital property for tax purposes. The original purchase price (cost) plus an adjustment for certain types of subsequent related expenses, e.g. costs of improvements, other than repairs, to a home or cottage that you own.

Administrator: The person appointed by the court to administer the estate. This occurs when there is no will, the will did not name an executor or the named executor has died or is unwilling or unable to act. Sometimes referred to as a "personal representative."

Affidavit: A sworn statement in writing, made before an authorized party, such as a lawyer or notary public.

Agent for Executor: Where a person or trust company is hired by the named executor for a fee to provide advice and/or administration services.

Alternate Appointment: An alternate executor appointed if the first named executor has died or is unwilling or unable to act.

Alternative Minimum Tax: Refer to regulations designed by the CRA to limit the tax advantage that an individual can obtain with certain tax incentives. For example annual RRSP contributions, capital gains and tax-shelter investments.

Annuity: A contract that provides for a series of payments to be made or received at regular intervals.

Any Occupation Disability: Disability from any suitable occupation, according to your education, training and/or experience. Most, but not all, group contracts specify an "any occupation" disability after the first two years of disability.

Assets: Property of a deceased person subject by law to payment of his or her debts and legacies.

Attorney: The person named in your power of attorney to act on your behalf. The term "attorney" does not mean a lawyer.

Attribution Rules: Under the *Income Tax Act*, the rules that govern attribution of income and/or capital gains in certain situations. For example, where property is transferred, directly or through a trust, for the benefit of a spouse or certain minor children, the income (and in some cases, capital gains) on that property may be deemed to be attributed as income or gains of the transferor rather than the person holding the property.

Autopsy: The medical examination to determine the cause of death.

Beneficiary: A person who receives a benefit or gift under a will, or a person for whose benefit a trust is created.

Bequest: A disposition in a will concerning property.

Capital: The money or property that is transferred by the settlor to the trustee. This could include realized capital gains. Trust agreements deal with how the capital will eventually be distributed and how the income of the trust will be dealt with.

Capital Beneficiary: A beneficiary who is entitled to the capital of the trust.

Capital Cost Allowance: The amount of tax relief that the CRA allows for depreciation, for example, for wear and tear on capital property. This would include an asset that has a useful but diminishing life over time, e.g., car, equipment, furniture, etc. Different assets have different amounts of annual depreciation, e.g., ranging from 4 percent to 100 percent.

Capital Gain: Gain earned on the sale of an asset or gain deemed to be realized on the death of an individual, as if the asset had been sold on the date of death, e.g., deemed disposition. The difference between a capital property's fair market value and its adjusted cost base—essentially what you've made on the investment.

Capital Loss: Loss experienced on the sale of an asset or loss deemed to be experienced on the death of an individual, as if the asset had been sold on the date of death.

Cash Surrender Value: The money paid out by an insurer upon cancellation of a life insurance policy.

Casket: A container, usually made of wood or metal, which holds the remains of the deceased. Also known as a coffin.

Charitable Gift Annuity: A life annuity issued by a charitable organization. It is based on an individual paying more than the expected annuity payments. At the time of the recipient's death, any capital remaining in the annuity reverts to the issuer for the benefit of the charity.

Charitable Remainder Trust: In this case, you would transfer property to a trust and name a charity as the capital beneficiary. Until your death you would be the income beneficiary, you can use the property and receive any income it generates.

Codicil: Change or addition to a will requiring all the formalities of signing and witnessing needed for a will.

Commissioner for Taking Oaths: An official appointed by law to take affidavits such as a lawyer or notary public or other government appointee.

Consanguinity: The relation or connection of persons descended from the same ancestor.

Continuing Power of Attorney: A power of attorney that contains a "continuing" or "enduring" clause so that it will remain effective even if you become mentally incapable.

Convertible Term Insurance: Allows the policy holder to change the term insurance policy to a whole life policy without providing evidence of insurability.

Coroner: A medical examiner who conducts an investigation to determine the cause of death.

CRA: Canada Revenue Agency, formerly known as Canada Customs and Revenue Agency, and before that, Revenue Canada. Responsible for collection of income tax and various other kinds of taxes imposed by the federal government.

Credit Life Insurance: Type of decreasing term insurance designed to pay the balance due on a loan if the borrower dies before the loan is repaid.

Creditor: Person to whom money is due.

Current Assumption Whole Life Insurance: Type of whole life insurance in which premium rates and cash values may vary according to assumptions regarding mortality, investment, and expense factors. Also called interest-sensitive whole life insurance.

Deemed Disposition: Means that the CRA deems that you have disposed of all your assets on your death. Any capital gains would be deemed realized and tax would therefore be due.

Deferred Gift: A charitable donation that you would arrange now for payment sometime in the future. The payment generally occurs after death.

Dependent Life Insurance: Group life insurance made available to group members to cover dependents of the group member.

Devise: A disposition of land by will.

Devolve: Pass by transmission or succession.

Digital Assets: Digitally stored content or online account owned by an individual.

Disability: The inability, due to illness or injury, to continue to work. Definitions of "disability" vary from contract to contract, and whether or not your policy will pay you benefits may well hinge on how it defines disability. Most contracts will define disability according to one of four types. Refer to the following definitions for disability: "own occupation"; "regular occupation"; "any occupation"; and "total and permanent."

Disability Income Insurance: Compensates the insured for a portion of the income they lose because of a disabling injury or illness. Refer to "disability."

Disclosure Statement: A document filed by the executor or administrator with the applicable provincial probate fees department.

Encroach (on Capital): The process of paying out to the beneficiary portions of the money or other assets (capital) being held for that beneficiary in trust. The agreement may provide the trustee(s) with the power to pay capital from the trust to a beneficiary if certain conditions for using the capital as outlined in the trust agreement or will are met. The encroachment power may be broad, such as "for the general benefit" of the beneficiary or limited to specific needs, such as "in case of sickness" or "for educational purposes." Many trust agreements provide for a specific person to get the income for life with the Capital ultimately going to someone else.

Endowment Fund: A donation made to fund a specific objective. The charity would then invest the donation and use the income generated to fund the specified project.

Enduring Power of Attorney: See "continuing power of attorney."

Escheat: The process by which the assets of a deceased person pass to the provincial government when he or she dies without a will and without a spouse and next-of-kin.

Estate: The right, title or interest that a person has in any property. Your estate consists of the assets owned by you at death.

Estate Freeze: A legal procedure that limits the growth in value of the freezor's estate. This is done by diverting the growth to a subsequent generation.

Exclusions and Limitations: Specified situations that are not covered by the insurance contract. Policies will often exclude disabilities caused by self-inflicted wounds or incurred during the course of illegal activities. Check your contract to see what exclusions and limitations apply.

Executor/Executrix: The person(s) or institution named under a will to administer, manage and/or transfer an estate, in accordance with the terms of the will. The executor will normally also be named as a trustee if the will requires a trust to be established, rather than having the assets distributed outright to the beneficiaries. Alternatively, the trustee could be a separate person or institution.

Fair Market Value: The price that the open market would pay in a normal time period situation between an arms-length (non-related) buyer and seller.

Family Income Life Insurance: Combination of whole life and decreasing term insurance, whereby a lump sum is paid when the insured dies, and an income is also paid for a specified period to help support the insured's family.

Fiduciary: An individual or institution under a legal obligation to act for the benefit of another party.

Fiduciary Duty: The level of obligation required of a trustee. A fiduciary duty implies a very high level and standard of care in dealing with assets on behalf of a beneficiary. If this duty and standard is not met, the trustee could be legally liable for the consequences.

General Power of Attorney: A document that gives your selected representative broad authority to make decisions relating to your assets.

Gift in Kind: A gift of an asset other than money.

Gift to the Crown: A donation to a provincial or federal government body or a Crown foundation. The recipient of the gift would be authorized to raise money for public institutions such as hospitals, universities, libraries and museums.

Grant of Probate: A certificate confirming the authority set out in a will to administer a particular estate; issued to an Executor by the court. Also called Grant of Letters Probate and Letters Probate.

Group Insurance: Insurance that provides coverage for several people under one insurance contract.

Group Ordinary Life Insurance: Group life insurance in which at least part of the coverage is permanent and builds a cash value.

Guardian: The person named to be legally responsible for the minor children should both parents die. Also used in many provinces for committing of a mentally incapable adult.

Health Care Practitioner: A person licensed or registered under provincial legislation to provide health and/or personal care and includes the administrator of a health care facility.

Health Insurance: Covers medical expenses or income loss resulting from injury or sickness.

Holograph Will: A will written completely in the handwriting of the person making it, having no witnesses to the signature of the testator.

Incapable/Incompetent: Terms used to indicate that a person is no longer able to understand the information that is relevant to making a decision and is not able to appreciate the "reasonable foreseeable consequences of the decision or lack of the decision." Each province has legal requirements for determining capability/competence. It is a court and/or health care practitioners who determine if a person is incapable/incompetent—in this context incapable of managing his or her legal and financial affairs, sometimes also personal affairs. Refer to "mental incapacity."

Income: The money generated through the investment of the capital. For example, dividends and interest.

Income Beneficiary: The person or persons entitled to the income generated by the trust property. The income includes dividends and interest. It does not commonly include capital gains, which become part of the capital. See "life tenant."

Indexed Life Insurance: Whole life insurance in which the death benefit and the premium increase automatically every year in accordance with any increase in the Consumer Price Index (CPI).

Internment: Another term for "burial."

Inter Vivos Trust: This type of trust document comes into effect during the lifetime of the settlor. Also known as a "living trust."

Intestate: The person who dies without a will. A partial intestacy is where a valid will does not deal with all of the estate.

Intestate Distribution: If a person dies without a will, the process of distribution of assets according to a pre-determined formula.

Irrevocable Trust: The person who created the trust cannot revoke it.

IRS: U.S. Internal Revenue Service. Tax collection arm of the United States federal government.

Issue: All persons who have descended from a common ancestor. It is a broader term than children, which is limited to one generation (e.g. grandchildren, great-grandchildren, etc.).

Joint Tenants: A form of joint ownership in which the death of one joint owner results in the immediate transfer of ownership to the surviving joint owner or owners. This transfer is deemed to have occurred at the time of death.

Key Person Insurance: Life insurance purchased by a business on the life of a person who is important to the continuing operations of the business, usually an employee.

Legacy: Personal property or money given by a will. Also called a "bequest."

Letters of Administration: The court grant appointing an administrator to administer the estate of an individual dying intestate.

Letters of Administration with Will Annexed: The court grant appointing an administrator to administer the estate of an individual who left a will, where the named executor has died or is unable or unwilling to act.

Letters Probate: The court grant confirming the appointment of an executor named in a will and confirming the validity of the will itself.

Life Insurance: Insurance that provides protection against the economic loss caused by the death of the person insured.

Life Interest: A benefit given to a beneficiary in a will that permits that beneficiary to enjoy or have the use of some property or some amount of money for the balance of the beneficiary's lifetime only.

Life Support: Machines used to keep a person alive by maintaining circulation and breathing.

Life Tenant: A beneficiary who has an interest in trust property for balance of that beneficiary's life (a life interest). For example, the beneficiary may be entitled to live in a house rent-free for life. On the death of the beneficiary, the trust property reverts to the capital beneficiary.

Limited Power of Attorney: A power of attorney that limits your attorney to specific transactions, such as banking, the sale of real estate, or negotiating securities.

Living Trust: A trust created by a settlor while he or she is alive. Also referred to as an *inter vivos* trust.

Living Will: Also referred to as a "health care directive" or an "advance medical care directive." This document explains to family, friends, doctors and other caregivers, your personal philosophy regarding medical treatment and health care. It also conveys your wishes with respect to procedures to prolong your life in the event of terminal illness.

Marker: A stone or bronze tablet that rests flush with the ground and identifies the grave.

Mausoleum: Also referred to as a tomb, this is generally an above-ground structure.

Mental Incapacity: The inability to understand information that is relevant to making decisions or the inability to appreciate the reasonably foreseeable consequences of making a decision. Refer to "incapable/incompetent."

Monument: An upright stone, or sometimes a combination of stone and bronze standing above ground, which identifies the grave. Also known as a "tombstone."

Natural Death: A commonly used phrase to indicate dying by a normal process, without any intervention that would prolong life. Put simply, "let my body die on its own." Most health care directives that include reference to dying a "natural death" do include the desire for comfort care and pain control.

Next of Kin: Blood relatives of a person dying intestate who inherit by reason of the applicable provincial legislation.

Notarized or Notarial Copy: True copy of an original document certified by a lawyer or notary public as being true copy.

Oath: Solemn affirmation of the truth of what is stated.

Own Occupation Disability: Disability from your own occupation only. Provided you are disabled from doing your own job and are under the care of a doctor, you qualify for benefits. Even if you went to work in another occupation, you may still qualify for benefits. Individual contracts may offer an "own occupation" clause to age 65.

Palliative Care: Health and/or personal care that relieves pain and the symptoms of disease, but does not attempt to cure it.

Persistent Vegetative State: A coma that results from the loss of brain functions relating to consciousness and feelings although the body may continue to function.

Personal Care: Assistance with bathing, grooming, dressing, mobility, eating/drinking, and other activities of daily life.

Personal Property: All property with the exception of real estate and buildings; also known as "personalty" (as opposed to "realty").

Personal Representative: The individual administering an estate, whether an executor or administrator.

Per Stirpes: A method of dividing assets of an estate. For example, if a member of the group among which the assets are being divided was dead at the time of the division. In this event, the children of that deceased member would divide among them the share that their parent would have received had she or he been alive.

Planned Giving: A charitable gift designed to maximize your tax and estate planning goals and benefits.

Power of Attorney: A written document by which you grant to someone the authority to act on your behalf on various matters. A power of attorney is different from a will, which provides for the orderly distribution of your estate after your death; a power of attorney terminates on your death. There are different types of powers of attorney dealing with specific or general financial or health issues.

Power of Attorney for Personal Care: A document that gives your stated representative expansive authority to make personal care decisions on your behalf if you become mentally incapacitated. This document may include instructions normally covered in a "living will."

Precedent: Guide or example that has been used before.

Pre-existing Condition: An ailment for which you sought medical advice in the six months (or one year, or two years, depending on the insurance contract) prior to applying for the disability policy, and which recurs within a specified period of time (for example, six months) from the policy date. Policies that have this clause exclude coverage for pre-existing conditions occurring within the prescribed time frame. Some group contracts have a pre-existing condition clause. It is also common in creditor's disability insurance.

Present Gift: A charitable donation in which you give the gift now, not in the future.

Probatable Assets: Those assets that pass through the estate. They are therefore governed by the probate process and subject to probate fees.

Probate: Formal proof before the appropriate officer or court that the will presented is the last will of the testator. In addition, the executor(s) named are formally confirmed.

Proceeds of Disposition: The actual proceeds from the sale of an asset (net of sale after expenses) and in some cases, it is a "deemed" amount where there is no actual sale.

Real Property: Land and buildings; also known as "real estate" or "realty."

Regular Occupation Disability: Disability from your own occupation, provided that you choose not to work in an alternative occupation.

Renewable Term Insurance: Type of term insurance that includes a renewal provision giving the policy owner the right to renew the insurance coverage at the end of the specified term without submitting evidence of insurability.

Residuary Beneficiary: The beneficiary to whom the residue of the estate is left.

Residue: That portion of an estate remaining after all specific bequests and specific devices have been made.

Revenue Canada: Now known as the Canada Revenue Agency (CRA).

Revocable Trust: A trust that can be revoked by the person who created the trust.

Second-to-Die Life Insurance: See "survivorship insurance."

Settlement: The transfer of property to a trust.

Settlor: The individual who establishes a trust.

Specific Bequest: A gift under a will of a specific item of personal property or a specific amount of cash.

Specific Devise: A gift under a will of a specific item of real property, personal property or cash.

Spousal Trust: A trust, under which the spouse is entitled to all of the income for his or her lifetime. Nobody but the spouse has a right to any of the capital while the spouse is alive. Spousal trusts are most commonly created as testamentary trusts, that is, taking effect on death and as part of the will. The major benefit of a spousal trust is that the transfer of property to the trust does not create a capital gain.

Surrogate Court: The court responsible for the appointment of personal representatives and generally involved with problems arising during the administration of estates.

Survivorship Insurance: Type of whole life insurance that insures two people and pays benefits only after the second person dies. Also called "second-to-die life insurance."

Terminally Ill: An irreversible condition that cannot be cured and will eventually result in death.

Term Life Insurance: Life insurance under which the benefit is payable only if the insured dies within a specified period.

Testamentary Trust: A trust that is created under a will.

Testate: Either the act of dying with a will or the name given to a person who dies leaving a will.

Testator: A person who makes a will.

Total and Permanent Disability: Some contracts require not only that you be totally disabled from working, but also that your disability be permanent.

Transfer: Act of conveying the title to property.

Transmission: Transfer of property to beneficiary after probate of will or letters of administration obtained.

Trust: A legal arrangement in which one person (the settlor) transfers legal title to a trustee (a fiduciary) to manage the property for the benefit of a person or institution (the beneficiaries). A testamentary trust is set up in a will and takes effect only after death. There are two main types of trust components. A living trust (*inter vivos*) is a trust set up during an individual's lifetime.

Trustee: A person who acts in a position of trust in administering assets on behalf of someone else. The person or institution who take legal title to the trust property and who are required to follow the terms of the trust. The trustee may be an individual or trust company or both (co-trustees). Often settlors will name joint or co-trustees with equal authority. For example, the individual advises on matters where the trustees have been given discretion about the distribution of funds, while the trust company manages the property and deals with various legal and tax matters.

Underwriting: The process by which a life insurance company determines whether or not it will accept your application for disability insurance and, if so, on what basis. Usually, this involves reviewing medical information and, in some cases, financial information as well.

Universal Life Insurance: Whole life insurance that often guarantees a minimum interest rate on the money in the policy's cash value, and in which the mortality, investment, and expense factors used to calculate premium rates and cash values are expressed separately in the policy.

Urn: A container for the cremated remains of the deceased.

Vault: A container, usually made of concrete, to protect a casket from the surrounding weight of earth.

Visitation Period: Also known as a wake, it usually takes place in a funeral home a few days before the service and allows people to pay their respects to the deceased and offer condolences to the family.

Waiver of Premium: During a period of disability, your premiums may be waived (suspended). Check your contract to see if this provision applies for periods of total disability only, or if it also applies during partial disability.

Whole Life Insurance: Life insurance that builds a cash value and that remains in force during the insured's entire lifetime, provided premiums are paid as specified in the policy.

Will: A written document conforming to strict provincial rules relating to form and signing. The purpose is to instruct the executors appointed under the will how the property of a deceased person should be distributed.

Wills Variation Act: The provincial statute permitting a spouse, child or others to obtain benefits from the estate of a deceased if not adequately provided for by the will.

INDEX

1971 Tax Reform, 135
21-year deemed disposition rule, 109–110, 215
30-day survivorship clause, 54

Accidental death insurance, 330
Accountants
    fees and costs, 289
    resolving disputes, 289–290
    selecting, 287–289
Accruing benefits plans, 14–15
Adams, Charles, 134
Adjusted cost base, 141–142, 225–226
Administrator bond, 51
Administrators, 116
    compensation, 75
    responsibilities, 116–126
    See also Executors
Advance directive. *See* Living wills
Advertising for creditors, 124, 131
Advisors. *See* Professional advisors
Allowance for surviving spouse, 11
Alter ego trusts, 5, 99
Alternate beneficiaries, 54
Alternative Minimum Tax (AMT), 161
Annuities, 17, 19–21
    charitable gift annuities, 247–248
    protecting against default, 26–27
Ashes from cremation, 328–329
Assets
    arranging immediate funds for survivors,
        118–119
    government pension plans, 10
    guaranteed income supplement (GIS), 10–11
    minimizing amount in estate, 77
    non-probatable assets, 131
    Old Age Security (OAS) pension, 10
    ongoing professional management, 123–124
    preparing a list of, 121–122
    probatable assets, 131
    protecting, 123–124
    using your home as additional source of
        income, 21–25
    See also Digital assets; Real estate; Trusts; Wills

Assuris, 26, 27
Attestation clause, 54
Autopsy, 320

Bank deposits, protecting against default, 26, 37
Bank power of attorney, 84
Banks, 299
Bare trusts, 109
Barristers. *See* Lawyers
Beneficial ownership, 97
Beneficiaries, 97
    capital beneficiary, 248
    income beneficiary, 248
    naming estate as beneficiary of RRSP, 154
    notifying, 120–121
    release from, 128
Bequests, 52
Bonds, 42–44
    See also Investments
Burial, 327–328
    documents, 321
    at sea, 329
    See also Funeral planning
Business. *See* Family-owned businesses;
        Home-based businesses; Privately-owned
        businesses

Canada Pension Plan, and funeral costs, 330
Canada Pension Plan (CPP), 11, 12
    death benefit, 13
    disability pension, 12
    living outside Canada, 37
    surviving spouse pension, 13
Canada Pension Survivor's Benefits, 332
Canada Revenue Agency (CRA), 15, 128
Canada Savings Bonds, 18
Canada/U.S. Tax Treaty. *See* Tax treaty
Canadian Deposit Insurance Corp. (CDIC), 26,
        28, 37
Canadian Investor Protection Fund (CIPF), 27
Canadian Life and Health Insurance Association
        (CLHIA), 30, 340
Capital gains taxes, 109–110, 135

$800,000 plus lifetime capital gains exemption, 230

calculating capital gain or loss, 139

calculating income tax on a capital gain, 142–143

calculating taxable capital gain or allowable capital loss, 139–140

claiming a capital gains reserve, 141

on death, 143–147

deemed disposition of assets, 148, 159

determining adjusted cost base, 141–142

determining proceeds of disposition, 140

estimating future capital gains taxes, 143

exemption for small business corporation shares, 175

on gifts, 147–150

offsetting capital losses against capital gains, 140

paying tax on vacation property now or later, 216

terminology, 137–139

See also Vacation properties

Care facilities, 308–310, 312, 399–403

Cash legacies, 53

Cash refund annuity, 20

Caskets, 324

Cemeteries, 324–325

Certificate of Death. *See* Medical Certificate of Death

Certified cultural property, gifts of, 245–246

Charitable giving and philanthropy

cash donations, 243

charitable gift annuities, 247–248

charitable remainder trusts, 100–101, 248

donation tax credit, 254

donations to organizations outside of Canada, 254–255

endowments, 252

and funeral planning, 318–319

gifts in kind, 243–245, 251–252

gifts of certified cultural property, 245–246

life insurance, 252–253

pitfalls to avoid, 250–253

planning tips, 249–250

private foundations, 248–249

special tax treatment for gifts of qualifying publicly-traded securities, 244–245

tax incentives for charitable gifts, 242–243

taxes, 160–161

using life insurance for charitable purposes, 246–247

Charitable remainder trusts, 100–101, 103, 248

Chartered Professional Accountants. *See* CPAs

Checklists

care facility comparison, 399–403

current and projected retirement monthly income and expenses, 384–386

current financial net worth, 382–384

duties and responsibilities of the executor, 391–394

personal information record, 363–381

projected financial needs, 387

retirement residence comparison, 394–398

where retirement income will come from, 388

will preparation, 389–391

Children

disinheriting a child, 55

protecting children's inheritance, 57

rights of dependents, 57

transfer of vacation property ownership to a child, 212

trusts for minors, 103

See also Family; Guardians

CLHIA. *See* Canadian Life and Health Insurance Association (CLHIA)

Codicils, 52, 346–347

Commissions. *See* Fees and costs

Committee, 82

Common-law couples, 73, 121, 128, 180

Company human resources personnel, 299

Compassionate travel policy, 331

Conditional trusts, 98

Continuing power of attorney

for personal care, 84–85, 86–87

for property, 84, 85–86, 87

Control premium, 144

Costs. *See* Fees and costs

CPAs, 63

Credit unions, 299

protecting deposit plans against default, 26

Creditor-proofing, 27, 234–237

Creditors, 128

advertising for, 124, 131

Cremation, 328–329
   documents, 321
   See also Funeral planning
Critical illness insurance, 273
Cultural Property Export and Import Act (CPEIA),
   245–246
Currency risk, 29

Death. *See specific topics*
Death benefit, 13
Death certificate, 118
   See also Medical Certificate of Death; Proof of
      Death Certificate
Death clock, 39
Death Registration Form, 321
Deemed disposition, 109–110, 138–139, 145, 229
   for capital gains purposes, 148, 159
   income taxes owing on capital gains resulting
      from, 161–162
Default, protecting investments against, 26–28
Deferral tax, 166
Deferred profit sharing plans (DPSPs), 16
Defined benefit plans, 14–15
Defined contribution plans, 15
Deflation, risk, 29
Dependents, rights of, 57
Deposit brokers, 301
Deposit plans, 16
Digital assets, 32–35
Digital executors, 35
Disability, pensions, 12
Disability insurance, 272–273
Discount brokers, 300–301
Disinheriting a child or spouse, 55
Disposition, 137–138
Diversification, 19, 31
Divorce, 75
   payments for divorce settlements, 102
   and revocation of a will, 60, 79
Documents. *See specific documents, such as* Wills
*The Duke of Westminster v. Commissioner of
   Inland Revenue,* 168
Durable power of attorney. *See* Enduring power
   of attorney

Economic risk, 31
Embalming, 326

Employer-funded pension plans, 14–16
Encroachment on capital, 56
Enduring power of attorney, 82, 89
Estate administration
   advertising for creditors, 124
   applying to probate the will, 124
   arranging immediate funds for survivors,
      118–119, 131
   distributing the estate, 125
   funeral arrangements, 118
   locating and reading wills, 117–118
   notifying beneficiaries and others, 120–121
   obtaining death certificate, 118
   paying debts and expenses, 124–125
   preparing a list of assets and liabilities, 121–123
   preparing and filing income tax returns, 124
   protecting assets, 123–124
   record-keeping, 125–126
   seeking professional advice, 164
   tax returns to be filed, 162–163
   winding up the estate, 163–164
Estate freezing, 111, 169, 176–178, 228,
   230–231, 240
Estate planning
   and digital assets, 32–35
   lifetime stages of, 2–5
   overview, 1
   pitfalls to avoid, 5–8
   and vacation properties, 207–209
Estate taxes, 135–136, 153, 196–200
   U.S. estate tax, 195
   See also Taxes, Canadian; Taxes, U.S.
Executors, 52, 116
   compensation, 75, 126
   digital executors, 35
   duties and responsibilities of the executor
      (checklist), 391–394
   potential liability, 127–128
   powers of, 55–56
   responsibilities, 116–126
   selecting, 70–71
Executor's year, 127
Expenses. *See* Fees and costs

Fair market value, 153
   determining, 144
   of privately-owned business, 225, 230

Family
    impact of family law legislation, 73–75
    joint ownership of property, 197–198
    lifetime stages of estate planning, 2–5
    providing for family members with special
        needs, 100
    rights of dependents, 57
    transactions between family members,
        149–150
    See also Children; Estate planning; Funeral
        planning; Guardians; Wills
Family trusts, 98–99, 100, 178
    transferring vacation property ownership to,
        213–215
    See also Living (inter vivos) trusts
Family-owned businesses
    $800,000 plus lifetime capital gains
        exemption, 230
    analyzing your financial situation, 225–226
    buy/sell agreements, 232–234, 236
    considering alternatives, 227
    creditor proofing your business, 234–237
    establishing realistic goals, 227–228
    estate freezing, 230–231, 240
    family farming business, 231
    implementing plan, 229
    importance of having a plan, 224–225
    leadership talent evaluation tools, 226–227
    planning tips, 237–238, 240
    reviewing plan regularly, 229
    shareholder agreements, 231–234
    spousal rollover, 231
    strategic planning, 227
    succession planning, 222–224
    SWOT analysis, 226
    tax planning, 229–231
Farm property rollover, 176
FATCA, 189
Federal Home Buyer's Plan, 160
Fees, trusts, 114
Fees and costs
    accountants, 289
    contesting fees, 76
    for executors, 126
    financial planners, 295–297
    funerals, 323–325
    joint ownership to avoid probate fees, 119–120

    lawyers, 286–287, 302
    paying debts and expenses, 124–125
    power of attorney (PA), 88
    probate, 76, 151, 358–359
    provincial and territorial government probate
        fees, 358–359
    reducing probate fees, 128–129
    RRSPs and RRIFs, 19
    trusts, 104
    wills, 75–76
Financial planners
    Certified Financial Planners (C.F.P.), 290
    Chartered Financial Analysts (C.F.A.), 291
    Chartered Financial Consultants (CH.F.C.),
        291
    fees and costs, 295–297
    resolving disputes, 297–298
    selecting, 63, 290–295, 303
Fixed-term payout, 18
Flat benefits plans, 15
Foreign accrual property income (FAPI),
    taxation of, 110–111
Foreign estate taxes, 151, 163
Foreign trusts, 110–111
Fraternal funeral services, 326–327, 331
Funeral instructions, 54, 57
Funeral planning
    autopsy, 320
    burial or cremation, 327–329
    and charitable giving, 318–319
    costs of, 323–325
    documents and permits, 320
    do-it-yourself, 321–322
    expressions of sympathy, 319–320
    financial assistance with, 330–332, 334
    funeral providers and organizations,
        322–323, 337
    monuments and markers, 329
    personalizing, 317–318
    pre-arranging, 314–317, 334
    public vs. private, 314
    support services, 321
    See also Burial; Cremation
Funeral providers and organizations,
    322–323, 337
Funeral services, 325–327
    executor making arrangements, 118

General anti-avoidance rule (GAAR), 168
General power of attorney, 82–83
Gift taxes, 135–137, 147, 153, 193–194
GIS. *See* Guaranteed Income Supplement (GIS)
Government offices, contact information, 335–336
Government pension plans, 10–14
Government policy risk, 30
Group RRSPs, 16
Guaranteed Income Supplement (GIS), 10–11, 332
Guaranteed Investment Certificates (GICs), 18, 28
Guardians
    appointment of for minor children, 53
    selecting, 72–73

Half-secret trusts, 102
Handwritten wills, 62
Health care directive. *See* Living wills
Heirs-at-law, 121
Holograph wills, 62
Home. *See* Real estate
Home-based businesses, 24–25

Immediate disposition, funeral, 326
Income tax. *See* Taxes, Canadian; Taxes, U.S.
Income Tax Act. See Taxes, Canadian
Indexed life annuity, 20–21
Indexed payout, 18
Inflation, 29, 37–38
Installment refund annuity, 20
Instruction directive, 92
Insurance
    accidental death, 330
    corporate-owned insurance, 233
    criss-cross insurance, 233
    critical illness insurance, 273
    disability, 272–273
    key person insurance, 234
    long-term care insurance, 273
    out-of-country emergency medical insurance, 274–276
    planning tips, 276
    to protect assets, 123
    split-dollar insurance, 233–234
    See also Life insurance; *specific types of insurance*

Insurance agents, 300
    selecting, 266–268
Insurance companies
    choosing a life insurance company, 268–269
    rating, 269
Integrated life annuity, 21
Inter vivos trusts. *See* Living (*inter vivos*) trusts
Interest rate risk, 29
Interest-only payout, 18
Internal Revenue Service, U.S. (IRS)
    Individual Taxpayer Identification Number (ITIN), 186–187
    mutual assistance with Canada in collection efforts, 189
    sharing information with the CRA, 187, 188–189
    what the IRS knows about you, 188
    See also Taxes, U.S.
Intestate (dying without a will), 50–51, 117–118, 180
    how assets are distributed, 355–357
Investing, 40, 41
Investment counsellors, 298–299
Investment Industry Regulatory Organization of Canada (IIROC), 27
Investments
    estimating future value of, 42–44
    and inflation, 37–38
    investing in U.S. securities through Canadian pooled fund corporations or Canadian mutual funds, 200
    protecting against default, 26–28
    risk, 28–32
    withdrawing money from, 44–46, 48

Joint and last survivor annuity, 20
Joint ownership, 119–120, 197–198
    vacation properties, 210
Joint partner trusts, 4–5, 99

Lack of diversification risk, 31
Lack of liquidity risk, 31
Last Post Fund for Veterans, 331
Lawyer-drawn wills, 63–64
Lawyers
    fees and costs, 286–287, 302
    resolving disputes, 287, 302
    selecting, 63, 284–286

Legal fees, 75–76
Letter of probate, 130
Letters of Administration, 130–131
Letters of Direction, 52
    See also Wills
Level payout, 18
Liabilities, preparing a list of, 123
Life annuities, 20–21
Life annuity with a guaranteed period, 20
Life Income Fund (LIF), 15–16, 17
Life insurance
    buying term life insurance, 198–199
    buying to cover future tax liabilities, 216–217
    choosing a life insurance company, 268–269
    choosing an agent, 266–268
    comparing group and individual insurance, 269
    comparison chart, 360–361
    death benefit, 270, 278
    face amount, 259
    funding a buy/sell agreement with, 233–234, 236
    and funeral costs, 330
    guaranteed policies, 268–269
    how much is enough, 258–259
    identifying the need for, 258–259
    income tax treatment of, 270–271
    permanent insurance, 259, 261–262, 278
    planning tips, 276
    policy loan, 271
    proceeds from cancellation, 270
    protecting deposit plans against default, 26, 27
    second-to-die insurance, 264–266
    tax-free accumulation of investment component, 270–271
    term insurance, 259, 260–261, 278
    Term to 100 insurance, 262–264
    types of, 259–266
    universal life insurance, 262
    using for charitable purposes, 246–247, 252–253
    for wealthy individuals, 259
    whole life insurance, 262
Life interest, 215–216, 248
Life tenants, 55
Limited power of attorney, 83–84

Liquidity, 19, 31
Living (*inter vivos*) trusts, 71, 72, 98
    alter ego trusts, 99
    avoiding probate, 101
    defined, 112
    family, 100
    family trusts, 98–99
    giving to charity, 100–101
    joint partner trusts, 99
    keeping a gift confidential, 101–102
    managing retirement needs through a trust, 101
    payments for divorce settlements, 102
    planning, 111
    providing for family members with special needs, 100
    tax implications of, 106
Living wills
    changing, 93
    discussing with professionals, 92–93
    instruction directive, 92
    legality of, 93–94
    need to follow, 93
    overview, 90, 96
    provincial organizations for information on, 338
    proxy directive, 91–92
    reasons to make, 91
    vs. regular will or power of attorney, 90
    sample, 350–354
    what to do with a living will, 95
    when residing part-time outside home province, 94
Locked in Retirement Funds (LRIFs), 17
Long-term care facilities, 339
Long-term care insurance, 273
Lump-sum withdrawls, 17

Managed funds, 27
Managed plans, 16–17
Marital status. *See* Divorce; Marriage; Separation; Spouse
Marital tax credit, 197
Market cycle risk, 31
Marriage
    common-law, 74
    and revocation of a will, 59–60, 79

same-sex, 74
traditional, 74
Medical Certificate of Death, 320, 321
Medical insurance
    critical illness insurance, 273
    out-of-country emergency, 274–276
Medical research
    body donated for, 332–333
    See also Organ donation
Memorandum, 52, 57–58
    See also Wills
Memorial services. *See* Funeral planning
Memorial societies, 323, 327
Military funeral services, 326–327
Minimum payout, 18
Minors. See Children
Mortgages
    placing a non-recourse mortgage on
        U.S. real estate, 199
    reverse mortgages, 22–23, 37
Mutual funds, 200
    agents, 300

Net worth, checklist, 382–384
Non-arm's length transactions, 148–149
Non-enduring power of attorney, 89
Non-probatable assets, 131
Notice of Assessment, 163–164

Official Administrator, 51
Old Age Security Act, 10
Old Age Security (OAS) pension, 10
    integrated with an annuity, 21
    living outside Canada, 37
Online vaults, 34
    See also Digital assets
Organ donation, 56, 332–333, 334, 339
Out-of-country emergency medical insurance,
    274–276

Paid vs. payable, 107
Pension Income Credit, 17
Pension plans
    funded by employers, 14–16
    government pension plans, 10–14
    tax-sheltered, 16–21
Pension risk, 32

Permanent insurance, 259, 261–262, 278
Personal information record, 363–381
Personal property, gift of, 194
Philanthropy. *See* Charitable giving and
    philanthropy
Pooled fund corporations, 200
Power of attorney (PA), 68
    bank power of attorney, 84
    choosing, 85–87
    committee, 82
    continuing power of attorney for personal
        care, 84–85, 86–87
    continuing power of attorney for property,
        84, 85–86
    defined, 82, 96
    enduring power of attorney, 82
    fees, 88
    general power of attorney, 82–83
    limited power of attorney, 83–84
    personal care, 349–350
    powers of, 87
    property, 347–349
    responsibilities, 87
    revoking, 88
    samples, 347–350
    specific power of attorney, 82
    validity for U.S. assets, 89–90, 96
    what happens without a power of attorney,
        82, 96
    what to do with a PA, 88–89
Preferred beneficiary election, 107
Preserving capital, 40, 41, 48
Private foundations, 248–249
Privately-owned businesses
    $800,000 plus lifetime capital gains
        exemption, 230
    analyzing your financial situation, 225–226
    buy/sell agreements, 232–234, 236
    considering alternatives, 227
    creditor proofing your business, 234–237
    establishing objectives, 226–228
    establishing realistic goals, 227–228
    estate freezing, 230–231, 240
    family farming business, 231
    implementing plan, 229
    importance of having a plan, 224–225
    leadership talent evaluation tools, 226–227

Privately-owned businesses (*Cont.*)
  planning tips, 237–238, 240
  reviewing plan regularly, 229
  shareholder agreements, 231–234
  spousal rollover, 231
  strategic planning, 227
  succession planning, 222–224
  SWOT analysis, 226
  tax planning, 229–231
Probatable assets, 131
Probate
  applying to probate the will, 124
  avoiding, 101
  defined, 116
  fees, 76, 151, 358–359
  joint ownership to avoid probate fees, 119–120
  letter of, 130
  reducing fees, 128–129
  See also Wills
Proceeds of disposition, 140
Professional advisors
  accountants, 287–290
  bank, trust company and credit union
    personnel, 299
  company human resources personnel, 299
  deposit brokers, 301
  discount brokers, 300–301
  factors to consider when selecting, 280–284, 302
  financial planners, 290–298, 303
  insurance agents, 300
  investment counsellors, 298–299
  lawyers, 284–287, 302
  mutual fund agents, 300
  overview, 279–280
  retirement counsellors, 299
  Society for Trust and Estate Practitioners
    (STEP), 281
  stockbrokers, 300
Proof of Death Certificate, 330
Provincial social security supplement
    programs, 11
Proxy directive, 91–92
Public Trustee, 51, 332

Qualified domestic trusts (QDOTs), 200
Quebec Pension Plan (QPP), 11
Quebec tax returns, 158

RAMs, 22–23
Real estate
  Federal Home Buyer's Plan, 160
  gift of U.S. real estate, 194
  giving property to beneficiaries during your
    lifetime, 200
  joint ownership, 197–198
  leaving U.S. property to a qualified domestic
    trust (QDOT), 200
  owning foreign real estate through a
    Canadian holding company, 199
  placing a non-recourse mortgage on U.S. real
    estate, 199
  principal residence exemption, 205–207,
    209–211
  purchasing through a Canadian partnership,
    199–200
  purchasing through an irrevocable non-U.S.
    trust, 199
  rental income from U.S. real estate, 190–192
  renting out part of your home, 23–24
  reverse mortgages, 22–23
  sale and leaseback, 198
  selling U.S. real estate, 192–193
  transfer of ownership to a child, 212
  transfer of vacation property ownership to a
    trust, 212–215
  using your home as additional source of
    income, 21–25
  See also Vacation properties
Record-keeping, 125–126
Registered Pension Plans (RPPs), 14–16
Registered Retirement Income Fund (RRIF),
    17–19
  diversification, 19
  fees, 19
  income tax on, 150–151
  liquidity, 19
  protecting against default, 26–27
  rate of return, 19
  safety, 18–19
  taxes, 160
  and wills, 56
  withdrawing money from, 18
Registered Retirement Savings Plan (RRSP),
    16–17
  contribution for year of death, 160

converting into an RRIF, 38
diversification, 19
estimating future value of, 42–44
Federal Home Buyer's Plan, 160
fees, 19
group RRSPs, 16
and income splitting, 12
income tax on, 150–151
liquidity, 19
protecting against default, 26–27
rate of return, 19
safety, 18–19
taxes, 160
and wills, 56
withdrawing money from, 17, 44–46, 48
Related persons, 149
Remainder interest, 215–216
Renting out part of your home, 23–24
Repayment risk, 30
Residuary clause, 53
Residue, 53
Resulting trust, 119
Retirement
    current and projected retirement monthly
        income and expenses, 384–386
    how long to continue working, 41–42
    managing retirement needs through a trust,
        101
    where retirement income will come from,
        388
Retirement counsellors, 299
Retirement residences, 306–308, 312, 394–398
Reverse mortgages, 22–23, 37
Rights or things return, 158
Risk, 28–32
Rollovers, 144, 171–172, 176, 231
    electing out of, 174–175
RRIF. See Registered Retirement Income Fund
    (RRIF)
RRSP. See Registered Retirement Savings Plan
    (RRSP)

Safe income dividends, 228
Same-sex couples, 73
Saving money, 40
Second-to-die insurance, 264–266
Secret trusts, 101

Securities. See Investments
Self-directed plans, 17, 27
Self-written wills, 62
Separation, 74–75
    and revocation of a will, 60
Settlor, 97
Small business corporations. See Family-owned
    businesses
Smoothed payout, 18
Social security programs, from other countries,
    13–14
Society for Trust and Estate Practitioners
    (STEP), 281
Solicitors. See Lawyers
Sources of information, 335–340
Special needs trusts, 100, 103–104
Specific power of attorney, 82
Spendthrift trusts, 3, 103
    defined, 113
Spousal rollover, 171–172, 180, 231
    electing out of, 174–175
Spousal trusts, 3, 102–103, 172–174
    property transferred to, 108
Spouse
    allowance for surviving spouse, 11
    avoiding spousal disputes, 73–75
    common-law spouse, 121, 128, 180
    CPP surviving spouse pension, 13
    disinheriting, 55
    joint ownership of property, 197–198
    transferring property to your spouse, 171–175
Sprinkling trusts, 3
Stockbrokers, 300
Stocks, 42–44
    See also Investments
Straight life annuity, 20
Succession duties, 136–137
Succession planning. See Privately-owned
    businesses
Supplemental benefits, funeral, 332
SWOT analysis, 226

Tax advantages, home-based businesses, 25
Tax avoidance, 169
Tax Clearance Certificate, 125, 163–164
Tax deferral, 170, 171
Tax evasion, 169

Tax planning, 166
  anti-avoidance rules, 168
  balancing tax factors against other considerations, 169
  estate freezing, 111, 169, 176–178
  exemption for small business corporation shares, 175
  family trusts, 178
  in the family-owned business, 229–231
  farm property rollover, 176
  goals, 170
  and high taxes, 168–169
  importance of professional advice, 169
  vs. tax avoidance or evasion, 167–168
  tips, 151–152, 164–165, 178–179
  transferring property to your spouse, 171–175
Tax reduction, income splitting, 12
Tax treaty, 196
  marital tax credit, 197
  U.S. estate tax credit, 196–197
Taxable events, 144
Taxation risk, 31–32
Taxes, Canadian, 202
  $800,000 plus lifetime capital gains exemption, 230
  on accrued income up to date of death, 159
  Alternative Minimum Tax (AMT), 161
  arising on death, 137
  calculating income tax on a capital gain, 142–143
  capital losses, 159
  charitable donations, 160–161
  deduction for attendant care, 161
  deemed disposition of assets for capital gains tax purposes, 159, 195
  disability tax credit, 161
  donation tax credit, 254
  elective income tax returns, 158
  on employment income up to date of death, 158–159
  final returns and Tax Clearance Certificates, 163–164
  final stub period income tax return for year of death, 156–157
  of foreign trusts, 110–111
  history of estate taxes in Canada, 134–137

income tax return for previous calendar year, 156
income taxes owing on capital gains resulting from deemed disposition, 161–162
marital tax credit, 197
medical expenses, 161
on pension benefits, 159
personal tax credits and exemptions, 161
preparation and filing by executor, 124
Quebec tax returns, 158
rights or things return, 158
RRSPs and RRIFs, 160
special tax treatment for gifts of qualifying publicly-traded securities, 244–245
T3 trust return for testamentary trusts, 162–163
T3 trust return for the estate, 162, 166
tax implications of trusts, 105–111
tax incentives for charitable gifts, 242–243
tax treatment of life insurance, 270–271
U.S. estate tax credit, 196–197
See also Capital gains taxes; Tax treaty
Taxes, U.S., 202
  Closer Connection Exception, 184–185, 189
  deadlines for filing, 189–190
  estate tax marital tax credit claim, 190
  estate taxes, 195, 196–200
  FIRPTA withholding taxes, 192–193
  foreign estate taxes, 151, 163
  gift taxes, 193–194
  guidelines for filing U.S. income tax return, 186
  income tax filing requirements for tax treaty Article IV claim, 186
  Individual Taxpayer Identification Number (ITIN), 186–187
  for individuals with green cards, 185
  marital tax credit, 197
  qualified domestic trust election, 189
  reducing U.S. estate tax on U.S. assets, 197–200
  on rental income from U.S. real estate, 190–192
  residency and the tax treaty, 185–186
  resident vs. non-resident alien tax status, 182–184
  substantial presence test, 185

when U.S. tax laws apply, 182–185
See also Internal Revenue Service, U.S. (IRS);
    Tax treaty
Tax-sheltered pension plans, 16–21
TCA90, 19–20
Term Certain Annuity to Age 90, 19–20
Term deposits, 18
Term life insurance, 198–199, 259, 260–261,
    278
Term to 100 insurance, 262–264
Terminology, 405–412
Testamentary donation, 246–247
Testamentary trusts, 71, 98, 102–104
    defined, 113
    T3 trust return for, 162–163
    tax implications of, 106
Testator, 51
Total return, 44
Trust companies, 299
    benefits of using, 64–67
    protecting deposit plans against default, 26
    wills, 64
Trustees, 52, 97
    fees, 76, 114
    powers of, 55–56
    selecting, 71–72, 113, 214–215
    See also Trust companies
Trusts, 54–55
    capital gains taxes, 109–110
    for charities, 103
    fees and costs, 104
    foreign trusts, 110–111
    for minors, 103
    outlining everything in a trust agreement,
      105
    planning, 111
    and privately-owned businesses, 237
    tax implications of, 105–111
    taxation as a flow through entity, 106–107
    taxation as a separate entity, 106
    transfer of assets into, 108–109
    transfer of property out of to a beneficiary,
      109
    transfer of vacation property ownership to a
      trust, 212–215
    types of, 98
    See also specific trusts; Wills

Universal life insurance, 262
Unrealized income, income tax on, 151
U.S. validity
    of power of attorney, 89–90, 96
    of wills, 61

Vacation properties
    buying life insurance to cover future tax
      liabilities, 216–217
    creating a life interest and a remainder
      interest, 215–216
    joint ownership, 210
    overview, 203–205
    paying tax now or later, 216
    planning tips, 217–218
    principal residence exemption, 205–207,
      209–211, 219
    transfer of ownership to a child, 212
    transfer of ownership to a trust, 212–215
    using a corporation to own, 217
    will planning and, 207–209
Validation, of power of attorney, 88
Vesting, 15–16
Veterans, 13, 325, 326–327, 330–331
Veterans Affairs Canada, 13
Veterans' Affairs Canada, 330–331

Wealth accumulation, 40–46
Websites and contact information, 335–340
Whole life insurance, 262
Widowed Spouse's Allowance, 332
Will registry, 117
Wills
    30-day survivorship clause, 54
    alternate beneficiaries, 54
    application for variation, 79
    attestation clause, 54
    avoiding spousal disputes, 73–75
    changing, 58–59, 79
    codicils, 52, 346–347
    disinheriting a child or spouse, 55
    and divorce, 59–60, 79
    encroachment on capital, 56
    fees and costs, 75–76
    funeral instructions, 54, 57
    holograph wills, 62
    how to avoid will being contested, 77

Wills (*Cont.*)
    keeping your will current, 58
    lawyer-drawn wills, 63–64
    life tenants, 55
    locating and reading, 117–118
    and marriage, 59–60, 79
    Memorandum, 52, 57–58
    organ donation, 56
    parts of a will, 51–54
    protecting children's inheritance, 57
    residuary clause, 53
    revoking, 59–60
    RRSPs and RRIFs, 56
    sample, 341–346
    search, 117
    self-written wills, 62
    special circumstances, 68–70
    trust company wills, 64–67
    vacation properties, 207–209
    will preparation checklist, 389–391
    witnesses, 79
    See also Executors; Probate; Trusts
Worker's Compensation Board, 332

Yield, 44

ABOUT THE AUTHORS

DOUGLAS GRAY, B.A., LL.B., is a Vancouver-based expert on estate and retirement planning. Formerly a practicing business and real estate lawyer, he is now a consultant, speaker, columnist and author of 25 bestselling business and personal finance books (published primarily by McGraw-Hill and John Wiley & Sons), including the "Top 10 National Best-Seller," *The Canadian Snowbird Guide.*

Many of these books have been published in other languages and adapted for foreign jurisdictions. Douglas has also designed a real estate investment software program for McGraw-Hill Ryerson and has been a regular expert contributor on personal finance issues for various Internet sites and CD-ROM products, including *Microsoft Money* and *QuickTax—Home and Business.* He has also been a regular contributor to the Microsoft Canada Small Business website and the Microsoft Network Canadian Money Central website.

Douglas has given seminars and presentations to over 250,000 people nationally and internationally in his various areas of expertise.

Frequently interviewed by the media as an authority on personal finance and retirement matters, Douglas has appeared many times on various CBC, CTV and Global TV programs. He has given over 1,500 media interviews. He has been a regular columnist for *Profit, Computer Paper, Canadian Computer Wholesaler, Canada News* and *Forever Young* and a nationally syndicated columnist for Southam Press. He has also been a periodic contributor to the *Globe and Mail, Toronto Star, House and Home, Macleans, Good Times, Canadian Moneysaver, Adviser's Edge, The Successful Investor* and many other publications.

His family of websites includes *estateplanning.ca, retirementplanning.ca, snowbird.ca, homebuyer.ca* and *smallbiz.ca.*

Douglas lives in Vancouver, B.C.

JOHN S. BUDD, T.E.P., F.C.P.A., F.C.A., is a financial and investment advisor in Toronto. He is one of the owners of Cumberland Partners Limited, a firm that provides investment management services to affluent families through its wholly-owned subsidiaries, Cumberland Private Wealth Management Inc. and Cumberland Associates Investment Counsel Inc.

John holds a Bachelor of Commerce (Honours) degree from the University of Toronto, and he is a Chartered Professional Accountant. John has been honoured by the Chartered Professional Accountants (Ontario) by being named a Fellow, in recognition of his contribution over many years to the CPA profession. For more than 25 years up to 1997, he specialized in tax and estate planning, including 18 years as a tax partner with Deloitte & Touche in Toronto. His clients included some of Canada's most affluent individuals and families. In addition, he served as national leader of Deloitte's estate planning service line.

While at Deloitte's, he authored *Second Property Strategies,* a bestselling book on capital gains tax planning for vacation properties and second residences. For many years, he was also the editor and co-author of Deloitte's *Canadian Guide to Personal Financial Management*, and a contributor to *How to Reduce the Tax You Pay*. In addition, John developed and instructed a number of specialized tax courses for the Canadian Institute of Chartered Accountants, including *CICA Personal Tax and Estate Planning, Using Trusts in Tax Planning*, and *CICA Advanced Tax Issues*.

John has been a member of the Toronto Estate Planning Council, and served as the Council's President in 2002/2003. He is also a member of the Canadian Tax Foundation and of the international Society of Trust and Estate Practitioners (STEP). John has been a guest speaker and/or chair of many tax conferences and seminars for the Canadian Tax Foundation, The Strategy Institute, Insight Conferences, and other organizations. He has also written numerous articles and has been frequently quoted by the media in the *Globe and Mail, National Post*, and *Financial Post Magazine*, and appeared several times on *CBC Business World*.

In 1997, John left public accounting to go into the wealth management business. In 2000, he joined Cumberland Private Wealth Management Inc. as a partner and client portfolio manager. John is a shareholder of Cumberland's parent company, Cumberland Partners Limited, and he serves on the firm's Board of Directors. His responsibilities have included business development, as well as the day-to-day management of the investment portfolios of a number of affluent clients located in Canada and abroad.

John lives with his wife and family in Toronto.

READER INPUT AND EDUCATIONAL SEMINARS

If you have thoughts or suggestions that you believe would be helpful for future editions of this book, or if you are interested in having one or both of the authors give a seminar or presentation to your group, association or company, please contact the authors directly (see below).

In addition you may be interested in the services provided by the Canadian Retirement Education Group Inc. This company offers a wide range of consulting services and objective educational programs. These are provided to the public and for organizations, associations, and companies throughout Canada on issues of particular interest to those over 40. Topics cover personal, retirement, financial and estate planning, charitable giving, money management, wills, powers of attorney, investment, taxes, real estate, and other topical, relevant subjects. Customized programs are also designed for corporations for their employees and executives. In addition, customized professional development programs are designed for the financial services industry and other related professionals.

Douglas Gray, B.A., LL.B.
c/o Canadian Retirement Education
    Group, Inc.
#300–3665 Kingsway
Vancouver, BC V5R 5W2
• E-mail: *advisors@shaw.ca*
• Website: *www.estateplanning.ca*

John S. Budd, T.E.P., F.C.P.A., F.C.A.
c/o Cumberland Private Wealth
    Management Inc.
Suite 300, 99 Yorkville Avenue
Toronto, ON M5R 3K5
• E-mail: *johnb@cpwm.ca*
• Website: *www.cumberlandprivate.com*